Oracle E-Business Suite Financials Administration

Shankaran Iyer

McGraw-Hill/Osborne

New York   Chicago   San Francisco
Lisbon   London   Madrid   Mexico City   Milan
New Delhi   San Juan   Seoul   Singapore   Sydney   Toronto

McGraw-Hill/Osborne
2600 Tenth Street
Berkeley, California 94710
USA

To arrange bulk purchase discounts for sales promotions, premiums, or fund-raisers, please contact **McGraw-Hill/Osborne** at the above address. For information on translations or book distributors outside the U.S.A., please see the International Contact Information page immediately following the index of this book.

Oracle E-Business Suite Financials Administration

1234567890 CUS CUS 01987654321

ISBN 0-07-213098-9

Publisher
Brandon A. Nordin

Vice President & Associate Publisher
Scott Rogers

Acquisitions Editor
Jeremy Judson

Project Editor
Jennifer Malnick

Acquisitions Coordinatorr
Athena Honore

Technical Editor
Raghu Vullaganti

Copy Editor
Lisa Theobald

Proofreader
Stefany Otis

Indexer
Valerie Robbins

Computer Designers
Mickey Galicia
Lucie Ericksen

Illustrator
Beth E. Young, Lyssa Sieben-Wald,
Robert Hansen, Michael Mueller

Series Design
Jani Beckwith

Cover Designer
Damore Johann Design, Inc.

This book was composed with Corel VENTURA ™ Publisher.

Dedicated to my father and mother
for their love, inspiration, and strength.

About the Author

Shankaran Iyer has more than sixteen years' experience in the IS Industry, and for the last thirteen years he has specialized in large mission-critical projects using Oracle Server, Application, and Tools. He has worked as a Financials Administrator and Technical Architect in a variety of environments.

Shankaran is a regular presenter at Oracle conferences in the U.S. and Europe. He has presented at Oracle Apps World, Oracle Open World, and IOUG-A Live conferences on topics like E-Business Technology, Database administration, and ERP issues.

Shankaran holds a master's degree in Computer Science and is currently working as Technology Manager in Renaissance Worldwide IT Consulting, Inc., in Bloomington, Minnesota.

Contents

PART I
Introduction

PART II
Setting Up the Financials Environment

PART III
Database Administration and Maintenance

PART IV

Tuning Your Environment

PART V
DBA Tools and Processes

PART VI

Miscellaneous Topics

Acknowledgments

Many people have helped and inspired me in writing this book and converting it from a dream to a reality. I would like to thank each one of them for their help and support. I want to gratefully acknowledge the help I received from several friends at Oracle Corporation, and also from the Metal Link and Oracle Technology Network. I would like to thank the friendly team at Osborne/McGraw Hill, including Acquisitions Editors Jeremy Judson and Scott Rogers, Project Editor Jennifer Malnick, and the entire Acquisition and Production teams, for painstakingly copyediting my work and getting those last-minute changes in while keeping on top of deliverable dates. It has been a great team effort. Special thanks to Jeremy for all his help and support.

I would like to sincerely thank Raghu Vullaganti and other members of the Technical Editorial team, who did an excellent job of reviewing the chapters and providing suggestions for improvements. Your time and expertise were really valuable and appreciated.

I also want to thank my wonderful wife, Sudha, who not only meticulously reviewed many of the chapters and provided feedback but was also very supportive and encouraging while I wrote this book. My special thanks are due to my dear daughter, Shruti, for being so understanding in spite of Dad putting in long writing hours in the home office. I am indebted to Sudha and Shruti for letting me write this book and encouraging me to make it a reality.

I would like to acknowledge the encouragement I received from my team at the Minneapolis Branch of Renaissance Worldwide, especially our leader, Bonnie Harris. Bonnie was really supportive right from the day I decided to write up till now.

I would also like to thank everyone I have worked with in the past, who directly or indirectly influenced my work and my thoughts.

Introduction

scalable and complex product like Oracle E-Business Suite bundles several new capabilities that benefit the business in a very positive way. The business requirements have been increasingly driving the technology requirements, and indeed the best use of technology is to add value to business by deploying easy-to-use, easily repeatable and scalable processes. Oracle E-Business Suite introduces several newer elements in its mix including Oracle8i, Oracle Application Server components, and business intelligence tools working together to deliver value.

Understanding these technical components along with the business requirements is a critical requirement for deploying various modules like financials, human resources, and so on. A Financial administrator fills this critical role with his understanding of the technology stack components, his ability to administer the database, and the application based on his understanding of the application components.

This book is designed to help an Oracle Financials DBA perform administration of the Oracle E-Business Suite Financials environment. It includes a plethora of tips and techniques, sample plans, step-by-step instructions for implementation, and also many scripts to help the Financials administrator perform her role in a very effective manner. It contains information on using AD utilities, managing application patches, and application-specific performance tuning tips, which can make any new DBA operational right away.

Audience and Scope

This book is mainly intended for intermediate-level Oracle DBAs, application technical team leads, and managers. It is ideal for DBAs aspiring to get into Oracle Applications work, and can also help the more experienced Oracle Financials DBAs to understand specific topics as a handbook for performing specific tasks. This book can help Oracle Financials DBAs perform their day-to-day work including installation, patch application, troubleshooting, and tuning as well as help them plan upgrade of application versions. They should have knowledge of Oracle (as a developer or DBA) and some basic understanding of the Oracle Financial Modules.

In addition, any Oracle user or DBA who has installed or supported an Oracle database will find this book interesting. The discussions in various chapters are targeted toward Oracle E-Business Suite administration and apply to both NT and UNIX environments. In addition, there are discussions about many new features that can be implemented for improving overall throughput.

This book is useful for technical managers, architects, and designers to help them understand various functions performed by the administrators.

How to Use This Book

This book covers all aspects of the Oracle E-Business Suite Financials administrator's role including installation and upgrading Oracle Financials Module binaries, applying various patches, installing and upgrading the database, tracing and tuning various critical application modules, managing customizations, and more. It contains real-world examples and step-by-step instructions to perform day-to-day Oracle E-Business Suite Financials administration activities, and is designed to be a mentor for new Oracle E-Business Suite Financials administrators and to help them implement newer database features and also provide troubleshooting tips, sample plan templates, and tuning actions.

This book provides in-depth information on Oracle Financials–specific issues like using AD utilities as well as issues like version control, patch management, etc., and covers Oracle Financials–specific performance tuning and capacity planning guidelines. These guidelines are really valuable since they are always required but are hard to get. It addresses the requirements of Oracle E-Business Suite administrators by providing them information about customization information as well as implementing standard functionality.

This book is divided into six parts.

Part I provides an introduction to Oracle E-Business Suite and some of its more important modules. It also includes a review of the architecture components of 11i. This section is important since there are several modules in Oracle E-Business Suite and each operates on a common architectural framework. It is important to understand the basic components and their interactions. Part I also has a good discussion on the roles and responsibilities of what we call Financials administrator, or database administrator, managing the Oracle Financials environment. The roles performed by the Financials administrator vary to a great extent and are largely dependent on the size and complexity of the implementation.

Here is a breakdown of Part I.

Chapter 1: Introduction to Oracle Applications 11i Suite

This chapter presents an introduction to Oracle Application Suite in general and specifically about 11i enhancements. It also includes a breakdown of Oracle Financials Modules, and a presentation of technical architecture explaining various components in a typical Oracle Financials setup.

Chapter 2: Roles and Responsibilities of a Financials DBA

This chapter discusses typical identified roles for a large Oracle Financials Implementation Project. Discussion includes upgrade projects as well as new implementations. With this as the basis, the importance of a DBA Roles for the Oracle Financials Implementation project is stressed, and a detailed list of the roles, duties, and responsibilities of Oracle Financials DBA is laid out, which lays the foundation for further chapters where the DBA functions are discussed in much more detail. Chapter 2 contains a section on how to succeed as an Oracle Financials DBA. It also presents guidelines to differentiate between customization, enhancements, and administration tasks.

Part II provides a discussion of the setup of Oracle E-Business Suite for a Financials implementation. The chapters in Part II discuss the Oracle Technology Stack and its components and how they operate in a three-tier architecture model. This is followed by a discussion of upgrading from older versions to Release 11i. The discussion covers many of technical differences like Cost-Based Optimization (CBO) as well as material to help the DBA deliver positively to an upgrade project. Part II also has a chapter on Managing the Financials Environment, which covers details about various utilities available for applying patches, linking application executables, printer setup issues, and more. The last chapter in this part discusses the concurrent manager best practices, tips, and techniques for ensuring maximum throughput from a concurrent manager setup.

Here is a breakdown of Part II.

Chapter 3: Installing and Configuring the Technology Stack

This chapter focuses on various database and application components and patches that need to be configured to create the Oracle Financials environment. The discussion covers installation aspects of the entire technology stack including

Developer Server, Forms Server, Reports Server, Application Server, Jdeveloper, and more.

Chapter 4 : Upgrading to Oracle Financials 11i

This chapter details upgrading existing Oracle Financials environments to 11i. The discussion includes impact analysis, technology issues, upgrade steps, and best practices, as well as utilization of Cost-Based Optimization.

The second section of this chapter discusses the DBA's tasks during the upgrade to 11i. This section contains typical deliverables expected out of a DBA and step-by-step information on preparing for the upgrades, installation process, various patches, post installation steps, and more.

Chapter 4 also refers to Chapter 18, Using Oracle8i Features, and highlights some of the features that can be turned on during upgrade.

Chapter 5: Managing the Financials Environment

This chapter lists various DBA Functions required for ongoing maintenance of Oracle Financials environment, and will provide step-by-step methods and best practices. Some of the functions discussed include:

- Creating development, test, and production environment
- Copy or refresh production data to development or test
- Using AD utilities like ADAIMGR, ADRELINK, and so on
- Applying and backing out patches
- Checklist of steps performed for removing all traces of an instance
- Printer setup issues

Chapter 6: Managing the Concurrent Manager

This chapter discusses the concepts and issues around using Concurrent Manager processes, setup issues, best practices, tuning tips, and configuration recommendations.

Part III is dedicated to database administration and maintenance tasks. It discusses issues close to the Financials administrator's heart including managing and tracking data growth, version control techniques, and patch management recommendations. This part also has a detailed chapter on how the administrator can use the Cost-Based Optimizer effectively as well as provides an introduction to various Open Interfaces, which can be implemented in an Oracle E-Business Suite environment.

Here is a breakdown of Part III.

Chapter 7: Managing Growth

This chapter covers issues like tracking data growth, sizing and organizing tables and indexes, fragmentation issues, index rebuild options, and so on.

Chapter 8: Change Control and Patch Management

This chapter includes information for keeping track of application changes as well as customizations. Many version control techniques are discussed.

The second section covers Patch Management issues including information on how patches work, types of drivers, why patch management is critical, working with patches in a multi-project implementation environment, and third-party tools for Patch Management.

Chapter 9: Managing CBO in a 11i Environment

This chapter discusses setting up the Financials to use CBO using the FND_STATS package.

Chapter 10: Open Interface

This chapter discusses Open Interfaces, tips for using the SQL Loader interface, PL/SQL, etc., and also data conversion strategies and File Manager Access Utility (FNDGFU).

Chapter 11: Troubleshooting

This chapter includes important tips and techniques on the most common problems and how to fix them in an Oracle Financials environment.

Part IV provides a discussion of another important facet of the administrator's responsibility—tuning. It discuss in detail the application tuning aspects and stresses the importance of collecting statistics for each layer of the technology stack, analyzing them, and then implementing changes. The next chapter covers the latest database statistics collection tool by Oracle called Statspack. Statspack provides important insights into the database resource consumption and is recommended in comparison to its predecessors, utlbstat and utlestat. Part IV concludes with a discussion of Capacity Planning and sizing for the application.

Here is a breakdown of Part IV.

Chapter 12: Application Performance Tuning

This chapter covers detailed information about performance audit and tuning methodology for Oracle Financials application and areas like database, network, internet, concurrent manager, forms/reports, and more. Both 11 and 11i are covered. A consolidated approach of collecting statistics, analyzing them, and making changes is discussed with step-by-step tuning steps. SQL Tuning is also discussed along with different values for init.ora parameters.

Chapter 13: Collecting Statistics Using Statspack

This chapter includes a step-by-step method of implementing Statspack for collecting performance statistics and performing reactive tuning.

Chapter 14: Capacity Planning and Sizing

This chapter includes planning for various hardware resources, defining a holistic equation for growth, coming up with optimal configuration, and other tips for capacity planning.

Part V discusses various tools and processes that are part of the Financials administrator's roles and responsibilities. The chapters in this part cover important aspects like discussion of toolkit for the administrator to perform various functions. The chapter on backup and recovery presents a high-level discussion of backup requirements for the administrator. The chapter on security provides an overview of the application security for both standard modules and custom module implementations. The last chapter in this section is an important one. It presents an in-depth discussion of Oracle8i features that can be leveraged in an Oracle E-Business Suite implementation.

Here is a breakdown of Part V.

Chapter 15: Financial Administrator's Toolkit

This chapter covers an evaluation of various tools like Oracle Enterprise Manager, Precise, and other tools that can be used for maintaining and monitoring the Oracle Financials Environment. The discussion also includes a wish list of the typical activities needed to be done versus how far a tool can help with that. It also contains important scripts to add to any administrator's tool chest.

Chapter 16: Backup and Recovery

This chapter reviews and discusses various backup issues and strategies. It also discusses availability issues, best practices, and evaluation requirements for a standby recovery database.

Chapter 17: Security

This chapter discusses security issues around Oracle Financials and issues like web security, data protection, and the fine-grained access control options available with Oracle8i in the context of Oracle Financials.

It will also include setting up users and responsibilities, privileges, security group, and more.

Chapter 18: Using Oracle8i Features

This chapter includes some important features of Oracle8i that can be leveraged by DBAs when setting Oracle Financials Environment. Features covered include partitioning, FGAC, Resource Manager Groups, and Parallel Query implementation.

Part VI covers some miscellaneous topics related to the function of the Financials administrator including a discussion of Oracle Portal, for deploying custom self-service modules; and Oracle Financial Analyzer, for implementing advanced analysis and forecasting of General Ledger data.

Here is a breakdown of Part VI

Chapter 19: Oracle Portal (WebDB)

This chapter discusses Oracle Portal features and functionality.

Chapter 20: Oracle Financial Analyzer

This chapter reviews the Oracle Financial Analyzer tool and how it can be integrated with Oracle General Ledger to get advanced forecasting and drilling functionality.

PART

I

Introduction

CHAPTER
1

Introduction to the Oracle Application Suite

- What's in the Oracle Application Suite
- Product suites
- Additional enhancements
- Internationalization support
- Introduction to file system

racle Application Suite version 11i combines several product modules, including Oracle Financials, Manufacturing, Conflict Resolution Manager, and Human Resources. It is based on Oracle's Internet Computing Architecture and provides the administrator with the ease and flexibility of managing a complex environment from a single point. This chapter introduces some of the features and enhancements of the Oracle Application Suite that will serve as background information for installing the suite or upgrading to the 11i release from a previous version.

What's in the Oracle Application Suite

Oracle Application Suite version 11i is completely Internet enabled and can be centrally managed from a single site. In addition, data centers can be consolidated, leading to fewer servers to maintain and reduced information fragmentation. Using the Oracle Application Suite, a global company can operate one data center with a single database instance rather than operating multiple data centers in different parts of the world.

The Oracle Application Suite helps achieve and support consolidation in your business. Some of the salient features of release 11i include the following:

- Internet Computing Architecture

- Additional enhancements

- Internationalization support

- Simplified file system

Internet Computing Architecture

The Internet Computing Architecture is a framework for three-tiered, distributed computing that supports the Oracle application environment. The Internet Computing Architecture distributes *services* (applications, requests) among as many *nodes* (machines) on a network as are required to support the processing load. Processes run in the background for application components such as Forms Server Listener and Report Server Listener, which listens for requests and processes them. The HTTP server runs in the background and listens for HTTP requests.

The three tiers in the architecture are called the Database tier (which includes the Oracle8i database), the Application or Middle tier (which manages Oracle applications and tools), and the Desktop tier (which provides the user interface). Figure 1-1 shows the three tiers and various components of a typical Oracle Application Suite implementation. In the Internet Computing Architecture, the Desktop tier contains only a plug-in to a standard browser. The application is accessed using a standard browser from a PC using an appropriate URL. A Java applet (Jinitiator) is downloaded

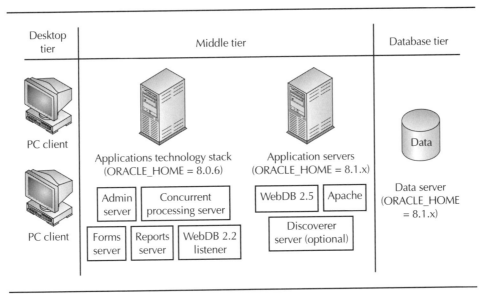

FIGURE 1-1.   *The three-tiered architecture in Oracle Application Suite 11i*

from the application server down to the PC. Oracle application software and other tools are deployed on the Application tier. This tier eliminates the need to install and maintain application software on each desktop client. The software on the Application tier also enables Oracle applications to scale with load and keep network traffic low.

Release 11i Product Suites

Release 11i includes two principal product suites: Enterprise Resource Planning (ERP) products and Customer Relationship Management (CRM) products.

The ERP products are the "back office" products familiar to users of earlier Oracle releases, such as Oracle Financials. In the ERP suite are more than 90 products that help your business manage important operations, including purchasing, inventory management, supplier interaction, order tracking, financial planning, and accounting. The ERP products are divided into several product families: Financials, Human Resources, Manufacturing and Distribution, and Process Manufacturing.

CRM products provide "front office" functions, such as call-center management service, e-commerce, and Internet sales and marketing. CRM products help your business build lasting customer relationships and increase customer satisfaction and loyalty.

Forms Server and Forms Client

The Application tier software used in most ERP and CRM products is the Forms server, which works between the Forms client (a Java applet running on the desktop) and the database in the Database tier. Both the Forms server and Forms client are components of Oracle Forms. The Forms server updates the database with changes that correspond to user input. The server and client exchange messages across a standard network connection, which may be either TCP/IP (Transmission Control Protocol/Internet Protocol) or HTTP (Hypertext Transfer Protocol), with or without SSL (Secure Sockets Layer). The Forms client can display any Oracle applications screen and provides field-level validation, multiple coordinated windows, and data entry aids such as list of values. A Java-enabled Web browser manages the downloading, startup, and execution of the Forms client on the desktop.

Another software component, the HTTP server, helps start a client session over the internal or external Web. The Apache HTTP Server is the HTTP server in release 11i. In installations with multiple Forms servers, only one of the Forms servers runs the HTTP server software. If more than one Forms server is used, Oracle Forms also provides a Common Gateway Interface (CGI) script that distributes the processing load among the servers.

HTML-Based Products

Release 11i also includes products that are based on Oracle Self-Service Web Applications technology, Oracle Workflow, and Oracle Business Intelligence System (BIS) products. These products do not use the Forms server as the Application tier software or the Forms client on the desktop; instead, they rely on HTTP-based servers on the Application tier and a Java-enabled Web browser on the desktop.

Oracle Self-Service Web Applications and Oracle Workflow   Self-Service Web Applications provide a fast and cost-effective way to get information to and from people within an organization. For example, a user can register himself to use a part of the application, rather than having to depend on a network administrator to do this for him. This leads to quick throughput for the end user, faster setup time, and less workload for the functional and technical folks in the project team.

Many Oracle applications use Oracle Workflow to enforce business rules and policies automatically and to provide a common notification system. Oracle Workflow monitors business processes, collects process data, and provides an e-mail and Web page notification system. Release 11i includes the full Oracle Workflow product and the license to customize any Oracle applications embedded in Workflow.

Most Oracle Self-Service Web Applications and Oracle Workflow applications are designed using authoring tools such as HTML, XML, and JavaScript. These applications operate via direct connection to the Apache HTTP Server. Logic is controlled through stored procedures executed by the PL/SQL cartridge and by Java servlets and JavaServer Pages (JSP) executed by the Apache JServ module. Apache communicates with the database using Java Data Base Connectivity (JDBC). The Apache HTTP Server can be the same machine used by Oracle Forms.

Business Intelligence System Products   BIS is a decision support solution integrated with the Oracle Application Suite. Using the BIS products, a manager can query the Oracle applications database to monitor recent business performance across multiple organizations. For instance, line managers can set sales or inventory goals for their units and then follow actual sales or inventory to keep track of the progress. The managers can also set thresholds using the BIS tools and can be informed when a particular threshold is crossed.

With the BIS Performance Manager Framework, some corrective actions can be performed automatically. BIS in ERP and CRM products do not use the Forms server or Forms client. Instead, BIS products use the Oracle Discoverer server and Oracle Reports server on the Application tier. A Java applet running on a desktop client communicates with the HTTP server, which connects to the Discoverer server or Reports server. The Discoverer server provides ad hoc analysis; then the Reports server supports data analysis and ad hoc queries, often using summary tables such as monthly aggregates of data, and returns them to the browser. The desktop browser initiates the request; the HTML server passes the request to the Discoverer or Reports server; and the Discoverer or Reports server gathers the data and returns it to the browser as HTML.

To support BIS in ERP products, release 11i includes a file that will generate an Oracle Discoverer End User Layer (EUL). When the EUL is generated, workbooks and queries can be saved to the database. You must, however, use the Oracle Discoverer Administrator's Edition, which is not included in release 11i, to generate this EUL. With the Administrator's Edition, you can also create additional EULs, administer security information, and set responsibilities.

Release 11i Enhancements

Release 11i provides the following enhancements that improve usability, increase performance, and simplify the installation and maintenance of Oracle applications:

- The Personal Homepage provides users with a single point of access to all Oracle applications.

- Release 11i leverages the power of Oracle8i to increase performance speed and reduce network traffic.

- Rapid Install automates installation and drastically reduces the time for getting Oracle applications online. In addition, internationalization support allows users to set language, date and time configurations, currency, and other formatting options that are location specific.

The following sections further review these enhancements.

Personal Homepage

In release 11i, each user logs in to the Oracle Applications Suite through the Personal Homepage on the desktop client. The Personal Homepage is the starting point from which you access all ERP, CRM, Self-Service Web Applications, and BIS products. Once logged into the Personal Homepage (see Figure 1-2), you need not sign on again

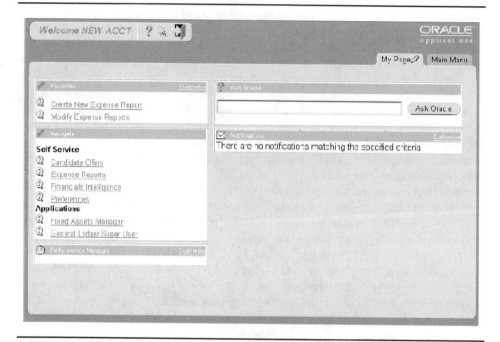

FIGURE 1-2. *A typical Oracle applications personal home page*

to access other parts of the system—in other words, you will not be prompted again for your user name and password, even when you navigate to other tools and products. Oracle applications also retains preferences as you navigate through the system.

Behind the scenes, the Personal Homepage is communicating with the Application tier server. For example, when you go to an Oracle Self-Service Web Applications page, the browser makes the URL request to an HTTP server Web listener. The listener in turn contacts a PL/SQL cartridge, which runs a stored procedure on the database server. You can customize the Personal Homepage to fit your individual needs and responsibilities

Customizing the Personal Homepage   In release 11i, each user can choose a preferred language, date format, and number style in a Personal Homepage. Users can also set an installed language as the default language and change to another language for any session. User preferences are stored in the Oracle8i database. When you log on, the Application tier servers read your user preferences from the database and then format information for you based on your preferences.

Before a user can customize or set preferences on the Personal Homepage, the system administrator must first define a user account, including a user name and default password, and assign the user responsibilities. The system administrator must also have defined "Preferences" as one of the user's responsibilities.

The Personal Homepage can contain one or more tab pages. Each tab page is laid out in regions, such as Navigate, Favorites, Ask Oracle, and Notifications. The default tab page, the Main Menu page, is automatically created for each user and cannot be deleted. The user can add or delete all other tab pages, and can thereby create an interface that clearly shows the products, responsibilities, and tools needed for daily operations.

The Navigate region of the Personal Homepage provides a list of responsibilities that the system administrator assigned to the user. Favorites can include links to frequently used Self-Service Web Applications or BIS product features, or to favorite URLs. The Ask Oracle region allows you to enter search criteria in the text box and returns a related set of links. Ask Oracle uses the Oracle8i *interMedia* engine to search for Oracle Self-Service Applications and BIS product functions. The Notifications region lists Workflow notifications sent to you.

You can customize each region on the tab page to expand or limit the information it contains, or to display the information in a different format. If Preferences is one of the responsibilities listed in the Navigate area, you can choose this item to change the session language, or to create an alias user name, specify a default language, and change date and number format. Each user can thereby set his or her own local preferences. Two users may have differing language and territory-specific sessions, whether they are located next to each other and sharing the same office or they are located on different continents.

Language Support

In the previous version of the Oracle Application Suite, you could specify only one language (called the *base* language). If more languages were required, customization was often necessary. With release 11, you could run Oracle applications in more than one language, but the set of available languages was limited to the languages supported by your character set.

In release 11, textual parts of Oracle applications, such as Forms, Reports, messages, help text, menu prompts, and lists of report names, were available in all active languages, but most data at the product level was available only in the base language. This meant, for example, that you could enter payment terms only in the base language, even though Forms would appear in a nonbase language. For additional multilingual support in the products, customization was often required.

In release 11i, however, support for the Unicode UTF8 character set removes the limitation on the number of supported languages that can be run in a single instance. The Unicode character set supports all characters in common use in all of the world's modern languages. The majority of Oracle applications (but not all) have been restructured in release 11i to provide multilingual support at the data level.

Languages and Character Sets on the Database Tier   The Oracle8i Database tier is installed in the US7ASCII character set by default, but it can be converted to run in any other supported character set. You choose the database character set when running Rapid Install, and Rapid Install converts the database to the new character set.

The US7ASCII character set supports only American English. Other character sets vary in the number of languages they support. For example, if you need to run Oracle applications in English and French, you might choose WE8ISO8859P15 as the database character set when running Rapid Install. WE8ISO8859P15 is a superset of US7ASCII, supports both English and French, and contains the Euro symbol. If you need to support English, French, Japanese, and Arabic, however, you must choose the UTF8 character set, because this is the only one that supports these four languages. You cannot change the character set while upgrading from an earlier release to release 11i. You must first upgrade to release 11i using the existing character set; after the upgrade, you can change the character set.

The extended multilingual support in the release 11i data model increases database storage requirements. For a new installation, consider the database space required for a single language and multiply this by the number of languages you will support. For an upgrade of an earlier natural language support (NLS) installation, some of the data currently in a single language structure will be converted to a multilingual structure, which will require additional storage.

Before installing the Oracle Application Suite, carefully consider the worldwide language requirements. The character set you choose determines the languages that you can support. Starting with version 8.1.7, Oracle provides a utility called *csscan* that can scan your database and point out specific tables and columns that may be affected by a character set change. It is certainly a good idea to evaluate the character set requirements before the implementation to avoid additional downtime, risks, and expenses.

Language and Character Sets on the Application Tier   The Application tier is installed in the US7ASCII character set by default, but it can be converted to run in any supported character set. You specify the Application tier character set when running Rapid Install. To prevent data loss, character sets on all tiers should either be the same or should be sets that can be converted to another character set. (Some character sets allow a conversion with no data loss because the character representation in one corresponds to an appropriate character representation in the other. For example, JA16SJIS and JA16EUC are both Japanese language character sets and allow for conversion with no data loss.) If a target character set does not contain all characters in the source data, replacement characters will be used and data is thereby lost. The HTTP servers on the Application tier must use a character set supported by the browsers on the Desktop tier. The browsers may not support all the character sets available for the HTTP server. This is the only compatibility requirement between the Desktop tier and Application tier. All other Application tier servers, such as the Concurrent Processing server, can be configured with any other character set that is compatible with the database server.

By default, Rapid Install installs American English on all servers in the Application tier. If you later install a NLS release on these servers, you must install all other licensed languages on all servers. All Application tier servers must have the same set of languages installed. As UTF8 is a superset of all other character sets, there are no other fully compatible character sets. If you use UTF8 on any tier, you must use UTF8 on all tiers.

Character Sets on the Desktop Tier   Language support, which includes support for data input methods and required character sets and fonts, must be available in the desktop client's operating system. If Unicode UTF8 is installed on the Application tier, the desktop client operating system must support Unicode. You must therefore license a UTF8 font and make it available to each desktop client. The desktop browser must be configured to input data in the required language and must handle any language-specific capabilities. The HTTP server sets the character set of the browser and should not be changed by users during their application session.

External Documents   *External* documents are documents intended for customers and trading partners, such as bills of lading, commercial invoices, and packing slips. In release 11i, you can produce many external documents in any of the active languages, simultaneously and with a single request. For example, a customer in Paris can receive her invoice printed in French. You can also print the documents to different printers based on language and route completion notifications to different people according to the requested language.

Territory and Organization Support   Each of the organizations within a worldwide enterprise may have its own set of local requirements. In a worldwide operation, all organizations in the enterprise must have these local requirements integrated in a single instance.

Country-Specific Functionality   The Oracle Application Suite has a single common core of functionality, with country-specific extensions to meet the statutory, legal, and cultural practices of different countries. Release 11i supports a worldwide enterprise by installing all these extensions in the same database instance without them overwriting or conflicting with each other. Although all country-specific extensions are installed, you must license each extension before you can use its country-specific functionality. Rapid Install lists all the countries that have extensions and licenses the extensions you choose.

Dates and Numbers

You can enter and view dates in any valid format, such as 11/25/01 or 11-25-2001. Any format for which SQL provides a mask is valid. The only exception to flexible date formats is that reports will always display the Y2K compliant format DD-MON-RRRR.

You can also enter and view numbers with either the period (full stop) character or a comma as the decimal separator. The only exception to flexible numeric formats is that Oracle Self-Service Web Applications always enters and displays numbers with the period as decimal separator and the comma as group separator.

Regardless of the various formats users may choose to enter dates and numbers, the actual values are stored in the database in uniform canonical formats. This allows date and number values to be entered in one format and viewed in another format by another user.

NLS-Independent Application Servers

In release 11, an Application tier server was required for each language and territory configuration a user might have. For example, to process French and German Forms requests, you needed to start one Forms server for French and one for German. Even if two users both ran French, but one set the territory to France and the other to Switzerland, you would need to install two Forms servers and two Reports servers to support these two users. In release 11i, you no longer need to set up a server for each user's set of NLS preferences. All Application tier server processes can start with any NLS configuration.

Application tier processes must be started with the same character set that was chosen for the server in Rapid Install. All other user NLS settings (such as language, territory, date style, and number format) are passed with each user request to the Application tier servers, and the server's start up sessions are configured with those NLS settings.

NLS Settings   Earlier releases relied on operating system environment settings for runtime NLS requirements. In release 11i, user runtime NLS settings are stored as *profile option* values in the database.

The profile options for language and territory are configured at site level when running Rapid Install. The language you choose for the base language is used for the language profile option. The default user territory you choose is used for the territory profile option. Rapid Install does not set date and numeric formats. Based on the territory profile setting, default Oracle8i date and numeric formats are used.

Although the system administrator can reset date and numeric formats after Rapid Install, we recommend that you accept the defaults provided by the territory setting. The site level profile values provide the default NLS settings for all end users. Users inherit these values the first time they log on to Oracle applications using the Personal Homepage. A user can continue to use the default values or change any of the four NLS settings to other values. The updated values are stored in the database at the profile user level.

Multiple Organization Architecture

You can define multiple organizations (Multi-Org) and the relationships among them in a single installation of the Oracle Application Suite. The organization model dictates how transactions flow through different organizations and how those organizations interact with each other. Generally, a complex enterprise has several organization models, such as Internal, Accounting, and Human Resources. You can define different structures to customize Oracle applications for your worldwide business needs.

Multi-Org is also the underlying technology for Multiple Reporting Currencies. The types of organizations that can be defined include business group, set of books, legal entity, balancing entity, operating unit, inventory organization, HR organization, and organizations in Oracle Projects and Oracle Fixed Assets. The set of books organization, for example, is a financial reporting entity that uses a particular chart of accounts, functional currency, and accounting calendar. A legal entity represents a legal company for which you prepare fiscal or tax reports. You assign tax identifiers and other legal entity information to this type of organization.

With the various organization types, you set up different organization models depending on your enterprise needs. For instance, using the accounting, distribution, and materials management functions, you can define the relationships among inventory organizations, operating units, legal entities, and sets of books to create a multilevel company structure or organization model.

When you run Oracle applications, you first choose an organization—either implicitly by choosing a responsibility or explicitly in a Choose Organization window. Each window and report then displays information just for your organization.

Multiple Reporting Currencies   The Multiple Reporting Currencies (MRC) feature allows you to report and maintain accounting records at the transaction level, in more than one functional currency. This can be done by defining one or more reporting sets of books, in addition to your primary set of books.

In your reporting sets of books, you maintain records in a functional currency other than your *primary functional currency*. Primary functional currency is the currency you use to record transactions and maintain your accounting data within Oracle applications. The primary functional currency is generally the currency in which you perform most of your business transactions and the one you use for legal reporting. A *reporting functional currency* is a currency other than your primary functional currency that you need for reports.

MRC is based on Multi-Org and requires a primary set of books and a reporting set of books. In the primary set of books, the functional currency is always the primary functional currency. The reporting set of books is a financial reporting entity associated with a primary set of books. The reporting set of books has the same chart of accounts and accounting calendar as the primary set of books, but the former usually has a different functional currency. The reporting set of books allows you to report in a different functional currency than that of your primary set of books. You must define a separate set of books for each of your reporting functional currencies. For each set of books you use with MRC, you need to specify which is the primary set of books and which are the reporting sets of books. You then assign the reporting sets of books to the primary set of books. You must also define a primary responsibility to correspond to your primary set of books and a reporting responsibility to correspond to each reporting set of books.

File System

In release 11i, no Oracle files are stored on the desktop client. In release 11i, the database server holds only database files. All Oracle Application Suite product files, technology stack files, common files, and Oracle Enterprise Manager files are held in the *file system* on the Application tier servers. *Environment settings* indicate the location of files in the file system. Refer to Figure 1-3 for an illustration of the file system on the Database and Application tiers.

Oracle applications use environment settings to control program execution. These settings are defined when you install the Oracle Application Suite. Many settings are defined by information you provide when running Rapid Install; other settings have constant values for all installations. In the sections that follow, braces (< and >) indicate the value that an environment setting contains. For example, *<dbname>* indicates the database name as contained in the ORACLE_SID or TWO_TASK environment setting. On UNIX servers, environment files hold the environment variable settings for each Applications TOP directory. Each Applications TOP directory has a main

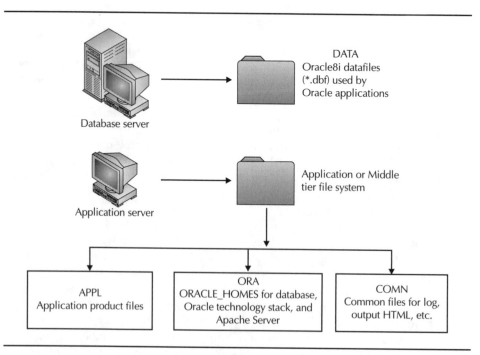

FIGURE 1-3. *Standard subdirectories created for Oracle applications for the database server and the application server*

environment file, *<dbname>*.env, which is named after the database instance associated with the installation.

Windows NT includes an additional main environment file called *<dbname>*.cmd. You may choose a different name for the main environment file with the AD Administration utility (adadmin—Application Development Administration Utility), but you cannot change the name when running Rapid Install. On Windows NT, environment settings are stored in the Registry under the following key:

```
HKEY_LOCAL_MACHINE/SOFTWARE/ORACLE/Applications/11.5.0/<dbname>
```

The *<dbname>*DATA Directory

The *<dbname>*DATA file system contains the .dbf files of the Oracle8i database. Rapid Install installs all the system, data, and index files in up to four different disks on the database server. You can specify mount points for these different disks and directory names on the database server during installation.

The Concurrent Managers use temporary files located on the Oracle8i server. You may specify up to three separate locations for these files when running Rapid Install, AutoUpgrade, or the adadmin utility. Most temporary files are written to the location specified by the APPLTMP environment setting, which is set by Rapid Install. If you choose, Oracle Reports temporary files can be directed to a separate location determined by the REPORTS60_TMP setting. Applications also produces temporary PL/SQL output files used in concurrent processing. These files are written to the location specified by the APPLPTMP environment setting. The APPLPTMP directory must be the same directory as specified by the utl_file_dir parameter in your database initialization file. Rapid Install sets both APPLPTMP and the utl_file_dir parameter to the same directory. During an upgrade with AutoUpgrade, you must provide the utl_file_dir parameter value for the APPLPTMP environment setting.

The *<dbname>*APPL Directory

Oracle applications files are stored in the *<dbname>*APPL directory. Rapid Install saves the name of this *<dbname>*APPL directory in the APPL_TOP environment setting.

Some Oracle application utilities use your operating system's default temporary directory even if you define alternative environment settings. Be sure that disk space is available for these default directories as well as those denoted by APPLTMP, REPORTS60_TMP, and APPLPTMP.

Figure 1-4 shows the location of the main environment file, the *<dbname>*.env file, and four product directories. Rapid Install creates a directory tree for every Oracle application in this APPL_TOP directory.

Within the APPL_TOP directory, files associated with a product are installed under the product's top-level directory, which is stored in the *<prod>*_TOP environment setting. The *<prod>* portion of this environment setting is the product's short name, such as *AD, AU, FND, GL,* and *INV*. The corresponding *<prod>*_TOP environment settings are AD_TOP, AU_TOP, FND_TOP, GL_TOP, and INV_TOP.

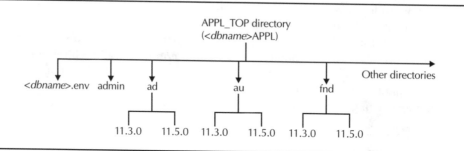

FIGURE 1-4. *The layout of the APPL_TOP directory*

For compatibility with earlier releases, Rapid Install creates another directory, named for the version number, within the product's short name directory. Therefore, as shown in Figure 1-4, the value contained in the AD_TOP environment setting is APPL_TOP/ad/11.5.0, and the AD_TOP environment setting points to the APPL_TOP/ad/11.5.0 directory. Similarly, the value of AU_TOP is APPL_TOP/au/11.5.0, and the AU_TOP environment setting points to the APPL_TOP/au/11.5.0 directory. This is the same for all directories except for the admin directory. Rapid Install creates a new Applications TOP directory when you upgrade. Rapid Install does not delete any existing product files from earlier releases, but it unloads new product files in a new <dbname>APPL directory tree.

Each Applications TOP directory is associated with a single Oracle database instance on the Oracle8i server. If you install both a Vision Demo environment and a test environment, you must use Rapid Install to lay down two file systems: one for each environment.

Vision Demo is a small and complete 11i application suite that comes with the Oracle Application Suite CDs. The Vision Demo can be used for reviewing and testing various functionality of various modules, and can be installed from the Rapid Install wizard. Vision Demo is also used for stress testing of the application for specific number of users before the actual production rollout.

Core Technology Directories

The admin, ad, au, and fnd directories are the *core technology directories*. The admin directory holds files used for the preliminary install or upgrade steps for all Oracle applications. Subdirectories in the admin directory hold the log and restart files that record the actions performed by installation and upgrade utilities and scripts.

The ad (Applications DBA) directory contains the installation and maintenance utilities such as AutoUpgrade, AutoPatch, and the adadmin utility. The au (Applications Utilities) directory contains PL/SQL libraries used by Oracle Forms and Oracle Reports, Oracle Forms source files, and a copy of all Java files used to generate the desktop client. The fnd (foundation) directory contains the forms, C object libraries, and scripts that are used to build the Oracle applications data dictionary.

Product Directories

Each *<prod>*_TOP directory, such as APPL_TOP/gl/11.5.0, contains subdirectories for product files. Product files include forms files, reports files, and some files used to install or upgrade the database (tables and other database objects are stored separately on the Oracle8i database server). To display data entry forms for Oracle General Ledger, for example, Oracle applications accesses files in the forms subdirectory under the 11.5.0 directory.

The *<dbname>*ORA Directory

The Oracle Application Suite supports running with data in a database of one version, while linking Oracle applications using the tools from a second or third version of the database server. This is known as *multiple Oracle home*s. This model allows Oracle to support features in later database server versions and still maintain compatibility with an earlier release.

The *database home* contains the files for creating and maintaining the Oracle8i database on the database server. The *technology stack home* contains library and object files the AD Relink Utility uses to link Oracle applications with forms-based tools on the Forms server and Report server. The *HTTP home* contains the object and library files used to link with the HTTP server.

The 11i database home and HTTP home contain Oracle8i object and library files. The 11i technology stack home uses libraries from the Oracle8 server technology stack, which includes Oracle Forms, Oracle Reports, Pro*C, PL/SQL, and SQL*Plus.

The *<dbname>*COMN Directory

The *<dbname>*COMN directory contains files that are used by several different Oracle applications (or all Oracle applications) or that are used with third-party products.

The admin directory in the *<dbname>*COMN directory contains the log and output directories for Concurrent Managers. When the Concurrent Managers run Oracle Reports, the default is to write the files to the log and out directories in the *<dbname>*COMN/admin/log and *<dbname>*COMN/admin/out directories. However, you can change the location to which the Concurrent Managers write these files, so that, for example, the log and output files are written to directories in each *<prod>*_TOP directory. The admin/assistants directory (known on Windows NT as the admin/assistant directory) of the admin directory contains the License Manager utility. You use the License Manager to license additional products or languages after installing the Oracle Application Suite. The admin/install directory contains scripts and log files used by Rapid Install during installation. The admin/scripts directory contains scripts to start and stop services such as listeners and Concurrent Managers.

The OAH_TOP environment setting points to the html directory. The Oracle Application Suite's HTML sign-on screen and Oracle Self-Service Web Applications HTML files are installed in the html directory. If you install a language other than American English, the html TOP directory contains subdirectories, named by language code, for the translated HTML files. The html directory also contains other files used by the HTML-based products, such as JavaServer Pages files, JavaScript files, XML files, and style sheets. Rapid Install copies the HTML-based product files from each *<prod>*_TOP directory to subdirectories in OAH_TOP.

The JAVA_TOP environment setting points to the java directory. Rapid Install installs all Oracle application class files in the Oracle namespace of this JAVA_TOP directory. The java directory holds third-party Java files used by Oracle applications as well as other zip files. Most Java code used by Oracle applications is version-controlled in the apps.zip file contained in the AU_TOP directory. Patches, for example, update individual classes in apps.zip under the AU_TOP directory, and from this apps.zip file, JAR files are generated both in the JAVA_TOP and the *<prod>*_TOP directories. The same apps.zip file exists in both the AU_TOP and JAVA_TOP directories.

The Java Archive (JAR) file format enables you to bundle multiple files into a single archive file. Typically, a JAR file will contain the class files and auxiliary resources associated with applets and applications. The JAR file format provides many benefits:

- **Security** You can digitally sign the contents of a JAR file. Users who recognize your signature can then optionally grant your software security privileges it wouldn't otherwise have. Decreased download time—If your applet is bundled in a JAR file, the applet's class files and associated resources can be downloaded to a browser in a single HTTP transaction without the need for opening a new connection for each file.

- **Compression** The JAR format allows you to compress your files for efficient storage. Packaging for extensions (version 1.2 - Not Supported in Webforms)—The extensions framework provides a means by which you can add functionality to the Java core platform, and the JAR file format defines the packaging for extensions. Java 3DTM and JavaMail are examples of extensions developed by Sun. By using the JAR file format, you can turn your software into extensions as well.

- **Package Sealing** Packages stored in JAR files can be optionally sealed so that the package can enforce version consistency. Sealing a package within a JAR file means that all classes defined in that package must be found in the same JAR file.

- **Package Versioning** A JAR file can hold data about the files it contains, such as vendor and version information.

- **Portability** The mechanism for handling JAR files is a standard part of the Java platform's core API.

The portal directory contains the Rapid Install Portal files. The Rapid Install Portal is a Web page that includes the post-install tasks that may be necessary for your installation, server administration scripts, installation documentation, and online help. Using a browser, you can view the Rapid Install Portal after you run Rapid Install.

The temp directory is used for caching by some processes such as Oracle Reports. The util directory contains the third-party utilities licensed to ship with Oracle applications. These include, for example, JRE, JDK (Java Developer Kit), and the unzip utility.

Oracle8i Features

Release 11i uses and leverages many features of Oracle8i to make the applications scalable and to improve performance. Using release 11i with Oracle8i creates a winning combination of application flexibility and database power. Chapter 18 of this book contains a detailed discussion of several useful Oracle8i features. A summary is provided here.

Cost-Based Optimization

The Oracle Optimizer evaluates many factors to calculate the most efficient way to execute a SQL statement. It uses either a *rule-based* or *cost-based* approach. Rule-based optimization was used in earlier Oracle releases, but the SQL used in release 11i is tuned for cost-based optimization, and release 11i requires that the Optimizer use cost-based optimization (CBO).

Using CBO, the Optimizer considers the available access paths and factors in statistical information for the tables and indexes that the SQL statement will access. CBO also considers hints, which are optimization suggestions placed in a comment of the SQL statement.

First, the Optimizer creates a set of potential execution plans for the SQL statement based on its available access paths and hints. Then the Optimizer estimates the *cost* of each execution plan based on statistics in the data dictionary for the data distribution and storage characteristics of the tables, indexes, and partitions. The Optimizer compares the costs of the execution plans and chooses the one with the smallest cost. For some operations, such as batch processing, release 11i uses CBO to achieve the best throughput, or the minimal resource use necessary to process all rows accessed by the statement. For other operations, such as accessing forms and communication with the desktop client, release 11i uses CBO to achieve the best response time, or the minimal resource use necessary to process the first row accessed by a SQL statement. Features like partitioning and materialized views also require the use of CBO.

Database Resource Manager

The Database Resource Manager in Oracle8i gives the system administrator more control over processing resources in a worldwide environment. For example, a user performing an inefficient query might impact other more important processes being performed by other users. With the Database Resource Manager, the system administrator can distribute access to the server central processing unit (CPU) based on business rules, thereby ensuring that the highest priority processing always has sufficient CPU time. Using the Database Resource Manager, the system administrator might, for example, limit ad hoc queries on the database to consume no more than 5 percent of CPU usage.

Partitioned Tables

Partitioning helps support very large tables and indexes by dividing them into smaller and more manageable pieces called *partitions*. After partitions are defined, SQL statements can access and manipulate the partitions rather than entire tables or indexes. Partitioning reduces access time, and partitions are especially useful in data warehouse applications, which often store and analyze large amounts of historical data. For example, operations that involve copying or deleting data are now improved because release 11i products use partitioned tables. Creating and deleting all rows of a partitioned table is a much faster operation than selectively inserting rows into and selectively deleting rows from an existing table. Operations in some products that in earlier releases could potentially take hours are now reduced to seconds.

Oracle Parallel Server

Oracle Parallel Server harnesses the processing power of multiple, interconnected computers all running Oracle8i and all attached to the same physical database. Servers (nodes) are clustered and attached to a *disk farm*. In an Oracle Parallel Server environment, all nodes concurrently execute transactions against the same database. Oracle Parallel Server coordinates each node's access to the shared data to provide consistency and integrity. By dividing a large task into subtasks and distributing the subtasks among multiple nodes, the task is completed faster than if only one node did the work. Oracle Parallel Server also provides increased performance to process larger workloads and accommodate the growing numbers of users of a worldwide operation.

In Oracle8i, Oracle Parallel Server allows an instance to share data that has been committed but not written to disk. Data may be in database buffers on one node and shipped over to another node to satisfy a query. This new architecture, called *cache fusion*, provides copies of blocks directly from the holding node's memory cache to the requesting node's memory cache. Cache fusion is useful when updates and queries on the same data tend to occur simultaneously.

Cache fusion, introduced in Oracle8i, provides a scalability breakthrough for Oracle Parallel Server. With cache fusion, you can also build redundancy into a worldwide operation. If one node goes down, there is no need to restore from backups, and the Oracle Application Suite will continue to be available despite the failure.

The Oracle Parallel Server option also has a Distributed Lock Manager (DLM) in the Oracle kernel. This allows Oracle to implement flexible, consistent, and portable solutions. The DLM introduces two new background processes:

- **LMON** Handles instance deaths and associated recovery for lock management

- **LMDN** Handles remote lock requests that originate from a different instance

Materialized Views

Materialized views increase the speed of queries on very large databases. Materialized views are schema objects that can be used to summarize, precompute, replicate, and distribute data. They are used to precompute and store aggregated data such as sums and averages. They provide better performance in Oracle applications, such as the BIS products that perform many queries on summary data. Cost-based optimization can use materialized views to improve query performance by automatically recognizing when one can and should be used to satisfy a request. The optimizer transparently rewrites the request to use the materialized view. Queries are then directed to the materialized view and not to the underlying detail tables or views. In distributed environments, materialized views are used to replicate data at distributed sites and synchronize updates at several sites with conflict resolution methods. As replicas, they provide local access to data that otherwise would have to be accessed from remote sites.

Temporary Tables

In addition to permanent tables, Oracle8i can create temporary tables to hold data that exists only for the duration of a transaction or session. The general ledger uses temporary tables for a session. In earlier releases, data from several users' sessions was written to one common table. A column in the table stored individual session IDs, so the information private to each user session could be selected from this common table. In Oracle8i, data in a temporary table is private to each user's session. Each session can see and modify only its own data. Locks are not acquired on the temporary table because each session has its own private data. Unlike permanent tables, SQL statements on temporary tables do not generate redo logs for the data changes. The older implementation also required additional housekeeping, such as deleting data from the table after a commit, which is not required with temporary tables. Data from the temporary table is automatically dropped when the session terminates.

Oracle Applications Manager

The Oracle Applications Manager provides a set of system administration functions on a new Oracle Enterprise Manager console. These functions include starting and stopping Concurrent Managers, administering Concurrent Managers and requests, and providing details on transaction managers. You can also define and edit managers and work shifts, and view concurrent request schedules and completion options, diagnostics, log and output files, statistics, and available managers. The Oracle Applications Manager also provides access to diagnostic and status information for concurrent processing that cannot be found in the Forms-based system administration interface.

Requests submitted within the standard Oracle applications windows can be viewed from the Oracle Applications Manager Console, and Concurrent Managers defined in the console can be accessed from within Forms-based Oracle applications.

Oracle Management Pack for Oracle Applications

The Oracle Management Pack for Oracle Applications extends the Oracle Enterprise Manager to include monitoring, diagnosing, and capacity planning of the Oracle applications environment. The Management Pack includes a set of tools that provide the following:

- An Oracle applications-specific library for event monitoring and problem detection

- An extensive array of real-time monitoring charts on all Concurrent Managers and Forms sessions

- Concurrent Manager performance consumption analysis and detection of performance anomalies

- Examination of historical processing information about Oracle concurrent processing requests and Concurrent Managers

Release 11i provides the enabling technology to create a single global instance that can be configured to meet the international requirements of the various organizations in your worldwide operation. International features include support for country-specific functionality, flexible dates and numbers, and multiple organizations and multiple reporting currencies.

Summary

The Oracle Application Suite provides a scalable architecture to support the environment from a single point. The architecture also makes use of the strengths of various technologies such as Forms, Reports, and the Oracle8i database to provide a winning combination of application and database. Release 11i provides for several welcome enhancements like the Personal Homepage, multilingual current support, and a simplified file system.

This chapter reviewed the Oracle Application Suite and enhancements to lay the groundwork for further discussions in subsequent chapters. We also reviewed some of the Oracle8i features leveraged by the Oracle Application Suite. In the next several chapters, we dig deeper into issues like installation and configuration of Oracle applications, upgrading and migrating from a previous version, managing various resources, changing control, and troubleshooting. We'll start by detailing the roles and responsibilities of an Oracle Financials administrator in the next chapter.

CHAPTER 2

Roles and Responsibilities of a Financials Administrator

- Define a Financials administrator
- Financials administrator's duties
- Skill sets of a Financials administrator
- Typical organization chart for Financials administration functions
- How to succeed as a Financials administrator

Financials administrator is a critical resource in any Oracle application implementation. No matter the size of the organization and the application, the administrator plays a crucial role in the creation and upkeep of the environment. A Financials administrator's duties are broad—responsibilities include day-to-day administration such as registering users, to more serious issues such as security and backup and recovery. In this chapter, we will consolidate the roles and responsibilities of a Financials administrator and define the skill sets required to fulfil this role.

In e-commerce environments, maintaining high availability and delivering consistent support and service are essential for sustaining business. If a company's response time degrades, additional costs are incurred, leading to a straight loss to the bottom line. E-commerce brings with it added complexity and interdependencies on one hand and increased user expectations on the other. The Financials administrator's role is critical in this context—and so complicated that it is difficult to list every role and responsibility of the administrator.

Who Is a Financials Administrator?

A Financials administrator is the person responsible for managing the operating system resources, capacity planning, and tuning activities. In the context of Oracle applications, the administrator is responsible for the upkeep of the environment. The responsibilities include a variety of activities, such as assigning user names and responsibilities, installing patches, and tuning performance.

A typical Oracle application implementation project has several identified roles, as described in the following list. These roles depend on the size of the implementation and the number of modules implemented. Often, two or more of these roles could be performed by a single person. Also, depending on the size of the operation, several folks could work on the same task as well.

- Project sponsor
- Project manager
- Project lead
- Functional and technical architects
- Developers
- Functional and technical administrator

A Financials administrator is a person or group of people who are responsible for controlling access and ensuring smooth day-to-day operations of the Oracle

Financials environment. Every Oracle Financials project should include a Financials administrator to perform tasks similar to the following:

- **Implementing security**   Define appropriate levels of access for each user and profile settings for each application. Determine which programs, functions, or reports can be accessed by each user.

- **Setting up new users**   Register application users via the setup provided by the Oracle applications and provide users access to forms, functions, and programs they need to perform their work.

- **Auditing users**   Monitor user activities—keep an eye on who is using the application and when. Decide which data should be audited.

- **Setting user profiles**   Set user profile—a set of changeable options that affects the way an Oracle application operates. Alter user profiles based on user application, responsibility, and levels.

- **Managing the concurrent processing**   Monitor, manage, and control the concurrent processing. Concurrent processing is Oracle's way of executing long-running, data-intensive programs in the batch mode to implement parallel processing and free up the online application to perform more useful work.

- **Tuning applications and databases**   Tune SQL statements or make database changes to ensure that the available system resources are utilized in a better way. The Financials administrator is the first point of contact for performance related issues.

- **Auditing system resources**   A Financials administrator is the first point of contact for issues relating to disk space availability, CPU, and memory resources and is also responsible for making sure that the assigned resources are available and are being properly utilized. More often, the Financials administrator works with the system administrators to achieve these objectives.

- **Incorporating custom programs**   Work with developers to move custom code into the environment. Responsible for migrating forms, reports, and batch programs when upgrading Oracle applications.

- **Sequencing documents**   Assign sequence to numbered documents using the Document Sequences window. A sequence's definition determines whether a document's number is automatically generated or manually entered by the user.

- **Managing printers**   Register printers to Oracle applications so that users can forward reports to specific printers.

Financial Administrator vs. Database Administrator

Oracle applications, as we will see in the following chapters, work in a three-tier mode: the database tier, the middle tier, and the desktop tier. When working with Oracle applications, note the following two distinctions:

- Oracle applications screens, forms, and processes that the users work with are typically part of the interface layers that form the middle layer, along with the Web server, form server, etc.

- The data manipulation occurs in the database tier.

A system administrator works with the user interface or application side of Oracle applications. An Oracle database administrator (DBA), however, is responsible for administering the database and maintaining the data in Oracle applications. Often this role is combined into a single role—the Financials administrator. A Financials administrator performs the administration role for Oracle applications not only on the application side but also on the database side.

Financials Administrator's Responsibilities

Every Oracle Financials project should have a Financials administrator. The Financials administrator has many responsibilities in achieving his overall mission of keeping the application environment running smoothly. In this section, we will review some of these responsibilities.

Technology Stack Installation and Configuration

The Financials administrator is involved with installing and configuring the Oracle Application Suite environment and installing various components of the technology stack. The administrator ensures that the components of the database, middle, and desktop tiers are properly installed. The administrator is also responsible for applying the latest available patches for each of the components. Often the Financials administrator is called in to recommend a feasible technical architecture based on available hardware resources and other site-specific requirements. Refer to Chapter 3 for more information on the various components of the technology stack.

Oracle Application Migration and Upgrade

The administrator plays a major role in Oracle application upgrades and migration. The administrator is responsible for ensuring compatibility of the database and application version with any third-party tools installed in the environment. Based on the compatibility, the administrator prepares a plan to upgrade the database and the application. The administrator also prepares a detailed list of patches to be applied for migration and ensures that the database and application are backed up before the upgrades. The administrator is also responsible for highlighting any application or database functionality that may be used to improve existing processes. The administrator makes decisions about upgrade or migration architecture in terms of number of application servers, server partitioning implementation, and other considerations. For a more detailed discussion on upgrading the Financials environment, refer to Chapter 4.

Financials Environment Management

After the upgrade or the installation has been performed and the environment has been prepared and deployed to production, the administrator is responsible for managing the upkeep and implementing best practices of the environment. The administrator is responsible for setting processes or scripts for automating repetitive tasks, such as creating instances based on standard OFA (Oracle Flexible Architecture) principles and site-specific sizes for production, testing, development, sandbox, and training environments. The sandbox environment is typically a different area from development, testing, or production and is used as an exploratory area for testing new functionality not yet implemented. The administrator is also in charge of defining procedures to refresh either the entire instance or specific schema from production to test or develop, based on the project requirements under the direction of project lead or functional team lead. The administrator utilizes the AD (Application Development) utilities for applying patches, relinking executables, and performing other functions. More details on managing the Financials environment is available in Chapter 5.

Concurrent Manager Control

The administrator must manage and control the Concurrent Manager programs, processes, and requests, setting best practices, tuning, maintaining history, and making scheduling decisions about which batch program can execute during which time for a particular module. The administrator makes these decisions based on his overall knowledge of concurrent requests and on how busy the system is during a particular time of the day. Refer to Chapter 6 for a discussion about the administrative tasks involved with Concurrent Managers.

Database Growth Management

The administrator must analyze, monitor, and tune the growth of various tables within the application area and proactively size them. When performing this activity, the administrator recommends better indexing strategies, index rebuild options, and other organizational options and keeps an eye on fragmentation. Chapter 7 offers more details on managing database growth.

Change Control and Patch Management

In a typical Oracle application environment, at least five environments must be maintained. They are demo, development, testing, training, and production. The administrator is responsible for implementing the change control process for the application so that changes are tracked for application enhancements and customizations. The administrator is also responsible for patch management. Refer to Chapter 8 for a discussion on implementing change control and patch management for your Oracle Applications environment.

Cost-Based Optimization Management

Starting with version 11i, Oracle applications make use of cost-based optimization (CBO) rather than rule-based optimization. The application tables and indexes must be analyzed periodically so that the application can effectively utilize the cost-based optimization. The administrator is responsible for ensuring this by implementing a process to gather statistics using either the Concurrent Manager process or using the FND_STATS package. Refer to Chapter 9 for more details.

Open Interface Implementation

Open interfaces are procedures that feed data from an external source into Oracle application tables. Depending on the customizations used in your environment, you may need to define custom open interface programs using techniques such as PL/SQL, SQL*Loader, and Java. The Financials administrator could help out with building and implementing open interfaces. Open interfaces are covered in more detail in Chapter 10.

Troubleshooting

The Financials administrator is the first point of contact for all application developers and end users when they have a problem. The administrator is involved in understanding and resolving the problem. Finding the resolution, in many cases, involves talking to Oracle technical support, and the administrator is responsible for serving as the liaison with Oracle. The administrator also prepares the environment for reproducing the error in the testing arena. Some troubleshooting tips and recommendations are discussed in Chapter 11.

Performance Tuning

The Financials administrator is responsible for monitoring, analyzing, and tuning the environment and implementing tuning recommendations. The Financials administrator typically implements a process for collecting performance or utilization statistics for various components such as the database- and middle-tier components, and then analyzes them. The Financials administrator also reviews expensive SQL statements for performance improvement and makes recommendations for improvement, such as adding a new index or changing some initialization parameter. Many of these tuning methods are discussed in Chapter 12.

Capacity Planning and Sizing

The administrator is responsible for providing statistics related to utilization of various hardware resources, including CPU, memory, network, and disk space, and he also evaluates whether sufficient capacity is available for sustaining projected growth or addition of new modules, customizations, or other functionality. The administrator plays a key role in evaluating the advantages and disadvantages of various architectures as well. Refer to Chapter 14 for a more detailed discussion on sizing and capacity planning.

Backup and Recovery Implementation

A Financials administrator implements a backup and recovery methodology for the Oracle Financials environment. In most cases, the Financials administrator must work with other administrators to evaluate various options for backup and recovery. The Financials administrator must provide for both file-level backup and options for object-level backups, which are useful for refreshing specific tables or schema. The Financials administrator is a critical resource for planning a maintenance window, for performing database recovery, and for restoring archived data for a special project. Backup and recovery is discussed in Chapter 16.

Security Implementation

Security, especially Internet security, is a critical component of Oracle applications. The administrator is responsible for setting up new users and access, deciding profiles, creating strategies for securing critical tables such as credit card tables, deciding privileges for users, and setting up security groups. The Financials administrator also has some extended responsibilities, as discussed next.

Methodology and Coordination

Financial administrators are involved in creating procedures and methods and making various processes repeatable. They also help coordination of administration efforts and are often the point person for the application team even for questions on areas not directly under their control.

- Coordinate and execute database and application upgrades
- Coordinate with teammates to resolve Oracle or operating system–specific issues
- Create error handling procedures
- Create naming convention for listener files
- Create a test plan for performing load testing on the test environment; could lead to understanding and working with automatic testing tools such as Load Runner
- Define and maintain enterprise-wide standards
- Help create Service Level Agreement (SLA) for application uptime
- Define methodology for database software integration
- Determine whether the new release of the database is stable enough to be used for the development environment
- Develop and test a strategy for data conversion involving validation, error handling, restartability, and performance
- Develop and coordinate procedures for implementing production processes and handing over tasks to shared services
- Develop migration procedures

Education, Training, and Mentoring

Financial administrators are looked upon for technical knowledge related to Oracle as well as applications. They need to keep their knowledge up-to-date by attending various events and keeping abreast with upcoming technology.

- Attend training sessions and user group conferences and Oracle Appsworld to keep on top of technical issues
- Evaluate new features of Oracle database- and middle-tier components
- Develop a good understanding of PL/SQL and Oracle utilities

- Develop a solid understanding of shell scripting and other operating system–specific commands and manipulation tricks

- Understand the functional aspect of Oracle Financials modules

- Understand Oracle provided open interfaces as well as Oracle provided APIs

- Understand Oracle internals, including latches and locks

- Develop performance tuning skills

- Stay abreast of current technology trends and consider various ways of performing a task

- Review technical pages on the Internet to get the latest scoop

Communication

Financials administrators need to have good communication skills to not only help them interact with business and functional counterparts in various projects but also for knowledge transfer to their peers.

- Assist developers in the project with SQL and PL/SQL information as well as help them with tracing statements and interpreting them

- Mentor other members of the DBA team in specific tasks

- Interface with Oracle and third-party vendors

- Explain status of various patches and other issues to developers, project leads, and other staff

Documentation

Financials administrators are often involved with technical documentations as well as documenting the operating procedures.

- Maintain ongoing documentation for patches applied and various instance levels

- Create and document information about Net8 bundles installed along with naming standards for various files

- Maintain an up-to-date picture of the Oracle application environment along with other related servers

Skill Sets of a Financial Administrator

In this section, we will review the required and preferred skill sets of a typical Financials administrator for a large application environment. A good Financials administrator should have a sufficient amount of experience in both the application and database areas and should be well versed with Internet deployment. When hiring a Financials administrator, it is essential that you ensure that the administrator has the necessary background, experience, and exposure to complete all the aforesaid roles and responsibilities successfully. It is critical for an Oracle Financials administrator to have exposure to Oracle Financials modules and not just be an Oracle DBA. Table 2-1 shows the skills that can prove valuable to the organization and that will also help reduce the learning curve to a great extent.

Skill	Expertise Rating
Knowledge of Oracle application architecture for the specific version	Very good or expert
Knowledge of application server technology	Highly desirable
Large installation experience	Very good or expert
Knowledge of Oracle Database Server (version 8.x preferred)	Very good or expert
Knowledge of the specific operating environment (both database tier and middle tier)	Good or very good
Database and application tuning experience	Very good
Oracle applications troubleshooting	Very good
PL/SQL, Java, PERL exposure	Preferable
Knowledge of shell scripting	Good
Hands-on experience with backup and recovery, using tools like RMAN	Highly desirable

TABLE 2-1. *Required Skills*

Characteristics of a Financials Administrator

Following is a list of characteristics of an accomplished Oracle Financials administrator:

- Sound technical background and experience
- Strong interpersonal skills and excellent communication skills
- Ability to work in teams and be a team player
- Ability to think analytically
- Quick learner and able to learn new applicationn and tools quickly
- Ability to interact with both technical staff and business and user community
- Great attitude and lots of patience
- Mentoring skills

Typical Tasks Performed by a Financials Administrator

A Financials administrator is involved in all aspects of the project cycle—from concept to completion of any Oracle application project. Using Rapid Install and other techniques, the project turnaround time has reduced considerably. With this in mind, it is recommended that the Financials administrators are involved early on in the implementation process so that they can get used to the environment and participate in training and knowledge transfer. Some of the tasks performed by the administrator are shown here:

- Planning
- Requirements gathering
- Design
- Setup and testing
- Implementation
- Support

Finding Success as a Financials Administrator

Oracle Corporation CEO Larry Ellison believes that *the Internet changes everything*. With the implementation of e-commerce and Internet-based technologies in the Oracle applications area, the Financials administrator must be well versed in a variety of new technologies. Although the list of knowledge a good administrator needs could be infinitely long and depends on the type of application he is working on and his professional background, the required skills described in Table 2-1 could be further broken down to the following:

- The administrator should be familiar with Web server, cartridge technology, HTML, Java, XML, and similar technologies. This knowledge will help him deploy solutions around the Oracle applications and become more useful to the organization.

- The administrator should be familiar with the concepts and implementation of self-service Web applications and the technologies behind it. The self-service Web application architecture consists of a Web browser, Web listener, HTML documents, Web request broker (WRB), and Common Gateway Interface (CGI) script. The three-tier architecture provides common, easy, browser-based access to the application, and the application server layer has all the application code. The self-service Web application provides an easy and scalable interface for deploying enhancements.

- The administrator should be familiar with the installation and configuration of database and application trees as well as patches. (For more information and latest release notes on these topics, see Oracle's Web site at **http://metalink.oracle.com**, or consult **http://appsnet.oracle.com**. You will need your CSI number to access the Knowledge Base.)

- The administrator should be conversant with copying, renaming, and refreshing Oracle instances and performing other standard SQL-based data manipulation.

- The administrator should be familiar with concurrent manager processes and requests. He should be familiar with commands to start and stop concurrent managers and able to change the status of a request using Oracle provided interfaces.

- The administrator should be aware of the more recent features of Oracle8i and should be able to leverage these in the environment whenever called for. Some of these features include function-based indexes, locally managed tablespaces, materialized views, and transportable tablespaces.

- The administrator should have experience using cost-based optimization and should be familiar with various troubleshooting procedures related to gathering statistics and setting appropriate initialization parameters.

- The administrator should have solid experience tuning extensive SQL statements and should be able to recommend ways of tuning performance based on an analysis of available statistics.

- The administrator should be familiar with third-party backup and recovery, media management, version control, and performance monitoring tools and should be able to provide an unbiased technical comparison with pros and cons of implementing them in the environment.

- The administrator should have experience implementing application security and performing capacity planning exercises.

Types of Financials Administrators

As scope, size, and complexity of systems expand, the Financials administrator role can be broken into several areas of responsibility. For smaller organizations, as discussed earlier, this role could be wrapped into one person. Larger implementation administrators tend to be associated with a line of specialty.

Operator   The operator is responsible for monitoring the database console, mounting tapes, and performing critical batch jobs. She also verifies that the backups ran correctly. The operator is paged if the archive area is nearly full. The operator then backs up the archive log files and creates space.

Systems Administrator   The systems administrator is a more experienced person and participates in database architecture meetings. He/she also plays a critical part in new projects and upgrades and is responsible for capacity planning. The systems administrator has knowledge of new features and makes implementation recommendations to the other administrators. The systems administrator also proactively monitors the database health in terms of I/O bottlenecks, CPU utilization, memory, and swap utilization.

Application Administrator   A typical application administrator supports various projects and is responsible for day-to-day operations of the environment, such as the Concurrent Manager, database upkeep, and application response issues. This administrator works closely with the functional leads, developers, and project team.

When defining a Project Team for Oracle Application implementation, the following salient points can be considered:

- Clearly define and update a team plan and get everyone's buy-in.

- Outline the team goal, targets, and deliverables.

- Define and maintain an operations plan.

- Conduct periodic reviews and lessons learned sessions and document results so these can be used for the next project implementation.

- Plan, plan, plan.

Summary

A Financials administrator is an important part of the Oracle Financials implementation team and takes part in this process from concept to completion. A Financials administrator has a wide range of responsibilities, including managing the concurrent requests, adding users and responsibilities, and backup and recovery. The primary goal of a Financials administrator is to ensure the successful implementation and smooth operation of an Oracle application environment. In this chapter, we reviewed various roles and responsibilities of a Financials administrator and discussed some of the skill sets required for being an Oracle Financials administrator. This chapter laid out an outline for our discussions in the next topics, which cover some of these responsibilities in greater detail.

PART
II

Setting Up the
Financials Environment

CHAPTER
3

Installing and Configuring the Technology Stack

- Provide information about changes and improvements in Oracle Financials 11i as compared to older application versions

- Provide an introduction to three-tier architecture in the context of Oracle Financials

- Discuss various components of the technology stack and how they fit into the overall environment

- Establish a foundation for creating the Oracle Financials environment (more details will be covered in Chapter 5)

- Provide an overview of Oracle9i Application Server

racle Application Suite is based on a number of technology layers, which are termed technology stacks. Each element of the technology stack has a specific set of functions from the point of view of Oracle Application Suite implementation, and the architecture involves leveraging the individual strengths of various technologies and yet getting all the functionality of the application suite. With this in mind, the objective of this chapter is to review the benefits of three-tier architecture and various components of the technology stack that make up the Oracle Application Suite. These technology stacks make up the environment for any Oracle Financials implementation, so it is important to understand the individual strengths and weaknesses of each member of the stack. Also, from the point of view of developing extensions or customizations, it is indeed essential to choose an appropriate tool from the available stack. There are several tools that could be used for a given situation and knowing about them makes all the difference in identifying the right one.

Improvements in Oracle Financials 11i

Oracle Financials 11i has several improvements and changes over previous versions. These improvements go a long way in making the application easy to use and scalable.

The earlier versions of Oracle Financials were based first on the character-based model and then on the client/server model. The Network Computing Architecture or NCA provided a three-tier architecture where specific add-on applications like Web Expenses or Web Customers could be implemented as self-service applications while keeping the main financials modules in the client/server mode. Setting up the client /server environment and keeping it going on a day-to-day environment presented a series of challenges. However, Oracle Financials 11i provides a single three-tier architecture based on a technology stack of the latest Oracle tools and database server. Following are some of the changes in Oracle Financials 11i:

- Oracle Financials provides a completely browser-based application, making it possible to manage from a centrally managed location.

- Being browser based, Oracle Financials is also much easier to navigate. It is easier to use and has a common look and feel from the user's perspective. The user community in general resists changes. With this in mind, managing a changeover to an Internet-based application environment is something that needs to be carefully managed. Thus, the benefits provided by this newest technology, in terms of ease of use and common look and feel, is a welcome change.

- Oracle Financials has new color scheme, tabs, and bubble help. There are several other product enhancements, such as indication of list of values

(LOV) availability on the field, mandatory field indication, and the ability to use the right mouse button for cutting, copying, pasting, and so on.

■ Several modules of Oracle Financials have features to attach text or documents along with a transaction and the ability to export data out of forms into a spreadsheet for further analysis.

■ Oracle Financials has a single sign-on mechanism. Once a user has signed on with his user ID and password, his preferences are retained throughout his navigation. Oracle generates a unique session ID which is passed on to all the processes used by the client.

■ Oracle's latest Application Suite—Oracle9i Application Server—is integrated to the existing technology stack for Oracle Financials. In a later section of this chapter, we will cover more details about various components of Oracle9i Application Server and how they can help leverage functionality and performance.

■ Oracle Application Suite supports self-service Web applications. Oracle Employees, Oracle Customers, and Oracle Purchasing work on this principle and provide users with more functionality using technology like Oracle Workflow, HTML Java-based front-end, and also dynamic generation of HTML pages using either PL/SQL (earlier called PL/SQL Cartridge) or Java Code.

■ Oracle Financials requires Oracle database version 8.1.6 or higher and utilizes new features such as cost-based optimization, partitioned tables, and invoker's rights. These features are powerful and help to make optimum utilization of available resources. You will find more information on some of these features in Chapter 18.

■ Oracle Financials provides multilingual support as well as multiple currency reporting (MRC) support in greater detail.

■ Oracle Financials can be configured to provide different levels of functionality for daily reporting, analytical reporting, or strategic reporting using Oracle Business Intelligence.

Three-Tier Architecture in Oracle Financials

Just like the NCA model, Oracle Financials is based on a three-tier architecture, consisting of the database tier, the middle tier, and the desktop tier. Oracle Financials leverages the advantages of various tools and products in the Oracle family by making use of Oracle Forms and Oracle Reports in the middle tier and Oracle8i Server on the database tier.

Oracle first released its one-hour install with version 11. The 11i installation process (also called Rapid Install or now AutoUpgrade) installs all the components of the technology stack, Oracle application, demonstration database, and starter database. The installation method is both fast and easy to operate.

A typical client/server Oracle Financials model has two components. The first component is the database server (ORACLE_HOME). The second component is the application (APPL_TOP). The application component could either be installed on the server side or on a client workstation. The connectivity layer is provided by SQL*Net. This model provides the flexibility to install specific modules for certain users. For example, you can choose to install GL for all GL users, GL and AP for others, and so on. Also, it is one improvement from the previous application model that was character based, and where both the database and application components were installed on the server side only. This model had two major drawbacks: performance of the application and scalability. For a typical large installation, a lot of the financial administrator's time could be spent in installing various application components and keeping them up and running.

Three-tier architecture alleviates many of the issues faced with the client/server model. The application layer has the application component and various listeners installed, reducing the need to install specific modules for specific users. Also, the application can be accessed using a standard Java-enabled browser. Scalability is addressed by having load-balancing mechanisms and adding more servers to manage listener requests from concurrent user loads.

Oracle Applications Technology Stack

Understanding the various pieces involved in setting up the Oracle Financials environment will provide a basis for further discussions about upgrading to 11i in Chapter 4 and managing the environment in Chapter 5. This section will also introduce the general strengths and architecture of each technology with a view to understanding more about how it affects the Oracle Financials environment.

Components of the Technology Stack

The following is a list of members of Oracle's technology stack:

- Oracle8 Enterprise Edition (Version 8.1.6) with Oracle Intermedia and Oracle Spatial components installed.

- Oracle Forms 6i, Oracle Reports 6i, Oracle Graphics and Portal 2.2 listener (8.0.6 Home).

- Application Servers Portal 2.5 (8.1.6 based) and Apache (1.3.9) with JServ (1.1).

- JRE (Java Runtime Environment) 1.1.8.

- JDK (Java Development Kit) 1.1.8.

- Jinitiator (1.1.7) on the PC client.

Oracle Application Suite delivers third-party components such as ILOG and RogueWare.

In addition, interoperability patches will be required based on the platform and the version you are using. See Figure 3-1 for an architecture diagram.

Figure 3-1 shows a typical three-tier Oracle Application Suite architecture with the three tiers being the desktop tier, the middle (or application) tier, and the database tier. Notice that there are several components installed on the middle tier to form the technology stack.

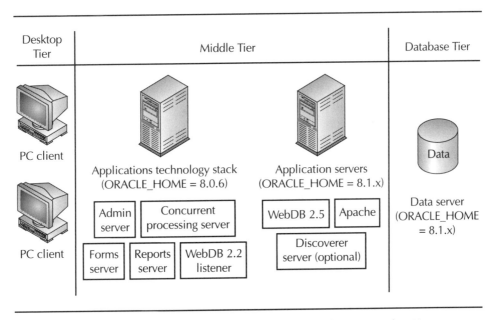

FIGURE 3-1. *Three-tier architecture introducing Oracle Financials 11i*

The concurrent processing server controls report generation and batch processing within Oracle applications. The server can be configured to allow administrators to limit system resources consumed during various times of the day. The concurrent processing server can have a number of processes running, and the administrators can tune the number of processes for optimum performance.

The admin server is used for maintaining data server objects with application DBA utilities like AutoPatch, FND_STATS, and so on. The FND_STATS utility is discussed in more detail in Chapter 9.

Client Workstation Configuration

The following client configuration is essential for running Oracle Financials modules:

- At least a 200 MHz processor

- At least 64MB RAM, 128MB preferred

- Windows 95, Windows 98, or Windows NT 4.0

- Netscape 4.5 or 4.73 or Internet Explorer 5.x

- Jinitiator 1.1.7

The application server and database server configuration are sized based on the volume of data, number of users, and other subsystem requirements. A multiprocessor server is recommended for both application server and database server with an ample amount of free memory. A robust networking infrastructure also helps improve overall performance of the application. The capacity planning issues are discussed in more detail in Chapter 14.

Server Partitioning

Server partitioning means that Oracle Server and Oracle Tools basically use different Oracle Homes. With server partitioning, you can use the functionality and features of both the server and the tools and keep current with the releases. Integrating the server partitioning concept in your technology stack, you can be more flexible in sharing Oracle8i database libraries with the tools. In Oracle Financials, server partitioning concepts are used by installing the applications technology stack in a separate Oracle Home (from 8.0.6 onward). The application server and the database server use a more recent Oracle Home (from 8.1.6 onward). For more details, refer back to Figure 3-1.

Server partitioning helps with scaling the application and also use of additional features on the server side.

Self-Service Web Applications

The self-service Web application architecture consists of a Web browser, Web listener, HTML documents, Web Request Broker (WRB), and Common Gateway Interface (CGI) (see Figure 3-2). The three-tier architecture provides a common, easy, browser-based access to the application, and the application server layer has all the application code. The application server and the database server are connected with the usual Net8 connection.

In Figure 3-2, you can see that the self-service Web application architecture is three-tiered, similar to the Oracle Application Suite. The architecture is simple to implement, scalable, and easy to administer.

Here are some additional components of self-service Web applications.

Web Application Dictionary   This is basically a repository of data, prompts, navigation, security, and other information about the self-service Web application. The Web application dictionary is stored in the Oracle database.

Oracle Web Application Server   The application server is required by self-service Web applications to provide a standard HTTP server that offers an open, extensible application development environment platform.

PL/SQL Agent   The PL/SQL agent helps in connecting to the database and executing stored procedures. The procedures can retrieve data and returns the result

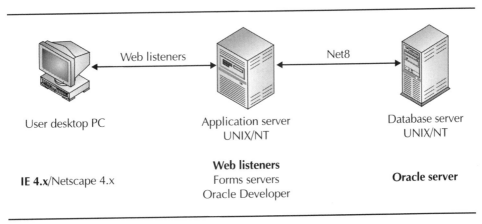

FIGURE 3-2.   *Self-service Web applications architecture*

in HTML format, displayed on the standard browser. The generated page can also contain JavaScript code.

Basic Steps in a Self-Service Web Application   Here are the steps for implementing self-service Web applications:

1. The user starts the application using a specific URL.

2. After validating user credentials, the application main menu is displayed.

3. The user reviews and edits the information.

4. The user submits the transaction.

5. The submitted transaction is validated and approved. Based on the type of the transaction a response is sent to the user as well as others.

6. The committed transaction passes over to the verification stage. This verification is done as part of the Oracle Financials function.

7. An import process is run to include the self-service transactions into the Oracle Financials tables.

8. Further processing of the transactions is done as part of the Oracle Financials transactions.

Report Server Architecture

Report server architecture is one of the several stacks of the Oracle Application Suite. The report server provides functionality to process and print reports on the Internet. It is based on Oracle Developer architecture, which is a three-tiered architecture similar to the one for the applications described earlier.

In a client/server implementation of Oracle Developer, most of the processing takes place on the desktop machines, which makes the client layer "fat." See Figure 3-3 for more details.

You can see that in the client/server model the Oracle tools such as PL/SQL, Forms, or Reports have to be installed on each of the nodes being used in the architecture. These nodes then access a common backend server using SQL*Net or Net8. Upgrading the software involves upgrading each and every client installation.

In the case of a three-tier implementation of Oracle Developer, the tools reside on the application server.

How Does Report Server Work?

An Oracle Report server is responsible for receiving reporting requests and getting them processed by communicating with the database tier. The following steps indicate briefly the working of the Oracle Report server.

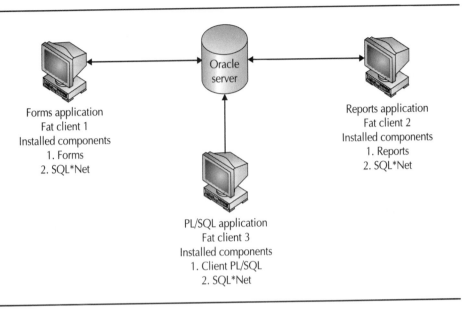

FIGURE 3-3. *Client/server implementation of Oracle forms and reports*

1. Using the browser, the user chooses a particular report to be executed.

2. The URL is sent over to the application server.

3. The Web server invokes the reports cartridge, which converts the request to a server command line.

4. The command line is sent over to the report server, which in turn queues it.

5. The command line is sent to the runtime engine when it becomes available.

6. The runtime engine connects to the database and executes the report.

7. The report output is sent to the report server by the runtime engine.

8. The report server passes it back to the Web server, which directs it to the client's browser.

Forms Server Architecture

The architecture of the forms server is similar to the report server. The forms server is based on three-tier architecture as well. The desktop tier consists of a browser running the Forms applet, the middle tier includes the forms server, and the database tier includes the Oracle server. See Figure 3-4 for more details.

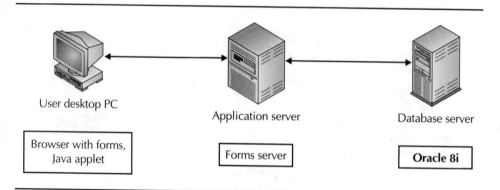

FIGURE 3-4. *Forms server architecture*

The forms client handles the display of the forms user interface. It also manages the communication between the user and the forms server.

The middle tier (or application server layer) handles the actual running of forms. The Forms Server Listener initiates the forms server runtime session. It connects between the forms server and the forms client.

The database tier could be on a different server and communicates with the application server using Net8.

How Does Forms Server Work?

An Oracle Forms server is responsible for receiving requests from the Web server and getting them processed by communicating with the database tier. The following steps briefly indicate the working of the Oracle Forms server.

1. The client browser sends the URL to the Web server.

2. The Web server generates the corresponding HTML page.

3. The HTML page is returned to the client browser.

4. The browser checks the applet tag and starts the Jinitiator plug-in.

5. The Jinitiator requests the Forms applet.

6. The Web server returns the Forms applet.

7. The Forms applet connects to the forms server.

8. The forms server spawns a forms runtime engine.

9. The forms runtime engine connects to the Forms applet.

10. The forms runtime engine loads the Forms applet.

11. The forms runtime engine connects to the database from the middle tier using Net8.

Oracle Portal (Formerly WebDB)

Oracle Portal implementation is another important component of the applications technology stack. The functionality of Portal has considerably improved across previous versions. Portal is also based on a three-tier architecture (see Figure 3-5).

This section offers a brief introduction to Portal. Chapter 19 contains a more detailed discussion of Portal and how it can be used in the area of financials administration as well as customizations.

The database server tier consists of an Oracle instance with procedural option (PL/SQL installed). The Web server tier can either run under Application Server 4.0 or use a lightweight listener which acts as a CGI-based PL/SQL gateway between the database and the browser. A lightweight listener can help deploy stand-alone applications. In the context of Oracle applications, running Portal under OAS provides better security.

The browser is used for viewing database content by end users.

Here are additional features of Portal:

■   The PL/SQL Web Toolkit that is installed as part of the Portal installation translates the user requests into dynamic HTML and JavaScript from the database and displays them on the browser.

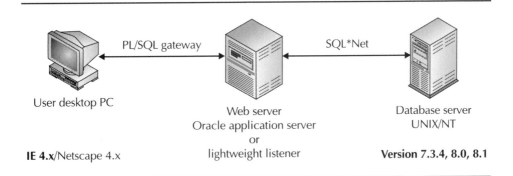

FIGURE 3-5.   *Oracle Portal (WebDB) architecture*

■ The PL/SQL gateway uses database access descriptors (DAD) for capturing the database connection information. The URL maps to DAD to execute the PL/SQL procedure. DAD can be maintained within Portal itself.

■ The PL/SQL gateway depends on Oracle Web Agent PL/SQL packages, which are part of the OAS 4.0 suite.

■ Portal does not require heavy SQL knowledge, so it is an ideal platform for functional teams. Portal does not require the skills of an experienced forms and reports developer.

There are two methods of Portal installation: automatic and manual. The manual method could be a preferred method in our case. This method involves installation of the following pieces:

■ PL/SQL Web Toolkit

■ Portal packages

Listener need not be configured separately since it is already configured as part of the application setup.

Discoverer Server

With e-commerce–based applications, business intelligence has gained importance as a tool for understanding your company's consumers and staying competitive. The ability to react to rapidly changing customer requirements—and moreover, responding to them—is critical.

Oracle Discoverer is a tool that could provide users with the answers they need, using a familiar browser-based interface. It is an easy-to-use, powerful tool for application users. Discoverer is a business intelligence tool and provides two layers: the administration layer (or edition) and the user layer (or edition). Complex business relationships can be handled in the administration layer and converted to simpler structures easily understood by the users of the user layer.

From the point of view of Oracle Financials, the advantage of using Oracle Discoverer is the ease with which reports can be generated and the ease of use by functional as well as some end-user communities. The developers and administrators can focus on more specialized tasks in the environment, and reports can be developed by people who will be using them.

The administration layer has a wizard interface and closely integrates with Oracle8i to provide a centralized, scalable repository. This layer also has features like automatic summary management. The administration layer creates the end-user layer, business areas, and folders.

Discoverer Server Architecture

The Discoverer server is useful for additional reporting as well as business intelligence reporting requirements of Financials users. The architecture for the Discoverer server is a three-tier architecture and is installed in a separate Oracle Home. Note that Oracle Discoverer is an optional piece of the technology stack.

Figure 3-6 shows the Discoverer server architecture.

Here is a brief overview of the architecture:

■ The user invokes Discoverer 3.x, using a URL from a Java-enabled browser via an HTTP server. The HTTP server could be installed either on a Windows NT or UNIX computer.

■ On its first use, a Java applet is downloaded onto the client and cached. The next time, the applet is downloaded only when there is a change in it.

■ The preference repository is part of the Discoverer server. It stores information such as the maximum number of rows fetched, client timeouts, and so on.

■ The user's data is cached in the session. The session determines if the required data is available in the cache before it gets it from the disk. This reduces network traffic.

■ The Discoverer client communicates directly with the Discoverer server using Common Object Request Broker Architecture (CORBA). This results in improved performance and better scalability.

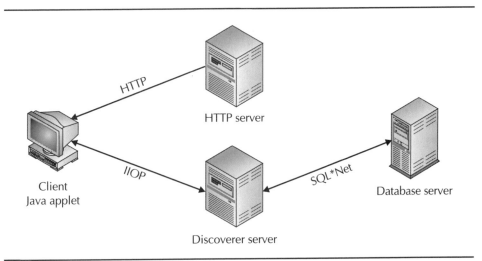

FIGURE 3-6. *Discoverer server architecture*

Other Tools

There are a few other important components of the technology stack which need to be mentioned. These components help the Oracle Financials implementation team, especially the administrators and customization teams. The components are:

- Oracle Designer
- PL/SQL
- SQL*Loader
- Oracle Workflow

Oracle Designer

Oracle Designer is a critical component for developing customizations. It helps with modeling the application as well as maintaining metadata information. Oracle Designer, when used with the application environment, can make the migration of customization and application hooks and add-ons easier. This is because you will have metadata information and programming information as part of the Designer repository and can plan an upgrade strategy for the custom code parallel to the application upgrade. Oracle Designer Release 2 has several additional features that can be utilized in conjunction with other layers of the technology stack.

PL/SQL

PL/SQL is an important component of both the middle tier and the database tier. The procedural language largely complements Forms, Reports, Java, and other tools. Oracle8i has several enhancements to PL/SQL, which can be usefully employed in the context of Oracle applications. Some of the features include autonomous transactions and Invoker's Right. We will discuss more about Oracle8i features in the applications context in Chapter 18. PL/SQL also provides an easy way to implement simple customizations to improve data integrity and validations. Database triggers coding through PL/SQL can be used to enforce the application logic.

SQL*Loader

SQL*Loader provides a method to bring data to the interface tables and then into the Financials environment. SQL*Loader scripts can run in either the conventional or direct model. The conventional model uses an array-based insert and is comparatively slower. The direct model is very fast since it writes out database buffers. However, there are advantages and disadvantages of each of them. If you use the direct model, for example, restarting the load from a particular key value is not easy. Typically, you have to restart your load by truncating the table.

Oracle Workflow

Oracle Workflow is an important component when implementing any self-service Web application. Oracle Workflow provides for a way of maintaining activities, events, and a notification mechanism. One of the components of Oracle Workflow is called the Workflow Monitor. Administrators who manage various activities within Workflow can use Workflow Monitor to review error cases and promote certain activities to the next stage after analyzing them. Oracle Workflow is used in Oracle Employees, Oracle Customers, and other Oracle application products utilizing the Workflow aspects.

Creating the Functional Environment

Oracle Financials 11i improves the flexibility and ease of use of the front end as compared to earlier versions. However, creating the environment in terms of installation, upgrades, and such on the back end demands constant attention and meticulous planning. We will cover more details about creating and managing the environment in Chapter 5.

The installation procedure in Oracle Financials 11i can be done using AutoUpgrade. AutoUpgrade was previously called Rapid Install. Typically, *at least* six instances need to be created based on the intended use—for example, development, testing, production, and so on. It is recommended to follow this pattern as a process.

- **Production**   This will be the main production instance and will be accessed by end users, batch programs, and concurrent requests.

- **Production Test**   This instance is typically refreshed periodically from production. It is useful for reproducing production problems for resolution, and also for testing patches before they are applied to production.

- **Vision Demo**   This instance is mainly used as a demonstration instance. It can be used for testing the default behavior and functionality.

- **Development**   This is the instance where newer submodules are implemented or additional customization projects are developed. Note that several development instances may be required depending on the number of projects and the scheduled rollout dates.

- **Sandbox**   A sandbox instance is a copy of the production instance. This instance is typically used for testing product functionality in a more "production-like" environment. This is the first place where patches are applied and tested.

- **Training**   A training instance is used for training end users on different new functionality. Typically, a training instance is a smaller subset of production data, or it could have additional functionality users need to be trained on. Refer to Chapter 5 for more details.

An Overview of Oracle9i Application Server

This section provides a glimpse of Oracle's newest Application Server implementation: Oracle9i Application Server, which is being integrated with the Oracle Application Suite. Oracle9i Application Server provides a highly secure, scalable, and reliable application server for any e-business implementation. Oracle9i makes managing the technical components easy and provides an integrated view of the middle tier. Further, Oracle9i Application Server can be deployed for small as well as very large e-business implementations with equal ease. Figure 3-7 provides an introduction to various services that are available with Oracle9i Application Server.

Oracle9i Application Server is a critical component of any Oracle E-Business application solutions and provides a number of services to help out various aspects of the E-Business Development Cycle. Some of the services provided by Application Server include:

- Content launch

- Content management

- Tools to build applications

- Building presentation layer

- Tight integration with Oracle Server

- Consistent user interface using Portal services

- Scalability using Web and database caching

- Environment management

- Understanding the application environment

Appendix A contains more information on Oracle9i Application Server and how it could be integrated into the Oracle Financials environment.

Summary

Oracle Application Suite is implemented using several powerful technologies working together in a single architecture. There are several technology stacks that make up the Oracle application environment. These stacks are divided into three main parts: the database tier, middle (or application) tier, and desktop tier. The database tier includes Oracle8i Server, which is implemented using server partitioning. The middle tier is the applications technology stack, which includes

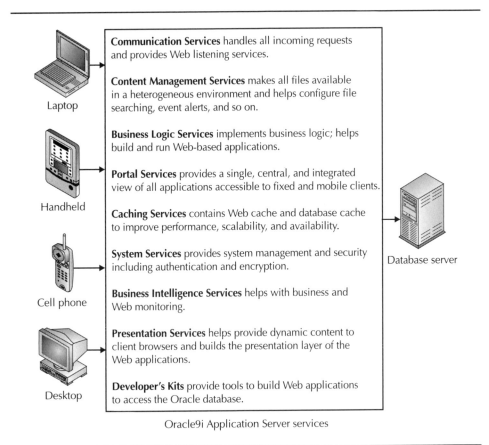

Communication Services handles all incoming requests and provides Web listening services.

Content Management Services makes all files available in a heterogeneous environment and helps configure file searching, event alerts, and so on.

Business Logic Services implements business logic; helps build and run Web-based applications.

Portal Services provides a single, central, and integrated view of all applications accessible to fixed and mobile clients.

Caching Services contains Web cache and database cache to improve performance, scalability, and availability.

System Services provides system management and security including authentication and encryption.

Business Intelligence Services helps with business and Web monitoring.

Presentation Services helps provide dynamic content to client browsers and builds the presentation layer of the Web applications.

Developer's Kits provide tools to build Web applications to access the Oracle database.

Laptop

Handheld

Cell phone

Desktop

Database server

Oracle9i Application Server services

FIGURE 3-7. *Oracle9i Application Server services overview*

Oracle Forms, Oracle Reports server, and Web server. The desktop tier includes a Java-enabled browser. This chapter was devoted to discussing various components in the technology stack and their features and functionality. This chapter also discussed self-service Web applications and other related technologies such as Oracle Designer, PL/SQL, and Workflow. The last section of the chapter covered Oracle9i Application Server, which is being integrated into the Oracle applications technology stack. In the next chapter, you will learn the issues, techniques, and best practices relating to upgrading to the Oracle Financials environment. We will also review Rapid Install and manual install procedures.

CHAPTER
4

Upgrading to Oracle Application Suite 11i

- Planning the upgrade
- Executing the upgrade
- Handling customizations
- Review of post-upgrade tasks

pgrading the Oracle Application Suite from a previous version, such as 10.7 SC, 10.7 NCA, or 11.0, is a complex task. Upgrades involve meticulous planning by functional and technical teams whose members work well together. Preparing for upgrades is important for controlling the time and the budget, and it limits downtime for the users of the application. A Financials administrator is a critical part of the team during the upgrade process. His or her inputs are required in the planning phase, implementation phase, and during the ongoing support of the application. The objective of this chapter is to review the upgrade of Oracle Financials 11i from an administrator's perspective.

The upgrades can be classified into two main sections:

- Upgrade from 10.7 to 11i
- Upgrade from 11.0 to 11i

Five major areas need to be addressed by the project lead to ensure success of an 11i upgrade project:

- Process
- People
- Technology
- Training
- Change management

Change management is critical. Because version 11i runs entirely on the Internet, some fundamental business changes are required, which implies that some old processes will need to be modified. Oracle Applications 11i provides many features, including multiple document interfaces (toolbar and menu attached), unique colors to indicate required fields, list of values indicator (fields with LOV [list of values] are specified), interruptible query (the user can abort a long query), and pop-up menus (right-click to cut, copy, paste). Flexible date format now allows the user to enter the date by their preference (no longer *dd-mon-yy*). Business Intelligence features a personal home page, including prebuilt content (reports and performance measures). In addition, version 11i has several module enhancements, including automatic journal scheduling and automatic journal reversal in the general ledger, payment enhancements, self-service expense reporting in accounts payable, credit memo workflow in receivables, and many more. These enhancements, and the fact that the entire application can be centrally controlled, are the main advantages of upgrading to 11i.

Upgrade Objectives

At the time of planning your upgrade, it will be useful for you to identify and prioritize your objectives. Some of the common objectives follow:

- Decrease support costs
- Reduce maintenance and customization
- Standardize and simplify patch application and management
- Simplify future upgrades
- Reduce product support and training time
- Simplify addition of new Oracle and third-party products and interfaces
- Increase business process support
- Utilize self-service features and Internet deployment
- Simplify user access
- Support new business initiatives with new and enhanced Oracle products
- Implement newer modules as required by business

A typical upgrade project cycle involves the following steps:

1. System review and initial project planning
2. Detailed project planning
3. Testing upgrade and support
4. Application testing
5. Enhancements and interface development and modifications
6. Training
7. System integration testing
8. Production upgrade and support

Reviewing and Planning for the Upgrade

Several resources must be carefully planned, verified, and available at the right time for any upgrade project to be successful.

- **Hardware** Plan to increase disk space by 25 to 30 percent: about 10 percent on network bandwidth, and about 15 percent increase in memory; make sure you factor in additional modules that you plan to implement

■ **Software** operating system, technology stack, Oracle application installation and configuration, version compatibility matrix

■ **Resources** Project management, functional, technical

■ **Enhancements and interfaces** Environment, user interface

Some amount of testing and quality assurance work are involved with any Oracle upgrade project. Testing not only ensures that the functional pieces of various modules work to satisfaction, but it also helps define stress levels. Testing can include functionality testing of enhancements and interfaces; new application database structure, functionality and tools; sizing; patches; user interface and access issues; and load and performance testing.

Training is an ongoing process for users of existing applications to keep everyone in the project up to speed. User training occurs with a new release for all employees using the new application. Such training covers technical and navigational features, new features and functionalities, business process changes, and change management.

Technical Planning Issues

From the technical perspective, an upgrade depends on several factors, including hardware availability through user connectivity. The technical project manager for the upgrade project should keep in mind the following points when planning the upgrade:

■ Ensure the availability of sufficient hardware for both the database and application server for development, testing, training, and production.

■ Ensure uninterrupted and sufficiently broad network/connectivity capacity.

■ Configure clients appropriately.

■ Ensure that the application is certified with the database version as well as the operating system version.

■ Make sure that the correct resources are available.

■ Plan and provide for the enhancements and customizations.

■ Ensure that the environment is stable.

■ Focus on new modules and prioritize the implementation schedule based on them.

■ Plan for sufficient user training.

Deciding When to Upgrade

An application upgrade is usually launched by technical experts in the company who are exposed to new product details and development issues and who are familiar with the functionality, usability, and performance issues relative to the upgrade. It is very useful for these experts to stay in touch with the Oracle Applications Users Group (OAUG), Oracle Applications Network (AppsNet), and other technical user groups to learn about new products and discuss implementation issues. Upgrades are also sometimes dictated by the requirements of a particular application. For example, if a required functionality is available only in the next release, and if that functionality is critical, the upgrade decision is driven by it. In such a case, the company can participate in product beta testing by partnering with Oracle.

Evaluation Phase   During the evaluation phase, several members of the company review the functionality of the product to make decisions about whether or not an upgrade suits the business requirements. Following are hints for a successful evaluation:

- Identify a project sponsor and choose a project leader and key evaluators. The evaluators should be from different backgrounds and should represent functional, technical, and business teams. The members of the evaluation teams are the best sources for learning a new functionality and whether or not to implement it.

- Decide on an implementation date in terms of earliest start and latest finish after the upgrade is implemented.

- Separate the work areas for evaluations so that several meetings can occur simultaneously, and allow demonstrations and testing to be performed in a lab.

- The evaluation report and presentation should be at two levels. A high-level presentation can communicate a go, no-go decision. A detailed presentation and white paper can serve as a bible for the application implementation team. The report should highlight the new version's features, the business's needs, what gaps and risks are involved, and customization needs. Here is an extract of an evaluation report specifying the need for a customization:

  Module Name: Accounts Payable
  Form/Object Name: Invoice Entry Form
  Business Owner: VP, Finance
  Applications Owner: Accounts Manager
  Customization Name: Split invoice details based on expense types
  Business Reason for the Customization: For implementing self-service expense reporting, accounts department must set up expense type budgets for a quarter and needs to track down invoice details for each of the expense types.

Oracle Standard Process: Include screen shots
Customization Description: Describe the customization in detail and include screen shots and the proposed technology for customization and the amount of time required.
11i Functionality: Included
Effort Required to Wholly or Partially Redo Customization: 0
11i User Training Needed: Minimal

■ The evaluation team should ensure that the recommended customizations are required, or if the same benefits can be achieved by the standard 11i functionality.

■ The evaluation team should provide guidelines for CPU, memory, and other resource utilization so that the implementation team can incorporate these in their plan.

Pre-Upgrade Considerations

After the planning phase has been completed, it's time to upgrade the software. In this section of the chapter, we will review the various steps in the upgrade process. We will discuss the components of the technology stack, upgrade scripts and batch files, database modifications, pre-upgrade categories, AutoUpgrade, and post-upgrade steps.

Technology Stack Components

During the upgrade process, Oracle's Rapid Install tool installs and configures required technology stack components:

■ Oracle8i Enterprise Edition (8.1.6)

■ Oracle Forms Server

■ Oracle Reports Server

■ Oracle Graphics (8.0.6 Oracle home)

■ Oracle HTTP Server

■ Jinitiator (1.1.7) on the PC client

NOTE
See Oracle's Certification Web page
*(**http://metalink.oracle.com**) for the latest*
information on certification requirements.

If you are upgrading from a character-mode environment, you need to consider a significant number infrastructure requirements. Rapid Install installs all components including the applications technology stack and Oracle Applications file systems and environment, and it sets up your Database Listeners, Web Listener, Web Server, Forms Server, and Reports Server.

An Overview of the 11i Development Environment

The development environment and the architecture of version 11i is more or less similar to that of either version 10.7 or 11.0. The version numbers of the various development tools have changed and the application needs to be developed, tested, and deployed for an Internet implementation. Following are some of the components of the 11i development environment.

- Oracle8i
- Oracle Forms Developer 6i
- Oracle Forms Server 6i
- PL/SQL Version 8
- Oracle Reports Developer 6i
- Oracle Application Object Library 11i

Refer to Figure 4-1 for an illustration of various components in the Oracle Financials 11i development environment.

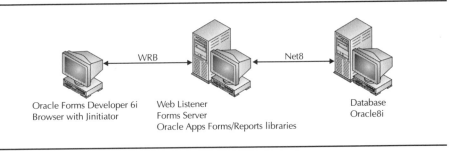

FIGURE 4-1. *Components in the Oracle Application 11i development environment*

Long-Running Scripts

Certain changes in functionality in release 11i have resulted in long-running scripts, which may require tuning to optimize performance during the upgrade. To identify long-running scripts, review $APPL_TOP/admin/<dbname>/out/adt00001.lst (UNIX) or %APPL_TOP%/admin/<dbname>/out/adt00001.lst (NT).

Long-running scripts have been identified in the following areas:

- Conversion of database from rules-based optimization of SQL queries to cost-based optimization

- Migration of existing date and noninteger data from character columns to date and number type columns

- Certain Oracle payables conversion scripts

Performance of some upgrade scripts can be significantly improved by changing some database settings for the duration of the upgrade. These settings include DB_BLOCK_BUFFER, SHARED_POOL_SIZE, SORT_AREA_SIZE, and so on.

Creating a Temporary Tablespace

A temporary tablespace should be created as a locally managed tablespace, using the temporary file option with a uniform allocation size. If your temporary tablespace is not defined in this way, you should delete the tablespace and re-create it using the following example as a template:

```
SQL> drop tablespace TEMP;
SQL> create TEMPORARY tablespace TEMP
tempfile 'ts_p_temp1.dbf' size 2028M
EXTENT MANAGEMENT LOCAL
UNIFORM SIZE 10M;
```

To verify that the temporary tablespace has been created, execute the following:

```
SQL> select CONTENTS,EXTENT_MANAGEMENT,ALLOCATION_TYPE
from dba_tablespaces
where tablespace_name='TEMP';
```

The query output should be

```
CONTENTS EXTENT_MANAGEMENT ALLOCATION_TYPE
------------ ------------------ ---------------
TEMPORARY LOCAL UNIFORM
```

Cost-Based Optimization (CBO)

Optimization is the process of choosing the most efficient way to execute a SQL statement. In the Oracle8i database and Oracle Financials 11i, the Oracle optimizer uses cost-based, rather than rule-based, optimization. *Cost-based optimization (CBO)* dynamically determines the most efficient access paths and join methods for executing SQL statements by taking into account statistics such as the size of each table and the selectivity of each query condition. The incorporation of CBO into release 11i improves performance and enables other database features that depend on cost-based optimization.

Release 11i represents a transition from rule-based to cost-based optimization. Because CBO is enabled during the AutoUpgrade process, the pre-upgrade steps in this book are rule-based, while steps performed after you run AutoUpgrade (post-upgrade) are cost-based. You may want to evaluate the impact of CBO on your custom code in your test system before you begin your upgrade. For more information on CBO, refer to Chapter 9.

Dropping Obsolete Columns

During the upgrade process, the Oracle8i **DROP COLUMN** command marks Oracle Financials columns as unused in the data dictionary, making it possible for the system administrator to drop the columns and reclaim the associated space. It is a good idea to plan this reclamation ahead of time with your users, because the process locks the associated tables. Once the space is reclaimed, the upgraded data model looks more like a fresh install (except for customizations). Note that **DROP COLUMN** has no effect on custom columns.

Changing Character Sets

If you need to change the character set of your APPL_TOP, you can do so before or after the upgrade. If you choose to change it before the upgrade, make the selection on the appropriate Rapid Install Wizard screen.

You must wait until *after* the upgrade to change the database character set. The character set of your APPL_TOP must be compatible with the database character set at all times—do not change it before the upgrade in anticipation of changing the database character set after the upgrade.

Preparation, AutoUpgrade, and Post-Installation Process Categories

The 11i upgrade spreadsheet can be downloaded from the Oracle Metalink Web site. This tool can help in planning an Oracle Applications upgrade to release 11i. The spreadsheet has a provision to enter start and end times when performing tests, which helps you track the time spent as well as downtime information. It can also be used as a benchmark for future upgrades. The upgrade occurs in six categories that include the AutoUpgrade process. Categories 1 through 3 are pre-upgrade steps and are performed before running AutoUpgrade. Categories 4 through 6 are done as part of the post-upgrade steps after AutoUpgrade is successful. Categories 4, 5, and 6 contribute to the crucial downtime for the application.

Category 1

The steps in Category 1 prepare for the AutoUpgrade and involve backing the existing database, renaming and backing up custom tables, and upgrading the database to a compatible version. All the Category 1 steps can be performed before receiving the Oracle application software and are done in preparing for the upgrade. Following are the database upgrade steps that need to be performed as part of Category 1.

Step	Action	For Version
Step 1	Back up the Oracle Applications database (recommended)	10.7, 11.0
Step 2	Maintain Multilingual tables (conditionally required)	11.0
Step 3	Verify operating system login (required)	10.7, 11.0
Step 4	Rename custom database objects with Applications prefixes (conditionally required)	10.7, 11.0
Step 5	Migrate or upgrade to Oracle8i Enterprise Edition (conditionally required)	10.7, 11.0
Step 6	Back up Oracle Applications and customizations (conditionally required)	10.7, 11.0

Notes for Category 1 Steps

■ Database object names should contain at least four characters for the product short name, followed by an underscore. Use only letters, digits, and underscores when naming database objects. For example, you could define your custom application to use the short name CUST, and database objects to use CUST_.

■ Releases 10.7 and 11.0 of the Oracle Applications Suite are both certified to run with Oracle8i Enterprise Edition release 8.1.6. It is recommended that you upgrade to Oracle8i before upgrading the application to 11i because this will avoid additional downtime.

1. Migrate or upgrade your database to Oracle8i Enterprise Edition release 8.1.6. The Oracle8i migration documentation contains instructions for migrating or upgrading your database.

2. Apply the Oracle8i Enterprise Edition release 8.1.6 interoperability patches. These patches are an integral part of your migration or upgrade. Applying the patches allows your 11.0 or 10.7 applications to run under the 8.1.6 version of the Oracle database. The patch README files contain complete instructions and describe other tasks necessary to complete the migration or upgrade. The patches are available on the Oracle Metalink Web site.

Following is a summary of other steps required to complete Category 1.

Applications Technology Products	For Version
System Administration Tasks	
Step 1　Verify Oracle schemas (required)	10.7, 11.0
Step 2　Rename custom value sets (required)	10.7, 11.0
Step 3　Determine attachment file upload directory (conditionally required)	10.7, 11.0
Step 4　Review current user responsibilities (conditionally required)	10.7
Step 5　Document concurrent program customizations (recommended)	10.7, 11.0
Step 6　Preserve menu customizations (recommended)	10.7, 11.0
Step 7　Preserve CUSTOM library customizations (conditionally required)	10.7, 11.0

Applications Technology Products	For Version

Application Object Library Tasks

Step 1	Transition custom forms to Oracle Forms 6i (conditionally required)	10.7, 11.0
Step 2	Convert custom reports that use SQL*Report (RPT), FlexRpt, and FlexSQL (conditionally required)	10.7
Step 3	Convert message dictionary functions (conditionally required)	10.7
Step 4	Convert user profile APIs in C concurrent programs (conditionally required)	10.7

Oracle Alert Tasks

| Step 1 | Run the Purge Alert and Action Set Checks alert (recommended) | 10.7, 11.0 |

Financials Product Family

Oracle Cash Management Tasks

| Step 1 | Back up customized Reconciliation Open Interface objects (conditionally required) | 10.7, 11.0 |

Oracle Payables Tasks

| Step 1 | Complete outstanding payment batches (required) | 10.7, 11.0 |

Oracle Projects Tasks

Step 1	Apply prerequisite patch (required)	10.7, 11.0
Step 2	Complete transfer and tieback of cost, revenue, and invoices (required)	10.7, 11.0
Step 3	Clear the Transaction Interface table (conditionally required)	10.7, 11.0
Step 4	Transfer asset lines and post mass additions (conditionally required)	10.7, 11.0
Step 5	Upgrade to the new summarization model (conditionally required)	10.7, 11.0

Applications Technology Products	For Version

Oracle Receivables Tasks

Step 1	Rename customized tax structure (conditionally required)	10.7, 11.0
Step 2	Create tax vendor extension view scripts (conditionally required)	10.7, 11.0
Step 3	Verify realized gains, realized losses, and rounding accounts (conditionally required)	10.7, 11.0
Step 4	Migrate customers as persons (conditionally required)	10.7, 11.0

Country-Specific Financials Product Family

Oracle Financials for the Americas Tasks

Step 1	Record the value of the JL: Inflation Ratio Precision profile option (required) (JL refers to the set of tables within the Application Object Library [AOL])	11.0
Step 2	Import outstanding bank collection documents (required)	11.0
Step 3	Restore all archived technical appraisals and adjustments (recommended)	11.0

HRMS Product Family

Oracle Human Resources Tasks

Step 1	Update custom code after removing obsolete synonyms (conditionally required)	10.7
Step 2	Update custom reports after dropping HRV (Human Resources views) and OTV views (conditionally required)	10.7, 11.0
Step 3	Check location of customized script for Salary Proposal view (conditionally required)	10.7
Step 4	Update custom code referring to positions (conditionally required)	10.7, 11.0
Step 5	Update user-defined FastFormula definitions (conditionally required)	10.7, 11.0

Applications Technology Products	For Version

Oracle Payroll (U.S.) Tasks

| Step 1 | Update custom code for U.S. tax information (W4) changes (conditionally required) | 10.7 |

Manufacturing and Distribution Product Family

Oracle Inventory/Cost Management/Work in Process Tasks

| Step 1 | Close discrete jobs - WIP (recommended) | 10.7, 11.0 |
| Step 2 | Purge discrete and repetitive data - WIP (recommended) | 10.7, 11.0 |

Oracle Release Management/Automotive Tasks

| Step 1 | Verify product installations (recommended) | 10.7, 11.0 |

Public Sector

Oracle Grants Accounting Tasks

| Step 1 | Run costing and funds check procedures (required) | 10.7, 11.0 |
| Step 2 | Run the update awards summary (required) | 10.7, 11.0 |

Oracle Labor Distribution Tasks

| Step 1 | Ensure that transactions are summarized and transferred (required) | 10.7, 11.0 |

Category 2

The steps in Category 2 are geared towards preparing your application schema for the older version for upgrading to 11i. There are steps to validate the APPS schema, set up tablespaces, and perform other preparation tasks. Category 2 steps are performed after receiving the Oracle Applications Suite software.

Step	Action	For Version
Step 1	Validate APPS schema(s) (recommended)	10.7, 11.0
Step 2	Set up tablespaces (conditionally required)	10.7, 11.0
Step 3	Drop custom schemas that match APPS% (required)	10.7, 11.0
Step 4	Verify custom index privileges (required)	10.7, 11.0
Step 5	Drop conflicting custom public synonyms (required)	10.7, 11.0

Here is a summary of other steps in Category 2.

Applications Technology Products	**For Version**

Oracle System Administration Tasks

Step 1	Delete unsuccessful login data (recommended)	10.7, 11.0
Step 2	Restrict access to administration directory on all servers except database (recommended)	10.7, 11.0
Step 3	Purge old concurrent requests (recommended)	10.7, 11.0

Oracle Flexbuilder/Account Generator Tasks

Step 1	Indicate use of Flexbuilder process for Account Generator (conditionally required)	10.7

Financials Product Family

Oracle General Ledger Tasks

Step 1	Review daily rates (conditionally required)	10.7
Step 2	Revise custom programs that automatically load daily rates (conditionally required)	10.7

Global Accounting Engine Tasks

Step 1	Verify accounting data model change (required)	11.0
Step 2	Ensure that all transactions are translated (required)	10.7, 11.0
Step 3	Confirm update of the balance calculation data model (required)	10.7
Step 4	Calculate and verify balances for all existing accounting lines (conditionally required)	10.7
Step 5	Close all accounting periods (required)	10.7, 11.0

Oracle Payables Tasks

Step 1	Upgrade supplier and supplier site bank data for multiple supplier banks (conditionally required)	10.7
Step 2	Choose payment method for future dated payments (conditionally required)	10.7, 11.0
Step 3	Evaluate use of recoverable tax (required)	10.7, 11.0

Applications Technology Products	For Version

Oracle Projects Tasks

Step 1	Correct the week ending date and month ending date for summarization data for multilingual support (required)	10.7, 11.0
Step 2	Correct excess revenue amounts data for hard limit funded agreements (conditionally required)	10.7, 11.0
Step 3	Correct excess revenue accrued for non-adjusting negative amount expenditure items (conditionally required)	10.7, 11.0
Step 4	Correct credit memo invoice dates (conditionally required)	10.7, 11.0
Step 5	Correct bill amount data stored on revenue distributions (conditionally required)	10.7, 11.0
Step 6	Correct billing hold data on reversing items (conditionally required)	10.7, 11.0
Step 7	Correct billable flag data for reversing items (required)	10.7, 11.0
Step 8	Run data fix scripts (conditionally required)	10.7

Oracle Purchasing Tasks

Step 1	Clear open interface tables (required)	10.7, 11.0

Country-Specific Financials Product Family

Oracle Financials for Asia/Pacific Tasks

Step 1	Record lookup codes and meanings that will be truncated or renamed (recommended)	10.7, 11.0
Step 2	Move government uniform invoice information for each organization (conditionally required)	10.7, 11.0
Step 3	Move customer uniform numbers and tax registration numbers (conditionally required)	10.7, 11.0
Step 4	Move supplier uniform numbers and tax registration numbers (conditionally required)	10.7, 11.0
Step 5	Record uniform numbers for your company (recommended)	10.7, 11.0
Step 6	Record Canadian tax setup (required)	10.7, 11.0
Step 7	Print tax rebate and rule listings (recommended)	10.7, 11.0

Applications Technology Products		**For Version**
Oracle Financials for Europe Tasks		
Step 1	Update Swedish EFT (Electronic Fund Transfer) payment format information (required)	11.0
Step 2	Pay Danish EFT invoices (conditionally required)	10.7, 11.0
Oracle Financials for the Americas Tasks		
Step 1	Upgrade Brazilian subledgers data structure (conditionally required)	11.0
Step 2	Identify and correct duplicate rows in JL_BR_LOOKUPS (conditionally required)	10.7, 11.0

HRMS Product Family

Oracle Human Resources Tasks		
Step 1	Update taskflow definitions (conditionally required)	10.7, 11.0

Manufacturing and Distribution Product Family

Oracle E-Commerce Gateway Tasks		
Step 1	Report output interface datafile definitions (conditionally required)	10.7, 11.0
Step 2	Report cross-reference data definitions (conditionally required)	10.7, 11.0
Oracle Inventory/Cost Management/Work in Process Tasks		
Step 1	Find and correct items with no primary unit of measure - INV (required)	10.7, 11.0
Step 2	Purge unwanted transaction history - INV (recommended)	10.7, 11.0
Step 3	Clear Open Job and Schedule Interface table - WIP (conditionally required)	10.7, 11.0
Oracle Order Management		
Step 1	Run Order Entry Interface programs (required)	10.7, 11.0
Step 2	Close eligible orders (required)	10.7, 11.0
Step 3	Run Order Import program (required)	10.7, 11.0
Step 4	Run Auto-create Installed Base program for Services (required)	10.7, 11.0

Applications Technology Products		For Version
Manufacturing and Distribution Product Family (continued)		
Oracle Order Management **(continued)**		
Step 5	Make sure orders are in a status supported by Order Management (required)	10.7, 11.0
Step 6	Close open pick slips/picking batches or open deliveries/departures (required)	10.7
Step 7	Run the Shipping Interface programs (required)	10.7
Step 8	Review Item Validation Org settings (required)	10.7, 11.0
Step 9	Validate inventory organization data (required)	10.7, 11.0
Step 10	Review cycles that may not be upgraded (required)	10.7, 11.0
Oracle Release Management/Automotive Tasks		
Step 1	Create Release Management Spreadsheets (recommended)	10.7, 11.0

Notes on Category 2 Steps

■ Convert tablespaces to local extent management to increase performance. To convert all non-SYSTEM tablespaces from data dictionary extent management to local extent management, run the following script:

```
$ cd $APPL_TOP/admin/preupg
$ sqlplus <SYSTEM username>/<SYSTEM password> @adtbscnv.pls \
<SYSTEM password>
```

■ Create tablespace for new products and resize existing product tablespace. To create tablespaces for your new and upgraded products, first run adgntbsp.sql to gather information about your current products and their tablespace sizes, and then run adcrtbsp.sql (created by adgntbsp.sql) to add or increase tablespaces for your upgraded installation. Running dgntbsp.sql requires a value for the **MODE** variable. **NEW** only adds tablespaces for new products. **ALL** adds new tablespaces and increases the size of existing tablespaces so that they are minimally sized.

```
$ cd $AD_TOP/patch/115/sql
$ sqlplus <APPS username>/<APPS password> @adgntbsp.sql <MODE>
```

Category 3

Category 3 includes steps to actually perform the upgrade. When performing these steps, your users cannot be connected and using the application.

Oracle Alert Tasks	**For Version**
Step 1 Drop event alert triggers in custom schemas (conditionally required)	10.7, 11.0

Oracle Common Modules Tasks

Step 1 Delete invalid AK data for non-Global Demo databases (conditionally required)	10.7
Step 2 Check for invalid AK data in non-Global Demo databases (conditionally required)	10.7, 11.0
Step 3 Fix invalid data in non-Global Demo databases (conditionally required)	10.7, 11.0

Oracle Workflow Tasks

Step 1 Update the protection and customization levels of seeded item types (recommended)	10.7, 11.0

System Administration Tasks (Performed after all product-specific Category 3 steps and before the Category 3 database steps)

Step 1 Determine potential Oracle schema conflicts (conditionally required)	10.7, 11.0
Step 2 Enable SYSADMIN user and password (required)	10.7, 11.0
Step 3 Ensure all concurrent requests are complete (required)	10.7, 11.0
Step 4 Disable AOL Audit Trail feature (conditionally required)	10.7, 11.0

Financials Product Family

Oracle Payables Tasks

Step 1 Update existing payment records (conditionally required)	11.0
Step 2 Determine exchange rates for new accounting data model (MRC) (conditionally required)	11.0
Step 3 Import and purge Payables Open Interface invoices (required)	11.0

Oracle Alert Tasks	**For Version**

Financials Product Family (continued)

Oracle Payables Tasks **(continued)**

Step 4	Import and purge Invoice Import Interface expense reports and invoices (required)	10.7, 11.0
Step 5	Transfer all data to General Ledger (MRC) (required)	10.7, 11.0

Oracle Projects Tasks

Step 1	Submit and obtain approval for all timecards entered in Project Time and Expense (PTE) (conditionally required)	10.7, 11.0
Step 2	Correct excess revenue accrued for negative amount events (conditionally required)	10.7, 11.0
Step 3	Back up custom client extension packages and views (conditionally required)	10.7, 11.0
Step 4	Perform Projects Category 1 and Category 2 steps again (required)	10.7, 11.0

Oracle Receivables Tasks

Step 1	Drop tax vendor synonyms (conditionally required)	10.7, 11.0
Step 2	Diagnose and correct pre-existing database problems (recommended)	10.7, 11.0

Country-Specific Financials Product Family

Oracle Common Countries Financials Tasks

Step 1	Partition EFT system formats information by operating unit (conditionally required)	10.7

HRMS Product Family

Oracle Payroll (U.S.) Tasks

Step 1	Remove triggers specific to PayMIX (required)	10.7, 11.0

Oracle Alert Tasks		For Version
Manufacturing and Distribution Product Family		
Oracle Inventory/Cost Management/Work in Process Tasks		
Step 1	Complete physical inventories in process - INV (recommended)	10.7, 11.0
Step 2	Process all data in temporary and interface tables - INV (required)	10.7, 11.0
Step 3	Verify that no uncosted transactions exist - Standard and Average Costing (required)	10.7, 11.0
Step 4	Run inventory valuation reports - INV (recommended)	10.7, 11.0
Step 5	Run WIP (Work-in-progress) Value report - Standard and Average Costing (recommended)	10.7, 11.0
Step 6	Close all accounting periods - Standard and Average Costing (required)	10.7, 11.0
Oracle Order Management		
Step 1	Repeat Category 2 "Oracle Order Management" steps 1–10 (required)	10.7, 11.0
Step 2	Set up **utl_file_dir** parameter (required)	10.7, 11.0
Oracle Purchasing Tasks		
Step 1	Set MRP profile options (conditionally required)	10.7
Step 2	Drop ICX index (conditionally required)	10.7, 11.0
Oracle Release Management/Automotive Tasks		
Step 1	Stop processing of inbound demand EDI transactions in CARaS (required)	10.7, 11.0
Step 2	Ensure that all demand in CARaS has been exported to Oracle Automotive (required)	10.7, 11.0
Step 3	Print Status Inquiry report (required)	10.7, 11.0
Step 4	Print Demand Status Inquiry report (required)	10.7, 11.0

Oracle Alert Tasks	**For Version**
Public Sector	
Oracle Grants Accounting Tasks	
Step 1 Rename the Grants Accounting tables (required)	10.7
Step 2 Run data correction script (required)	10.7, 11.0
Oracle U.S. Federal Financials Tasks	
Step 1 Drop obsolete seed data (required)	10.7, 11.0
Step 2 Drop obsolete database objects (required)	10.7, 11.0
Step 3 Upgrade menus (required)	10.7, 11.0
Step 4 Drop indices (required)	10.7, 11.0
Database Upgrade Steps	
Database Upgrade Tasks	
Step 1 Shut down all applications listeners and concurrent managers (required)	10.7, 11.0
Step 2 Migrate or upgrade to Oracle8i Enterprise Edition (required)	10.7, 11.0
Step 3 Set up Net8 - database server (required)	10.7, 11.0
Step 4 Run preparatory scripts - database server (required)	10.7, 11.0
Step 5 Gather database statistics for CBO.	10.7, 11.0
Step 6 Install database objects for the Oracle HTTP Server (required)	10.7, 11.0
Step 7 Gather database information (recommended)	10.7, 11.0
Step 8 Check SQL*Plus options (required)	10.7, 11.0

Oracle Alert Tasks	For Version
Database Upgrade Steps (continued)	
Database Upgrade Tasks **(continued)**	
Step 9 Verify rollback segment sizing (required)	10.7, 11.0
Step 10 Turn off automatic archive logging (recommended)	10.7, 11.0
Step 11 Disable custom triggers, constraints, and indexes (conditionally required)	10.7, 11.0
Step 12 Run preparatory scripts – admin server (required)	10.7, 11.0
Step 13 Back up the Oracle Applications database (recommended)	10.7, 11.0
Step 14 Complete database upgrade steps for NLS databases (conditionally required)	10.7, 11.0

AutoUpgrade

After completing the Category 3 steps, you can execute the AutoUpgrade command to upgrade the application to Release 11i.

Batch Commit Size

Batch commit size affects system performance during an upgrade. It determines the number of rows to commit at one time when certain scripts run. When you start AutoUpgrade, it prompts you to enter a batch commit size. If you do not specify a value, AutoUpgrade defaults to a relatively small value to accommodate systems with small rollback segments. To take advantage of large rollback segments, specify a batch commit size larger than the default value.

Category 4

The Category 4 scripts should be performed after the application is upgraded and is categorized as post-upgrade tasks. These tasks should be performed before starting to use the application. Following is a summary of various database upgrade steps involved in Category 4.

Step	Action	For Version
Step 1	Install NLS translated software (conditionally required)	10.7, 11.0
Step 2	Gather database statistics for CBO (required)	10.7, 11.0
Step 3	Reset Oracle schema passwords (recommended)	10.7, 11.0
Step 4	Run Rapid Install to configure and start server processes (required)	10.7, 11.0
Step 5	Reapply product customizations to environment and files (conditionally required)	10.7, 11.0
Step 6	Set rollback segments for normal use (required)	10.7, 11.0
Step 7	Install XML Parser for PL/SQL (required)	10.7, 11.0
Step 8	Validate and compile APPS schema(s) (recommended)	10.7, 11.0
Step 9	Integrate custom objects and schemas (conditionally required)	10.7, 11.0
Step 10	Re-enable custom triggers, constraints, and indexes (conditionally required)	10.7, 11.0
Step 11	Back up Oracle Applications (recommended)	10.7, 11.0

Following are more steps in this category.

Upgrading Multiple Reporting Currencies (MRC)	**For Version**

Multiple Reporting Currencies Tasks

Step	Action	For Version
Step 1	Validate and compile APPS schema(s) (conditionally required)	11.0
Step 2	Maintain MRC schema(s) (conditionally required)	11.0
Step 3	Verify your MRC installation (conditionally required)	11.0

Upgrading Multiple Reporting Currencies (MRC)	For Version

Applications Technology Products

System Administration Tasks

Step 1	Fix Flexfield cross-validation rules (required)	10.7
Step 2	Set profile options (required)	10.7, 11.0
Step 3	Clone Date and DateTime value sets (required)	10.7, 11.0
Step 4	Upgrade Flexfield date and number data (required)	10.7, 11.0
Step 5	Set up custom data groups (conditionally required)	10.7, 11.0
Step 6	Set up electronic mail for use by Concurrent Managers (required)	10.7, 11.0
Step 7	Reconnect spawned concurrent programs (conditionally required)	10.7, 11.0
Step 8	Re-create/validate custom menus (conditionally required)	10.7, 11.0
Step 9	Verify installation group numbers for custom IDs (conditionally required)	10.7, 11.0
Step 10	Update/verify custom responsibilities (conditionally required)	10.7
Step 11	Copy and re-customize previously modified scripts or reports (conditionally required)	10.7, 11.0
Step 12	Regenerate CUSTOM library customizations (conditionally required)	10.7, 11.0
Step 13	Define custom concurrent managers startup parameters (required)	10.7, 11.0
Step 14	Restrict access to concurrent processing servers (required)	10.7, 11.0
Step 15	Load attachment files into database (conditionally required)	10.7, 11.0

Upgrading Multiple Reporting Currencies (MRC)	For Version

Oracle FlexBuilder/Account Generator Tasks

Step 1	Complete installation steps for Oracle Workflow (required)	10.7
Step 2	Complete installation steps for Oracle Workflow Builder (conditionally required)	10.7
Step 3	Associate Flexbuilder rules for Accounting Flexfield structure and Workflow item type (conditionally required)	10.7
Step 4	Customize Account Generator process (conditionally required)	10.7

Oracle Workflow Tasks

| Step 1 | Link WFMAILOO (conditionally required) | 10.7, 11.0 |

Country-Specific Financials Product Family

Oracle Financials for Asia/Pacific Tasks

| Step 1 | Modify migrated lookups and customized modules (conditionally required) | 10.7, 11.0 |

Oracle Financials Common Country Features Tasks

| Step 1 | Upgrade descriptive Flexfield dates to use the new AOL date validation (conditionally required) | 10.7 |

Manufacturing and Distribution Product Family

Oracle E-Commerce Gateway Tasks

| Step 1 | Report output interface datafile definitions (conditionally required) | 10.7, 11.0 |
| Step 2 | Report cross-reference data definitions (conditionally required) | 10.7, 11.0 |

Public Sector

Oracle Grants Accounting Tasks

Step 1	Apply Grants Accounting data migration patch (required)	10.7, 11.0
Step 2	Verify billing amounts (required)	10.7, 11.0
Step 3	Verify award balances (required)	10.7, 11.0

Category 5

Category 5 includes various steps that are required for finishing the installation. Some of these steps are product specific and need to be done only if you are installing a particular product.

Applications Technology Products	For Version

Application Implementation Wizard Tasks

Step 1	Check past implementation status (conditionally required)	11.0
Step 2	Purge invalid wizard tasks (conditionally required)	11.0
Step 3	Verify application server database access descriptors (DAD) for Oracle Applications (conditionally required)	11.0

Oracle Self-Service Web Applications (and Expenses) Tasks

Step 1	Reapply extensions and customizations (conditionally required)	10.7, 11.0

Financials Product Family

Oracle General Ledger Tasks

Step 1	Migrate conflicting daily rates to new or existing rate types (conditionally required)	10.7

Global Accounting Engine Tasks

Step 1	Migrate existing date and noninteger data from character columns to date and number type columns (required)	10.7, 11.0
Step 2	Update existing balances to comply with the Archive and Purge data model and the new balance calculation model (required)	10.7, 11.0
Step 3	Migrate obsolete event types and document statuses to new event types and document statuses (required)	10.7, 11.0
Step 4	Upgrade the Transfer to GL (General Ledger) posted flag from the accounting line level to the accounting header level (required)	10.7, 11.0
Step 5	Populate tax information for accounting lines (required)	10.7, 11.0

Applications Technology Products	For Version

Oracle Payables Tasks

Step 1	Remodify payment formats (conditionally required)	10.7
Step 2	Create or modify data for data model changes for MRC (conditionally required)	11.0
Step 3	Set up prepayment payment terms (recommended)	10.7, 11.0

Oracle Projects Tasks

Step 1	Review organization hierarchies and uses of organizations (required)	10.7
Step 2	Update project status values (required)	10.7
Step 3	Update customized billing extensions with changes in predefined procedures (conditionally required)	10.7
Step 4	Review and update billing cycle names (conditionally required)	10.7
Step 5	Convert custom overtime calculation program to PL/SQL (conditionally required)	10.7
Step 6	Populate billing title for employee assignments (conditionally required)	10.7
Step 7	Set up the invoice rounding account (conditionally required)	10.7, 11.0
Step 8	Add new parameters to customized invoice-related client extensions (conditionally required)	11.0
Step 9	Add new parameters to customized transaction control extension (conditionally required)	10.7, 11.0
Step 10	Add new currencies and nonrecoverable tax amounts to commitment views (conditionally required)	10.7, 11.0
Step 11	Update custom code that populates the Transaction Interface table (conditionally required)	10.7, 11.0
Step 12	Reinstall customized client extension packages and views (conditionally required)	10.7, 11.0
Step 13	Correct FIFO marking of expenditure items for projects using event billing (conditionally required)	10.7, 11.0

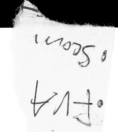

Applications Technology Products	For Version

Oracle Projects Tasks (continued)

Step 14	Update custom code that uses Oracle Activity Management Gateway APIs (recommended)	10.7, 11.0
Step 15	Update the currency and the billing and shipping addresses of draft invoices (conditionally required)	10.7, 11.0
Step 16	Drop invalidated packages (conditionally required)	10.7, 11.0

Oracle Receivables Tasks

Step 1	Create indexes on transaction Flexfield columns (conditionally required)	10.7, 11.0
Step 2	Re-create customized tax vendor extension views (conditionally required)	10.7, 11.0
Step 3	Update tax vendor descriptive Flexfield information (conditionally required)	10.7, 11.0
Step 4	Set up Tax Accounting (recommended)	10.7, 11.0
Step 5	Create contexts and segments for new Flexfields (required)	10.7, 11.0
Step 6	Create database objects required for the upgrade of data for MRC (conditionally required)	11.0
Step 7	Create or modify data for data model changes for MRC (conditionally required)	11.0

Country-Specific Financials Product Family

Oracle Financials Common Countries Features Tasks

Step 1	Update customized menus that use JG submenus (conditionally required)	10.7, 11.0
Step 2	Set up EFT system format information (conditionally required)	10.7
Step 3	Enable the Swift Code field in the Enter Banks window (conditionally required)	10.7

Applications Technology Products	For Version

Oracle Financials for Asia/Pacific Tasks

Step 1	Correct existing data before reporting tax information (conditionally required)	10.7, 11.0

Oracle Financials for Europe Tasks

Step 1	Upgrade character-mode responsibilities (recommended)	10.7
Step 2	Update customized menus that use JE submenus (conditionally required) (JE refers to a set of libraries required at install time)	10.7, 11.0

Oracle Financials for the Americas Tasks

Step 1	Set the value of the JL: Inflation Ratio Precision profile option (required) (JL is a list of tables which are compiled as part of AOL [Application Object Library] at the time of installation)	11.0
Step 2	Create new lookup codes (required)	10.7, 11.0
Step 3	Set tax system options (required)	10.7
Step 4	Update sales orders and invoices (required)	10.7
Step 5	Ensure that a valid inventory organization is defined for profile options (required)	10.7, 11.0
Step 6	Manually associate tax information for each inventory organization location (required)	11.0
Step 7	Associate tax groups and tax categories (required)	11.0
Step 8	Cancel and re-enter all unapproved and unposted invoices (conditionally required)	11.0
Step 9	Archive restored technical appraisals (conditionally required)	11.0

HRMS Product Family

Oracle Human Resources Tasks (U.S., U.K., and Japan)

Step 1	Select legislative and college data with DataInstall (required)	10.7, 11.0
Step 2	Run the global legislation driver (required)	10.7, 11.0
Step 3	Run the exchange rate migration script (conditionally required)	10.7, 11.0

Applications Technology Products		For Version

Oracle Payroll Tasks (U.S., U.K., and Japan)

Step 1	Ensure that DataInstall has been run (required)	10.7, 11.0
Step 2	Ensure that the global legislation driver has been run (required)	10.7, 11.0
Step 3	Ensure that the exchange rate migration script has been run (conditionally required)	10.7, 11.0

Manufacturing and Distribution Product Family

Oracle Inventory/Cost Management/Work in Process Tasks

Step 1	Review and correct organization default accounts - INV (recommended)	10.7, 11.0
Step 2	Define profile option, if not already defined - INV (conditionally required)	10.7
Step 3	Verify inventory valuation - INV (recommended)	10.7, 11.0
Step 4	Run WIP Value report (if WIP is installed) and/or inventory valuation reports (recommended)	10.7, 11.0
Step 5	Define default material subelement - Average Costing (conditionally required)	10.7, 11.0
Step 6	Define Average Rates cost type - Average Costing (conditionally required)	10.7, 11.0

Oracle Master Scheduling/MRP and Supply Chain Planning Tasks

Step 1	Start the Planning Manager (required)	10.7, 11.0

Oracle Order Management

Step 1	Document errors that occurred during upgrade (recommended)	10.7, 11.0
Step 2	Create OM (Order Management) profile option for the Cycles to Workflow upgrade (required)	10.7, 11.0
Step 3	Set up responsibilities for order creation/manipulation (required)	10.7, 11.0
Step 4	Review upgraded transaction types (required)	10.7, 11.0
Step 5	Set up processing constraints (required)	10.7, 11.0
Step 6	Set up Flexfield definitions (required)	10.7, 11.0

Applications Technology Products		For Version

Manufacturing and Distribution Product Family (continued)

Oracle Order Management (continued)

Step 7	Review seeded attributes and their sequences (required)	10.7, 11.0
Step 8	Set up pricing profiles (required)	10.7, 11.0
Step 9	Define pick slip grouping rules (required)	10.7, 11.0
Step 10	Define release sequence rules (required)	10.7, 11.0
Step 11	Define shipping parameters for inventory organizations (required)	10.7, 11.0
Step 12	Define ship methods and carrier mappings (required)	10.7, 11.0
Step 13	Set up shipping execution profiles and menus (required)	10.7, 11.0
Step 14	Set up invoice source and nondelivery invoice source (required)	10.7, 11.0
Step 15	Set up Workflow notification approver and update Workflow item attributes (required)	10.7, 11.0
Step 16	Review Shipping Execution upgrade errors (recommended)	10.7, 11.0

Oracle Purchasing Tasks

Step 1	Activate transaction managers (required)	10.7, 11.0
Step 2	Upgrade notifications (conditionally required)	10.7
Step 3	Set MRP profile options (conditionally required)	10.7
Step 4	Verify and modify sourcing rules (conditionally required)	10.7
Step 5	Verify date formats (required)	10.7, 11.0
Step 6	Verify RMA upgrade (conditionally required)	10.7, 11.0
Step 7	Perform additional setup steps (conditionally required)	10.7, 11.0

Applications Technology Products	**For Version**

Public Sector

Oracle Labor Distribution Tasks

Step 1	Upgrade Labor Distribution and remove obsolete objects (required)	10.7, 11.0

Oracle U.S. Federal Financials Tasks

Step 1	Migrate data to new tables (required)	10.7, 11.0
Step 2	Load seed data (required)	10.7, 11.0

NLS Database Considerations

Each language capability that you add to the database may take up to 200MB of space in the NLS (natural language support) database. If there is not enough space to accommodate this growth, you will encounter an error during the upgrade or while applying the translations. If you receive an error due to lack of space, simply increase the affected tablespace and restart the process.

You must retain your original language configuration until the entire upgrade is complete (including the post-upgrade and finishing steps). After you complete the upgrade, you can use the License Manager to change your language configuration.

Category 6

Category 6 includes steps that are part of the post-upgrade steps. These steps can be completed when users are logged in, but they cannot use specific features unless these steps are completed.

Applications Technology Products	**For Version**

System Administration Tasks

Step 1	Set up report security groups (conditionally recommended)	10.7, 11.0
Step 2	Upgrade accounting calendar (conditionally required)	10.7, 11.0

Application Object Library Tasks

Step 1	Update custom code using Flexfield values in FND_LOOKUPS (conditionally required)	10.7
Step 2	Update custom calls to FND_DESCR_FLEX_ CONTEXT_TL (conditionally required)	10.7
Step 3	Rename the /srw directory to /reports for custom applications (conditionally required)	10.7
Step 4	Copy custom forms libraries to AU_TOP (conditionally required)	10.7, 11.0
Step 5	Copy custom .fmb files to AU_TOP (conditionally required)	10.7, 11.0
Step 6	Convert character-mode messages to GUI for custom applications (conditionally required)	10.7
Step 7	Regenerate, recompile, and relink custom concurrent program libraries (conditionally required)	10.7, 11.0

Applications Technology Products	For Version

Oracle Alert Tasks

Step 1	Associate organization names to pre-existing custom Alert definitions (conditionally required)	10.7
Step 2	Disable and re-enable all custom alerts to re-create triggers (conditionally required)	10.7

Oracle Common Modules Tasks

Step 1	Upload and back up customized data for non-demonstration databases (conditionally required)	10.7, 11.0

Financials Product Family

Oracle Cash Management Tasks

Step 1	Reinstall customized Reconciliation Open Interface objects (conditionally required)	10.7, 11.0
Step 2	Prepare Cash Management for Payroll Reconciliation (conditionally required)	10.7, 11.0

Oracle General Ledger Tasks

Step 1	Preserve GL account combinations affected by the Segment Value Inheritance program (required)	10.7, 11.0
Step 2	Ensure that account segment values use correct account type (conditionally required)	10.7
Step 3	Review period rates (conditionally required)	10.7, 11.0
Step 4	Define Owners Equity Translation Rule profile option (conditionally required)	10.7
Step 5	Define income statement accounts revaluation profile option (conditionally required)	10.7, 11.0
Step 6	Review AutoPost criteria (conditionally required)	10.7
Step 7	Define GIS conversion rates and rate types (conditionally required)	11.0
Step 8	Verify program submission parameters for mass funds check/reservation (conditionally required)	10.7

Applications Technology Products		For Version

Financials Product Family (continued)

Oracle General Ledger Tasks **(continued)**

Step 9	Set function security for journal posting and reversing functions (recommended)	10.7
Step 10	Define Daily Rates profile option (recommended)	10.7
Step 11	Set up intercompany balancing (recommended)	10.7, 11.0
Step 12	Define new consolidation mapping rules (recommended)	10.7
Step 13	Review concurrent program controls (recommended)	10.7
Step 14	Define Archive and Purge profile option (recommended)	10.7, 11.0
Step 15	Define GL Summarization profile options (recommended)	10.7, 11.0

Oracle Payables Tasks

Step 1	Set up Offset taxes (conditionally required)	10.7, 11.0
Step 2	Set up the future dated payment account (conditionally required)	10.7, 11.0
Step 3	Set up taxes to be partially recoverable (conditionally required)	10.7, 11.0
Step 4	Link GL records and AP records (required)	10.7, 11.0

Oracle Projects Tasks

Step 1	Implement Self-Service Time (conditionally required)	10.7, 11.0
Step 2	Implement cross charge (conditionally required)	10.7, 11.0

Oracle Receivables Tasks

Step 1	Define Application Rule Set (recommended)	10.7, 11.0
Step 2	Define GL tax assignments for Natural Account tax codes (conditionally required)	10.7, 11.0
Step 3	Set up Internet Receivables (recommended)	10.7, 11.0
Step 4	Enable Header Level Rounding (recommended)	10.7, 11.0
Step 5	Enable credit card processing (recommended)	10.7, 11.0

Applications Technology Products	**For Version**

Financials Product Family (continued)

Oracle Receivables Tasks (continued)

Step 6	Enable cross-currency lockbox (recommended)	10.7, 11.0
Step 7	Set Up Bills of Exchange (recommended)	10.7, 11.0
Step 8	Link GL and AR records (required)	10.7, 11.0

Country-Specific Financials Product Family

Oracle Financials for Asia/Pacific Tasks

Step 1	Define additional company information—Taiwan (required)	10.7, 11.0
Step 2	Define additional company information—Singapore (conditionally required)	11.0
Step 3	Update tax types (conditionally required)	11.0

Oracle Common Countries Financials Tasks

Step 1	Set up Appreciation QuickCode (recommended)	10.7, 11.0
Step 2	Upgrade Appreciation (recommended)	10.7, 11.0
Step 3	Assign request groups to your responsibilities (recommended)	10.7, 11.0

Oracle Financials for Europe Tasks

Step 1	Update Polish and Turkish journal line sequence numbers (conditionally required)	11.0
Step 2	Update Spanish globalization Flexfield contexts (conditionally required)	11.0
Step 3	Update Danish EFT invoices to use EDI Flexfield (required)	10.7, 11.0
Step 4	Re-create French income tax types (conditionally required)	10.7, 11.0
Step 5	Update French deductible VAT invoices (conditionally required)	10.7, 11.0
Step 6	Update Italian VAT transactions (conditionally required)	10.7, 11.0
Step 7	Create Italian inventory tax types (conditionally required)	10.7

Applications Technology Products	For Version

Country-Specific Financials Product Family (continued)

Oracle Financials for Europe Tasks (continued)

Step 8	Update taxable amounts for custom bills and self invoices (required)	10.7, 11.0
Step 9	Update Hungarian VAT transactions (conditionally required)	10.7, 11.0
Step 10	Enable the Additional Information for Hungary globalization Flexfield on the Transaction Types window (conditionally required)	10.7, 11.0
Step 11	Enable the Tax Code field in the Receipts window (conditionally required)	10.7

Oracle Financials for the Americas Tasks

Step 1	Update Colombian journal line third-party information (conditionally required)	11.0

HRMS Product Family

Oracle Human Resources Tasks

Step 1	Reapply customization to script for Salary Proposal view (conditionally required)	10.7
Step 2	Drop obsolete Oracle users (recommended)	10.7

Oracle Payroll (U.S.) Tasks

Step 1	Check for invalid U.S. address information (conditionally required)	10.7, 11.0

Manufacturing and Distribution Product Family

Oracle Inventory/Cost Management/Work in Process Tasks

Step 1	Create indexes on Flexfield segment columns - INV (recommended)	10.7, 11.0
Step 2	Summarize demand history - INV (recommended)	10.7, 11.0
Step 3	Define Item Catalog Description profile option - INV (required)	10.7, 11.0
Step 4	Update item descriptions - INV (conditionally required)	10.7, 11.0

Applications Technology Products	For Version
Oracle Quality Tasks	
Step 1 Configure new profile options (1) (conditionally required)	10.7
Step 2 Configure new profile options (2) (conditionally required)	10.7, 11.0
Oracle Release Management/Automotive Tasks	
Step 1 Create sourcing rules (recommended)	10.7, 11.0
Step 2 Validate release 11i Demand Status Inquiry report (required)	10.7, 11.0
Step 3 Verify all setup data (required)	10.7, 11.0
Step 4 Create cumulative (CUM) keys for shipped sales order lines (recommended)	10.7, 11.0
Step 5 Run CUM Key assignment script (recommended)	10.7, 11.0
Step 6 Verify CUM shipped quantities of Ship-from Customer Items (recommended)	10.7, 11.0
Step 7 If CUM does not match, enter CUM adjustments (recommended)	10.7, 11.0
Step 8 Evaluate forecasts (recommended)	10.7, 11.0
Public Sector	
Oracle Grants Accounting Tasks	
Step 1 Drop obsolete tables (optional)	10.7, 11.0
Public Sector Budgeting Tasks	
Step 1 Ensure account segment values use correct account type (conditionally required)	10.7
Step 2 Convert dates stored in character columns into canonical format (required)	10.7, 11.0
Step 3 Convert real numbers stored in character columns into multiradix format (required)	10.7, 11.0

Applications Technology Products		For Version
Public Sector		
Public Sector Budgeting Tasks (continued)		
Step 4	Create baseline budgets from historical worksheets for use in budget revisions for line items and positions (required)	10.7, 11.0
Step 5	Enable Excel interface functionality (conditionally required)	10.7, 11.0
Step 6	Enable Oracle Financial Analyzer functionality (conditionally required)	10.7, 11.0
Oracle U.S. Federal Financials Tasks		
Step 1	Reset the profile options (conditionally required)	10.7, 11.0
Step 2	Set up holiday and non-working days (required)	10.7, 11.0

Upgrade Case Study

A Financials administrator helps other members of the upgrade team to prepare a list of steps required for the upgrade. It is recommended that this list be as detailed as possible to include all the steps as well as the time taken to perform them. Here is a case study report from a typical installation upgrade for 10.7 to 11i.

Step	Action	Time Taken/Notes
1.1	Migrate database to Oracle 8.1.6.	
1.2	Back up the database.	
1.3	Perform Category 1 steps described in the Upgrading Oracle Applications Release 11i manual.	
2.1	Use Rapid Install to install Oracle Financials Release 11i on the new hardware (the application tier). Choose Upgrade Existing Applications instance to lay out and configure the APPL_TOP and corresponding technology stack components. Follow instructions on installation manual.	

Step	Action	Time Taken/Notes
2.2	Create Net8 alias for the database instance running on the database tier and set the TWO_TASK environment variable on UNIX to point to it.	
2.3	Perform Category 2 and 3 steps described in the Upgrading Oracle Applications Release 11i manual	

Handling Customizations

A critical part of any Oracle Financials project is making sure that the database and development components of the custom applications are migrated to the upgraded environment as well. Time and resources required for this activity depend on the number of customizations. More often, an existing customization is already available as a standard feature and does not have to be migrated.

Some of the customization may be phased out after the upgrade has been completed if those programs are not used on a day-to-day basis. Custom programs built using the following tools should be reviewed after migration:

■   Oracle Developer 4.5 (Forms 4.5 and Reports 2.5)

■   PL/SQL components, including functions, stored procedures, and triggers

Oracle Customization Toolset

Following are the additional components of the Oracle Technology Stack. These components should be reviewed in Oracle Financials 11i in this context.

■   Oracle Forms Server 6i

■   Oracle Developer 6i

■   Oracle8i

■   PL/SQL version 8

In general, the following steps are required to upgrade existing 10.7 or 11.0 custom components:

1. Upgrade custom libraries and forms using Oracle Developer 6i. On your developer client machine, convert your Oracle Forms 4.5 forms to Oracle Forms 6i forms using the Forms Generator and make changes related to converting to PL/SQL 8. Any library files that are attached to the forms need to be converted first.

2. Run the upgrade utility *flint60* on custom forms. Move the converted 6i forms to the Forms Server in the $AU_TOP/forms/US directory. Then run flint60 to apply changes that help your form conform to release 11i standards. Note that flint60 can be run multiple times against a custom-developed form as part of any development process. The flint60 utility is used only for customizations to forms.

3. Make certain manual changes (cannot be avoided).

4. Test the functionality.

5. Compile the program using Oracle Developer 6i.

NOTE
It is recommended that you perform testing after migrating an old Forms 4.5 form to a Forms 6i form and then test it again after running flint60. This will help identify issues either to the form development or to the 11i integration issues, and it will help identify problems sooner and fix various issues.

The flint60 utility creates a new form file called *.fmb.new. The original *.fmb file is not touched and can be reused. The flint60 utility logs all the actions in a log file. The log file is created under $AU_TOP/forms/US/*.fmb.html; this file can be reviewed using a standard browser. The flint60 utility requires a configuration file, flint60.ora, to hold the database user name and password and other information. The flint60.ora file is a simple text file that should include the following information:

- server_host=
- message_file=
- connect=[y|n]
- userid=[usr/pwd]

The Web server host name that will be used to access the .html log files the virtual path and filename of the message description file, fnderr.html, is a boolean that indicates whether you should verify blocks against the database. If connect=y, this is the Oracle user name and password you should use to connect to the database.

The flint60 utility can accept one, two, or no switches on the command line as follows:

```
flint60 -uc <module1>.fmb <module2>.fmb
where -u is the upgrade mode
c indicates don't clear out the text hints for reusing with flint60
```

The log file generated by the flint60 utility includes details of all the activities. Following are some of the message types found in the log file:

- **Status**   An informational message

- **Action**   Each action taken by the utility

- **Warning**   Could indicate a problem

- **Fatal**   Fatal flint60 issue needs immediate attention

Some of the conversions automatically occur when upgrading Oracle Forms 4.5 forms to Oracle Forms 6i. These changes include the following:

- CHAR(1) is converted to VARCHAR2(1)

- LENGTH(field) is converted to NVL(LENGTH(field),0)

- NULL is added to RETURN statements

Setting Environment Variables

When using the flint60 utility, ensure that the environment variable called FLINT60_CONFIG (for UNIX) is set and points to the flint60.ora configuration file. If this is not done, flint60 looks for the configuration file in the current directory.

You should also ensure that you define the following environment variables when working with the 11i development environment:

- FORMS60_PATH

- REPORTS60_PATH

- FORMS60_USER_DATE[TIME]_FORMAT

- REPORTS60_USER_DATE[TIME]_FORMAT

- NLS_DATE_FORMAT   Should be set to *dd-mon-rr*

Further Reference

For details on upgrading custom forms as well as coding standards for the applications, refer to the following Oracle manuals:

- Oracle Applications Developer's Guide for 11i
- Oracle Applications User Interface Standards for Forms-Based Products for Release 11i

Summary

Upgrading to release 11i is critical from the point of view of using added production functionality, staying current with versions, and supportability. Upgrading is a complex activity and needs to be planned to minute details before upgrade begins. A decision to upgrade should be followed by an evaluation process, in which an evaluation team identifies business requirements and how various modules can service them, and identifies gaps. The report produced by the evaluation team in terms of product strengths and customization requirements are valuable to the implementation team. A smooth upgrade depends on how critical resources such as hardware, software, people, and processes are managed and also how the team reacts to various unforeseen problems. In this chapter, we reviewed a summary of pre-installation, AutoUpgrade, and post-installation steps needed to upgrade to release 11i. In addition, we also discussed ways of handling customization and incorporating it seamlessly in the development environment. In the next chapter, we will review some of the techniques for managing the 11i environment we just created.

CHAPTER
5

Managing the
Financials Environment

- Introduction to commonly used Oracle Applications utilities or AD utilities
- Using AD Administration utilities
- Using the AutoPatch utility
- Analyzing the database
- Changing a password
- Migrating the Oracle Financials database
- Using components of Oracle Workflow
- Managing Oracle Workflow notifications
- Setting up notification mailer
- Using Workflow scripts
- Tips and techniques

T he successful Oracle Financials administrator should understand his environment thoroughly and should be able to react to technical issues quickly and confidently. Given the complexity of Oracle applications, it is important for the administrator to spell out best practices and processes for managing the environment so that standards are followed and deviations from standards are documented and understood by all the stakeholders in the environment.

This chapter focuses on two aspects of management that the administrator deals with on a day-to-day basis: Active Directory (AD) utilities and Oracle Workflow "gotchas."

AD Utilities

AD utilities are a group of tools designed to install, upgrade, maintain, and patch a specific set of products contained in a release of Oracle Financials. This section discusses some commonly used AD utilities. The objectives of the section are to provide you with a basic understanding of the AD utilities along with how to manage the Oracle Financials environment using AD utilities.

Commonly Used AD Utilities

The three most common AD utilities are AD Administration, AutoUpgrade, and AutoPatch. These utilities may call many other utilities to perform specific tasks.

AD Administration Utility

AD Administration (adadmin) performs maintenance tasks and can also be used to complete runtime tasks during an installation or upgrade, or at any time thereafter. The tasks performed with this utility fall into two categories: database and file system tasks. Like AutoUpgrade and AutoPatch, AD Administration can run parallel workstations for most database tasks and some file system tasks.

AD Administration has two main menus that help you perform the following functions.

Maintain Database Objects Menu   You can perform the following tasks from this menu:

- Validate the APPS schema(s)
- Compile the APPS schema(s)
- Re-create grants and synonyms for the APPS schema(s)

- Compile Flexfield data in Application Object Library (AOL) tables

- Maintain multilingual tables

- Check the DUAL table

- Maintain Multiple Reporting Currencies schema(s)

- Convert to Multi-Org

- Convert to Multiple Reporting Currencies

Maintain Applications Files Menu   You can perform the following tasks from this menu:

- Create an applications environment file

- Relink application programs

- Copy files to destinations

- Verify files necessary for runtime

- Generate message files

- Generate form files

- Generate report files

- Generate graphics files

- Generate product JAR (Java Archive) files

AutoUpgrade Utility

The AutoUpgrade utility can be run after you complete the basic installation tasks. It performs such tasks as updating database objects, adding a localization, and the like. We won't be focusing on this utility in this chapter. For more details on AutoUpgrade, refer to Chapter 4.

AutoPatch Utility (adpatch or adpatch.exe)

AutoPatch is used to apply patches, mini-packs, or maintenance packs. A *mini-pack* or *patch set* is a collection of individual patches for a product, while a *maintenance pack* or *update* is a collection of *mini-packs* for all application products. Any patches that accompany a release are installed using AutoPatch. In addition to maintaining existing products, AutoPatch is used during the process of installing additional tasks, such as adding a language or a new product that was not a part of the base release.

Running AD Utilities

To run the AD utilities, perform the following tasks:

1. Log in as APPLMGR.
2. Type **$APPL_TOP/APPSORA.env**.
3. Set the appropriate ORACLE_SID using the .oraenv shell script.
4. Make sure that sufficient temporary disk space exists in the TEMP file systems.

You can set up an e-mail notification to notify you or your group when a workstation fails at any time. For more details about various options available with running AD utilities, refer to *Oracle Applications - Maintaining Oracle Applications* (Part No. A87339-01).

Table 5-1 shows the configuration and environment files used by various AD utilities.

File Name	Default Location	Description
adconfig.txt	$APPL_TOP/admin	Contains environment information for all installed modules
def.txt	$APPL_TOP/admin/<ORACLE_SID>	Contains defaults used by AutoPatch and AD Administration for non-interactive operation
applprod.txt	$APPL_TOP/admin	Contains AD utilities product description file to identify products and their dependencies
applterr.txt	$APPL_TOP/admin	Contains all supported territories and localizations
applora.txt	$APPL_TOP/admin	Required runtime init.ora parameters
applorau.txt	$APPL_TOP/admin	Required install/upgrade init.ora parameters
<db-name>.env	$APPL_TOP	Main environment file created by Rapid Install
adovars.env	$APPL_TOP/admin	Environment file for Java and HTML
fndenv.env	$APPL_TOP/admin	Additional environment variables for AOL

TABLE 5-1. *AD Utility Configuration and Environment Files*

AD Timing Report

The AD Timing Report (adt<*session_id*>.lst, where <*session_id*> is your AD program session ID) is produced by AutoUpgrade, AutoPatch, and AD Administration utilities. This report provides information on long-running processes during the operation of these three utilities. The output is placed in $APPL_TOP/admin/<*db_name*>/out. NT users will find it in %APPL_TOP%/admin/<*db_name*>/out. It contains the following information:

- Time-consuming jobs

- Failed jobs

- Incomplete jobs

- Total run time

- Percent usage by product

- Percent usage by phase and product

The report can also be generated manually during an upgrade or anytime thereafter to view timing statistics from a prior session.

```
$ cd $AD_TOP/admin/sql
$ sqlplus <APPS username>/<APPS password> @adtimrpt.sql <session id> \
```

Running the AD Administration Utility

This section contains information about using the AD Administration utility. It contains information for running AD Administration in interactive and non-interactive mode.

AD Administration (adadmin) performs maintenance tasks on an installed Oracle Financials system to ensure that it runs smoothly. These tasks fall into two categories: database and file system. Like AutoUpgrade and AutoPatch, AD Administration can run on parallel workstations for most database tasks and some file system tasks.

Performing Database Tasks

Database tasks are performed from the Maintain Applications Database Objects menu. These tasks are performed with installed database objects, and include the following:

- Validate APPS schema(s)

- Compile APPS schema(s)

- Re-create grants and synonyms for APPS schema(s)

- Compile Flexfield data in AOL tables

- Maintain multilingual tables

- Check DUAL table

- Maintain Multiple Reporting Currencies schema(s)

- Convert to Multiple Reporting Currencies

- Convert to Multi-Org

Performing File System Tasks

File system tasks are performed for product files from the Maintain Applications Files menu. Many of the following tasks require database access:

- Create applications environment file

- Relink application programs

- Copy files to destinations

- Verify files necessary for runtime

- Generate message files

- Generate form files

- Generate report files

- Generate graphics files

- Generate product JAR files

Running AD Administration Interactively

AD Administration can be initiated interactively by typing the following command:

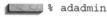 `% adadmin`

   You'll see a menu with options different from those described earlier, from which you can select the appropriate task to perform the job. AD Administration validates the init.ora parameter against applora.txt only the first time a task is performed. It does not recheck whether other tasks from the Database Objects menu were selected in the same AD Administration session. Following are the options found on the menu.

Validate APPS Schemas   Using this option, you can verify the integrity of the schema. This option executes the advrfapp.sql schema to check certain specific conditions. You should run this after an upgrade or after applying a patch. You may also want to run this task whenever you receive a runtime error that suggests a problem from the AD_DDL package. This can also be done from the SQL*Plus prompt.

Compile APPS Schema(s)   This option tells parallel workstations to compile invalid database objects in the APPS schemas. It uses the same parallel compile phases as AutoUpgrade. You can run this task at any time, but it is most effective after custom packages are moved to the APPS schema and need to be compiled after applying patches that alter packages in the APPS schema. Oracle11i utilizes Invoker's Rights in selected PL/SQL procedures and packages. By accepting the default of non-incremental mode, AD Administration will perform Invoker's Rights processing on every package in the APPS schema. If you type **yes** at the prompt, Invoker's Rights processing will be run only on packages that have changed since Invoker's Rights processing was last run.

Re-create Grants and Synonyms for APPS Schema(s)   This option identifies missing grants from a base product schema to the corresponding APPS schema or it identifies missing synonyms in the APPS schema for the object. This option re-creates the grants and synonyms for the Oracle Application Suite's public schema (APPLSYSPUB), re-creates grants on some packages from SYSTEM to APPS, and then spawns parallel workstations to re-create grants and synonyms linking sequences and tables in the base schemas to the APPS schemas. Run this option when grants and synonyms are missing from an installation. This may occur as a result of custom development, incomplete database migrations (exports/imports), or AD utility sessions that failed to run successfully to completion.

Compile Flexfield Data in AOL Tables   This option compiles Flexfield data structures in Oracle Application Object Library (AOL) tables. If you choose not to compile the structures, each one is compiled the first time any user accesses the Flexfield. This task should be run after applying a patch that changes the setup of Flexfields.

Check DUAL Table   This option verifies that the DUAL table exists in the SYS schema, is accessible by applications, and contains only one row.

Maintain Multiple Reporting Currencies Schema(s)   This option appears as a menu choice on the Database Objects menu *only* if Multiple Reporting Currencies (MRC) functionality is installed in your database. If you do not already have MRC installed, you will see a Convert to Multiple Reporting Currencies option. You can use that option to install MRC. For each APPS schema, MRC is implemented using an extra schema, called an *adjunct schema*, which contains synonyms to objects in the APPS schema, exact copies of some objects in the APPS schema, and modified copies of other objects in the APPS schema.

Once AD Administration completes this process, check the log file (adadmin.log) in the $APPL_TOP/admin/<*db_name*>/out directory and correct all problems. Rerun this report as you make changes until no more problems are listed. Choose this task after applying any database patches to synchronize the database objects in your MRC schemas with those that may have been updated in your APPS schemas.

Convert to Multiple Reporting Currencies This option appears on the Database Objects menu *only* if Multiple Reporting Currencies functionality is *not* installed in your database. The Convert to Multiple Reporting Currencies task accepts a number of parallel workstations, creates Multiple Reporting Currencies schema, sets up data groups, and performs similar tasks.

Convert to Multi-Org This option displays on the Database Objects menu *only* if Multi-Org and/or Multiple Sets of Books Architecture are *not* installed in your database. This task converts a standard product group (not Multiple Sets of Books Architecture and not Multi-Org) into a Multi-Org product group with one operating unit defined at the site level. Before running this step, you must define an operating unit and set the site-level AOL profile option MO: Operating Unit to use your new operating unit. This profile option tells AD Administration what operating unit it should use when converting your existing data. This site-level profile option must remain set at all times.

The Convert to Multi-Org task performs the following functions:

- Asks for the number of parallel workstations (for compiling invalid objects in parallel)

- Confirms that you want to run this task

- Creates scripts to disable and re-enable triggers in the APPS schema

- Disables all triggers in the APPS schema

- Converts seed data and transaction data to Multi-Org in parallel

- Re-enables all previously enabled triggers in the APPS schema

Maintaining Applications Files

The Maintain Applications Files menu in the AD Administration utility is used to perform tasks related to Oracle application product files. From this menu, the following tasks can be accessed:

Create Applications Environment File Using this option, you can create an environment file that defines Oracle application environment variables. The file has an .env extension. After the utility generates the environment file, you can make customizations in adovars.env and run the generated environment file as necessary.

Relink Application Programs   Using this option, you can relink Oracle Financials executable programs with the database server (Oracle8i) libraries so that they function with the database. Relinking can be done for all products or for specific ones. You should relink application programs when you upgrade the database version or when you relink the database binaries. It should be noted that AD Administration does not link executables for the product AD—that needs to be done using the adrelink.sh utility manually.

Copy Files to Destinations   This option copies files from each product area to a central location where they can be easily referenced by application programs. Existing files can be overwritten or you can choose to install files in a separate location.

Verify Files Necessary for Runtime   This option verifies whether all files required to run Oracle applications for the current configuration are in APPL_TOP.

Generate Message Files   Using this option, you can generate message binary files from Oracle Application Object Library tables. Usually this activity is done only when a specific patch instructs you to do so.

Generate Form Files   This option generates binary Oracle forms files (.fmx) from the definition files (.fmb). You can specify several parameters such as number of parallel workstations, character sets, and language-specific generation.

Generate Report Files   This option generates binary Oracle reports files (.rdf) from the definition files. You can specify several parameters, such as number of parallel workstations, character set, and language-specific generation.

Generate Graphics Files   This option generates binary Oracle graphics files (.ogd) from the definition files (.ogx). You can specify several parameters, such as number of parallel workstations, character set, and language-specific generation.

Generate Product JAR Files   This option is used when you apply an Oracle forms patch. This task does the following:

- Generates all JAR files that are out of date
- With the force option, generates all JAR files for all products
- Generates product JAR files in APPL_TOP and JAVA_TOP
- Signs JAR files, if on the Web server

Running the AutoPatch Utility

AutoPatch is used to apply individual patches, mini-packs, or maintenance packs. A *mini-pack* (or *patchset*) is a collection of individual patches for a product, while a *maintenance pack* (or *release update*) is a collection of mini-packs for all products in the Oracle Applications Suite.

In this section, we'll cover the following topics:

- How AutoPatch works
- Starting and running AutoPatch
- Applying Java patches

How AutoPatch Works

In addition to maintaining existing products, AutoPatch is used for additional tasks such as adding a language or a new product that was not a part of the base release. AutoPatch resides in the AD_TOP/bin directory. AutoPatch replaces some of the existing product files with new versions of those files that are included with the patch. It may also make changes to your Oracle Applications database objects.

If you are installing Oracle applications in a multiple-server environment, you must run AutoPatch on all relevant machines to install the necessary files. In preparation for running AutoPatch, perform these steps:

1. Log in as applmgr and set up your environment.

2. Copy the patch files to a directory on your file system by unzipping the archived patch file. The directory created by unzipping the archived patch file is called the PATCH_TOP directory.

3. Start AutoPatch from a Bourne or Korn shell.

4. Answer the AutoPatch questions. AutoPatch identifies the Oracle applications products that need to be updated.

After you have answered the AutoPatch questions, the utility performs these steps:

1. Extracts the appropriate files from each product's C library.

2. Compares the extracted object modules with their corresponding files in the patch directory. It also makes this type of comparison with files such as forms, reports, and SQL scripts.

3. If a file in the patch directory is a more recent version than the product's current file, AutoPatch backs up the product's current file into a subdirectory of your patch directory. Specifically, it backs up the following:

```
<PROD>_TOP/<subdir(s)>/<old_file_name> to
<patch_dir>/backup/<env_name>/<appl_top_name> -
/<prod>/<subdir(s)>/<old_file_name>.
```

Where *<patch_dir>* is the patch directory, *<env_name>* is the applications environment name, *<appl_top_name>* is the APPL_TOP name, and *<prod>* is the name of the product being patched.

4. AutoPatch replaces each product's outdated files with newer files from the patch directory.

5. It applies changed Java class files and regenerates JAR files as needed.

6. It loads the new object modules into the C libraries.

7. AutoPatch backs up any files you listed in adlinkbk.txt and is relinked.

8. It relinks the Oracle applications products with the Oracle8 Server.

9. It runs SQL scripts and execute commands, which change Oracle applications database objects. By default, AutoPatch does this in parallel.

10. AutoPatch copies any specified HTML or media files to their respective destinations.

11. It generates Oracle Forms files, Oracle Reports files, and Oracle Graphics files.

12. It appends a record of how it changed your system to applptch.txt in the $APPL_TOP/admin/*<db_name>* directory, where *<db_name>* is the value of your ORACLE_SID or TWO_TASK variable. For NT, the file is located in %APPL_TOP%/admin/*<db_name>*, where *<db_name>* is the value of your ORACLE_SID or LOCAL variable.

13. AutoPatch records summary information of actions actually performed to applpsum.txt located under APPL_TOP/admin.

Patches should always be applied in their entirety. When applying a patch to a multiple-server environment, make sure you apply the patch on all servers. Before applying any patch, make sure to read the readme.txt file in full. The readme.txt file contains information such as

- Bug number
- Patch description
- Special instructions

AutoPatch is started by using the following command:

```
% adpatch
```

Based on the nature of the patch, you may decide to shut down the Concurrent Manager before applying the patch. If the files on the Forms server are going to be relinked, make sure all users log off the application before proceeding.

Running AutoPatch Again

You can run AutoPatch as many times as necessary until the patch is successfully applied. You can then run AutoPatch to update other servers in your environment or another Oracle applications product group.

Running a Session to Completion   If you aborted your AutoPatch session or it did not run to completion, restart AutoPatch. AutoPatch first prompts for the name of the log file. If you specify the log file from the previous session, AutoPatch adds the message

```
****Start of AutoPatch Session****
```

to the end of that file and appends the messages from the new session as they are generated.

If you specify a new file name, AutoPatch creates a new main log file for this session. However, it does not create new versions of the other log files, such as admvcode.log or adrelink.log. It appends new messages to the existing versions of these files. AutoPatch then asks whether you want to complete the previous session. If you respond No, AutoPatch asks you to confirm your choice and then restarts from the beginning. If you respond Yes, AutoPatch restarts where the previous session stopped.

Using the AD Merge Patch Utility

AD Merge Patch (admrgpch) is designed to merge multiple AutoPatch compatible patches into a single integrated patch. It is an executable located in the bin directory of AD_TOP. To merge two or more patches into a single integrated patch, run admrgpch with the following arguments:

```
$ admrgpch <source directory> <destination directory>
```

The *<source directory>* is the directory in which the patches to merge have been unloaded. This utility reads the c*<patchnum>*.drv, readme.txt, d*<patchnum>*.drv, and g*<patchnum>*.drv for each patch in the source directory and merges them to create cmerged.drv, readme.txt, dbmerged.drv, and gmerged.drv files in the destination directory. It also merges the set of files contained in the individual patches under the source directory according to file revision and copies them to the destination directory. If a file is contained in more than one source patch, only the highest revision of the file is copied to the destination directory. Actions in the merged patches are grouped by product and then by patch number. Comments in the merged readme.txt are also ordered by product and then by patch number.

After admrgpch runs, you should check the admrgpch.log file for errors. The file is located in your APPL_TOP in the log directory under admin. If you do not find any errors, look in the readme.txt file in the destination directory for instructions on applying the merged patch using AutoPatch.

Patching Java Files

The copy driver file for a Java patch contains one or more **jcopy** commands. The **jcopy** command takes the content of the Java patch file j<*patchnum*>.zip and merges it with the apps.zip file located in the java directory under AU_TOP. This process replaces the old class files in the existing apps.zip and updates it with the new files in j<*patchnum*>.zip. It then updates the public apps.zip file located under JAVA_TOP.

apps.zip   Apps.zip is a patchable archive of all Java class files required by Oracle Financials. Individual Java class files are never present in the file system. Apps.zip is located in the java directory under AU_TOP, and a public copy is stored under JAVA_TOP. The public copy is the one used in a Web server environment, as the Web server can see the apps.zip in JAVA_TOP but, for security reasons, cannot access the apps.zip in APPL_TOP.

Regenerate JAR Files   The generation portion of the Java patch process regenerates the JAR (Java Archive) files in both APPL_TOP and JAVA_TOP. The JAR files in APPL_TOP are located in $<PROD>_TOP/java/jar (%<PROD>_TOP%\java\jar for NT) and the JAR files in JAVA_TOP are located in JAVA_TOP/oracle/apps/<prod>/jar (JAVA_TOP\oracle\apps\<prod>\jar forNT).

Signing JAR Files   The final step of the Java patching process is to sign all JAR files with the customer's digital signature. This is an inherent part of the Java patching process, and no user intervention is required. AutoPatch maintains JAR files on all servers but signs them only on the Web server. Signing all Oracle applications JAR files can take considerably longer than generating the JAR files without signing. Fortunately, most Oracle applications patches affect only a subset of all JAR files and AutoPatch re-creates and signs only the JAR files affected by a given patch.

Java Release Infrastructure   The Java Release Infrastructure (JRI) is a framework used by Oracle applications to develop, release, patch, and maintain Oracle applications Java code. Much of the functionality of JRI is invisible. The only direct interaction you may have is during the Java patching process when AutoPatch uses the **jcopy** command to merge the Java archive patch file with the apps.zip file and during the maintaining process when AD Administration is used to regenerate JAR files.

Other AD Utilities

In addition to AD Administration, AutoUpgrade, and AutoPatch, many other AD utilities are used for configuration, patching, upgrade and maintenance of the Oracle application environment. This section reviews some of these AD utilities.

- AD Controller (adctrl)

- AD Configuration (adutconf.sql)

- AD File Identification (adident)

- AD Splicer (adsplice)

- File Character Set Conversion (adncnv)

- ODF Comparison (adodfcmp)

- AD Relink (adrelink.sh)

- DataMerge (addmimp)

- AD Run SQL (adurs)

- AD Rebase (adrebase.exe)

- License Manager (LicenseMgr)

AD Controller (adctrl)

By using AD Controller, you can determine the status of AutoUpgrade, AD Administration, or AutoPatch workstations and restart failed tasks. Before you start the utility, perform these preparation steps:

1. Log in as applmgr.

2. Run the product group's environment file for UNIX. Set APPL_CONFIG to the name of the product group registry subkey for NT.

3. Start AD Controller by typing **adctrl** at the prompt. You will be prompted to do the following:

- Confirm the value of APPL_TOP.

- Specify an AD Controller log file (the default is adctrl.log). The log file resides in $APPL_TOP/admin/*<db_name>*/log, where *<db_name>* is the value of your ORACLE_SID or TWO_TASK variable.

- For NT, the file is located in %APPL_TOP%\admin*<db_name>*\log, where *<db_name>* is the value of ORACLE_SID or LOCAL.

4. Supply the Oracle Application Object Library user name and password of the product group. AD Controller displays the main menu.

AD Configuration (adutconf.sql)

This utility is a SQL script that reports standard information about the installed configuration of Oracle applications. This script generates a file called adutconf.lst that contains the following information about the product group:

- Whether Multi-Org is installed

- Whether Multiple Reporting Currency (MRC) is installed

- Information about all installed products, including shared and dependent products

- Information on all registered schemas

- The base language and other installed languages

- NLS environment variables

- Rollback segment information

- SQL*Plus PAUSE and NEWPAGE settings

- Useful information on referential integrity issues

Use the following command to run this script:

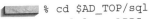

```
% cd $AD_TOP/sql
% sqlplus <APPS schema username>/<APPS schema password> @adutconf.sql
```

The output file, adutconf.lst, will be placed in your current working directory. You may need this information for debugging or to document the status of your installation when you contact Oracle Support Services.

AD File Identification (adident)

With AD File Identification, you can identify the version of one or more Oracle applications files. This information is used by AutoPatch to determine whether a file in a patch is newer than the on-site version. This utility is also useful for collecting information about your site when contacting Oracle Support Services. Use the following command to run the program:

```
$ adident Header <file 1> [ <file 2> <file 3> ... ]
```

The *<file n>* arguments should be the name of any applications text file, binary object file (extension .o for UNIX and .obj for NT), library file (extension .a for UNIX and .lib for NT), dynamic link library (.dll for NT), or executable program (.exe for NT). You may provide any number of file names as arguments. When you give adident the name of a library file or executable, it lists all of the files that make up the library or executable and their respective versions. For example,

```
$ adident Header $FND_TOP/lib/wfload.o $FND_TOP/lib/libfnd.a
wfload.o:
wfload.oc 115.5.1100.3
libfnd.a:
fdacon.lc 115.0
fdatat.lc 115.0
fdastr.lc 115.0
```

AD Splicer (adsplice)

Products introduced after a given release (those not on the base Oracle Application Suite CD for that release) can be difficult to install or maintain because the AD utilities do not recognize them as valid Oracle applications products. Therefore, they may be ignored or fail. AD Splicer resolves this difficulty by modifying your APPL_TOP and database so that AutoPatch and AD Administration recognize the off-cycle product(s) as being a valid Oracle Financials product(s) for the given release. Note that only the AutoPatch and AD Administration utilities recognize products added by AD Splicer. AutoUpgrade deliberately ignores products for the existing release that have been added by AD Splicer.

File Character Set Conversion (adncnv)

The File Character Set Conversion is used to convert files from one character set to another. This may be required for any text files shipped by applications, including SQL*Plus scripts, PL/SQL scripts, loader files, driver files, ODF files, header files, and HTML files. In general, you do not need to run this utility manually because AutoPatch and Rapid Install perform all required character set conversion for you.

You can convert one file at a time with this command:

```
$ adncnv <source file> <source char set> <destination file> <dest char set>
```

All parameters are required. The path and file name for the source and the destination files can be the same if the source file's directory and the APPLTMP directory are on the same file system. In general, it is simpler and safer to use different source and destination file names. Note that if you cannot convert to the same file name, convert to a different file name or change APPLTMP to a directory on the same file system as the source file directory.

ODF Comparison (adodfcmp)

ODF Comparison is used to compare the data model of a customer's database with the standard data model from the current release of the Oracle Application Suite and optionally modify the customer's database objects to match the standard data model. Each Oracle applications product is composed of functional building blocks. For example, Journal Entry is one building block of Oracle General Ledger. Each building block has an object description file (ODF) that describes its tables, views, indexes, sequences, and privilege sets. Privilege sets are grants that other schemas needed in earlier releases, before the introduction of the APPS schema. ODF Comparison compares a building block to its description file. A log file records any missing, extra, or incorrectly defined objects in the database. You can set the changedb parameter to have adodfcmp create missing objects, grants, and synonyms automatically. The changedb parameter set to *yes* will create the missing objects automatically. When set, the message in the log file after the 'CREATE . . . .' will be

```
Statement Executed.
```

AD Relink (adrelink.sh)

AD Relink is used to relink Oracle applications executable programs with the Oracle8 Server product libraries. Executable programs can also be relinked through the Relink Applications Programs task from the Maintain Applications File menu of AD Administration. If an error occurred during relinking, or if you are not sure that the relinking was successful, review the file adrelink.log. Note that in release 11i, you should use AD Administration to relink executables for most products. You must use adrelink.sh to relink AD executables because AD Administration does not relink AD executables. You can delete the adrelink.log file if it is large and contains no necessary information. A new adrelink.log file is created the next time adrelink.sh runs.

DataMerge (addmimp)

DataMerge is similar to the import utility. It allows you to import data into the Applications database. Sometimes Oracle Support Services will ask you to run DataMerge to work around problems encountered while upgrading your Oracle Applications database. However, in general, you should not run DataMerge manually unless instructed to do so by Oracle Support Services.

If you are running DataMerge to work around or reproduce an upgrade problem, go to the import directory under admin in the <PROD>_TOP of the product that owns the DataMerge files that failed. Run the same database command that you found in your AD worker log file. You may wish to specify different file names for the DataMerge log and summary file as follows:

```
$ cd $<PROD>_TOP/admin/import
```

Where *<PROD>* is the product short name of the product that owns the DataMerge file you want to run.

```
$ addmimp <parameter>=<value> [<parameter>=<value> . . .]
```

You can see instructions about DataMerge syntax by typing **addmimp** at the prompt.

AD Run SQL (adurs)

AD Run SQL is a utility that allows you to run a specified file in AutoUpgrade (AutoPatch) SQL mode. SQL mode is an interpreter that reads in your SQL script and then executes the statements it understands directly. SQL mode provides automatic error handling that is more robust than that of SQL*Plus. When AutoUpgrade and AutoPatch run SQL scripts, they use AD SQL mode for most SQL scripts unless the SQL script includes PL/SQL.

Rebase (adrebase.exe)

The AD Rebase utility is an NT-only utility that optimizes memory utilization of applications, RDBMS, and tools executable programs. Applications executables are automatically optimized when delivered by way of Rapid Install, AutoPatch, or adrelink.sh. You may wish to rerun the AD Rebase utility after upgrading the Oracle tools or the RDBMS. To run AD Rebase, type the following command:

```
adrebase
```

License Manager (LicenseMgr)

When you want to add products or languages to your Oracle applications installation, you can use the License Manager. Once you have contacted your Oracle sales representative, or set up your new license agreements online through the OracleStore, you are ready to "turn on" your new products and languages.

To begin:

```
$ cd COMMON_TOP/admin/assistants/licmgr
$ LicenseMgr
```

The location of COMMON_TOP is defined during the Rapid Install process. When License Manager displays the login screen, make sure your DISPLAY environment is properly set.

Analyzing the Database

Oracle11i uses cost-based optimization as a method for choosing the execution plan for SQL statements executed in the application. For cost-based optimization to run properly, it needs to regularly analyze the objects to gather statistics on them. This ensures that Oracle can pick up the execution path that fetches minimum cost for a given query.

Gathering statistics is recommended in the following circumstances:

- For a new system that already has a lot of data stored in the tables

- Before an upgrade

- During an upgrade

- As part of regular maintenance

Statistics can be collected by logging on as a system administrator, navigating to the Submit Request window, and submitting the Gather Schema Statistics program.

Changing the Oracle Applications Password

The Oracle applications password should be changed regularly for ensuring security. Note that user names cannot be changed after installation. Also, for changing the APPS password, ensure that the Concurrent Manager is taken down first.

To change the password, log on with system administrator's responsibility and perform the following steps:

- Navigate to the Oracle Users form (Security | Oracle | Register).

- Start a query by choosing View | Query by Example and then pressing ENTER.

- Enter the Database User Name for which you want to change the password.

- Run the query. Choose View | Query by Example, and then click Run.

- Enter a new password. Enter the password a second time to verify it.
- Commit the changes. (File | Save).

Migrating the Oracle Applications Database

In some situations, such as the following, you may need to move your application database:

- Moving to a different platform
- Upgrading the version of the Oracle Server you are using
- Moving to a split configuration
- After upgrading Oracle Applications, installing a higher version of the Oracle Server
- Improving scalability or performance
- Reorganizing database objects into different tablespaces
- Changing your database block size
- Changing your database character set

Oracle Server upgrades are possible using the Migration Utility that Oracle provides for that purpose.

Managing Oracle Workflow

Oracle Workflow is embedded in Oracle11i. Several manual setups are required to configure and manage Oracle Workflow. This section reviews the following aspects of Oracle Workflow:

- Components of Oracle Workflow
- Managing Oracle Workflow notifications
- Setup of Notification Mailer
- Useful Workflow scripts
- Miscellaneous tips and techniques

Components of Oracle Workflow

Oracle Workflow is installed as part of the Application Object Library (AOL) installation. The installation consists of two tiers: Workflow Client and Workflow Server. The Workflow Builder is used by Workflow developers to create or modify custom workflows. Builder is installed on Windows 95/NT/2000 clients only. The Workflow Client uses Net8 to connect to Oracle8i database on the server.

   The Workflow Server component is installed on the server side and includes the components discussed in the following sections.

The Workflow Engine

This component monitors workflow states and coordinates the routing of activities for a process. Changes in workflow state, such as the completion of workflow activities, are signaled to the engine via a PL/SQL API or a Java API. Based on flexibly defined workflow rules, the engine determines which activities are eligible to run and then runs them. The Workflow Engine supports sophisticated workflow rules, including looping, branching, parallel flows, and subflows.

Workflow Notification Mailer

Notification Mailer ensures that users can receive e-mail notifications for outstanding work items and can respond to those notifications using their e-mail application of choice. An e-mail notification can include an attachment that provides another means of responding to the notification.

Workflow Definitions Loader

The Workflow Definitions Loader is a utility that moves workflow definitions between database and corresponding flat-file representations. You can use it to move workflow definitions from a development to a production database, or to apply upgrades to existing definitions. In addition to being a stand-alone server program, the Workflow Definitions Loader is also integrated into Oracle Workflow Builder, allowing you to open and save workflow definitions in both a database and a file.

Workflow Monitor

Workflow administrators and users can view the progress of a work item in a workflow process by connecting to the Workflow Monitor using a standard Web browser that supports Java. The Workflow Monitor displays an annotated view of the process diagram for a particular instance of a workflow process, so that users can get a graphical depiction of their work item status. The Workflow Monitor also displays a separate status summary for the work item, the process, and each activity in the process.

Workflow Background Engine

Also called Workflow Background Process Concurrent Program, Workflow Background Engine is a supplemental Workflow Engine that processes deferred or timeout activities. This program can be accessed by a system administrator. At least one Workflow Background Engine should be scheduled to handle deferred and timeout activities.

Purge Obsolete Workflow Runtime Data Concurrent Program

This concurrent program accepts the following parameters:

Item Type   Item type associated with the obsolete runtime data you want to delete. Leave this argument set to null to delete obsolete runtime data for all item types.

Item Num   A string generated from the application object's primary key. The string uniquely identifies the item within an item type. If null, the program purges all items in the specified item type.

Age   Minimum age of data to purge, in days, if x_persistence_type is set to "TEMP". The default is 0.

X_persistence   Persistence type to be purged, either "TEMP" type for Temporary or "PERM" for Permanent. The default is "TEMP".

Managing Workflow Notifications

You can configure and manage Oracle Workflow. Oracle provides two methods by which users can use Workflow Notifications: the Web-based self-service method and e-mail notification method.

The WF_ROLES view provides a view of the HR and FND_USERS tables that list all users that can participate in a Workflow. The WF_ROLES view does a select on the WF_USERS view and uses the STATUS column to determine whether the user/ role participates in Workflow processes. If WF_USERS.STATUS = 'ACTIVE', a user can participate in Workflow. For Workflow users to receive e-mail notifications, the WF_ROLES view must be able to retrieve a user's valid e-mail address and is based upon their NOTIFICATION_PREFERENCE—ie., QUERY will not send an e-mail.

```
select name, email_address, status from wf_roles where name=<'NAME'>;
```

Oracle11i allows users to update their Notification Preference via the User Preference screen on the Web. In Oracle Workflow up to and including release 2.5.1, notifications are sent from the WF_NOTIFICATIONS table based on this query:

```
SELECT notification_id, recipient_role, message_type,
message_name FROM
```

```
wf_notifications WHERE status = 'OPEN' AND
mail_status in ('MAIL','INVALID');
```

When you start the mailer, notifications that are open and have not been sent are sent. To avoid sending old messages and to have only the new ones picked up, use the following command:

```
UPDATE wf_notifications SET status ='CLOSED', mail_status ='SENT',
end_date =<given_date> WHERE mail_status='MAIL';
```

Use the following script to send/resend notification for testing:

```
UPDATE wf_notifications SET status ='OPEN', mail_status ='MAIL',
end_date = NULL WHERE notification_id=<given notification ID>;
```

Set Up the Notification Mailer

If you want to have notifications automatically e-mailed to users (as opposed to having users access the Notifications Web page), you need to configure the Notification Mailer. Follow these steps for setting up the Notification Mailer.

1. Create an e-mail account to send and receive your e-mail notifications. It is recommended that this account be different from either the applmgr or oracle account to ensure that the workflow e-mail does not in any way disturb the e-mails for other accounts.

2. Create three folders for this account: discard, processed, and unprocessed. Different names may be used for these folders, but it is recommended to use the default names if possible.

3. Update and verify the $FND_TOP/resource/wfmail.cfg based on a sample available. The CONNECT, ACCOUNT, HTMLAGENT, and TAGFILE variables will need to be changed. The CONNECT variable should be set to the database login information for the account where the Oracle Workflow server is installed. The ACCOUNT variable holds the information necessary to connect to the e-mail account that will be used to send the notification messages. On a UNIX machine using Sendmail, you would need to provide the full path of the outgoing mail spool account file, which should be the same account from which you start the notification mailer. The TAGFILE variable lists the file that will be used as your Tag File. A Tag File lists strings of text that may be found in unusual messages such as an auto-reply or bounced message. It also lists the status to assign to that message according to the test string. Oracle supplies a starter tag file at $FND_TOP/resource/wfmail.tag. Make sure that the TAGFILE variable reflects the correct path to this file. This file may be edited as necessary for your installation. Note that if you used a different name for any of the three folders in your e-mail

account (discard, processed, or unprocessed) you will need to change the variables DISCARD, PROCESSED, or UNPROCESSED, respectively, to reflect the correct folder name.

4. Start the Notification Mailer, which runs in the background and sends the e-mail notifications as well as takes the correct course of action when a response is received. The Notification Mailer is set up as a concurrent program in the Oracle Application Suite. This concurrent program can be used only when using Workflow with UNIX Sendmail. You will need to supply the path and file name of your configuration file as a parameter to the concurrent program. In UNIX, you may also start the Notification Mailer from the command line with the command

```
WFMAIL APPS/<pwd> 0 Y <config_file> &
```

where *<pwd>* is the password for the APPS schema of your database and *<config_file>* is the complete path and file name to your configuration file.

5. Start at least one Workflow Background Engine. The Workflow Background Engine manages the state of all activities, executes functions, and sends notifications. It keeps a history of all the completed activities as well as completing all error processing. It is implemented as a PL/SQL Server package. Running the concurrent program named Workflow Background Process starts the Workflow Background Engine.

Useful Workflow Scripts

Oracle provides for many scripts to help you identify and fix issues with the Workflow. This section discusses some of these scripts.

- To see how many activities are waiting to be processed by the background engine, use the script

  ```
  $FND_TOP/sql/wfbkgchk.sql
  ```

- To see a list of items with their status, use this command:

  ```
  SELECT item_type,activity_status, COUNT(*) FROM wf_item_activity_statuses
     GROUP BY item_type,activity_status;
  ```

- To see a list of item types attribute values, use this command:

  ```
  SELECT item_type,count(*) FROM wf_item_attribute_values GROUP BY item_type;
  ```

■ To identify and fix errors with a specific item, you can log on with Workflow administrator's responsibility, view the waiting notification, and check the content. Based on the nature of the error, further action can be taken. If you have many errors, consider using wfretry.sql instead.

■ The Workflow can be run in debug mode to generate audit information, and status is saved in Workflow history tables. If you run the Workflow without this option, no log is generated and it runs faster because no history is being generated.

■ Use the following script to check conditions in your data model for consistency:

```
$FND_TOP/sql/wfdirchk.sql
```

It checks for the following conditions:

■ Invalid internal names that contain the character #, :, or / in WF_USERS

■ Invalid compound names in WF_USERS or WF_ROLES

■ Duplicate or missing names in WF_USERS or WF_ROLES

■ Multiple names in WF_USERS or WF_ROLES linked to the same row in the original repository

■ Invalid Notification Preference or null e-mail address if the Notification Preference is MAILTEXT, MAILHTML, or SUMMARY in WF_USERS or WF_ROLES

■ Invalid Status in WF_USERS

■ Rows in WF_USERS that do not have a corresponding row in WF_ROLES

■ Invalid internal names in WF_ROLES that contain the character # or ' or have a length greater than 30 characters

■ Invalid user/role foreign key in WF_USER_ROLES

■ Missing user/role in WF_USER_ROLES (every user must participate in its own role)

■ Duplicate rows in WF_USER_ROLES; wfdirchk.sql should return no rows to ensure that your directory service data model is correct

■ wfntfsh.sql can be used to display status information about a particular notification based on its notification ID:

```
sqlplus <user/pwd> @wfntfsh <notification ID>
```

- wfrefchk.sql can be used to check for invalid workflow data that is missing primary key data for a foreign key:

```
sqlplus <user/pwd> @wferfchk
```

- wfretry.sql can be used to display a list of activities that have encountered an error for a given process instance and then specify whether to skip, retry, or reset any one of those erroneous activities:

```
sqlplus <user/pwd> @wfretry <item_type> <item_key>
```

You must provide an item type and item key to uniquely identify an item or process instance. The script first returns the list of erroneous activities by label name. The script then prompts you for the label name of an activity that you wish to skip, retry, or reset. If you choose skip, you must also specify the result that you want the skipped activity to have.

- wfstatus.sql provides a status report for the end user about an item:

```
sqlplus <user/pwd> @wfstatus <item_type> <item_key>
```

- wfstdchk.sql can be used to check and report any problems found in the Oracle Workflow data model:

```
sqlplus <user/pwd> @wfstdchk
```

- wfver.sql can be used to display the version of the Oracle Workflow Server, the status and version of the Oracle Workflow PL/SQL packages, and the version of the Oracle Workflow views installed:

```
sqlplus <user/pwd> @wfver
```

- wfverchk.sql can help to identify if issues exist in your Workflow model due to multiple versions of workflow running simultaneously:

```
sqlplus <user/pwd> @wfverchk
```

- wfverupd.sql can be used to correct such problems. This script identifies and corrects multi version issues:

```
sqlplus <user/pwd> @wfverupd
```

- wfbkg can be used to start the background engine for the specified amount of time:

```
sqlplus <user/pwd> @wfbkg <minutes><seconds>
```

where *<minutes>* is the number of minutes for the background engine to run and *<seconds>* is the number of seconds between calls.

■ wfrmitms.sql can be used to delete item status information for items that match the supplied type and key patterns:

```
sqlplus <user>/<pwd> @wfrmitms <item_type> <item_key>
```

■ wfrmtype.sql deletes all runtime data associated with a given item type.

■ wfrmita.sql deletes all Workflow information for a specified item attribute.

■ wfrmitt.sql deletes all Workflow information for a specified item type.

■ wfrmall.sql deletes all Workflow information.

Reassigning the Workflow Administrator Role

The Workflow Administrator Role, by default, belongs to the SYSADMIN user. Users can reassign this role to the Oracle Applications Workflow Administrator responsibility by logging into Oracle Applications or the Personal Home Page as the SYSADMIN user:

1. Choose Workflow | Global Preferences.

2. Click the Update button.

3. Click LOV for Workflow Administrator.

4. Choose the Workflow Administrator% and click the Find button.

5. Select either Workflow Administrator or Workflow.

6. Choose Administrator Web Applications.

7. Click OK.

The Workflow administrator can change the course, reassign steps to other users, and suspend and expedite a workflow. These actions are useful in managing self-service processes, such as expense reporting. To change to default settings, modifications to the Workflow configuration file is made on the Database tier. This can be done by editing the file called $FND_TOP/resource/US/wfcfg.msg.

This file contains an entry like the following WFTKN WF_ADMIN_ROLE 0 *

This entry should be changed to the following after the initial setup

```
WFTKN WF_ADMIN_ROLE   0 SYSADMIN
```

You will need to verify that the Oracle Applications Profile option Applications Web Agent exactly matches the URL for your PL/SQL Web Agent entered into the Workflow Configuration file and define the Workflow Administration Role in the file wfcfg.msg. By setting this role, you are defining which Oracle applications users have access to Workflow's Administrative features. By default, this is set to the role of SYSADMIN but may be changed by editing the following line in $FND_TOP/resource/US/wfcfg.msg file:

```
WFTKN WF_ADMIN_ROLE 0 SYSADMIN
```

SYSADMIN may be replaced by the name of a different role, or the asterisk (*) may be used to signify all roles, as in the following example:

```
WFTKN WF_ADMIN_ROLE 0 *
```

Next, you can run the Workflow Resource Generator to update your database with the Workflow. You can do this either from the command line or as a concurrent program. When running as a concurrent program, the WFRESGEN program accepts the following parameters:

- **Destination Type**   Should be set to DATABASE to indicate that you want to upload seed data to the database.
- **Destination**   Should be left blank.
- **Source**   Should be the full path and file name to the file wfcfg.msg.

To run the Workflow Resource Generator from the command line, use the following command:

```
WFRESGEN usr/pwd 0 Y DATABASE <source_file>
```

where *<source_file>* indicates the full path and file name for the file wfcfg.msg.
To verify that the data was successfully loaded into the database, you can run the following queries against the APPS schema of your database:

```
SELECT  name,text FROM wf_resources
WHERE name = 'WF_WEB_AGENT';
```

and

```
SELECT name,text FROM wf_resources
WHERE name = 'WF_ADMIN_ROLE';
```

FNDWFPR   FNDWFPR "Purge Obsolete Workflow Runtime Data" is used to purge old data from Oracle Workflow runtime tables. In Oracle Applications, you can navigate to the Submit Requests form and submit this concurrent program. This program should be added to a request security group for the responsibility that is required to run this program. The FNDWFPR has the following arguments:

- **Item Type**   The item type to purge. Leaving this field blank defaults to purging the runtime data for all item types.

- **Item Key**   The item key to purge. Leaving this field blank defaults to purging the runtime data for all item keys.

- **Age**   Minimum age of data to purge, in days.

Checking for a Successful Installation

Oracle Workflow 11i/2.6 has two new Global Preferences:

- **Local System**   The system name for the database in which Oracle Workflow is installed

- **System Status**   The Business Event System Status. Value can be Enabled, Disabled, Local Only, or External Only.

You can view the Global Preferences settings by logging in to Oracle Financials as a user with access to the Workflow Administrator Web Applications Responsibility. Select the Workflow Administrator Web Applications Responsibility, and then select the Global Preferences function.

To verify that the upgrade to Oracle Workflow 11i/2.6 was successful, from the command line execute the following:

```
sqlplus <user>/<pwd> @$FND_TOP/sql/wfver
```

Verify the following based on the output of this script:

- The Workflow Server version is 2.6.0.

- The Local System Name status is ASSIGNED.

- The Local System status is ENABLED.

- The XML Parser PL/SQL Package Installation status is INSTALLED.

- The XML Parser Schema Java class version is xmlparser_2.0.2.9_production.

- The queues WF_IN, WF_OUT, and WF_ERROR were created and available for enqueue and dequeue.

- The PL/SQL Status Information contains no uncompiled packages or package bodies. If required, run the ADADMIN Compile Schema utility and recheck.

Workflow PING/Acknowledge Test

To confirm that the Workflow Business Event System has been set up correctly, a simple Workflow process is included, which routes an event message from a local outbound agent to any inbound agents on local or external systems. These processes will not complete until an acknowledgement event message is received after the event message on the inbound agent has been processed.

To complete the Workflow PING/Acknowledge:

1. Select the Workflow Administrator Web Applications responsibility.

2. From the Check Event Manager Setup screen, confirm that the JOB_QUEUE_PROCESSES parameter is set to at least 5. Note: If this value is set too low, while database propagation may be submitted, no processes will be available for the propagation processes, and messages will not be propagated.

3. Submit Local Database Propagation from the Check Event Manager Setup screen. Example values are Duration set to 10 seconds, Run Every 60 seconds, Latency of 0 seconds.

4. Submit the Workflow Agent Listen process for the WF_IN Agent from the Concurrent Manager.

5. From the Launch Processes screen, select the Workflow Agent PING/Acknowledge item type.

6. On the Initiate Workflow screen, enter a unique item key and select Master PING as the process.

7. Click Submit. Note that at least two workflow processes have been launched: a master process and a detail process.

8. To confirm the processing of the PING/Acknowledge event messages, navigate to the Event Queue Summary screen to see the event names and statuses of event messages on the WF_IN and WF_OUT queues.

9. For each inbound agent, a detail PING process is launched. The detail process will send the oracle.apps.wf.event.test.ping event message from an outbound agent on the local system to the inbound agent.

10. The PING message is placed on the outbound agent addressed to the inbound agent.

11. Oracle Advanced Queuing propagation will transmit the PING message from the outbound agent to the inbound agent.

12. Once the PING message is on the inbound agent, the Workflow Agent Listener concurrent program will dequeue the PING message the next time it runs.

13. The Agent Listener will determine the event that has been dequeued, in this case the oracle.apps.wf.event.test.ping event, and pass the event message to the dispatcher.

14. The dispatcher will look for any active subscriptions for this business event with a source type of External.

15. The dispatcher will execute the seeded subscription to this event. The rule function run by this subscription will send an acknowledgement oracle.apps.wf.event.test.ack event message back to the system from which the PING message originated.

16. The acknowledgement message will be placed on an outbound agent addressed to an inbound agent on the originating system.

17. Oracle Advanced Queue propagation will transmit the acknowledgement message from the outbound agent to the inbound agent on the originating system.

18. Once the acknowledgement message is on the inbound agent on the originating system, the Agent Listener database job on this system will dequeue the acknowledgement message the next time it runs.

19. The Agent Listener will determine the event that has been dequeued, in this case the oracle.apps.wf.event.test.ack event, and pass the event message to the dispatcher.

20. The dispatcher will look for any active subscriptions for this business event with a source type of External.

21. The dispatcher will execute the seeded subscription to this event. This subscription will pass the message back to the Workflow Engine.

22. The Workflow Engine will complete the detail PING process, matching the event message to the running workflow process using the correlation ID in the event message, and the item type and process name defined in the event subscription.

23. When all detail workflow processes complete, the master workflow process will also complete.

This completes the Workflow Agent PING/Acknowledge test. If you do not require local database propagation, delete the Local Propagation you submitted for the WF_OUT Agent in step 3.

Summary

An Oracle Financials administrator has a critical responsibility of not only performing capacity planning and sizing calculations but also day-to-day management activities. These activities typically include instance level activities such as creating test, development, sandbox, demo, and production instances; refreshing instances; renaming instances; load balancing of application servers; applying patches; printer setups; and fixing issues with workflow. This chapter focussed on AD Administration, AutoPatch, and other utilities as well as Oracle Workflow issues.

CHAPTER
6

Managing the
Concurrent Manager

■ What is Concurrent Manager?

■ Concurrent Manager architecture

■ Usage basics of Concurrent Manager

■ Use the Management Pack for Oracle Applications for managing
Concurrent Manager

■ Decide the number of Concurrent Manager processes to run

■ Setup issues and troubleshooting tips

■ Tuning recommendations

I n the previous chapters, we reviewed the Oracle Application Suite along with the Oracle technology stack components. We also discussed roles and responsibilities of the financial administrator and started to discuss these roles in more detail by first talking about upgrading to Oracle Financials 11i (Chapter 4) and then different methods the administrator uses for managing the environment (Chapter 5). In this chapter, we will discuss concepts and issues around Concurrent Manager. We talk about the setup issues and tuning recommendations and also see how you can use Oracle's latest Management Pack for managing the Concurrent Manager process. This chapter is designed to help DBAs and financial administrators get a better understanding of how the Concurrent Manager works and will provide them with information for tuning and troubleshooting day-to-day issues.

What Is Concurrent Manager?

Concurrent Manager is a process or mechanism to control the processing of batch programs and reports run in the background within the Oracle Application area. Concurrent Manager basically runs concurrent programs. Concurrent Manager can be configured to be generic (to run any concurrent program) or specialized (to run only specific types of programs). Concurrent Manager essentially schedules and controls your background jobs and frees up your workstation to perform other tasks. The number of Concurrent Managers can be tuned and has a direct effect on resource utilization as well as the available capacity of the server. The Internal Concurrent Manager (ICM) controls all of the other Concurrent Managers. The Conflict Resolution Manager resolves possible conflicts. The Standard Manager is generic and can accept any request. It does not have any special rules to govern it.

Concurrent Manager Architecture

As we discussed earlier, Concurrent Manager allows application administrators to limit and control system resources consumed by batch processes and reporting requests. The number of processes for each of the Concurrent Managers needs to be appropriately set by keeping in mind the minimum, maximum, and average number of user requests on one hand, and available resources in terms of free memory, processing capacity, and so on, on the other. In this section of the chapter, we will review the architecture to understand various terms involved with configuring and using Concurrent Manager.

1. At the time of initial installation, the static data for the Concurrent Managers is in tables like FND_CONCURRENT_QUEUES and

FND_CONCURRENT_PROGRAMS. These tables contain information about how many Concurrent Managers should be started, number of processes, and so on, and are changed when the administrator makes modifications to any of these statistics. When a user runs a report, a record is inserted into FND_CONCURRENT_REQUESTS.

2. The Internal Concurrent Manager is a special Concurrent Manager to control other Concurrent Managers. The startup of Concurrent Manager actually starts the Internal Concurrent Manager, which in turn starts other Concurrent Managers as defined in the configuration. Each queue can spawn multiple processes and a particular queue can be deactivated at any time.

3. The Conflict Resolution Manager handles program inconsistencies and conflicts.

4. Each of the running queues wakes up every now and then to check for pending requests. If there are requests, the Internal Concurrent Manager checks for compatibility. The queue checks if there are available processes to run the request. If there are, the request is processed, otherwise the request waits for the next check.

5. Every request passes through four phases. They are PENDING, RUNNING, COMPLETED, and INACTIVE. As a request goes through various phases the request table FND_CONCURRENT_REQUEST is constantly updated to reflect the change and can be queried by users to see where they stand in the request queue.

Refer to Figure 6-1 for an overview of how concurrent requests are processed using this Concurrent Manager architecture.

Concurrent Manager Terminology

When a user runs a report, a request to run the report is generated. The command to run the report is a concurrent request. The program that generates the report is a concurrent program. The Concurrent Manager starts concurrent programs, and the administrator can control how many concurrent programs to run and how many resources they utilize.

Concurrent Program   A concurrent program is an executable file that runs simultaneously with other concurrent programs and with online operations. A concurrent program is typically a batch job or a long-running program or report. Concurrent programs can be Oracle-provided or custom. They can be coded in SQL, PL/SQL, and Pro*C in addition to Oracle Forms and Oracle Reports.

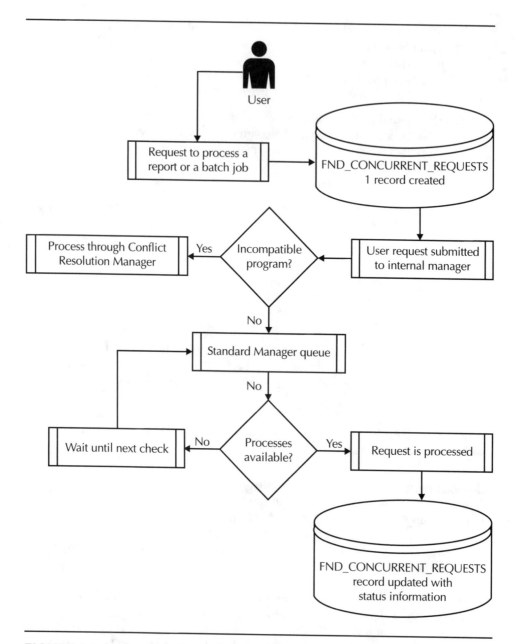

FIGURE 6-1. *Flowchart showing concurrent request processing using Concurrent Manager architecture*

Concurrent Requests   Execution of concurrent programs can be requested by setting up request groups and request sets. A request group is a collection of reports or concurrent programs defined by an administrator to control user access. A request set defines run, print, and other parameters for running the concurrent programs. An administrator can set privileges for end users for setting up request sets. Concurrent requests are a set of requests for executing concurrent programs. Concurrent requests are submitted using the CONCSUB program.

Specializing Managers   For every concurrent program that is run, a request is inserted into a database table. Concurrent Managers read from this table and act on it based on the request type and parameters. Without specializing rules, a manager reads requests to start any concurrent program. However, if you configure a specialize manager, you have the ability to read only certain requests. For example, you can define a specialize manager for AP programs or another specialize manager for all request for a certain user. A special type of specialization rule is the combined specialization rule, which can combine more than one action to define a single rule. For more details on how to set up a specialize manager and combined specializing manager, please refer to the Oracle documentation, especially the Oracle Application System Administrator's Guide.

Usage Basics of Concurrent Manager

Let us first review the procedure to check if Concurrent Manager is up and running. There are three methods that can be used to check if the Concurrent Manager is running.

Checking the Status of Concurrent Managers: Method 1

Log in with System Administrator responsibility and go to the Concurrent Manager Administration page (Concurrent Manager | Administrator). Then check the Processes column to see if the Target and Actual columns list the same number (greater than 0). The Target column lists the number of processes that should be running for each manager for a particular work shift. The Actual column, on the other hand, shows the number of processes that are actually running. If any of these numbers are zero, it means there are no processes running for this manager. If they are not zero, it means the Concurrent Manager processes are up and running.

Checking the Status of Concurrent Managers: Method 2

Log in to SQL*Plus as apps and execute the following script:

```
SQL>$FND_TOP/sql/afimchk.sql
```

The output of this script will tell you if the Concurrent Manager is running on your Oracle instance.

Checking the Status of Concurrent Managers: Method 3

The Concurrent Managers create a FNDLIBR process on the server machine. To check if the Concurrent Managers are up, you can use the following UNIX command:

```
ps -ef |grep FNDLIBR
```

On Windows NT, you can go to the Task Manager, then to the Processes tab and look for the FNDLIBR process.

The Internal Concurrent Manager generates a process in addition to the number of FNDLIBR processes—one for every Standard Manager.

How to Start the Concurrent Manager

Use the following command from the command line to start the Concurrent Manager:

```
startmgr sysmgr=apps/<password>
```

If you are on Windows NT, you can start Concurrent Manager with a service using the following command:

```
cmsrvadm add <APPL_CONFIG> [automatic/manual]
```

You can then use Start | Settings | Control Panel | Services and start the Concurrent Manager.

How to Stop the Concurrent Manager

Use the following command to stop the Concurrent Manager:

```
CONCSUB apps/<password> SYSADMIN 'System Administrator' SYSADMIN CONCURRENT FND DEACTIVATE
```

Using DEACTIVATE means that your current requests will be completed before the Concurrent Manager comes down. This is a cleaner and more graceful method to stop the Concurrent Manager.

You can also use the ABORT command as follows:

```
CONCSUB apps/<password> SYSADMIN 'System Administrator' SYSADMIN CONCURRENT FND ABORT
```

Using ABORT means that your current requests will be terminated and return to pending status.

If you are on Windows NT, you can select Start | Settings | Control Panel | Services and then stop the Concurrent Manager service.

Purging Concurrent Manager Tables

Concurrent Manager tables should be purged periodically to proactively handle performance issues and also as a maintenance effort. This section describes the method for this clean-up activity, step by step:

1. Connect to SQL*Plus using APPLSYS.

2. Execute the following command:

```
SQL>UPDATE FND_CONCURRENT_QUEUES
        SET RUNNING_PROCESSES=0, MAX_PROCESSES = 0;
```

3. Execute the following command:

```
SQL>TRUNCATE TABLE FND_CONCURRENT_PROCESSES;
```

4. If terminating requests are left in the concurrent request table, they can prevent the Concurrent Manager from starting. To take care of this, execute the following command:

```
SQL> DELETE FROM FND_CONCURRENT_REQUESTS WHERE STATUS_CODE='T';
```

5. To delete all the completed requests, use this command:

```
SQL> DELETE FROM FND_CONCURRENT_REQUESTS WHERE STATUS_CODE='C';
```

6. Also, make sure that the table FND_DUAL has only one row in it. If there are more rows, delete them using the following command:

```
SQL>DELETE FROM FND_DUAL WHERE
        ROWNUM < (SELECT MAX(ROWNUM) FROM FND_DUAL);
```

Concurrent Manager Log Files

If $APPLCSF is set, the concurrent manager log files are created under $APPLCSF/$APPLLOG and the output files are created under $APPLCSF/$APPLOUT. $APPLCSF is the complete directory path and $APPLOUT is the directory name.

If $APPLCSF is not set, Oracle places the files under the product top of the application associated with the request. So for the AP module, the log files will go under $AP_TOP/$APPLLOG and the output files will go under $AP_TOP/$APPLOUT.

Using the Management Pack for Oracle Applications for Managing Concurrent Manager

Concurrent Manager can be effectively managed using Oracle Enterprise Manager as well. Administrators can start and stop Concurrent Managers from the managed node and also perform other functions from a central console. Using these new tools, DBAs and administrators can administer Concurrent Managers, processes, and requests and also do capacity planning analysis. Oracle provides a new Management Pack for Oracle Applications with several useful modules, including Oracle Performance Manager, Capacity Planner, Concurrent Processing Tuning Assistant, and Oracle Applications Manager. If you are already running Oracle Enterprise Manager and are used to its features and capabilities, you can seamlessly transition to the Management Pack. If you are new to Oracle Enterprise Manager, you can refer to the following documentation for help in setting it up:

- Oracle Enterprise Manager Concepts Guide
- Oracle Enterprise Manager Configuration Guide
- Oracle Enterprise Manager Administrator's Guide

Oracle Applications Manager

Oracle Application Suite has integrated its Concurrent Manager administrative interface with Oracle Enterprise Manager, enabling administrators to better manage their systems. The Oracle Applications Manager console provides an applications DBA-oriented subset of the current Oracle Application Suite system administration functions. These functions include administration of Concurrent Managers, processes, and requests. The Oracle Applications Manager is available for releases 11.0 and 11i. This new functionality is in addition to the multiwindow Oracle Application Suite forms, and administrators can choose which tools to use. Requests submitted within the standard Oracle Application Suite windows can be viewed from the Oracle Applications Manager console. Likewise, Concurrent Managers defined in the console can be accessed from within the Oracle Application Suite windows. The Oracle Applications Manager can be found in the Windows Start menu under Oracle Applications or under the Enterprise Manager Tools menu under Application Management.

The Oracle Applications Manager can be used for releases 11 and 11i. For further information, you can also refer to the following documentation provided with the Management Pack CD:

- Oracle Intelligent Agent User's Guide Release 8.1.7, Part No. A85251-01
- Oracle Enterprise Manager: Getting Started with the Oracle Management Pack for Oracle Applications Release 2.2, Part No. A85229-01
- Oracle Enterprise Manager: Oracle Management Pack for Oracle Applications Installation Release 2.2 for Windows and Solaris Platforms, Part No. A85227-01

This section describes the configuration of Oracle Applications Manager. The first step is to install the Oracle Enterprise Manager along with the Intelligent Agent and then install Oracle Applications Manager. These pieces need to be installed on the following nodes:

- Managed node (where Concurrent Manager is running)

- Oracle Management Server node

On the managed node, the following configuration should be completed:

1. Apply the Oracle Applications Manager Interoperability Patch for Release 11.

2. Configure Net8 and verify for the Intelligent Agent's ORACLE_HOME.

3. Configure the oapps.ora file for discovering the Oracle application.

4. Configure Windows NT security for the Enterprise Manager Job System.

The oapps.ora File   The oapps.ora file is installed in the following directory in the Intelligent Agent's ORACLE_HOME: $ORACLE_HOME/network/agent/config. This file is used to discover Oracle application information. The format of the file is as follows:

<type> <WS> <dbname> <WS> <envfile> <WS> <startup information> <NL>

- **type**   Entry type (such as cmanager).

- **WS**   White space (blanks or tabs).

- **dbname**   Application database name (same as the entry in tnsnames.ora in Net8).

- **envfile**   Fully qualified path to the application environment file. The file defines all the environment variables for the application environment, including all variables defined in the APPL_TOP directory.

- **startup information**   For NT, the name of the ICM service in the NT Services panel. In UNIX, this refers to a fully qualified ICM startup script such as:

  ```
  $FND_TOP/bin/oemstart.sh
  ```

- **NL**   Refers to newline.

Configuring Window NT Security for the Enterprise Manager Job System
Oracle Intelligent Agent can be used to perform administrative activities relating to
Concurrent Manager, such as starting and stopping Concurrent Manager. To use this
feature, however, you need to have the Window NT Log On As A Batch Job privilege.
This privilege needs to be granted for all users who will be running jobs using
Concurrent Manager. You can follow these step-by-step instructions to grant
this privilege:

1. Select Start | Programs | Administrative Tools | User Manager.

2. Highlight the user to be granted the privilege.

3. Choose Policies | User Rights.

4. Check the Show Advanced User Rights option.

5. Select Log On As A Batch Job Right.

6. Click Add.

If any user who does not have this privilege submits a job, the job fails with a
"Vni Authentication Error."

Concurrent Processing Tuning Assistant
The Concurrent Processing Tuning Assistant reports historical information about
Concurrent Managers, concurrent programs, and concurrent processing requests.
You can use these reports to achieve better throughput and performance. Unlike
other Management Packs for Oracle Application Suite tools, the Tuning Assistant
does not connect to the Oracle Management Server. Instead you log in directly to
the database schema containing the Oracle Application Object Library tables for
the subsystems you want to tune.
The Tuning Assistant provides the following reports:

- Time periods with greatest wait times

- Requests that waited during those time periods

- Time periods with excess Concurrent Manager capacity

The Tuning Assistant provides several reports that can be used for proactively
tuning concurrent requests for your busy application environment. Some of the
more important reports are:

- Hourly Analysis of Concurrent Manager

- Program-Wise Usage of Concurrent Manager

- Program Wait Summary

- Long-Running Reports

- Request Run Summary by Month

- Drill-Down Reports

Setup Issues and Troubleshooting Tips

Oracle provides a number of scripts that can help you diagnose Concurrent Manager problems. These scripts are located under $FND_TOP/sql. For example, *afrqscm.sql* prints log file names of managers that can run a given request. It can be used to check possible errors when a request stays in pending status. Another example is *afrqstat.sql,* which prints a summary of completed concurrent requests grouped by completion status and execution type. This script accepts number of days prior to the current day as a parameter. These and other scripts help troubleshooting issues and identifying and fixing setup problems. In this section, we will cover a few troubleshooting tips.

How do I handle Concurrent Manager errors?   The Concurrent Manager log files are located under $APPLCSF/$APPLLOG. Log files are usually named std.mgr or CCM name.mgr. Look at the error details in the log file and then look up these errors in the metalink. The metalink is a very good source to get the latest information about error handling and patches.

     If you do not find any hit or resolution from the metalink, you can then file an iTar with Oracle with all information about the error.

Can I rebuild the Concurrent Manager views?   It is okay to rebuild the view if required. This can be done by executing the command FNDCPBWV:

```
FNDLIBR FND FNDCPBWV apps/<password> SYSADMIN 'System Administrator' SYSADMIN
```

I have too many concurrent requests. Is there a way I can archive and purge the information?   The best way to do this is to write a database trigger to move records from FND_CONCURRENT_REQUESTS to another history table, such as APPSCUSTOM.FND_CONCURRENT_REQUESTS_HIST. The trigger could be a "before delete trigger" on the FND_CONCURRENT_REQUEST table and could insert into the custom table when the purge process deletes records. The trigger can also be specified as an event trigger (a feature available with Oracle8i), which can fire off every day at a time when there is not much going on in the system. You can also define a custom view which will be defined on top of FND_CONCURRENT_REQUESTS and

APPSCUSTOM.FND_CONCURRENT_REQUEST_HIST. This view can provide you with a complete view of the requests for your analysis.

How do I set the PMON method?   To check the PMON method, execute the following steps:

```
cd $FND_TOP/sql
SQLPLUS apps/<password> @afimchk.sql
```

To set the PMON method, execute the following steps.

First, shut down the Concurrent Manager using the CONCSUB command. Then use the following:

```
cd $FND_TOP/sql
SQLPLUS apps/<password> @afimpmon.sql LOCK
```

Tuning Recommendations

Setting up and using Concurrent Manager presents the administrator with numerous options and flexibility in configuration. Tuning of Concurrent Manager is required to ensure that the optimum number of processes are configured to run in batch along with the online load. The other objective in tuning is to ensure that sufficient hardware resources exist to run the general and specialty managers. This section of the chapter provides some tuning recommendations.

The main key to tuning Concurrent Manager is to understand and plan the daily, weekly, and monthly activities in terms of jobs that need to run as well as daily online user volume and ad hoc usage estimates. The other important component for the administrator is available hardware resources. Armed with these two pieces of information, the administrator can set up concurrent requests and processes that best fit the given environment. The planning is critical since AP users may be running important reporting information right about when the General Ledger users are running their monthly closing. This can cause both the job sets to go slowly.

The administrator should set up various categories of tasks such as user-requested reports, batch programs, batch reports, and so on, and also be able to identify which Concurrent Manager program falls under each of these categories. The administrator can follow the good old 80-20 principle in determining this. This means that he can only look at programs that take more than, say, 15 minutes and then work with users of different modules to schedule it without affecting the system response in an adverse manner.

Administrators can fine-tune the sleep time (in seconds) to determine how often each queue will wake up to check if there are requests. In general, this timing could be anything from two seconds to five minutes. When deciding an appropriate sleep time interval for standard as well as custom queues, consider the following points:

- Average number of requests in the queue during a particular time

- Average time taken by various reports and batch programs

- Number of processes required

- Average wait time

Make sure you review the history of the queue using the Tuning Assistant before making decisions to drastically change the sleep time interval. It is often okay to change the interval to a smaller value for a specific purpose, especially when the administrator is aware that several small requests are expected around a particular time.

Deciding the Number of Concurrent Managers to Run

Oracle Application Suite has a default configuration for the Concurrent Manager already in place when the application software is installed. This is based on some static data in the metadata tables that may or may not be correct for your environment. The configuration should ideally be decided based on the number of modules you have installed, the number of users and programs to be run, work shift details, and so on. The workload in terms of OLTP, reporting, batch users, and ad hoc users are also critical deciding factors, and the default configuration will not really reflect correct values. If you use the default configuration, you are either set up for modules you have not implemented or you may be wasting system resources which could be effectively redirected.

You can create a Fast Requests Manager and move jobs that always run fast to it from the standard queue. This way you can free up the bottleneck in the standard queue.

You need to strike a balance between the number of concurrent requests you can process and the number of online users. This balance depends on the amount of resources you have at your disposal. You have to closely monitor resource utilization in terms of memory, swap, and CPU cycles to make sure that the concurrent processes are not eating up all your resources, thus making online user response slow. The Tuning Assistant provides several reports (discussed in the previous section) that can help monitor and tune concurrent processes.

In general, it is advisable to have at least two processes running for each Concurrent Manager. The real challenge is to study your environment and decide on the number of Concurrent Managers and processes associated with it.

Summary

Concurrent Manager provides a way to control and schedule the batch and reporting requirements of your users and free up their workstations for more important work. The administrator needs to understand, coordinate, and plan the more critical reports and jobs in daily, weekly, and monthly schedules of various user communities and match them with available resources. Administrators can fine-tune several parameters in Concurrent Manager, such as the number of Concurrent Managers, processes for a Concurrent Manager, and the sleep interval. The administrator should ideally have a history of how busy each of the Concurrent Managers is during the day and night and also over the weekend. This will help him or her make tuning decisions. Oracle has a new product called Management Pack for Oracle Applications which has a module called Tuning Assistant. Tuning Assistant can help analyze the Concurrent Manager requests by hour, by program, and by status and also provides drill-down features. SQL scripts can also be used to get information from the FND tables about concurrent requests as well. The Applications Manager option can be used to start and stop Concurrent Managers. The objective of this chapter was to review the concepts around Concurrent Manager and discuss recommendations, tips, and solutions. In the next chapter, we will focus on different ways a financial administrator can track growth, size various tablespaces, and set up various processes to proactively manage growth.

PART

III

Database Administration and Maintenance

CHAPTER 7

Managing Database Growth

- Components of database growth
- Advantages of managing database growth
- Track and handle database growth
- Techniques for managing growth
- Tips for administrators

I t is said that a successful database administrator "knows the data," and the importance of this cannot be overstated. The Financials administrator should have a solid understanding of the type of transactions, main tables, important batch jobs, critical reporting requirements, number and types of users, and other important data. This knowledge enables the Financials administrator to perform the day-to-day work of maintenance, upkeep of the environment, and above all troubleshooting a problem. Financials administrators who know their data and the environment are often more productive and proactive in planning for a contingency and in taking steps to circumvent it.

Database growth—in terms of volume of data, number of transactions, number of users, and consideration of hardware components—is a critical part of the "know your data" paradigm for the DBA. This chapter is devoted to a discussion of various components of growth and discusses the processes that Financials administrators should set up for monitoring growth. The chapter also discusses certain techniques for proactively managing growth.

Components of Database Growth

The critical components of a database are tables, indexes, and tablespaces. Depending on the application size, the sizes of tables and indexes can grow to hundreds of gigabytes. Table and index partitioning schemes address a way of distributing the data so that it can be more effectively managed, and they can improve throughput for the end users, since Internet-based applications require continued data availability. Also, most administrators suffer a pretty narrow maintenance window in which they must complete maintenance tasks using traditional procedures. During database maintenance, of course, the entire database is often affected and is sometimes unavailable for the duration. All the applications using the set of tables in the database are also unavailable—which inevitably leads to decreased productivity. Time is of the essence, and as any good DBA knows, keeping a database up to date and running efficiently requires lots of maintenance time.

Advantages of Managing Database Growth

Properly tracking, managing, and monitoring database growth can go a long way toward ensuring end user satisfaction in terms of increased data availability. It is important to manage the human relationships as well as database relationships, and upgrading and implementing Oracle Financials is complex and needs careful planning to ensure that you and your end users are happy with the results. Managing database changes and timing plays a critical part in keeping users happy, and upgrading to increase availability via proactive database management goes a long way in this endeavor. Managing the growth of tables, indexes, tablespaces, and other aspects of the database have other benefits as well, including the following:

- **Better planning** Statistics about your organization's growth are helpful to consider when adding new modules or when upgrading to new versions. These statistics form the basis of the DBA's calculation worksheet when planning an upgrade.

- **Troubleshooting** Based on growth statistics, DBAs can forecast hardware capacity issues and initiate the procedures for handling problems well in advance of problems occurring. DBAs can also take short-term measures by reclaiming space from some unused objects and allocating that space to tables that are likely to grow heavily in the near future.

- **Proactive maintenance** Tablespace maintenance can be performed more effectively if DBAs can access usage statistics, including information about free space and used space and a history of growth during the past few months.

- **Predicting future growth** Growth statistics can also be used for performing trend analyses to estimate disk space requirements for sustaining existing applications and users as well as adding new projects and functionality to the environment.

Tables and indexes need to be appropriately sized because their default settings may not be optimal for your particular environment. Because most Oracle application tables are sized for generic usage, DBAs should resize the most critical tables and indexes by rebuilding them with correct initial and next extents. Doing so will affect the throughput in a positive way. In addition, the DBA should size the rollback segments based on the nature of the batch jobs, online transactions, and the number of users accessing the application.

Using Database Statistics to Monitor Growth

Database storage statistics are included as part of the data dictionary (a database that contains data about all the databases in the system). These statistics contain useful information that describes the objects within each database instance. Database statistics take two forms: *permanent* and *volatile*. Permanent statistics include information about the physical definitions of the objects that make up the database, such as tables, indexes, and so on, and can offer critical growth-related information such as storage location and sizes. These statistics are valuable in tracking growth and can also be helpful in making remedial plans for handling future database growth.

'Volatile statistics, on the other hand, provide information about the environment that changes with time. Some of the examples are wait statistics, sessions, and SQL statements running during a particular time. Being volatile, these statistics convey the state of the database at a particular point. Volatile statistics like waits, locks, latches, and session statistics can be used for trending growth information of the application and also for capacity planning for making decisions for additional hardware like memory or CPU.

Statistics are generated and maintained either automatically by the database or by using an analyze or gather statistics method such as FND_STAT (for more information about FND_STAT, refer to Chapter 9). Most of the information in the data dictionary is maintained automatically when a database is up and running. Since no manual intervention is required for automatic collection, this is by far the most accurate method of collecting statistics.

However, the statistics collected by the gather statistics method such as FND_STATS involves manual intervention in terms of setting up a process to refresh statistics periodically on the instance. This step is critical when cost-based optimization is the preferred optimization mode, as it is in the Oracle Application Suite. When you run FND_STATS for a table or a user, Oracle updates the data dictionary with important information, such as the number of rows and blocks used, based on the contents of the table while FND_STATS is running. These statistics remain in the dictionary until the next time FND_STATS is executed or until they are specifically deleted. Table 7-1 shows some of the statistics collected by analyzing a table.

Column Name	Description
NUM_ROWS	Number of rows returned
BLOCKS	Number of blocks used to store this table
EMPTY_BLOCKS	Number of blocks not used but allocated to the table; this statistic gives the value of unutilized space
AVG_SPACE	Average available space in the table
CHAIN_CNT	Number of chained rows; should be 0, and row chaining should be avoided by appropriate table sizing
AVG_ROW_LEN	Average row length including row overhead
AVG_SPACE_FREELIST_BLOCKS	Average free space of all blocks on a freelist
NUM_FREELIST_BLOCKS	Number of blocks on the freelist

TABLE 7-1. *Statistics Collected During Table Analysis*

Using Script to Track Database Growth

In Chapter 9, we review the FND_STAT package that is used for gathering statistics for the Oracle Application Suite. FND_STAT includes several procedures for analyzing index columns, gathering column statistics, restoring table statistics, and other functions. To track the growth of a database, the DBA must develop a process to run weekly, biweekly, or monthly to review all objects that correspond to the Oracle application's core modules as well as custom objects. This information is collected in a table, making it easy to track growth rates from month to month during a period of time. This process can be implemented not just for the production environment but for all environments on the system, enabling the DBA to better plan and control the entire application.

Using the APPLSYS.FND_STATTAB Table

This table is created by the FND_STATS.CREATE_STAT_TABLE procedure. The purpose of the table is to back up table and index statistics so that they can be restored to the main application tables as required. Note that a periodic gather statistics procedure should be run as a concurrent process to ensure that statistics are refreshed for all the application tables. Statistics backed up in the FND_STATTAB table can be used to populate a custom table called APPSC_STATISTICS. This table can contain the history information for all the tables and will be of the form shown in Table 7-2. This APPSC_STATISTICS table can become the source for trend analysis and reporting of growth patterns.

Column Name	Column Type and Size	Notes
STAT_ID	NUMBER(10)	/* Can be populated using a sequence */
STAT_DATE	DATE	
OBJECT_NAME	VARCHAR2(30)	/* Table or Index Name */
OBJECT_TYPE	VARCHAR2(10)	/* Table or Index */
TS_NAME	VARCHAR2(30)	/* Tablespace Name */
USERNAME	VARCHAR2(30)	/* Schema owner */
NUM_ROWS	NUMBER(10)	
BLOCKS	NUMBER(10,2)	
EMPTY_BLOCKS	NUMBER(10,2)	

TABLE 7-2. *An APPSC_STATISTICS Table*

Using the Table or Index Statistics Directly

DBAs can get the statistics directly from DBA_TABLES and DBA_INDEXES data dictionary views. The DBA can then write a script to run after the gather statistics concurrent program completes to review the DBA_TABLES and DBA_INDEXES tables and populate the APPSC_STATISTICS table with all the required information.

Using Growth Statistics

After realizing the need to collect database statistics and defining a process to collect periodic statistics for production, test, sandbox, and development environments, the DBA has collected several sets of statistics that are ready for use. This section discusses two uses of these statistics: one for database administration and the other for planning future capacity.

Fragmentation

When a table or an index in a database is modified and added in the normal course of its life, the object becomes *fragmented*. This means that the object has been physically distributed throughout CPU memory. Oracle technology does not put restrictions on the number of *extents*, or blocks of stored fragments, that an object can have. However, when a DBA begins fine tuning the database, it's helpful to know which blocks of data are contiguous to enable fine tuning of multiblock extents. It is generally good practice to store objects in a contiguous fashion in a minimum possible extents and to avoid dynamic extension of objects, which leads to different types of fragmentation. Administrators should take time to plan the initial sizing of tables and extents based on the number of rows and database growth rate. Fragmentation can occur at the extent level, block level, and index level.

Extent Fragmentation

Extent fragmentation occurs when the table or index is contained in multiple extents that are noncontiguous. Extent fragmentation reduces the storage efficiency of the tablespace and can affect performance. A DBA can avoid extent fragmentation by using the following two options:

1. *The tiling approach: choose equal size extents.* Based on an initial study of the tables and indexes, the administrator can choose standard size extents for the environment. For example, while upgrading from 11.0 to 11i, standard initial extent and next extent sizes can be determined based on the current schema for various existing tables. This will eliminate extent fragmentation since all extents will be of the same size. The size of the standard extent depends on a number of factors, and studies recommend a variety of values. The bottom line should be to make effective use of the tablespace by avoiding overallocation and to keep the number of extents to

the minimum. Usually, the administrator can classify tables into the following categories:

Table/Index Category	Standard Extent Size
SMALL	1MB
MEDIUM	10MB
LARGE	50MB
X-LARGE	100MB

These standard extent sizes are only recommendations—the most important issue being that the administrator classifies the tables into standard sizes and derives a script to generate tablespaces based on standard size extents. This will be a step towards automating this process.

2. *Use locally managed tablespace along with the prededing recommendation of standard size extents.* Locally managed tablespace extents (discussed in more detail in Chapter 18) are managed at the datafile level using bitmaps to keep track of free or used status of the block. Locally managed tablespaces have several advantages over dictionary managed tablespaces; they

■ Reduce recursive space management operations

■ Eliminate the need to coalesce free extents

■ Free up the data dictionary to perform more useful operations

Avoid ST (Space Management Transaction) lock contention and enable better performance. This is because the Space Management Transaction (ST) enqueue is acquired by any process allocating, freeing, or coalescing free space. It is used to serialize space transactions across all instances, which are executed within a transaction when space requires allocation or de-allocation. They are also acquired by SMON or foreground processes when two or more physically adjacent free extents are coalesced back into one extent.

Block Fragmentation

Block fragmentation can result from row migration and row chaining. Row migration occurs during update statements, when the total length of the new row no longer fits the current block size and has to be migrated to a new block. Row chaining occurs when a row is stored in multiple blocks that may not be contiguous. In this case, several blocks have to be read to read one logical row, leading to higher I/O rate.

Excessive row chaining could indicate that block size might not be correct. The database would need to be re-created to change the block size, and that could be a detailed task. Row migration can be handled either by reorganization, which can be implemented using export or import, or by moving the table to a different tablespace.

Index Fragmentation

Indexes create an access tree comprising a B-Tree structure of the data based on the range of data in the index column. If the values in the index column grow unevenly, or the range of values change, the depth of the B-Tree increases, making index operations less efficient. The data dictionary view DBA_INDEXES contains information about index fragmentation. You can execute a command similar to the following to get an idea about fragmented indexes in your application:

```
SELECT owner,index_name,blevel FROM DBA_INDEXES WHERE blevel > 5
```

If an index has a BLEVEL greater than 5, you may consider rebuilding that index to fix the index fragmentation.

Capacity Planning Using Growth Statistics

The history of the table and index sizing information is a great source for capacity planning. This information can be useful in making future decisions, such as those for increasing disk capacity, current rate of utilization, and the like. Figure 7-1 shows a typical trending graph that can be used to extrapolate how much disk space will be required in the next 6 to 12 months.

The monthly total space utilized is calculated by aggregating the space allocated for all the tablespaces. Similar graphs can be plotted for different modules, such as AP Growth, AR Growth, GL Growth, and so on. This process will highlight how each of the modules is growing. This could be a basis of cost absorption for the business units. Table 7-3 shows an example of wise disk-space utilization.

Capacity planning issues are discussed in more detail in Chapter 14.

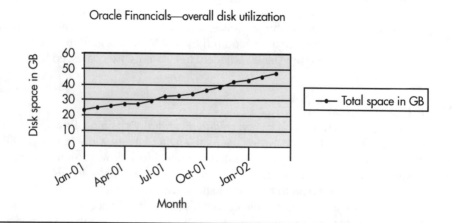

FIGURE 7-1. *Overall disk utilization graph*

Date	Total in GB	AP	AR	GL	Others
Jan-00	23.4	7.3	4.2	2.1	9.8
Feb-00	24.6	8.4	5.2	2.8	8.2
Mar-00	25.3	8.8	6.1	3.2	7.2
Apr-00	26.8	9.4	7.1	3.6	6.7
May-00	28.0	10.0	8.0	4.2	5.8
Jun-00	29.5	11.2	7.0	5.0	6.3
Jul-00	32.0	12.3	8.0	5.2	6.5
Aug-00	33.3	14.2	9.0	5.6	4.5
Sep-00	34.7	15.9	11.0	6.1	1.7
Oct-00	37.3	16.3	12.0	6.3	2.7
Nov-00	39.0	17.6	14.3	6.9	0.2
Dec-00	42.0	18.2	14.8	7.1	1.9
Jan-01	43.3	19.0	15.6	7.3	1.4
Feb-01	46.0	21.1	16.7	7.6	0.6
Mar-01	48.0	22.0	17.0	8.1	0.9

TABLE 7-3.   *Oracle Financials Module Wise Disk-Space Utilization*

Techniques for Managing Growth

Administrators play a key role not only in proactively monitoring the growth of data, users, and other critical resources, but in managing the growth by deploying scalability techniques to improve throughput. Downtimes are expensive, and in an Internet economy it may not be prudent to have frequent and lengthy maintenance windows to deal with fragmentation and performance tuning. With this in mind, administrators should spend a lot of time planning and sizing various objects so that day-to-day management involves managing the exceptions—not the entire environment. Administrators can deploy several methods and techniques for handling fast and drastic database growth. This section describes some of the indexing and materialized view options.

Using Indexing Options

Oracle8i provides a number of enhancements in the area of indexes. Bitmap indexes, and reverse-key indexes are additional types of indexes that may be suitable for specific types of application modules. Also, the index rebuild feature is enhanced. The Financial administrator should implement this feature carefully and choose the indexing strategy appropriately. In this section, we will review various new indexing options.

Bitmap Indexes

Bitmap indexes are suitable for tables that are used primarily for reporting and do not need frequent updates or inserts. In bitmap indexes, the index is stored in sorted bitmapped segments, each containing distinct values. Each bit in the uncompressed bitmap corresponds to a ROWID value. A mapping function converts the bit position back to a ROWID. Because the bitmap is compressed before it is stored in the index, to change a value, the bitmap is uncompressed and then compressed again after the change is done. Refer to Figure 7-2 for an illustration of a bitmap index and its contents.

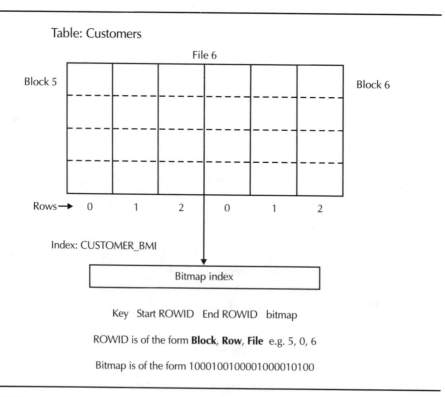

FIGURE 7-2. *A bitmap index and its contents*

Bitmap indexes are suitable for cases in which the key has few distinct values. The advantages of using bitmap indexes are as follows:

- A bitmap index takes much less space than a normal index

- Creation is much faster than creating a B-Tree index

- Certain queries are performed faster

When deciding how to structure the columns in a bitmap index, consider the columns that will be most often accessed together in a single query and create a composite bitmap index on them rather than a B-Tree index.

Here is the syntax for creating a bitmap index:

```
CREATE BITMAP INDEX APC_EXPENSES1 ON APC_EXPENSES(INVOICE_NUM);
```

Bitmap indexes should be used for retrieving rows from a table. Avoid using bitmap indexes for UPDATE and INSERT intensive tables because these operations involve excessive decompression and compression of the bitmap. This compression/decompression is required because the bitmap is compressed before it is stored in the index and must be decompressed before changes can be made. Bitmap indexes are suitable for reporting tables or for situations in which concurrent transactions are unlikely. For improving performance of certain batch jobs, you can drop the bitmap index before populating a table with values, and then re-create the bitmap index. The table can then be released for reporting activities.

Certain initialization parameters can affect your implementation of bitmap indexes:

- **CREATE_BITMAP_AREA_SIZE** This parameter determines the amount of memory allocated for bitmap creation. The larger the value, the faster the index creation. This parameter should be increased if the cardinality is higher. This parameter cannot be changed at session level.

- **BITMAP_MERGE_AREA_SIZE** This parameter fixes the amount of memory used to merge bitmaps retrieved from a range scan of the index. The default value is 1MB, and setting it to a higher value can improve performance. Again, this parameter cannot be dynamically modified at session level.

NOTE
Bitmap indexes require cost-based optimization and cannot be used for referential integrity checks or for checking data integrity such as B-Tree indexes. Note also that a bitmap index on a partitioned table must be a local index.

Reverse-Key Indexes

A reverse-key index is a new index type in Oracle8i. The bytes of each indexed column except the ROWID are reversed while keeping the column order. The idea of a reverse-key index is to distribute insertion across all the leaf keys in the index. If activities on a table are clustered in a single block or area of the table—for example, the key is generated using a sequence number and many users insert rows into the table simultaneously—creating a reverse-key index can improve the speed of queries. By reversing the key value, reverse key indexes ensure a more evenly distributed index and reduce the likelihood of having some index paths densely populated and others sparsely populated. See Figure 7-3 for an illustration of the reverse-key index.

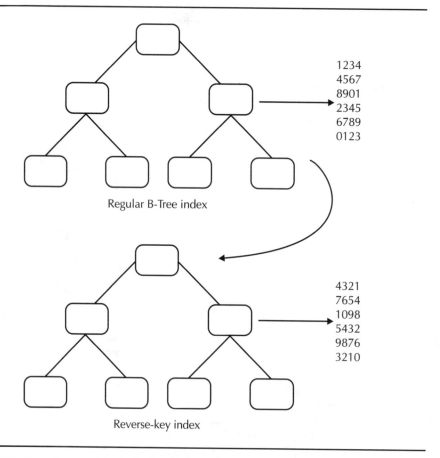

FIGURE 7-3. *Reverse-key indexing*

Reverse-key indexing is beneficial in an OPS (Oracle Parallel Server) environment. In this case, contention for the same leaf block when handling multiple inserts/updates could cause multiinstance pinging, which could result in heavy I/O activity. Implementing a reverse-key index in this situation can drastically improve performance.

Before you use reverse-key indexing, you should do some benchmarks and make sure your query or application gives better throughputs before implementing in production. With so many index options available in Oracle8i, it is important to choose the appropriate one and to verify that the chosen option does its job effectively.

A regular index can be altered to a reverse-key index using the following command:

```
ALTER INDEX my_index REBUILD REVERSE;
```

Similarly, a reverse-key index can be converted to a regular B-Tree index using the following command:

```
ALTER INDEX my_index REBUILD NOREVERSE;
```

The syntax for creating a reverse-key index is shown here:

```
CREATE INDEX customer_index ON customer (cust_num) REVERSE
TABLESPACE ...
```

Some of the limitations of a reverse-key indexes are as follows:

- Bitmap indexes cannot be reversed.

- An index-organized table cannot be reversed.

- A reverse-key index cannot be used in queries involving a range scan.

- Reverse-key indexes are also B-Tree indexes and have all the restrictions of B-Tree indexes, including rebuild requirement and space requirement.

Function-Based Indexes

Starting with Oracle version 8.1.5, you can use functions and expressions as keys for creating an index. Doing this can dramatically improve performance for a number of long queries. A number of performance issues can arise in the application environment where creating function-based indexes can significantly improve query performance. Here is an example of a function-based index:

```
CREATE INDEX vendor_master_index ON vendor_master(UPPER(vendor_name));
```

With this index created, the following SELECT statement will use the index:

```
SELECT vendor_name FROM vendor_master WHERE UPPER(vendor_name)='MCDONALD';
```

Consider using function-based indexes for a long-running query, using expressions in the query as the key values. Note that the WHERE statement should contain the expression on which the table is indexed for the function-based index to be used by the optimizer. Here is an example of a function-based index using an expression:

```
CREATE INDEX order_history_index ON order_history(ord_qty * ord_rate);
```

The following statement will use an indexed search:

```
SELECT * FROM order_history WHERE ord_qty * ord_rate < 100;
```

In the context of applications, function-based indexes can also be used when deploying different NLS (National Language Set) collating sequences. Note that a function-based index can be created as a bitmap index.

To enable a function-based index, execute the following:

1. Log in to sqlplus as internal.

2. Type the following:

    ```
    SQL> ALTER SESSION SET QUERY_REWRITE_ENABLED = TRUE;
    ```

3. Now type the following:

    ```
    SQL> ALTER SESSION SET QUERY_REWRITE_INTEGRITY = TRUSTED;
    ```

Function-based indexes are recommended for range scans or functions in ORDER BY clauses. Function-based indexes are useful when the values in a field are in mixed case, when without a function-based index you would either have to specify the field exactly in your query or the query would do a full table scan.

In Oracle8i, you can specify different columns for the columns that are indexed. This can help the sort performance of queries that require a different ordering sequence in the ORDER BY clause. Here is an example:

```
CREATE INDEX items_index ON items (item_code ASC, qty*rate DESC);
```

With this index in place, the following query will run much faster:

```
SELECT item_code, qty*rate value FROM ITEMS
ORDER BY item ASC, value DESC;
```

Index Rebuilds

Re-creating indexes for a large table can be very time consuming. The table must be unavailable during the index creation process, and this increases application downtime. Prior to Oracle version 8, creating or rebuilding indexes on a table required a lock on the table, and this prevented concurrent DML (Data Manipulation Language) operations on the table when the index was being created. However, since the release of Oracle8i, administrators can rebuild indexes when users are accessing the table, so downtime is reduced, and maintenance operations can be planned without planning for a downtime. However, it is advisable to plan and schedule these activities when the load on the system is not at the peak; a performance hit can result otherwise. The online index rebuild feature helps to achieve 24-7 availability for the Oracle applications. Rebuilding involves only minimal table locking for a short duration of time. When rebuilding an index, Oracle uses up additional space in the index tablespace for completing the rebuild since the existing index is not affected. Administrators must ensure that sufficient free space is available on the index tablespace (more than twice the size of the index being rebuilt) prior to a rebuild.

Index rebuilds can be done for most types of indexes, such as partitioned or nonpartitioned B-Tree indexes. Index rebuilds cannot be done for bitmap indexes. Rebuilds can be done in parallel.

Rebuilding on an index occurs in the following three stages:

1. **Prepare**   In this stage, table locks are acquired briefly to create index structure and place entries in the data dictionary.

2. **Build**   Index is populated in this phase, and this is a time-consuming step. Changes made to the table at the time of the build are placed in what is called a *journal table*. The journal table is structured like a B-Tree so that multiple operations on the same table data can be detected and resolved.

3. **Merge**   In this phase, the rows in the journal table are merged into the index. The table can be online when the merging occurs. As the journal rows are merged, they are deleted if they are not locked and new entries are still permitted. Hence, the merge phase is iterative. If after a few passes, more entries have been included in the journal, the table is locked and the rest of the journal is applied. Both the table and index are then brought back online.

Using Materialized Views

A *materialized view* can be considered an instantiation of the result set of a query. The materialized view provides functionality similar to Oracle's snapshot technology, which provides a way to replicate or distribute data periodically across various Oracle instances. A materialized view similarly allows a view's results to be stored in the database for use in subsequent SQL statements. This view can be periodically refreshed. Unlike standard views, materialized views can be permanently stored in a tablespace, and you can also create indexes on them. The technology is useful in the context of Oracle application implementation, and the administrator should review and understand the materialized view concepts and procedures. A materialized view stores both the definition of a view and the rows of the execution of the view. It uses a query as the basis (just like a normal view), but the query is executed at the time the view is created and the results are stored in a table (unlike the normal view concept).

Materialized views can help improve performance of queries that perform data aggregation. Here is an example of a materialized view:

```
CREATE MATERIALZED VIEW item_summary
   REFRESH START WITH SYSDATE NEXT SYSDATE + 1 AS
   SELECT item_code, item_name, count(*) total_items,
              SUM(qty*rate) total_value FROM item
    WHERE item_type = 'TV'
    GROUP BY item_code,item_name;
```

This example defines a materialized view called item_summary, which will be refreshed daily. The view is defined on top of the item table and summarizes all items of type 'TV'. The total number and total value of each item is calculated.

- Storage attributes like PCTFREE, PCTUSED, INITRANS, MAXTRANS, TABLESPACE, and CACHE can be included in the materialized view syntax.

- Oracle recommends that the materialized view name be less than 19 characters in length. This is to help ensure that the Oracle-generated name is less than the specified 30 characters.

- REFRESH controls the rate of reloading. START WITH specifies the first refresh, and NEXT specifies the periodicity of the next one. Some of the other options for REFRESH include FAST, COMPLETE, FORCE, ON COMMIT, ON DEMAND, and USING ROLLBACK SEGMENT.

- Starting with Oracle 8.1.6, you can use an ORDER BY clause in the query. You can also specify INSERT....SELECT into a materialized view with ORDER BY phrase.

A materialized view can be based on a prebuilt table. In the following case, the underlying table and the materialized view should have the same name and schema:

```
CREATE TABLE item_summary AS
SELECT item_code, item_name, count(*) total_items,
                SUM(qty*rate) total_value FROM item
   WHERE item_type = 'TV'
   GROUP BY item_code,item_name;

CREATE MATERIALZED VIEW item_summary
  ON PREBUILT TABLE WITH REDUCED PRECISION
  REFRESH START WITH SYSDATE NEXT SYSDATE + 1 AS
  SELECT item_code, item_name, count(*) total_items,
                SUM(qty*rate) total_value FROM item
   WHERE item_type = 'TV'
   GROUP BY item_code,item_name;
```

The phrase WITH REDUCED PRECISION enables the REFRESH to work even if some columns generate different precision than originally defined.

REFRESH can be done using either a manual method or an automatic method. To refresh an existing table manually, you can use the Oracle provided PL/SQL packages called DBMS_MVIEW as follows:

```
EXECUTE DBMS_MVIEW.REFRESH('ITEM_SUMMARY');
```

The DBMS_MVIEW packages provides many other useful procedures, such as REFRESH_DEPENDENT and REFRESH_ALL_MVIEWS.

Automatic REFRESH can be performed in the following ways:

- **ON COMMIT** If this option is specified, the materialized view gets updated whenever the base table transactions are committed. This commit is asynchronous.

- **Time based** REFRESH can be scheduled to occur at specified times of the day using the START WITH and NEXT clauses. To be able to use this functionality, the JOB_QUEUE_PROCESSES parameter should be set.

Oracle's cost-based optimizer takes advantage of the existence of a materialized view when it encounters a query that could be most efficient if the corresponding materialized view can be used instead of the objects specified in the query itself. This is done using the query rewrite feature, where the optimizer transparently rewrites the query to use the materialized view. The query rewrite can be enabled either at session level or at instance level using the initialization parameter QUERY_REWRITE_ENABLE. To enable or disable individual materialized views, the user must have GLOBAL QUERY REWRITE or QUERY REWRITE system privilege. GLOBAL QUERY REWRITE privilege allows users to enable any materialized view they own, while the QUERY REWRITE privilege requires the base tables as well as the view to be owned by the user's schema itself.

Materialized views are useful in the following situations:

■ Materialized views help reduce scripting complexities in situations where the source tables are constantly being modified or the summary report (created using a materialized view) is frequently accessed by the user community.

■ Improves performance of standard reporting of a query and also reduces the code maintenance cost; especially true for complex join queries

■ Queries that will be executed often in the database are possible candidates for creating a materialized view because when a query can be satisfied with data in a materialized view, the Oracle Server transforms the query to reference the view rather than the base tables. Thus, expensive operations such as joins and aggregations need not be re-executed for each of the queries running on the server. For example, a string manipulation of customer name and address lines.

The downside of using a materialized view is the additional space required to store the table and indexes created and the overhead associated with keeping the data refreshed in the materialized view. It is recommended that you implement the query rewrite feature along with the materialized view to reap its full benefits. Most of the time, accessing a materialized view may be significantly faster than accessing the underlying base tables, so the optimizer will rewrite a query to access a view when the query allows it. The query rewrite is transparent to the application. Without using the query rewrite feature, the materialized view will essentially serve as a standard view, which will be periodically refreshed from the base tables. A careful study of the cost of implementing and maintaining a materialized view should be completed and compared with the cost of not implementing this functionality. In general, the Oracle Financials implementation does involve many resource-intensive queries, many of which aggregate and summarize data.

A REFRESH operation is used to synchronize the contents of the materialized view with the data in the base tables. How often you need to refresh depends on how often the base tables change and the accuracy of the required information. The refresh process in materialized views is similar to that of snapshot technology. Snapshots were used in Oracle Replication to replicate parts of changes of one Oracle instance over regular intervals to another instance. The refresh options are complete, fast, force, and never.

A *complete* REFRESH of a materialized view involves truncating existing data and reinserting all the data based on the base table by re-executing the query definition from the CREATE command. A *fast* refresh applies only to changes made since the last refresh. Certain restrictions apply while using fast refreshes; for a complete discussion, refer to the Oracle8i Replication Manual. There are two flavors of fast refresh:

- *Fast refresh using materialized view logs.* All changes to the base table corresponding to the materialized view are saved to a log and then applied back to the materialized view.

- *Fast refresh using ROWID range.* This type of fast refresh is suitable for direct loader logs. In this method, a materialized view is refreshed after direct path loads, based on the ROWIDs of the new rows.

Force is the default for the refresh option. The *never* option suppresses all refreshes on the materialized view.

Using Transportable Tablespaces

When your database is growing at a fast pace, you may need to move a subset of the database from the production environment into either a reporting instance or even a sandbox environment or test instance. The transportable tablespace can be used for handling or balancing a tablespace as part of growth or as part of regular testing and maintenance of the application environment. The ability to work on only a piece of the entire database is critical when you are conducting major testing, which necessitates that you repeatedly REFRESH a portion of the tablespaces (or objects) from production for testing. An entire REFRESH of a production database will not really suit this situation, because you may not have that much space in the target instance or you simply do not require use of the entire database. Transportable tablespaces, an Oracle8i feature, can be used for this REFRESH procedure. Transportable tablespaces are also helpful when you want to remove a portion of the database from your production instance and make it part of another database. This would be a good method for implementing application recoverability as well as ensuring that availability of the data is maximized for all your user communities. This section contains more details about transportable tablespaces and will help you understand the basics of implementing transportable tablespaces and some restrictions. Some of the other ways of moving data from one Oracle instance to another include export and import utilities, COPY command using parallel DML, direct path SQL*Load, and using extraction and loading tools such as Informatica for loading data from source instance to the target instance. Each of these methods has its advantages and disadvantages and each should be chosen according to the needs of specific instances. For instance, you must consider time constraints, as export and import methods will take quite some time when you are dealing with a huge volume of data.

Transportable tablespace involves copying the datafiles corresponding to the tablespaces from the server of the source instance to the server of the target instance. Copying metadata from the source to the target using the familiar export/import feature is an example of this. Indexes can also be transported just like the table datafiles.

Using transportable tablespaces involves a few restrictions, some of which depend on the version of the Oracle instance you are using as well as the operating system. As a general guideline, here are some of the main restrictions:

- The source and target databases must have the same block size.

- The source and target databases must have the same character set.

- The source and target databases must have compatible platforms.

- Function-based indexes and replication/snapshots are not supported.

Note that the ROWIDs are not the same in the source and the target databases. This means that when you transport tablespaces, the ROWID will change. In addition, partitioned tables can be transported so long as all the tablespaces corresponding to a table for the tablespace are set. Incomplete partitioned tables cannot be transported.

Five Steps to Implement Transportable Tablespaces

Following are the five steps used to implement transportable tablespaces:

1. Identify a self-contained set of tablespaces. Change them to read-only.

   After identifying the tablespaces, use the Oracle-provided PL/SQL procedure called DBMS_TTS to ensure that the procedures are self-contained. Use the procedure TRANSPORT_SET_CHECK with arguments as the list of tablespaces and TRUE as the second parameter indicating whether or not you want to consider the constraints. Then run the following command to check any violations:

   ```
   SELECT * FROM transport_set_violations;
   ```

   Run the script called dbmssplts.sql from $ORACLE_HOME/rdbms/admin to create a DBMS_TTS package. This script should run as part of your catproc.sql in your standard installation. If you have problems finding the script, you can run it separately by logging on to Oracle as internal.

2. Generate scripts to identify the datafiles that correspond to the identified tablespaces, and copy the datafiles over to the target server. Also write a control script to export metadata information.

   The first script can be generated using a SQL similar to the following:

```
SELECT 'cp '||file_name||' '||file_name||';' FROM dba_data_files

   WHERE tablespace_name IN ('A','B','C');
```

Note that this script must be modified to include the server name. You can also directly ftp the identified data files over to appropriate areas in the target server with appropriate names.

Next, to generate the tablespace metadata you can write a parameter file for export similar to this:

```
transportable_tablespaces=yes
tablespaces=A,B,C
```

3. Execute the copy script to copy the datafiles to the target server. Then create the export file containing the metadata and copy it to the target server as well.

4. After the datafiles are copied, run an import control file on the target file similar to the following:

```
transportable_tablespaces=yes
tablespace=A,B,C
datafiles=(a.dbf,b.dbf,c.dbf)
tts_owners=(11iPROD)
```

5. If you want to be able to use the transported tablespaces on the source instance also, make them read/write. You now have both instances available for use in a fraction of the time it takes to import objects for specific tablespaces.

```
ALTER TABLESPACE A READ WRITE;
```

Consider transportable tablespaces for moving data from the core Oracle applications module to a reporting instance. The reporting instance can be used for all reporting needs, and using it will improve availability and performance of the core modules because the load will be distributed.

Tips for Administrators

Let's review some tips and recommendations that will be useful for the Financials administrator in day-to-day operations. DBAs should attempt to reduce and eliminate issues during company off hours—that is, hours in which database use is at a minimum. Much of this involves following up on various on-call issues and making efforts to fix these problems so that they do not recur.

Key to Success

The key to successful database administration is not only to administer the database proactively to prevent problems from happening but also to ensure that problems are followed up and remedied. Band-aid solutions amount to postponing the real solution and compound the problem. The saying "A stitch in time saves nine" is true in this context. If you have a team of DBAs managing your Oracle application environment, you can implement a common communication using an acceptable source like e-mail or a support.log to manage issues and their resolutions.

Relocating or Reorganizing a Large Table

Oracle8i provides the means for moving a nonpartitioned table without needing to export and import. DBAs can use this option to move a table from one tablespace to another or to reorganize a table to eliminate row migration. The command to do this is as follows:

```
ALTER TABLE items MOVE TABLESPACE ts1;
```

Note that in case you want to reorganize the table, you can move it to the same tablespace so long as free space is available in the tablespace. This is because this operation creates a new segment, populates the table, and then drops the old segment. This method can also be used to rebuild an index-organized table.

When a table is being moved, the users are still able to query the table but cannot insert, update, or delete from the table. The indexes on the table are rendered invalid and hence must be rebuilt after the table move is completed. This can be achieved using the ALTER INDEX REBUILD ... option. Here is an example for the index rebuild:

```
ALTER INDEX apc_invoices REBUILD UNRECOVERABLE
TABLESPACE apc STORAGE (INITIAL 10M NEXT 10M PCTINCREASE 0);
```

Marking a Column as Unused

You can mark a column as unusable and leave the data in the table using this option. The advantage of using the unused option as compared to removing a column for the table (discussed in the next section) is that this method is faster and does not involve rebuilding the table. However, this method does not reclaim disk space. Unused columns act as if they are not part of the table. Queries cannot "see" the data in the unused columns and the DESCRIBE command does not show these columns. To remove the unused column, you can export the table and then import it. Or you can move the table via the method discussed in the previous section.

Oracle provides a data dictionary view called DBA_UNUSED_COL_TABS that can be queried to obtain the names of tables that have unused columns and the number of columns that are marked as unused. You can query this view for a particular schema using a command like this:

```
SELECT TABLE_NAME,COUNT FROM DBA_UNUSED_COL_TABS
WHERE OWNER='APPS';
```

Dropping a Column for a Table

In Oracle8i, you can drop a column from a table. The drop functionality complies with the SQL92 Transactional Level specification. The basic syntax for dropping a columns is as follows:

```
ALTER TABLE items DROP COLUMN in_stock_from
CASCADE CONSTRAINTS;
```

You can handle dependent objects and constraints in various ways, and the drop column syntax provides for them. Following is a brief explanation.

- **DROP**   When the column is explicitly dropped, all columns currently marked as unused in the target table are dropped at the same time.

- **DROP UNUSED COLUMNS**   Specifying this option removes all columns currently marked as unused from the table. This can be used for reclaiming space used by UNUSED columns.

- **CASCADE CONSTRAINTS**   The option drops all the referential integrity constraints that refer to the primary and unique keys defined on the dropped columns.

- **INVALIDATE**   Invalidates dependent objects such as views, triggers, packages, procedures, and functions.

Monitoring Long-Running Processes

For real application implementation, some operations like queries, index creation, DDL (Data Definition Language), data loads, exports, backups, and recoveries could take a long time to complete. Until Oracle 8.0, there was no way of knowing how much of an operation was complete and one could not estimate when a job or process would be finished.

In version 8i, Oracle has provided an enhanced data dictionary view called V$SESSION_LONGOPS. This view contains useful information about several long-running operations. You can query this view to obtain such information as how much of a process is completed. There are two ways to use this view:

■ Oracle adds a record for many long-running processes such as SQL execution, sorting, and so on. This view can be queried to obtain information about those operations. No setup is required for using this feature.

■ You can add a record in this view through the PL/SQL program and track execution of critical programs yourself using the DBMS_APPLICATION_ INFO package. To use this method, you modify your application (package or stored procedure) to add calls to this package with appropriate values. The procedure is called SET_SESSION_LONGOPS. This feature can be used for tracking long-running jobs such as the following:

   ■ Index creation

   ■ Backup and recovery

   ■ Export

   ■ SQL queries

   ■ DDL (eg., CREATE TABLE AS SELECT *...)

   ■ User-defined stored packages and procedures

   ■ SQL loader

   ■ ANALYZE using DBMS_STAT (standard analyze command can also be monitored)

   ■ Full table scan

The V$SESSION_LONGOPS View

Oracle stores information about long-running transactions in this view. For a complete description of the view refer to the Oracle8i Reference Manual (search for "V$SESSION_LONGOPS"). The V$SESSION_LONGOPS view can be used in two ways:

■ To obtain information about how much of a job has completed and expected completion time (see script)

■ To obtain session-level information to help you track the status of a job, process ID, and other information

Table 7-4 shows some useful fields in the view. Note that enhancements to this view are included with every release of Oracle8i.

The V$RECOVERY_PROGRESS view is based on the V$SESSION_LONGOPS view. This view is used for tracking recovery operations—it can be used to

Column Name	Data Type	Description
SID	NUMBER	Session identifier
SERIAL#	NUMBER	Session serial number
OPNAME	VARCHAR2(64)	Operation name like SQL Execution or Sort Output
SOFAR	NUMBER	Units completed so far
TOTALWORK	NUMBER	Total units of work
START_TIME	DATE	Starting time of OPNAME
USERNAME	VARCHAR2(30)	Schema owner

TABLE 7-4.   *Useful Fields in V$SESSION_LONGOPS View*

determine whether the recovery is still running or stalled and also to determine estimated completion time.

Scripts for Monitoring Long-Running Jobs

This section discusses two scripts—one for tracking down specific long-running tasks and the other for monitoring all the long-running tasks. The monitoring script also helps estimate when various tasks will complete. These programs use the V$SESSION_LONGOPS to get this information.

■   **TRACKING**   To track long-running jobs and get information about the program name, osuser, and other information. This script can be useful to obtain information about resource consuming/long jobs:

```
select opname,
       to_char(start_time,'mm/dd/yy hh:mi:ss') start_time,
       to_char(last_update_time,'mm/dd/yy hh:mi:ss') last_update_time,
       sofar,
       totalwork,
       b.osuser osuser,
       -- b.command command,
       b.schemaname schemaname,
       b.program program,
       b.status status,
       b.process process,
       round((sofar/totalwork)*100,3) pct_complete,
       to_char(
         start_time +
```

```
         (sysdate - start_time)/(sofar/totalwork)
         , 'mm/dd/yy hh:mi:ss')                    est_completion_time
from v$session_longops a
,v$session b where a.serial# = b.serial#
 and (sofar/totalwork)*100 < 100;
```

Note that the script does not select cases where sofar = totalwork, because in that instance the job is 100 percent complete. This script provides output like the following:

```
Operation        Start Time        Last Upd Time      SoFar    TotalWork
OSUsr      DBUsr   Program                     Status      Cmpted    %    Est
Cmpl Time
-----------------------------------------------------------------------------
-------------------------------------------

SQL Execution   10/12/01 03:14:23  10/12/01 03:14:32   14752    28370
oracle     SIYER   sqlplus@finp11i (TNS V1-V3)     INACTIVE  22207       52
10/12/01 03:48:10
Sort Output     10/12/01 03:14:38 10/12/01 03:31:37    143      685
oracle     SIYER   sqlplus@finp11i (TNS V1-V3)     INACTIVE  22207       21
10/12/01 04:37:35
```

■ **MONITORING** The following script could be used for monitoring long-running jobs to obtain estimated completion time:

```
select opname,
       to_char(start_time,'mm/dd/yy hh:mi:ss') start_time,
       round((sofar/totalwork)*100,3) pct_complete,
       to_char(
         start_time +
         (sysdate - start_time)/(sofar/totalwork)
         , 'mm/dd/yy hh:mi:ss') est_completion_time
from v$session_longops a
,v$session b where a.serial# = b.serial#
 and (sofar/totalwork)*100 < 100;
```

The output of this query looks like this:

```
Operation       Start Time        % Cmp    Est Cmp Time
------------------------------------------------------------
SQL Execution  10/12/01 03:14:23    52     10/12/01 03:30:00
Sort Output    10/12/01 03:14:38     9     10/12/01 04:37:32
```

Notes on Implementing Long-Operations Monitor

■ Oracle internally calculates totalwork for long operations like SQL execution, sort/merge, and sort output in blocks.

- The V$SESSION_LONGOPS is cleared up only when an instance is bounced. All older operations (even completed ones) are stored in the view.

- Import operation *does not* generate an entry in the v$session_longops view. In practice, it is import (not export) that takes a lot more time, and statistics on import would be helpful.

- There is no way to start and stop the collection of monitoring statistics. Also, completed activities stay in the view until the instance is restarted.

- Consider using this feature for monitoring index creation, long scripts, and similar activities.

Summary

Tables and indexes are two critical components of a growing Oracle database application. Developing a process to track, analyze, and monitor the growth of the application leads to better planning, improved troubleshooting, and proactive maintenance, and it helps predict future growth. DBAs should spend time resizing the initial and next extents and other storage parameters of the tables and indexes.

This chapter discussed ideas about how growth can be tracked using the statistics information to record a history of weekly, biweekly, or monthly growth for capacity planning as well as for analyzing module growth over a period of time. This analysis will be of immense use to the application architects and project technical leads in planning their projects. We also reviewed some techniques for managing growth, such as indexing options, materialized views, and transportable tablespaces for moving data to a reporting instance. In the next chapter, we will review change control and patch management.

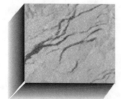

CHAPTER
8

Change Control
and Patch Management

- Introducing patches and upgrades
- Change management
- Change management tools

n this chapter we will discuss patches, upgrades, and change management. This chapter introduces you to patches and how you can apply them. Then, it discusses how upgrades can best suit your business needs and infrastructure. The chapter also covers managing change and introduces you to some change management tools.

Any organization can develop an application from scratch and get all the specific functionality it requires. The only disadvantage of this approach is that it might be expensive and time consuming to develop such applications. An alternative solution is to purchase packaged or generic applications and customize them. Doing so not only reduces development time, but it also reduces cost. An additional advantage is that external resources that are familiar with these applications can be made available to assist with implementation. A distinct disadvantage of these applications is that they do not suit every organization's business requirements.

To a large extent, selecting an application depends on how well-matched the application is to the requirements of each organization. In most cases, the best option is to purchase a combination of packaged applications and customize them accordingly to attain the required capabilities without incurring the expense of developing these applications from scratch.

Business requirements change dynamically, which leads to a constant and varied demand from users for new features to be incorporated in their existing applications. It is not always possible for software vendors to keep pace with the demands of the users and develop standard application packages that meet every business requirement. In doing so, they might compromise the quality of the software while delivering it at such a rapid pace. The more demanding the schedule and complex the technology, the greater the chances of poor design and bugs in the software. As a result, software vendors constantly release patches and upgrades for their software to fix bugs and add new functionality.

Introducing Patches and Upgrades

A *patch* is a fix provided by the software vendor that is used to resolve problems, or bugs, that are reported in an existing application package. The software vendor can release a single patch to solve one or more problems. Patches enable customers to receive the most up-to-date software with the fewest number of bugs. Patches can be freely downloaded and applied to an application. However, it is essential that you have a tight control on applying patches to a production system, as a patch can affect one or more programs, may affect the functionality of the system, and might even affect existing data or make new data incompatible with existing data.

An *upgrade*, on the other hand, is a new version of an application. As with patches, you need to have a proper plan in place for upgrading your application.

The most common problem faced with upgrading software is data incompatibility between the older and newer versions of the software.

The following sections discuss patches and upgrades in detail.

Patches, in Depth

When you apply a patch, in addition to fixing the bug, the patch may also impact other functional areas of an application. Detecting the areas of the application affected by a patch is not an easy task. You can experience the impact of a patch only after you have applied it. In addition, some changes or problems occur only after you have started using the application.

The impact of patches is more severe for customized applications, because the standard patches released by the vendors cannot be applied directly to customized software. In such situations, you need to customize the patches to fix the problems.

To make the best use of patches, keep the following things in mind:

- Define a patch strategy, including information relating to patch management, application, and testing.

- Apply a patch only when you need it—such as if you are using a specific combination of application modules.

The most important question that needs to be answered by an administrator is "Which patch should be applied?" There are two answers to this question: First, don't change anything in the system if everything is working fine. There is no need to spend a great deal of time in testing and applying a patch that will not yield any benefit to the system. Second, if you're using the latest release of the application and the patch is for a previous release, don't use it. The bug addressed in the patch was probably fixed in the new release.

You can get the information on the changes brought about by patches from a number of sources, including these:

- **Oracle Support**   You can refer to the Oracle Web site at **www.oracle.com**, which provides various white papers on new releases and enhancements.

- **Metalink**   Metalink is a self-service application that provides information on patches, certifications, reference materials, and product installs. You can access Metalink by requesting the Oracle World Wide Support Web pages at **www.oracle.com**.

- **Oracle Release Notes**   These notes contain information on new and old functionality and system requirements. You can download Oracle Product Release Notes from Metalink.

- **Oracle Applications Users Group Web sites**   You can also get the information from Oracle Applications Users Group Web sites (**http://www.oaug.com**), and Oracle applications forums (**http://www.oaug.com/public/online_ help.htm**).

- **Readme.txt**   Before applying a patch, it is recommended that you always read the readme.txt file included with most patches. This text file contains instructions for the patch.

- **Driver files**   The driver files give you the names of the file system objects that are run by a patch. These objects might be actual programs, such as reports and forms, or libraries and scripts that create and change database objects.

NOTE
When you refer to the driver files, you need to interpret the specific file objects to which the patch applies. After the object is found, you must determine whether this object is used in the customization.

Installing a Patch

You need to perform the following steps to install a patch:

1. Verify that the patch works by installing it in a test environment and testing it.

2. From the production host nodes, make a backup of the Oracle installation files.

3. Use the *shutdown transactional* statement to shut down the secondary database server that is running. The primary server takes over the job of processing all user requests.

4. On the secondary database server, install the patch. (Remember not to bring up the database instance and Listener.)

5. Use the *shutdown transactional* statement to shut down the primary database server.

6. Start the secondary database and Listener and make it available to the users.

7. On the primary database server, install the patch.

8. Start the primary database server.

9. Finally, back up all the installation files again.

Simply applying a patch is not enough. You need to have a proper patch strategy in place to apply, test, and manage patch information. In addition, you need to ensure that patches are successfully applied to all the environments and that they are tested in the same conditions as the environment where they will be implemented.

Patch Strategy

An effective patch strategy helps in successfully implementing patches. It should include the following:

- Patch application

- Patch testing

- Patch information management

Patch Application   Patch application lays down certain guidelines that you need to follow while applying patches. Some of these guidelines are shown here:

- Restrict the number of people who have permissions to apply patches. Restricting the number of permissions makes the process of patch application more consistent and in control.

- Implement patches in a test environment first.

- Always use a standard log file name convention.

- Synchronize all environments before applying a patch.

- Make a backup of all installation files before applying a patch.

- The Concurrent Manager should be shut down.

- All users should be logged off.

- Drivers should be applied in the correct sequence.

- Readme.txt should be read thoroughly for any additional information.

- After patch application, all invalid objects should be checked.

- Apply drivers in the correct sequence.

Patch Testing   It is always recommended that patches be tested not only before their actual application but also after they have been applied. Testing not only helps you determine the success of the patch but also helps you identify any changes that have occurred as a result of patch application. You should create an environment strictly for testing patches. Testing patches and their associated changes should always be carried out on every environment before actual implementation.

Testing should be carried out in a systematic process where you test not only from a technical perspective but also from a functional perspective. Testing from a technical perspective involves:

- Successful completion of adpatch (the standard patching utility)

- Update of the applptch.txt file

- Detection of errors in the log files

- Detection of any extra invalid objects

Testing from a functional perspective involves:

- Test the areas affected by the patch. The testing should be based on the information in the readme.txt file.

- Check whether the patch was successful in fixing the problem.

- Check whether the patch affected anything else.

- Check the effect of the patch on any customizations.

Patch Information Management   Whenever you apply a patch, you need to document details relating to patch application. Some of the information that needs to be documented is shown here:

- The environments to which the patch was applied

- The date and time when the patch was applied

- Testing and approval information about the patch

- The list of files that were modified and their version numbers

NOTE
Fatal errors during the application of a patch can cause adpatch to exit immediately. This usually creates a restart file. You can restart adpatch after fixing the problem.

After you have formulated a patch strategy, you need to have a system that supports your strategy. One such system is the Patch Control System.

For Solaris systems, you can download patches from **http://www.sun.com/ solaris/java**. However, the application of a particular patch in Solaris depends on the version of Solaris that you are using. To view a list of patches installed on your system you issue the command

```
showrev -p
```

To install the patches you require, perform the following steps:

1. Extract the patch tar file that corresponds to the version of Solaris that you are using. The following are the Solaris versions and their corresponding patch tar files:

   - Solaris 2.5.1: $ tar xvf 1.1.8_10_patches_sparc_5.5.1.tar

   - Solaris 2.6: $ tar xvf 1.1.8_10_patches_sparc_5.6.tar

   - Solaris 7: $ tar xvf 1.1.8_10_patches_sparc_5.7.tar

   This results in creation of a number of patch archives with names like *<patch-id>*.tar.Z.

2. Uncompress and extract patch archives that are required to be installed. When you do so, a directory with the name of the patch-id is created, such as $ zcat *<patch-id>*.tar.Z | tar –xvf.

3. After the directory has been created, log in to the system as root and install the patch.

Patch Control

To prevent a patch from adversely affecting your application, you must first know what the patch changes. This involves *patch prediction*. To study the affects of patches, you need to conduct a thorough patch prediction analysis to determine any impacts caused by applying a patch. Patch prediction analysis involves two levels, discussed here.

Patch Prediction, Level 1   You can use Oracle's standard patching utility, adpatch, for a patch impact prediction. Adpatch verifies the versions of files in the patch driver. It then creates an adpatch log file, called adpatch.log, which lists all the files that will be changed on application of the patch. The adpatch log file also lists the actions that will be performed in the production mode, such as copying, linking, generating, and executing each file. The adpatch.log file is located in the directory $APPL_TOP/install/log. Adpatch uses the internal file version to determine whether a file will be changed.

For Windows NT/Intel, the Oracle Applications release 11.0.1 Patch sets are available as self-extracting archives on the installation CD. Before applying patches, you need to extract them to a temporary staging location by running appll1101.exe. The temporary staging directory includes the AutoPatch executable (ADPATCH.EXE) and FNDCORE.DLL. You use AutoPatch to apply all the patches in the Applications release 11.0.1 Patch sets. To use AutoPatch you need to apply patch drivers from the rel1101 directory. These patch drivers should be applied in the following order:

1. cr1101.drv (all tiers)

2. dr1101.drv (only on admin tier)

In case the Oracle Human Resources that you are using is licensed, you can use the AutoPatch utility for applying patch drivers from rel1101 directory in the following order:

1. cr1101hr.drv (all tiers)

2. dr1101hr.drv (only on admin tier)

However, before you apply these patches, you also need to apply the following patches, in the following order:

1. AD patch: Patch 692951, located in the pre1101\692951 directory

2. FND patches:

   ■ Patch 701255, located in the pre1101\701255 directory

   ■ Patch 701399, located in the pre1101\701399 directory

   ■ Patch 693219, located in the pre1101\693219 directory

3. PER patch: Patch 696537, located in the pre1101\696537 directory

After applying these prerequisite patches, run the adsysapp.sql script. In this script, you need to pass the SYSTEM password as an argument.

When invoking adpatch, include the command *apply=no* to run adpatch in test mode.

Patch Prediction, Level 2   You can perform patch prediction not only for file versions but also for the contents of the file. In addition to knowing which files will be modified by adpatch, you can also review what those changes will be. Patch prediction allows you to obtain reports about complete impact of the patch, such as the forms and reports that will be changed. In addition, you need to be aware of any modifications that are required to keep the customizations synchronized with the new code introduced by the latest patch. This information helps you in determining the time of application of patches—that is, whether certain patches can be applied immediately or later.

Patch Impact Analysis

You can also determine the impact of patches by analyzing reports that provide you with a list of objects, actions, and new versions of the object that have been affected by patch application. This lets you know immediately which forms, reports, and concurrent programs are to be tested.

By using tools such as PVCS Change Manager, you can determine the actual changes made inside the files and database objects. You can use these identified changes to update customizations that are not in sync with your requirements. By performing a comparison of the Oracle Financials schemas against a baseline, PVCS Change Manager can also determine which tables or views have extra or missing columns that could cause problems.

NOTE
Even if you do not want to perform patch prediction before applying patches, you can still be alerted about the changes made by a patch. For example, after applying patch 233333, you can receive an e-mail notification that the standard form XYZ has been overwritten by a newer version.

Error Messages in Patch Application

You can encounter errors during the application of a patch. These errors can be fatal or non-fatal. If the errors are non-fatal, you can continue with applying the patch. This section discusses some common error messages in patch application. The error messages generated during the patch application process are noted in the log files: adpatch.log and adworkxx.log. You can look up the explanation for an error by using the *oerr* utility. The syntax of the oerr utility is:

    oerr ora <error number>

where *error number* is the number that has been generated by the system. Some common errors are listed here:

- **ORA-1858**   A non-numeric character was found where a numeric was expected.

- **ORA-04020**   Deadlock detected while trying to lock object.

If the installation fails, you can always apply a patch again. If the patch makes no database updates, you can back out of a patch. For example, if a report or form was updated, you can use the .bak files and the .O files to recover the old version. Changes to a database by a patch can be made by using the database restore option.

Managing Patches

To manage patches, you need software tools that can work in diverse environments, have predefined control procedures, and provide you with complete information about the patch applications. In addition, these tools should provide for the following:

- Security on who can apply and approve patches

- Workflow rules to make it impossible to apply a patch in a production environment before applying it to the testing environment

- Viewing of log files to identify errors if any

- Information on the environment, date, and time when the patch was applied; details on who approved the patch and which files were modified

Upgrades, in Depth

An *upgrade* is the latest version of software released by a vendor. Unlike a patch, which is just a fix for a particular bug encountered in an application, an upgrade is a totally new version of the application. It caters to all aspects of the application and not just a single entity or bug. Upgrades introduce new functionality into existing applications and enhance their capabilities.

Upgrades can also severely affect customizations and make them obsolete. An upgrade may totally replace the customization or it may affect only a portion. Most cases are a combined effect when the new functionality replaces only a part of the customization. However, the new code must first be examined and analyzed. Then you must determine whether to apply the customizations to the new program or apply the upgrade to the custom code. For example, if Oracle changes the form or report upon which the customized version is based, those changes will have to be incorporated into the customized version. If Oracle changes the data structures that custom applications use, the custom applications need to be adapted. Oracle's changed code must be analyzed to determine what is new and how it fits in with the custom code.

You need to analyze the following points when performing an upgrade:

- Changes between the new and the earlier versions.

- Changes resulting from customizations versus the new code. You can then determine the degree to which the customizations have been affected.

■ Changes in requirements with respect to the new version. This could be done by adding custom code to the new version of Oracle's code, adjusting Oracle's new code into the customization, doing away with the customization, or starting anew.

With any new software release, there are bugs. Not only must you test any new software, but you must also convert the data, train users on new functionality, update procedures, and manage customizations. To minimize problems, the DBA must first perform multiple test installs before performing the actual upgrade on the production system. With each of these test runs, every single patch will have to be reapplied.

The technical analysts have to do a comparative analysis of the new code with the customizations. When it is found that the customizations must be continued, the migration, implementation, and testing must be considered.

The following points must be answered before performing the upgrade:

■ Does the upgrade offer enhanced functionality that benefits the user in his or her business environment?

■ Will the benefits of the upgrade outweigh the time and expense of the upgrade?

■ Is the upgrade required by Oracle to maintain ongoing support of the Oracle applications?

Before applying a new release or upgrade, you must learn as much as possible about the contents of the upgrade. You should consult some of the numerous sources of information on the Oracle database and Oracle application products. You then create an upgrade plan that can be followed to track the progress of the upgrade from start to finish. One of the most important factors that needs to be considered in this plan is the *infrastructure plan*.

Infrastructure Plan

You need to have a well laid out infrastructure plan for implementing an upgrade:

■ Analyze the existing infrastructure while researching for the upgraded contents. A thorough understanding of the hardware, software, and business practices is needed to determine the impact of the current upgrade and subsequent upgrades. This analysis should identify the physical location of all hardware and software components and how they communicate.

■ The computing environment analysis should include identification of all mainframes, LANs, servers, stand-alone computers, network/communications, and software packages in use. You can create a network diagram of the operating environment that depicts all applications and the flow of data between them.

- The analysis should include the number of concurrent users utilizing the applications, the methods used to access the applications, and the security access measures used to protect data, such as encryption software used for data transfers.

- Define how the applications transmit data across different platforms.

- Identify all points where data enters and exits the Oracle applications into other non-Oracle software products.

After the data on the current and future infrastructures has been collected, the next step is to compare the two structures and identify any differences. You need to determine whether the structure of the new operating environment can be supported by the existing infrastructure. The decision regarding the upgrade should be made on the basis of whether the existing hardware and software will be able to support the new upgrade. In case the new architecture will require the acquisition of additional hardware and software, it is important to identify purchase requirements early to decrease the lead time on hardware and software purchases. This process involves the following points:

- Identifying the impact to existing systems and how many custom interfaces and reports will need to be rewritten.

- Identifying how many custom reports can be replaced with standard Oracle reports or query functions.

- Identifying any interfaces that need to be replaced.

Periodically when applying an upgrade, existing functionality is permanently or temporarily lost. It is important to determine whether any losses of functionality will negatively impact the day-to-day operations of the business entity. Upgrades may need to be postponed until a later date, when the functionality has been restored or an alternative method has been developed.

The key points that need to be considered when deciding to upgrade are

- Determining how many instances will be needed for testing, migration, training, and production.

- Determining the type of upgrade. Identifying whether it is a database, applications, or desktop upgrade, or a combination.

- Determining whether upgrades are required for network/communications, e-commerce/EDI software, encryption, and security software.

- Identifying the impact of integration with non-Oracle software products.

- Identifying the number of concurrent users for each application and the number of logins that need to be created for these users.

- Identifying whether the number of users will increase due to the upgrade.

NOTE
To upgrade a database you need to run SQL scripts depending on the database that you want to upgrade. These scripts are located in ORACLE_HOME\ RDBMS\ADMIN. The upgrade files are stored in %ORACLE_HOME%\RDBMS\ADMIN\, where %ORACLE_HOME% represents the drive letter of your computer.

Testing is the most important part of an upgrade. Testing helps you to validate the functionality of the Oracle applications, after the upgrade has been applied. Just as for patches, upgrades should also be tested in a test environment before applying them to the live environment. You can design test cases for testing if the new and existing functions are functioning as desired.

You can also construct a test thread for validating transactions that are vital for business activities. In addition, you can write test cases with complete instructions and the expected outcome of the test. Test cases can then be distributed to multiple users for test-verification purposes. The test cases should be entered into the applications and the results compared to the expected outcome of the test. If the outcome does not match the original expectation, the test should be reviewed to determine whether there is a problem with the expected outcome or whether the system is not performing properly.

You should also define an acceptance criterion for test cases. This criterion should include a contingency plan in case the upgrade contains unresolved bugs or invalid test results. A final go-ahead or no-go decision on the upgrade should be given at the end of testing. A predefined sign-off criteria can assist in making this decision.

You need to have a backup and restore plan in place for the upgrade process. All databases and applications should be backed up before the upgrade is applied so that data can be restored if there are problems with the upgrade. It is not recommended that you apply upgrades directly into the production environment. The upgrade should first be applied to a test environment and after testing is complete and signed off, the upgrade can be applied to the live production environment.

Optimizing Strategic Business Processes

Three areas need to be considered when evaluating the business value of an upgrade—business gains, technology gains, and market gains. Business gains lead to increases in productivity or efficiency. Technical gains lead to an increase in maintainability of the applications or cost savings from a new technology. Market gains include the demand for new products and services or partner product collaborations that enhance or complement application functionality.

Before opting for an upgrade, you need to analyze your business processes. Business practices should be analyzed for the following:

- Duplicated functions and non-value added functions. You should develop a consistent set of business practices that optimize the performance of the organization as a whole.

- New application functionality to determine whether it is applicable to your business requirements.

- Steps that do not add value. Always check whether the step adds value and whether the value outweighs the cost of the step. If no value is added, modify or eliminate the step.

Aligning the Business Organization

After you have defined the optimal business processes, it is time to assess the organizational readiness for change. Check whether the organization is willing to accept and implement the processes necessary to maximize the new application architecture and functionality. It is often necessary to realign the business organization to optimize the benefits of the upgrade.

By breaking down the upgrade process into small business-oriented tasks, you can manage and successfully execute an upgrade:

- Research the new release.

- Develop a business case.

- Analyze the infrastructure.

- Develop the testing strategies.

- Establish the cut-over and contingency plans.

- Align business processes.

- Establish the support organization.

Dealing with Change

Change is effective only when you know its impact and can anticipate it. Lack of knowledge about the impact of change can lead to unpredictable results and thus an unstable system. In addition, this lack of knowledge about the impact of change can also cause changes in functionality and problems with the data. The overall result can be a shutdown of the mission-critical systems resulting in revenue losses. The functionality changes can cause users to lose time due to lack of awareness on how to handle change.

In the case of new software, one of the major reasons for the effects of unknown changes is improper pre-testing of the software. The other and more likely cause is lack of proper control on changes being put into force. Changes affect standard applications and customized applications equally. In such a scenario, it becomes imperative for you to study the effect of change on both the standard application and the customized part of the application.

Effect of Change on Customization

The level of customizing an application varies from one business need to another. While some companies may customize just the design of the application, other companies may decide to customize the entire application. Customizing the entire application involves customization of the code behind an application. Any customized code is not a stand-alone application, but impacts the functioning of a number of objects such as forms, reports, libraries, and database schemas. Customized code is also prone to the same set of problems regarding fixes and upgrades that are faced by packaged software.

Most companies have spent enormous amounts of time, resources, and money creating customizations to improve their business functions, stay ahead of competition, and create functionality that Oracle doesn't provide. This in turn translates to spending an enormous amount of time identifying and analyzing environments that include customizations every time a change is introduced in the system.

It is a well-known fact that developers/consultants do not document their work, which leaves a majority of companies without good documentation for their customizations. Performing a full system test to check for changes is a time-consuming task. Further, due to lack of appropriate documentation, companies spend hours trying to identify the impact of a patch or upgrades against their customizations. In most cases, companies take the approach of adding or *recustomizing* their code every time a new patch or upgrade is released.

This also leads to a situation where many companies do not apply patches and upgrades when everything seems to be working fine in their systems. The decision to apply the latest available patch is a crucial technical as well as business decision.

While it is certainly recommended to keep up with the latest available patch sets, the decision to apply a particular patch is often dictated by

- Project deadlines and time that has already gone in to create an environment
- Budget set aside for implementation of a particular module
- A fix being available for a given issue

Often companies have to trade off between applying patches in a timely manner and deferring it until there is an absolute requirement. Time and budget permitting, every effort should be made to stay up to date with Oracle-recommended patch set levels. Not applying the patches can lead to bigger problems for companies as they run the risk of having their software turn obsolete if they can't maintain the current releases of the software.

Also, as Oracle starts to de-support older versions of applications, customers must either get to the current supported level or re-implement the latest version of the applications.

The problem with customizations to Oracle applications is that they generate a large amount of code that needs to be managed. This code could reside either on the client, the server, or the Oracle database. An average Oracle applications form can contain about 4000 objects, 90,000 lines of code, 35 attached libraries, and 10 referenced forms. Among all these objects it is difficult to identify the location of the customizations and the impact of an upgrade on the customizations. Also, at this point the other factors that need to be accounted for are identifying the changes that have been made by Oracle, the missing objects, and the objects that are no longer needed.

Controlling Change

The effects of change must be reduced to lower the total cost to the company. You need to have control on what is changing. In case it is not possible to directly control all that is changing, you should always know what is changing and you should have control over when it is released. Overall, you must always be sure that the change is correct.

Managing change requires improved processes. This includes better tracking of change; better impact analysis of patches, upgrades, and new releases; and the reduction of manual processes that are error prone and slower. Processes such as manually applying patches and migrating code from one environment to another are not only time consuming but also susceptible to human error. What is required in the present business scenario is the ability to see the full impact of proposed change (new customizations, patches, updates, etc.). To see the full impact of proposed change you must be able to identify not only the files affected by the change but the detailed property levels within the file that are being affected by the change.

To do this you need information regarding patches and upgrades, especially how it relates to the customizations and procedures to control the release of tested software. Let us look at a few key functions of change management:

- **Process management**   Controls the flow of application components through a sequence of states.

- **Version management**   Tracks the evolution of each component of an application by individually storing its successive versions.

- **Workspace management**   Creates work areas in which developers create and test changes without disturbing concurrent development.

- **Build management**   Supervises the compilation, translation, and linking steps involved in turning source components into deliverable applications.

- **Parallel development**   Allows several developers to work simultaneously on alternate versions of application components while pursuing distinct goals.

- **Distributed development**   Coordinates changes to shared application components made by developers in multiple sites.

- **Issue tracking**   Manages the collection of bug reports and change requests for an application.

Instead of relying on IT staff, who are usually too busy to focus on the tedious work of assessing change impact, tools are available that can do this for them. Oracle provides change-management support within the Application Object Library. The Application Object Library is a repository in which all program files, reports, and forms are registered. The Application Object Library stores all revision information and displays log files to help organizations determine which patches have been applied and whether or not they were successful.

The Application Object Library also provides support for tracking every version of a file and the particular patch builds in which those files are included, as well as support for analyzing developer-tested patches, recording the configuration, and building the patches on multiple hardware platforms. Within the Application Object Library, the AutoPatch utility can be used to confirm that a particular patch is appropriate for a specific installation. It helps organizations determine the versions of customer files and database objects currently installed and compares these with the versions being delivered via the patch.

Some of the most common problems related to managing changes in Oracle are covered next.

Change Identification   You cannot determine, in a timely manner, what changes have been made to forms, reports, libraries, or databases. In fact, it is not immediately apparent what Oracle has changed, or what you have customized, without investigation into coding. Furthermore, database administrators and developers may spend hours attempting to find out why code works in a test environment but not in a production environment.

The many features and flexibility of Oracle applications produce a complex product and therefore make patches necessary. If you prepare in advance, you can minimize project delays caused by patches.

Assessing Impacts of Change   It is not possible to perform impact analysis on modification to forms, libraries, and database objects in a timely manner. This affects the other parts of the application, leading to downtime and research time to resolve the problem. Inconsistencies might appear in the application due to some modules needing modification not being updated. Additionally, it is difficult to determine which areas of the customized application need testing after installing patches or upgrades. A full system test can solve the problem, but it is time consuming. Foregoing testing can cause downtime and frustration for end users.

Processing Changes   It is difficult to manage change across the multiple promotion level environments such as development, testing, and production. The manual method is error-prone and becomes more so as workload increases. In addition, there is no method to verify that daily installation of software was successful. Taking shortcuts such as deploying the same executable across multiple environments can turn compilation errors into runtime errors. This is the leading frustration for the end users, because it creates sporadic failures.

Managing Change

Customized forms, reports, libraries, and other files are valuable assets that are costly to replace if they are inadvertently overwritten or lost. Additionally, most customized systems are poorly documented, making maintenance unnecessarily difficult and costly. The cumulative effect of these problems is that if implementing a patch or update, customizations can break and there will be no way to know where or how, because it is not possible to track or perform version control and manage the changes.

This situation leaves a choice between two options: upgrading and re-creating all customizations, which could impact the schedule, or wait to see what doesn't function and then fix those options. A third option is to simply leave applications where they are, and ignore patches and upgrades. But then, the option of benefiting from valuable new functionality is taken away, and this is not acceptable in today's fast-paced environment.

The obvious solution is to impose some kind of application change management discipline that is essential for managing and transferring customized financial applications.

You use an Application Change Manager (ACM) to identify the changes that have occurred within a form, report, library, or schema, as compared to its previous state. However, in Oracle Financials the analysis of the internal structure of Oracle's database and program objects is quite complex. In addition, the constituent characteristics and properties of databases and programs have complex interrelationships and result in unanticipated impacts caused by changes elsewhere.

More so, there needs to be a means to convey the knowledge of these changes and dependencies to developers, so that developers can easily ascertain which changes are noteworthy and which can be ignored. The goal is to manage change migration within all Oracle environments. By *change migration*, we mean being able to migrate changes created by customizations changes from patches and changes from new revisions to and from all environments with dependencies on those changes. This prevents changes from getting out of sync and causing customizations to fail.

To manage the change means to be able to identify the change, assess the impact of the change, process the change, and safeguard the change. The migration of custom code requires that the individual doing the migration must know all of the interdependencies associated with the files being moved. If the interdependencies aren't known or aren't checked for accuracy, end users will see more runtime errors and possibly more down time. When dealing with mission-critical activity, you must be able to migrate code quickly and report any failures accurately to ensure quick resolution and completion of the migration.

Change and patch management tools such as RingMaster from Cinap and Merant's ERP Change Manager can identify, analyze, and summarize the patch impact in a format readable by the functional people, and it can identify differences for database objects and changed code of new versions.

Change management tools can enforce procedures and automatically create documentation. You can use these tools to remove the manual steps out of patch applications and help in customizations across disparate platforms.

PVCS ERP Change Manager

PVCS ERP Change Manager solves the upgrade dilemma by automatically capturing the customizations and making it easy to upgrade to the next release. PVCS ERP Change Manager enables you to see where and when changes were made, including custom queries based on date and specific type of action. The Change Manager also enables you to see what versions are running in each Oracle environment.

Some of the features of PVCS Change Manager are listed here:

■ *Accelerates the adoption of new releases and capabilities.* PVCS ERP Change Manager makes it easier to see changes and their impact, so you can make decisions about what to implement, what to change, and what to leave undisturbed.

■ *Helps identify what needs to be changed and evaluate the impact of change.* Most changes to Oracle applications affect not just the software code and the database, but what the end user sees and uses at the desktop. It is impossible to manually identify each and every customized program, form, report, library, or database object affected by a patch or upgrade. PVCS ERP Change Manager automates the change identification process, indicating every line of customized code and helping you determine the implications of a patch or upgrade to their changes.

■ *Automate the migration of customized applications.* PVCS ERP Change Manager lets you see changes before you decide to upgrade and helps you identify potential problems before they occur.

The system requirements for PVCS ERP Change Manager are

■ Oracle Database version 7.x

■ Workstation or server with Windows 95/98 or Windows NT

■ 64MB RAM, 133MHz or higher processor

■ Workstation disk space requirement 30MB

■ Oracle Developer/2000 version 1.6

■ Forms, Reports, and SQL*Plus installed on each PC and PVCS ERP Change Manager server

The Server Requirements for PVCS Manager are

■ 100MB disk space for Developer/2000 and PVCS ERP Change Manager tables/indexes (based on 10 named users)

■ 400MB of table space for each APPS schema (Oracle Financials customers only) to be monitored

■ 200MB table space for indexes in the PVCS ERP Change Manager database (all other database schemas will vary in the required amount of table space needed)

■ Disk space adequate to contain Automated Versioning archives (will vary depending on the number of versions to be stored)

■ Disk space to hold a previous version (one copy) of every source code file to perform comparisons on new versions of a file

■ NFS Gateway or SAMBA to gain access to any UNIX servers containing application source code

PVCS ERP Change Manager is composed of the following six integrated components.

Change Finder   The Change Finder Difference Report lets you see where and when changes were made. It eliminates time spent on tedious line-by-line reviews of code. Change Finder has the following features:

- Identifies changes made to forms, reports, libraries, SQL scripts, text files, database objects, and entire database schemas

- Allows for easy resolution of differences between the client environment and the changes made to a given form, report, or library

- Identifies differences between database schemas

- Compares database schema and objects residing on a separate machine in any location

- Determines the differences between the client code and server code

Automated Change Finder   The Automated Change Finder extends PVCS ERP Change Manager's Change Finder abilities to monitor the environments automatically and run reports to identify changes made every day. The features of Automated Change Finder are

- Automatically monitor the environment

- Generates difference reports whenever changes are made to the forms, reports, libraries, and other text-based files

- Customization reports show what has been customized in the Oracle module

- Version change reports show the changes that have taken place between the versions of a given module

- Oracle change reports show the changes made by Oracle in new releases and patches

- Allows for easy drag-and-drop of the customizations into new modules shipped by Oracle

Automated Generation   Automated Generation has the following features:

- Automates the installation and generation of the application

- Works across all of the Oracle environments (development, test, production, etc.)

■ Interfaces with PVCS Version Manager to ensure that promoted database objects and program modules are installed properly in each environment

■ Automatic e-mail notifications alert assigned people of installation and upgrade statuses and of any errors that occurred during installation

Object Finder   The Object Finder lets you see where objects and libraries are used throughout the Oracle application, so you can more easily determine the impact of changes. Object Finder has the following features:

■ Enables you to perform impact analysis on changes being made to forms, reports, libraries, and PL/SQL

■ Helps you determine what would happen to a form or library where there are dependencies on other forms or libraries

■ Determines what modules a library is attached to

■ Enables text string search throughout the entire application and database

Automated Versioning   Automated Versioning saves developer time and keeps a backup of the Oracle Application changes through time. Automated Versioning has the following features:

■ Automatically versions software as changes occur—developers do not even need to know that the PVCS ERP Change Manager server exists

■ Provides built-in backup/recovery of the customizations

■ Triggers Automated Generation to install code at different times throughout the day or night

Automated Publishing   Automated Publishing has the following features:

■ Provides comprehensive documentation of the Oracle database and Developer/2000 software

■ Includes forms, reports, and libraries

■ Provides drill-down abilities to find the exact location of a given text string in forms, reports, libraries, and server code

■ Allows the generation of custom reports for showing specific information for forms, reports, and libraries

PVCS Version Manager

PVCS Version Manager offers an easy to use version management environment to manage the full spectrum of client/server development objects, including source code files, word processing files, online help files, graphics, and spreadsheet files. Version Manager automates common tasks and communication throughout a project's life cycle. Multiple workgroups can store files for an application at the same or different locations. The program oversees changes to all elements, automatically logs the time and date when the files were changed, recording the name of the person who "checked out" the files, and records when actions were performed, what changes were made, and when files were "checked in." Earlier versions of the software system can be reconstructed at any time. Version Manager improves developer productivity and reduces the complexity of version management. The program can also be configured to optimize performance on different types of binary files.

Summary

In this chapter, you learned about the basics of patches and upgrades. You learned that unlike a patch, which is just a fix for a particular bug encountered in an application, an upgrade is altogether a new version of an application. You learned that to apply a patch successfully you need to have a patch application strategy in place. You also learned that by breaking down the upgrade process into smaller tasks you can manage and successfully execute an upgrade. You learned about change management and that change is effective only when you know its impact and can anticipate it. Lack of knowledge about the impact of change can lead to unpredictable results and thus an unstable system.

We also reviewed a few key functions of change management.

Finally, you learned about change management tools. These tools can enforce procedures and automatically create documentation. You can use these tools to remove the manual steps out of patch application and help in customizations across disparate platforms.

CHAPTER
9

Managing CBO in an Oracle11i Environment

- Rule-based optimization (RBO) vs. cost-based optimization (CBO)
- Why is CBO required for Oracle11i?
- Set the optimizer mode
- CBO architecture
- Methods of collecting statistics
- Set initialization parameters for implementing CBO in Oracle11i
- Understand plan stability

his chapter covers cost-based optimization (CBO), a required component for implementing Oracle11i applications, and plan stability. Plan stability is a critical component of any application that involves significant customization efforts. It enables administrators to move seamlessly from rule-based to cost-based environments with custom modules and to continue using CBO for the core modules.

Rule-Based Optimization vs. Cost-Based Optimization

In Oracle, a SQL statement passes through three main phases—parse, execute, and fetch.

During the parse phase, the Oracle Server searches for the statement in the shared pool, checks the syntax and semantics, and then determines the execution plan. It scans the statement for bind variables and assigns a value to each variable. In the execute phase the Oracle Server applies the parse tree to the data buffers, performs necessary I/O and sorts for DML statements. In the fetch phase the Oracle Server retrieves rows for a SELECT statement during the fetch phase. Each fetch retrieves multiple rows, using an array fetch. The execution plan for a query is determined during the Fetch phase.

The *execution plan* defines how the data is to be accessed from the database. For example, the plan defines whether a table must be accessed using a full table scan or whether an index will be used. The execution plan also includes a join order for various tables and explains how subqueries will be merged into main queries. The execution plan directly influences the performance of the query.

Your application's execution plan should be based on the optimizer mode as well as on the statistics in the tables. The Oracle Optimizer uses either a rule-based approach (via RBO) or a cost-based approach (via CBO). RBO was used in Oracle versions 10.7 and 11.0. RBO processes tables of a query in the order they are specified in the FROM clause. RBO also ranks execution plans based on their relative cost in the list, regardless of the data stored in the table. In RBO, the developer needs to understand fully the data and its distribution.

Starting with release 11i, however, Oracle uses CBO—in fact, Oracle11i is tuned for CBO and requires that you use CBO. This means that at execution time, the optimizer considers and evaluates several access paths, available statistical information, and created indexes before an execution plan is determined. The optimizer also considers *hints* placed in SQL statements as well as any outlines created for that SQL statement (refer to "Understanding Plan Stability," later in this chapter, for more information on hints and SQL statements). The optimizer does all this by creating a set of available execution plans along with the cost of each execution plan based on the statistics available in the data dictionary. The costs are determined by statistics that the optimizer has collected on various objects by analyzing tables, table columns, partitions, indexes, and index columns.

In the context of Oracle applications, you must use the FND_STATS package or the Gather Schema Statistics Concurrent Program to collect statistics (both of these are discussed in more detail in the "Methods of Collecting Statistics" section). The FND_STATS package calls the DBMS_STATS package internally to collect these statistics. After analysis, the optimizer chooses the execution plan that corresponds to minimum cost. The CBO uses object-level statistics on tables, indexes, and partitions to determine selectivity, cardinality, and execution costs.

It is critical that you understand the way the CBO works. Doing so will help you tune generic as well as custom application modules effectively within the Oracle11i Application Suite.

Why Is CBO Required for Oracle11i?

Moving to CBO allows Oracle applications to utilize such key database features as partitioning, materialized views, function-based indexes, and index-only tables. For batch processing operations, 11i uses CBO to achieve best throughput. For client-based operations like forms or Java, 11i uses CBO to get the fastest response time. Oracle11i also makes use of partitioning and function-based index features, which make use of CBO mandatory.

Setting the Optimizer Mode

You can set the optimizer mode by specifying the Oracle initialization parameter called OPTIMIZER_MODE. The possible values for the OPTIMIZER_MODE parameter are RULE, CHOOSE, ALL_ROWS, and FIRST_ROWS. The default value for the OPTIMIZER_MODE parameter in the init.ora file is CHOOSE. This means that the optimizer gets to choose whether RBO or CBO will be used, depending on whether or not statistics exist on the objects. If even one of the tables in a SQL statement is analyzed, the optimizer will use CBO—unless a *stored outline* is defined for that SQL statement. In that event, Oracle chooses an execution plan that corresponds to the *hints* of that outline. (For more information about hints and stored outlines and how they can be implemented, refer to the section "Understanding Plan Stability," later in the chapter.)

The CBO approach can use one of two types of optimization: first rows (FIRST_ROWS) and all rows (ALL_ROWS). The FIRST_ROWS parameter is used to ensure fast response time, and ALL_ROWS is used to minimize the overall execution time. The FIRST_ROWS parameter is best suited for OLTP types of queries, where a quick response is often expected. In this case, the optimizer eliminates hash joins or sort-merge joins. The ALL_ROWS parameter is suitable for concurrent requests in which overall throughput needs to be optimized. Oracle11i applications can use the CHOOSE or ALL_ROWS method of optimization. Full table scans and merge joins are weighted higher in case of ALL_ROWS.

Initialization Parameter	Notes	Recommended Value
optimizer_features_enable	Specifies the Oracle release cost-based optimizer will use in terms of its features	8.1.6
query_rewrite_enable	Should be set to TRUE to use materialized view features	TRUE
_optimizer_mode_force	Forces recursive SQL to use the current environment's OPTMIZER_MODE	TRUE
_fast_full_scan_enabled	Disables index fast full scans (which could be expensive since the entire index is traversed)	FALSE
optimizer_max_permutations	Sets an upper limit for number of join permutations that the optimizer will consider	79000 or less
_push_join_predicate	Turns on the push join predicate	TRUE

TABLE 9-1. *CBO Initialization Parameters*

Table 9-1 shows initialization parameters that relate to implementing CBO. You can also run the script $FND_TOP/sql/AFCHKCBO.sql to see the current settings of the initialization parameters.

CBO Architecture

CBO uses a sophisticated and complex set of algorithms to determine the cost of various execution plans. Several factors and parameters affect the choice of the most optimal plan. Some of the most critical factors are these:

- The CBO calculates the cost of using a full table scan as well as of using an index-based search. If the full table scan is less expensive than the indexed search, the CBO chooses that option.

- It is critical that the statistics on the tables, indexes, and partitions are refreshed. If the statistics are regularly refreshed then the CBO (cost-based optimizers) can make a realistic estimate of the execution plan and estimate of the execution path.

■ When performing a full table scan, the value of the init.ora parameter DB_FILE_MULTIBLOCK_READ_COUNT is critical. This parameter indicates that Oracle will read a specified number of blocks per I/O, thereby making a full table scan faster. The optimal value for Oracle11i applications is 8 (the default value). This will ensure that the optimizer does not frequently choose a full table scan for the SQL statements. Note that the init.ora parameter can be changed at a session level using the command

```
alter session set db_file_multiblock_read_count=32;
```

You can change the value of this parameter for specific custom applications after thorough testing. This way, you can still force the optimizer to use full table scan in certain cases and maintain better control of your environment.

CBO Terminology

Following are some of the important terms you need to understand in the context of working with CBO:

■ **Cost**   CBO assigns a cost to each operation, such as access methods, joins, sorts, merges, and I/O.

■ **Cardinality**   The number of rows in a table; the expected number of rows returned from a query.

■ **Selectivity**   The ratio of number of rows returned to the total number of rows in the table.

■ **Histogram**   CBO, by default, assumes a normal or even distribution of data across each table. If the actual data is skewed, CBO can make a better choice of an execution plan using the histogram information. The CBO uses height-based histograms to identify data distribution. Histogram information is stored in data dictionary views such as DBA_HISTOGRAMS and DBA_PART_HISTOGRAMS.

Methods of Collecting Statistics

CBO uses object-level statistics on tables and indexes to generate optimal execution plan costs. It is critical that you define a regular method for analyzing your tables and indexes to refresh these statistics. If the statistics are not refreshed often, CBO plans will be based on old statistics, which may not be correct.

Ideally, you should devise a plan for refreshing each group of tables. Statistics on tables that are highly volatile (change frequently) should be refreshed more often than those on static tables. Your plan should include groups of tables that are refreshed daily, weekly, biweekly, monthly, and quarterly. You can then set up concurrent programs to refresh statistics automatically on those tables. Note that the Gather Schema Statistics Concurrent Program can be used in parallel to fit the available time window for refreshing statistics.

You can analyze objects and gather statistics for Oracle11i objects in two ways:

- Use the FND_STATS package
- Use the Gather Schema Statistics Concurrent Program

NOTE
Do not use the ANALYZE command or the DBMS_STATS package to gather statistics directly. These methods do not use the SEED data for interface tables that is used by FND_STATS and the Gather Schema Statistics Concurrent Program. Using ANALYZE or DBMS_STATS is not recommended and could result in incorrect statistics generation.

The FND_STATS Package

The FND_STATS package provides a number of procedures that are used for performing specific functions, such as creating a statistics table, populating table or schema statistics, or validating statistics. You can execute the FND_STATS package from the SQL*Plus prompt using the appropriate parameters. Following are details about each of the procedures available in the FND_STATS package.

For more information on the different procedures available within FND_STATS and also a complete list of parameters, you can refer to Maintaining Oracle Applications Release 11i Manual.

CREATE_STAT_TABLE   This procedure creates a table in which the statistics can be backed up. This feature can be used to transport statistics from production to other instances for testing purposes. The table is created in the APPLSYS schema and is called FND_STATTAB. The table can store multiple versions of statistics for the same table, user, or database—each identified by a statid. Backing up statistics in a table is advantageous for several reasons, including the ability to export and import the table to another instance and for analysis of performance issues.

BACKUP_TABLE_STATS   This procedure can be used to back up the table statistics into FND_STATTAB. Note that the default statid is BACKUP. You can also back up index statistics.

BACKUP_SCHEMA_STATS This procedure can be used for backing up table and index statistics for an *entire schema* in the FND_STATTAB table. The default statid is null, and you can keep multiple version backups as long as you use a different statid for each.

RESTORE_SCHEMA_STATS This procedure can be used to restore the backed up statistics for an entire schema.

RESTORE_TABLE_STATS This procedure restores table statistics for a given table and a given statid. The default statid is BACKUP. Statistics can be gathered for *all* products or separately for each application. The restore table statistics help in restoring the previous statistics for a specified time period. This can be helpful when you're trying to analyze performance issues.

RESTORE_COLUMN_STATS This procedure restores statistics for a particular column and a particular statid from FND_STATTAB into the data dictionary.

GATHER_SCHEMA_STATS This procedure gathers statistics for all objects in a schema. A backup of existing statistics is kept. The procedure also creates a histogram for specified columns in a FND_HISTOGRAM_COLS table and populates the default statistics for tables specified in FND_EXCLUDE_TABLE_STATS.

GATHER_SCHEMA_STATISTICS This procedure is a wrapper for calling GATHER_SCHEMA_STATS from the SQL prompt. This should be run for a particular schema only.

GATHER_INDEX_STATS This procedure gathers index statistics. It is equivalent to running this:

```
ANALYZE INDEX[ownname.]indname [PARTITION partname]
COMPUTE STATISTICS | ESTIMATE STATISTICS SAMPLE estimate_percent PERCENT 10
```

GATHER_TABLE_STATS This procedure gathers table, table columns, index, and index columns statistics. It can be executed in parallel with another procedure. The results are stored in FND_STATTAB. Statistics can be gathered for *all* installed products (from the FND_PRODUCT_INSTALLATIONS) or for a specific application. Before gathering the statistics, this procedure also keeps a backup of the earlier statistics that can be restored to previous status if the application runs slower after the statistics are gathered.

GATHER_ALL_COLUMN_STATS This procedure gathers the column statistics on all the columns for a given schema, as listed in the

FND_HISTOGRAM_COLS table. FND_HISTOGRAM_COLS can be populated using the LOAD_HISTOGRAM_COLS procedure.

ANALYZE_ALL_COLUMNS This procedure analyzes all the indexed columns for all the tables in a given schema. The concurrent request equivalent is "Analyze All Index Columns." This procedure is similar to executing an ANALYZE with a FOR ALL INDEXED COLUMNS option. In this case, Oracle creates histogram information for all indexed columns of a table. This improves query performance and also speeds up the gather statistics process since the nonindex columns will be eliminated.

LOAD_XCLUD_STATS This procedure loads the default statistics as specified in the SEED data table.

LOAD_XCLUD_TAB This procedure is used for SEED data manipulation for interface tables. It is meant for Oracle internal use only.

FND_EXCLUDE_TABLE_STATS Two versions of this procedure exist. One loads statistics for all the tables for a particular schema and the other loads statistics for a given table in a given schema.

LOAD_HISTOGRAM_COLS This procedure is used for SEED data manipulation for interface tables. It is meant for Oracle internal use only.

CHECK_HISTOGRAM_COLS This procedure produces a report on which indexed columns for a list of given tables is a good candidate for histograms. For a given list of comma-separated tables, this procedure checks the data in all the leading columns of all the nonunique indexes of those tables and determines whether histograms need to be created for those columns.

VERIFY_STATS This procedure produces a report on the statistics of the given list of objects. For a given list of comma-separated tables, or for the given schema name, this procedure reports the statistics in the data dictionary tables for the tables, indexes, and histograms. FND_STATS.VERIFY_STATS can be executed to check information about last statistics gathered.

CBO Trace To produce a CBO Trace, use the following method. First, run the FND_CTL package using

```
sqlplus apps/pwd
sql>execute fnd_ctl
```

Then submit a Concurrent Manager program called Monitor CBO Activity.

The CBO Trace shows the execution plan, query text, and parameters used by the optimizer and displays information about object statistics.

Using the Concurrent Manager to Gather Statistics

Gather Schema Statistics Concurrent Program can also be used to collect object statistics. Following are the steps to implement this:

1. Log on to the Oracle Application Suite as system administrator.

2. Navigate to the Submit Request window.

3. Fill out the appropriate parameters.

4. Submit the request.

Note that if the schema name is ALL, statistics for all objects in the applications-specific schema are collected. These applications are identified in the FND_PRODUCT_INSTALLATIONS table. This procedure gathers table-level statistics, index-level statistics, and column-level histogram statistics for all columns listed in the FND_HISTOGRAM_COLS table.

Table 9-2 shows Concurrent Manager programs that can be used.

Program Name	Description
FNDGAICST	Analyze all index column statistics
FNDBKTST	Backup table statistics
FNDRSTST	Restore table statistics
FNDGCLST	Gather column statistics
FNDGACST	Gather all column statistics
FNDGTST	Gather table statistics
FNDGSCST	Gather schema statistics

TABLE 9-2. *Concurrent Manager Programs*

Initialization Parameters for Implementing CBO in Oracle11i

Various initialization parameters must be set for CBO to function properly in Oracle11i. The current settings can be inspected by running $FND_TOP/sql/ afchkcbo.sql. You can also look at the init.ora parameters manually by selecting them from v$parameter or by editing the $ORACLE_HOME/dbs/init<ORACLE_SID>.ora file. Table 9-3 shows the initialization parameters used for implementing CBO.

Parameter	Set To	Explanation
COMPATIBLE	8.1	Set to the current release to allow you to use the latest features.
OPTIMIZER_ FEATURES_ENABLE	8.1	Set to the current release so that the latest optimization is utilized.
DB_BLOCK_ MULTIBLOCK_ READ_COUNT	8	Signifies the number of blocks read in one I/O operation during sequential scans. If set to a higher value, full table scans will be chosen.
SORT_AREA_SIZE	Set appropriately to minimize disk sorts	A large sort area size means that larger sorts run faster, involving less writes to the temporary tablespace. Size this parameter so that less than 2 percent of your sorts are disk based.
QUERY_REWRITE_ ENABLED	TRUE	11i uses materialized views and function-based indexes. Both these features need the query rewrite feature turned on.
OPTIMIZER_MODE	CHOOSE or ALL_ROWS	Consider using ALL_ROWS for a reporting instance and CHOOSE or FIRST_ROWS for the production instance.

TABLE 9-3.   *Initialization Parameters Used for Implementing CBO*

Understanding Plan Stability

You know that CBO is the preferred and accepted optimization method for Oracle11i modules. One of the critical milestones of any upgrade to 11i is the seamless migration of custom code. The number and complexity of custom programs in your environment are the critical factors that will affect your migration schedule and milestones. Custom applications need to be effectively migrated to the 11i environment without affecting performance. If the custom modules have been developed in a version prior to 11i, they have probably been optimized and tuned for a rule-based environment. Changing to CBO as part of the upgrade will undoubtedly affect many of the modules. Implementing the custom programs using RBO and implementing the core modules using CBO would alleviate the immediate need to test each and every custom program to make it work in the cost-based world.

Plan stability allows upgrades to move seamlessly from rule-based to cost-based environments with custom modules, and it allows CBO to be used for the core modules. Using plan stability, you can influence the optimizer to pick up an execution plan that you have chosen as the best for optimal performance. This plan will override all other plans. Plan stability allows

- Well-tuned applications to force the use of the desired SQL access path

- The execution plan to be consistently maintained despite database changes

- The execution plan to be controlled without the use of hints. Hints are specified within the SQL statement itself with a purpose of influencing Oracle's optimizer to use a particular execution plan.

The execution plan is implemented using *stored outlines*, which allow execution plans for SQL to be stored so that the plan remains consistent throughout schema changes, database reorganizations, and data volume changes. After the outline has been created, when the SQL statement is executed, a stored outline can be invoked to force the optimizer to use that plan. You can generate a stored outline for one statement or for all statements.

You might consider implementing stored outlines for critical reports/processing when you believe it's necessary to insulate external factors. For example, a daily morning custom business report containing information about product-wise/region-wise sales may be used for critical decision making. Using a stored outline would assure the DBA of performance stability on this report.

NOTE
When you are using stored outlines, Oracle uses hints to the CBO for influencing the execution plan. Usage of plan stability is restricted by how effectively you can control the execution plan using hints. This means that you need to implement CBO to use plan stability effectively.

When you generate a stored outline for a SQL statement, the following information is stored about the query:

- Access methods

- Join order and methods

- View/subquery merging

TIP
Because there is a one-to-one mapping between SQL text and a stored outline, Oracle opens a different outline even if two SQL statements differ by a space or case. Always use bind variables instead of literals in your SQL code. (This recommendation/ restriction is similar to writing a similar SQL statement to avoid reparsing.)

Benefits of Plan Stability

Plan stability and CBO complement one another. You can think of plan stability as a way of enforcing the execution plan for SQL statements that run best using that plan. Identifying those statements is key.

Oracle maintains the plan outlines for SQL statements through

- Migrating from one version of Oracle to another version

- New statistics on the objects (ANALYZE TABLE/INDEX)

- init.ora parameter changes (OPTIMIZER_MODE, SORT_AREA_SIZE)

- Database reorganization (export/import)

- Schema changes

NOTE
*In general, plan stability should not be implemented
for every SQL statement in an application. This will
defeat the CBOs' purpose. When transitioning from
RBO to CBO, old (existing) SQL statements can
continue to use RBO (using stored outlines) but
newer development projects can use CBO. Consider
implementing stored outlines as a planned phase for
moving to CBO. RBO will be unsupported by
Oracle eventually.*

TIP
*Consider using a stored outline when transitioning
from RBO to CBO. Until the complete transition
occurs (and even beyond that), certain statements
can use stored outlines. For example, the statistics
may not be refreshed or may have been accidentally
deleted during transition, thus causing the execution
plan to change drastically, causing a degradation.
This can be avoided by using stored outlines.*

Plan stability can also be helpful in ensuring that certain critical SQL statements
suffer no performance glitches because of changes in the environment, such as
database reorganizations, optimizer mode setting, and sort area size setting.

NOTE
*Remember that plan stability is limited by the
capability of hints. Any optimizer (however
sophisticated) does have its list of glorious
uncertainties.*

The plan stability feature is also useful for packaged applications. If the
application vendor distributes outlines along with the application code, plan stability
will ensure performance of the application, regardless of what kind of optimization is
followed. Plan stability can also be used for mass-distribution of software.

- When you update your version of Oracle, you can use plan stability to ensure
  that the migration does not impact critical queries by creating a stored outline
  for the entire application or critical processes, exporting the processes to a
  dump file, and then using them (if and when required) after migration.

■ You can benchmark query performance on a smaller test environment by using a combination of plan stability features and migrating production statistics to test instances. In this way, you can eliminate creating a large test instance.

TIP
It is generally recommended that you initiate implementing stored outlines at the time of development (custom applications) or setup and deployment (purchased application). The bottom line should be to plan well and avoid ad hoc deployment.

Creating, Using, and Managing Stored Outlines

You create stored outlines by using a create outline command or by using the CREATE_STORED_OUTLINE session parameter.

For the create outline command, use this script:

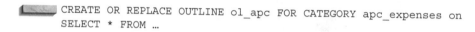

```
CREATE OR REPLACE OUTLINE ol_apc FOR CATEGORY apc_expenses on
SELECT * FROM …
```

CATEGORY indicates the way you want to group stored outlines. If CATEGORY is not specified, Oracle uses the DEFAULT category. A SQL statement can have any number of outlines as long as each outline is in a different category. Note that this command requires the CREATE ANY OUTLINE privilege.

NOTE
Using the naming conventions in this example, OL_ for all outlines and APC_ for all the Accounts Payable Custom categories, lets you track and identify any category to a stored outline and helps you identify an object as an outline.

To use the CREATE_STORED_OUTLINE session parameter, use this script:

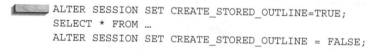

```
ALTER SESSION SET CREATE_STORED_OUTLINE=TRUE;
SELECT * FROM …
ALTER SESSION SET CREATE_STORED_OUTLINE = FALSE;
```

In this method, the stored outline name is system generated. If CATEGORY is not specified, Oracle again generates a category called DEFAULT. Because Oracle does not use stored outlines by default, after the outline has been created for a specific query, Oracle must be told to use the outline. You do this by setting the use_stored_outline session-level parameter. You can set it to TRUE, FALSE, or to a category name. For example,

```
ALTER SESSION SET USE_STORED_OUTLINES TRUE/FALSE/APC;
```

The category name need not be set in quotes. Note that USE_STORED_OUTLINES and CREATE_STORED_OUTLINES cannot be specified at the instance level. They can be implemented at session level only.

NOTE
CREATE_STORED_OUTLINES and USE_STORED_OUTLINES are session-level parameters and cannot be included in the init.ora file or set for the entire instance.

TIP
Consider enabling USE_STORED_OUTLINES for all users or for certain users when they log in by using an AFTER LOGON TO DATABASE trigger. This trigger is invoked after a user connects to a database. By using this trigger, you can force the use of outlines by users.

Managing outlines involves dropping, updating, and purging stored outlines within a category. Oracle provides a package called OUTLN_PKG to help you achieve this. To exercise control, only DBAs should be allowed to execute this package. Here are some examples that show you how the package can be used:

■ To drop all the outlines for the category ol_hr:
```
EXECUTE OUTLN_PKG.DROP_BY_CAT('APC');
```

■ To change all outlines of one category to another category:
```
EXECUTE OUTLN_PKG.UPDATE_BY_CAT('DEFAULT','ARC');
```

This command can be used to move outlines from the testing mode to production-like mode.

Examples of Using Plan Stability

Following are some examples that demonstrate use of the plan stability feature. The first example contains a procedure that uses plan stability for migrating from one version of Oracle to the next. The method consists of exporting the stored hints and saving them. The second example discusses a method of using production statistics on a test instance.

Example 1: Transporting Stored Outlines

This example demonstrates use of plan stability to preserve the outlines before performing database upgrades. All stored outlines (or specific categories) can be exported and preserved before upgrading. After upgrades, if any changes in the execution plan or performance bottlenecks are observed, specific outlines or categories can be imported to ensure that the execution plan is maintained. You can export outlines using any of the following three options:

- **All outlines**   Export full table OL$ and OL$HINTS

- **For a specific category or categories**   Specify QUERY='WHERE CATEGORY="HR_BENEFITS"' in the export command

- **For a specific outline or outlines**   Specify QUERY='WHERE OL_NAME="HR_BENEFITS"' in the export command

TIP
Consider using stored outlines for applications that are deployed at different locations. In this case, you can use plan stability to ensure that all customers are using the same execution plan.

The OUTLN schema contains two tables: OL$ and OL$HINTS. These tables are created in the default tablespace for SYS schema. If you are going to implement many outlines, it is recommended that you move these tables to a separate tablespace using the export/import method. Follow these simple steps:

1. Export the tables OL$ and OL$HINTS using

   ```
   exp USERID=OUTLN/pwd     FILE=outline_file   TABLES=OL$,OL$HINTS
   ```

2. Drop tables OL$ and OL$HINTS from the OUTLN schema.

3. Create a new tablespace called OUTLINES, and change the default tablespace for user OUTLN to tablespace OUTLINES.

4. Import the two tables into the new tablespace.

```
imp USERID=OUTLN/pwd  FILE=outline_file TABLES=OL$,OL$HINTS
```

NOTE
*The schema OUTLN is not intended to be used as
a schema for administering stored outlines. Oracle
grants only two system privileges to this schema:
execute any procedure and unlimited tablespace.
The OUTLN schema is used only for exporting and
importing the two outline tables—for example, from
test instance to production instance.*

Example 2: Copying Production Statistics to a Test Instance

By copying production statistics to a test instance, you can tune and benchmark
queries with smaller amounts of data and still be able to simulate the production
environment by moving only the statistics and stored outlines from a production
instance. You don't need to create a test instance that is similar in size to the
production instance.

Following is a step-by-step procedure that simulates a production environment
on a test instance for query execution testing. Your objective here is to use the test
instance to find the best execution plan, create outlines for the statements, and then
use the outlines in production.

1. Use FND_STATS.CREATE_STAT_TABLE to create a statistics table.

2. Export the statistics table to create a dump file, and import the statistics into
the test instance.

3. Use DBMS_STAT.IMPORT_SCHEMA_STAT to import statistics into the
test instance.

After testing the application, you can identify the outlines to be used and then
export these outlines back to the production instance using the following steps.

1. Test the application on the TEST instance and create stored outlines:

- Use EXPLAIN PLAN and Oracle Trace to identify a good execution plan.

- Create a category and stored plans under that category.

2. Move identified stored outlines from test to production:

Use a standard export utility to export stored outline tables and import them
into a production instance. When executing the import, you may want to

use the IGNORE = YES option. This will ensure that the rows you import are appended into various tables and will retain the rows already existing.

TIP
Plan stability involves identifying a best execution plan for a query and always using it. It may not be effective for environments in which lots of changes (e.g., data type change, index change, etc.) occur. Implement plan stability only in a stable environment.

Data Dictionary Views, Stored Packages, and Other References

This section provides details on methods that you can use to look up various outlines in the data dictionary. It also contains information about the Oracle provided package that lets you drop outlines, plus other reference material on plan stability.

The dictionary views for stored outlines are DBA_OUTLINES and DBA_OUTLINE_HINTS. In addition, ALL_OUTLINES, ALL_ OUTLINE_HINTS, USER_OUTLINES, and USER_OUTLINE_HINTS views are available.

To query all the outlines for a given category, use the following command:

```
SELECT name, category FROM DBA_CATEGORY WHERE category ='APC_EXPENSES';
```

To query all the hints for a given outline, use the following command:

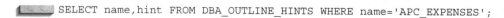
```
SELECT name,hint FROM DBA_OUTLINE_HINTS WHERE name='APC_EXPENSES';
```

Note the following:

- Stored outline and category names are not part of Oracle objects and cannot be found in DBA_OBJECTS.

- A schema called OUTLN is created during installation of Oracle8i. This schema owns the two tables required for maintaining stored outlines. Use the OUTLN schema to manage stored outlines centrally. This schema also helps export and import stored outlines across different instances. The default password for OUTLN schema is OUTLN. It is recommended that the password of this schema be changed for security reasons. Also, make sure that the default tablespace for the OUTLN schema is changed.

- If CREATE_STORED_OUTLINES is set to TRUE and a lot of SQL statements involving literals are being executed, the default system tablespace could get full. To fix this situation, delete the unused procedure using this command:

  `EXECUTE OUTLN_PKG.DROP_UNUSED;`

  In the DBA_OUTLINES view, a column called "Used" indicates whether a stored procedure is used or unused. When a stored outline is created, this column value is set to UNUSED and it remains UNUSED until a query uses the stored outline. At that point, the column value is changed to USED and remains that way. The procedure DROP_UNUSED provides a method of dropping stored outlines that are never used.

- Always create outlines under named categories. Also, always provide a specific name for the outline so that it can be uniquely identified. If the outlines are not named, CREATE OUTLINE statements could give the following error:

  ORA-18004 error outline already exists

  Providing names to category and outlines helps to control and track them.

- SQL_TRACE does not indicate whether a stored outline was used. TKPROF does provide an indication that the outline was used.

- Oracle does not keep track of the relationship between SQL Text and OUTLINE.

Summary

Cost-based optimization in Oracle11i is much more efficient than rule-based optimization. Using CBO enables Oracle applications to make use of such features as partitioning, function-based indexes, materialized views, and other Oracle8i features. The optimizer mode initialization parameter (OPTIMIZER_MODE) should be set either to CHOOSE or ALL_ROWS. The core tables for 11i should be analyzed to gather statistics periodically. There are two ways to collect statistics in 11i—using a package called FND_STATS and using the Gather Schema Statistics concurrent request. FND_STATS has features that store statistics for a table or schema in a table and transport it to another schema. (Note that you cannot import schema statistics into a schema with a different name. For example, you cannot export statistics for a schema called TEST and import it into a schema called TEST1.)

Plan stability provides a viable solution to move the custom code from the rule-based to the cost-based world gradually and yet upgrade to 11i. Plan stability is implemented by creating stored outlines. Stored outlines are stored in a schema called OUTLN in the form of hints. Stored outlines can be invoked in custom modules. OUTLN schema is created as part of the installation of Oracle 8.1.x and should not be deleted.

This chapter provided an overview of CBO in the context of Oracle11i. For more information on some of the Oracle8i features in the context of applications, refer to Chapter 18.

CHAPTER
10

Open Interfaces

- What are open interfaces?
- Review of Oracle Financials open interfaces
- Build your own open interface
- Overview of programming techniques
- Tune the interface programs

racle open interfaces provide a method of importing data from other sources, such as legacy applications, into the Oracle Financials environment. In this chapter, we will discuss concepts of, terminology for, and types of open interfaces. In addition, we will discuss a typical architecture plan for setting up open interfaces to help you customize your interfaces. We will evaluate various techniques that can be used for implementing open interfaces, and we'll discuss some of the main features, using examples. We will list steps to build a good open interface and also look at some tuning opportunities around some of these custom-built open interface programs. The main objective of this chapter is to help you understand Oracle open interfaces and provide you with some techniques that could help you deploy similar interfaces in your environment.

What Are Open Interfaces?

Open interfaces are used for moving data from external sources, such as legacy applications, into Oracle Financials applications. Open interfaces also help you integrate new applications such as payroll, accounts payable, and accounts receivable with Oracle Financial applications. For example, using the Payables open interface program, you can import invoice data from external sources into Oracle's interface tables. Oracle provides concurrent programs to import data applications using interface tables. Using open interfaces, you can import data into the application as well as load mass data through a batch program.

Oracle does provide many open interfaces, but it does not always provide coordination of related tables. In addition, some of the tables do not have open interfaces. In such circumstances, custom interfaces can be developed to support business functionality.

Here are the steps involved in a typical custom interface solution:

1. Create and transfer the data files from external sources.

2. Perform data validations to weed out bad data.

3. Define error-handling routines to ensure that bad records are fixed and fed back into the system.

4. Populate interface tables with clean data.

There are two types of open interfaces: inbound and outbound. This process flow applies to inbound interfaces only.

Oracle Financials Open Interfaces

Oracle provides interfaces for several tables in the Financials area. It also provides programs for importing data that can be run as concurrent programs and integrated with the applications environment. Always review these programs to determine whether they fulfil your requirements. It is advisable to resort to custom interface solutions only if your business requires specific changes not supported by these programs.

Here are some advantages of using Oracle provided interface programs:

- Data is automatically converted and mapping is automatic as long as you feed in correct input data.

- These programs can take input from various sources.

- They provide a way to review load results and identify error records.

- They provide a feature to archive source data when importing.

The custom *feeder program* is used for importing detailed accounting transactions from an external system into Oracle Financials interface tables. A typical feeder program could be written using SQL, PL/SQL, or the SQL Loader utility. Feeder programs can be written in many ways, using the techniques described in "Overview of Programming Techniques," later in this chapter.

The following open interfaces are available in Oracle11i:

- **Oracle General Ledger**

    - Budget upload

    - Importing journals

    - Loading daily rates

- **Oracle Payables**

    - Credit card transaction interface

    - Payables open interface

    - Purchase order matching

    - Invoice import

- **Oracle Purchasing**
    - Requisitions open interface
    - Purchasing documents open interface
    - Receiving open interface
- **Oracle Receivables**
    - AutoInvoice
    - AutoLockbox
    - Customer interface
    - Sales Tax Rate interface
    - Tax Vendor extension
- **Oracle Projects**
    - Activity Management Gateway
    - Client extensions
    - Transaction imports
    - Missing interfaces information
- **Oracle Assets**
    - ACE interface
    - Budget open interface
    - Mass Additions interface
- **Physical Inventory/Cash Management**
    - Bank Statements open interface
    - Forecasting
    - Reconciliation

Building Your Own Open Interface

Custom solutions can be built to implement open interface functionality, especially when Oracle does not provide an interface to fit your specific business requirement. Building a custom interface option opens up several new and exciting areas and technologies. For example, the validation and loading process could be coded using procedures written in PL/SQL or Java. The custom interface solution could be automated to include scheduling abilities as well as loading internal Oracle tables from the interface tables using concurrent program abilities.

Any open interface architecture should have the following four features:

- Ability to perform validation of input data from the Oracle lookup tables

- Ability to handle data errors

- Ability to restart the program to continue from a particular point

- Provision for detailed log statistics

Your choice of the tools used for developing interfaces should be based on the factors of validation, error handling, restartability, and logging features.

Overview of Programming Techniques

The interface programs or the feeder programs can be developed using a variety of languages and techniques. It is, however, a good idea to use a standard set of tools to improve portability and ease of maintenance. Also, the setup procedure should be documented so that it can be redone at the time of application upgrades. This section provides more details on some of the programming techniques. The section also contains more information on new features available since Oracle8i that can enhance the functionality of the interface.

SQL Loader

SQL Loader is a good choice for mapping source data (from a flat file) into temporary tables in Oracle. SQL Loader works using a control script that contains a mapping of the source data and the Oracle table. The control script contains positional information and can also be delimited by special character, such as the comma (,). SQL Loader can be executed in UNRECOVERABLE mode as well. In this mode, no log information is collected, and this method is suitable for loading large volumes of data. The load script can also be executed using a Korn shell script wrapper. It is usually invoked from the command line.

PL/SQL Scripts and Stored Programs

PL/SQL programs are standalone blocks that are coded in PL/SQL. Subprograms are also coded in PL/SQL and can be functions, procedures, or packages. *Functions* typically accept specific arguments and return a transformed value. Procedures are

PL/SQL blocks that accept specific input and output arguments and are mainly used for performing a repetitive task. *Packages* are functions and *procedures* grouped together. The advantage of using a package is that all functions and procedures that form the package are cached together resulting in better throughput. In the context of interface development, this method is optimal for the following reasons:

- The PL/SQL Engine is part of the Oracle RDBMS and hence gives better performance.

- Validation of data can be done using PL/SQL. Hence, invalid data can be identified in the same program that loads into the interface tables.

- PL/SQL programs can be run as concurrent programs and scheduled.

- PL/SQL provides several features that could be useful for error handling (see the section "Autonomous Transactions"), the ability to execute packages with the permissions of the person who runs the package (see the section "Invoker's Rights"), and a bulk binding facility (see the section "Bulk Binding in PL/SQL").

- Functions provide a convenient way to implement lookups.

- PL/SQL provides the ability to restart a load that is incomplete. It also provides speed, validation facility, and great logging facility.

Korn Shell Scripting

Shell scripting provides a method of wrapping around the interface or feeder programs. Shell scripts also provide a way to schedule the job in the background.

XML Scripting

XML (eXtensible Markup Language) technology is increasingly supported by Oracle products and is a standard for Internet-based transactions. XML can describe any type of transaction and provides custom extensions without using proprietary data format. XML provides portable data, which is critical for any Internet-based application. XML is more robust and affordable as compared to Electronic Data Interchange (EDI). Consider using XML as a long-term interface solution.

Autonomous Transactions

The *autonomous transactions* feature has been available in PL/SQL since version 8.1. This feature could be useful in developing error tracking as well as logging facility in the context of developing a feeder program or custom interface programs. The concept is good to know for an administrator in areas other than applications as well.

The autonomous transactions feature in Oracle8i provides PL/SQL developers with a way to suspend their main transaction (T1), perform SQL operations (T2), commit or rollback those operations, and then resume the main transaction (T1). Transaction T2 is committed even if changes in Transaction T1 have to be rolled back. Further, any changes made in transaction T2 are immediately visible to other transactions regardless of whether transaction T1 commits or not.

Following is a simple example of an autonomous transaction. Note that the boldface clause identifies the procedure log_error as an autonomous transaction.

```
CREATE OR PROCEDURE log_error IS
    (vSQLCODE NUMBER)
PRAGMA AUTONOMOUS_TRANSACTION;
vERROR_MSG VARCHAR2(100);
BEGIN
    vERROR_MSG := SQLERRM(vSQLCODE);
    INSERT INTO error_file VALUES (vSQLCODE, vERROR_MSG,SYSDATE);
    COMMIT;
END;
/
```

This procedure can be called from any other procedure whenever an error is encountered. For example, in our main PL/SQL block, we can say

```
...
WHEN OTHERS THEN
    log_error(SQLCODE);
END;
...
```

Even if the main transaction is rolled back, procedure *log_error* always commits and we can track all the error logs. Note that a procedure is defined as an autonomous transaction by including the line *PRAGMA AUTONOMOUS_TRANSACTION* in the declarative section.

Once an autonomous transaction is started, it executes totally independent of the main transaction. In addition, one autonomous procedure can call another autonomous procedure. The only limits on this are resource limits. Every autonomous transaction opens a new transaction, so you need to watch out for the number of transactions and control the number of transactions using the init.ora parameter *TRANSACTIONS*.

Oracle already uses similar functionality internally to handle updates of system resources. It is called *recursive transactions*. For example, when an application uses a noncached sequence, the next sequence number is updated in the database regardless of whether the application using the sequence has committed or not.

Following are the benefits of using autonomous transactions:

- Autonomous transactions are truly independent of the main transactions. This makes them useful for logging events and errors.

- The main transaction need not know about the called procedure's autonomous operation. For example, in the preceding code example, any procedure that calls *log_error* does not know that it is an autonomous transaction. This helps you write modular code.

- Autonomous transactions are fully functional and are available in PL/SQL only. Oracle plans to make this feature available for OCI (Oracle Call Interface) as well in a later version.

Examples of Autonomous Transactions

The first example shows how autonomous transactions can be used for auditing certain tables by duplicating values in Audit Tables (regardless of whether or not the changes are committed). This example shows implementing autonomous transactions using a database trigger.

The following script uses a table called PARTS and creates an autonomous PRE-INSERT trigger on it to duplicate or shadow records into the PARTS_LOG. Even if the insert transaction is rolled back, PARTS_LOG is still updated with the information along with a data stamp and a user name.

```
-- NOTES
-- This script demonstrates the use of autonomous transactions for
-- auditing certain critical tables (in this case the PARTS table).
-- This is implemented by creating a-- trigger on PARTS table.  The
trigger
is a PRE-INSERT autonomous
-- trigger. The trigger
-- adds certain fields as well as the timestamp and username in
-- the audit table PARTS_LOG.
-- This script also demonstrates an example of autonomous triggers.
-- Note that usually COMMIT is not allowed in triggers but it is
-- allowed in autonomous triggers.

-- create a main table and its shadow table
REM -- Change name of the spool file
spool auto_tran_example1.rep
DROP TABLE parts;
DROP TABLE parts_log;
CREATE TABLE parts (pnum NUMBER(4), pname VARCHAR2(15));
CREATE TABLE parts_log (pnum NUMBER(4), pname VARCHAR2(15),
    creation_date date, created_by varchar2(30));
```

```
-- Trigger to insert shadow rows in PARTS_LOG table whenever
-- rows are inserted in PARTS
CREATE OR REPLACE TRIGGER parts_trig
BEFORE INSERT ON parts FOR EACH ROW
DECLARE
    PRAGMA AUTONOMOUS_TRANSACTION;
BEGIN
    INSERT INTO parts_log VALUES (:new.pnum,:new.pname,sysdate,
             sys_context('userenv','session_user'));
    COMMIT;
END;
/
prompt Test Results - Auditing using Autonomous Trigger
prompt First Insert a record into parts table and COMMIT
INSERT INTO parts VALUES (1333,'Item 1333');
COMMIT;
prompt Next Insert a record into parts table and this time ROLLBACK
INSERT INTO parts VALUES (2444,'Item 2444');
ROLLBACK;
prompt Note that the original table contains only the first row
prompt But the log table contains both records along with information like
prompt date stamp and the user-id.

SELECT * FROM parts ORDER BY pnum;
     PNUM PNAME
--------- ---------------
     1333 Item
SELECT * FROM parts_log ORDER BY pnum;
PNUM          PNAME            CREATION_DT        CREATED_BY
1333          Item 1333        20-MAR-01             SIYER
2444          Item 2444        21-FEB-01             SIYER
```

The next example illustrates using an autonomous procedure to implement error logging:

```
-- NOTES
-- This script demonstrates the use of autonomous transactions for
-- logging errors (in this case when INSERTING into PARTS table).
-- This is implemented by creating a table called MODULE_ERRORS
-- and an autonomous procedure called LOG_ERROR.  The main body contains an
-- insert statement.  Whenever there is an error, a record
-- is generated and committed in the MODULE_ERRORS table even if the
-- transaction is rolled back.
-- Note that if we did not have autonomous transaction feature,
-- we would not have been able to commit a record to the MODULE_ERROR but
-- ROLLBACK the entire INSERT operation.
-- *****   STEP 0 : SETUP TEST ENVIRONMENT
```

```
REM -- Change the spool file name
spool auto_tran_example2.rep
DROP TABLE module_errors;
CREATE TABLE module_errors
(key           VARCHAR2(30),
 key_value     VARCHAR2(30),
 msg           VARCHAR2(30),
 module_name VARCHAR2(30),
 program_name VARCHAR2(30),
 error_dt     DATE,
 usr_id       VARCHAR2(30)
);
-- *****   STEP 1 : CREATE autonomous procedure called LOG_ERROR
CREATE OR REPLACE PROCEDURE log_error
( vKEY            VARCHAR2,
  vKEY_VALUE      VARCHAR2,
  vMSG            VARCHAR2,
  vMODULE_NAME    VARCHAR2,
  vPROGRAM_NAME   VARCHAR2,
  vERROR_DT       DATE,
  vUSR_ID         VARCHAR2
) IS
PRAGMA AUTONOMOUS_TRANSACTION;
BEGIN
  INSERT INTO module_errors values
  (vKEY, vKEY_VALUE, vMSG, vMODULE_NAME, vPROGRAM_NAME,
   vERROR_DT, vUSR_ID);
  COMMIT;
END log_error;
/
-- ***** STEP 2:  MAIN ROUTINE WHICH CALLS AUTONOMOUS PROCEDURE LOG_ERROR
DECLARE
   CURSOR c1 is
   select PNUM,PNAME FROM PARTS_LOG order by pnum desc;
   vPNUM NUMBER;
BEGIN
  FOR C1REC IN C1 LOOP
     vPNUM := C1REC.PNUM;
     INSERT INTO PARTS VALUES
         (C1REC.PNUM,C1REC.PNAME,500);
--   If the INSERT is valid then commit the changes;
     COMMIT;
  END LOOP;
EXCEPTION
  WHEN OTHERS THEN
--    If there is any error in INSERT then add a record to the
-- MODULE_ERROR table
--    Calling an autonomous procedure to log this error.
```

```
    log_error('PNUM',vPNUM,'Dup Value','INV',
    'check_bal.pls',sysdate,sys_context('userenv','session_user')
              );
    ROLLBACK;
RAISE;
END;
/
```

Executing the main procedure gives the following output:

```
DECLARE
*
ERROR at line 1:
ORA-00001: unique constraint (SIYER.PARTS_PNUM) violated
ORA-06512: at line 21
SELECT * FROM parts;
PNUM PNAME              BALANCE
--------- --------------- ---------
    1333Item 1333          1000
    2444 Item 2444          500
SELECT * FROM parts_log;
PNUM PNAME            CREATION_ CREATED_BY
--------- --------------- --------- ------------------------------
    1333 Item 1333      29-SEP-99 SIYER
    2444 Item 2444      29-SEP-99 SIYER
SELECT * FROM module_errors;
KEY                             KEY_VALUE                    MSG
------------------------------- ----------------------------- -----------
-------------------
MODULE_NAME                     PROGRAM_NAME                 ERROR_DT
------------------------------- ----------------------------- ---------
USR_ID
-------------------------------
PNUM                            2444                         Dup Value
INV                             check_bal.pls                20-Mar-01
SIYER
```

Notice that the insert on the table PARTS fails and the transaction is rolled back, but the log table MODULE_ERRORS is still populated and is committed.

References on Autonomous Transactions
This section contains some useful reference information on autonomous transactions.

- There is no special way to identify all autonomous transactions for an instance. However, administrators can identify the autonomous

transactions built into stored procedures, functions, and packages using
the following command:

```
SELECT name,type FROM dba_source WHERE
UPPER(text) LIKE '%AUTONOMOUS%'
```

There is no log of autonomous transactions when they are used as part of
an anonymous PL/SQL Block.

- Unlike normal database triggers, COMMIT/ROLLBACK statements are
allowed in case of an autonomous trigger. This feature can be used for
implementing certain audit functionality.

- Increase the TRANSACTIONS parameter in init.ora based on the number of
autonomous procedures open at any time. Autonomous transactions add to
the number of transactions.

- It is important to COMMIT or ROLLBACK at the end of an autonomous
transaction. If this is not done, the entire autonomous transaction is rolled
back with the following error:

```
ORA-06519: active autonomous transaction detected and rolled back
```

If there is no open transaction to commit, the code may be successful.

- SAVEPOINTS can be used with autonomous transactions. Note that rolling
back to a savepoint set before an autonomous transaction will not rollback
the autonomous transaction. This is because the savepoints are distinct for
each transaction and autonomous transaction is a different transaction.

- Only individual procedures or functions can be declared as autonomous.
This means that we cannot declare the entire package as autonomous.
For example,

```
CREATE OR REPLACE PACKAGE log_error AS
        PRAGMA AUTONOMOUS_TRANSACTION;
        PROCEDURE get_error(vSQLCODE NUMBER);
    END log_error;
Warning: Package created with compilation errors
SQL> show error
PLS-00710 - PRAGMA AUTONOMOUS_TRANSACTION cannot be declared here
```

However, we can individually declare ALL (or some) procedures and
functions of a package as autonomous. For example, the following code
is VALID:

```
CREATE PACKAGE BODY PK1…
   CREATE PROCEDURE P1 (..,..)
   PRAGMA AUTONOMOUS_TRANSACTION;
```

```
      BEGIN
         ...
      END P1;
      CREATE FUNCTION F1 (...,...)
      PRAGMA AUTONOMOUS_TRANSACTION;
      BEGIN
         ...
      END F1;
   END PK1;
   /
```

■ In addition to PL/SQL, feeder programs can be developed using Pro*C/C++ , Pro*Cobol, and Java scripts. The choice of the tool depends on the number of transactions, availability of skilled development, and support staff. In some situations, use of extraction, transformation, and loading tools like PowerMart by Informatica may also be considered. Restartability, validation, error handling, ease of use, and cost play critical roles in choosing the right tool to use to create feeder programs.

Invoker's Rights

In the pre–Oracle8i versions, stored programs such as procedures, packages, and functions were executed with *definer's rights*. This means that the object names were resolved and privileges depended on the owner of the PL/SQL code.

In Oracle8i, however, stored procedures can also be defined to use *invoker's rights*. With this feature, you can use the privileges and object resolution of the schema executing the object rather than the object owner. In the context of developing a custom interface program, you could use this facility if you choose to create a separate schema for executing your interfaces, which will have lower privileges than schema such as GL, AP, or PO. By using invoker's rights, you can create a single set of interface procedures or packages and yet execute it with different schemas.

The syntax for using invoker's rights in a PL/SQL block is shown here:

```
PROCEDURE my_proc(mytable_name VARCHAR2)
IS
AUTHID CURRENT_USER
```

Specifying AUTHID CURRENT_USER indicates that the user running the package should be able to perform all the actions required within the body of the package.

The syntax for using definer's rights in a PL/SQL block is shown here:

```
PROCEDURE my_proc(mytable_name VARCHAR2)
IS
AUTHID DEFINER
```

The AUTHID DEFINER is an optional parameter.

By default, when a package or procedure executes, the code is run under the security domain of the schema who owns the compile code. The owner for a package my_package can be found out by running this command:

```
SELECT owner FROM DBA_OBJECTS
WHERE OBJECT_NAME='MY_PACKAGE' AND
          OBJECT_TYPE='PACKAGE';
```

Other users of this package cannot perform specific database actions directly but can get indirect permission by executing the package. This is useful for performing certain types of tasks, but on some occasion it may be beneficial to provide more security or conditional security to the executor of the package.

The Oracle Application Suite makes use of the invoker's rights feature by implementing the same set of PL/SQL based packages used for multiple currency and multiple set of books architecture.

Bulk Binding in PL/SQL

Bulk binding provides improved performance for large loading jobs. Bulk binding is implemented using the NOCOPY flag and improves performance of programs since collection of data is passed between PL/SQL routines instead of one at a time. This reduces context switches between the PL/SQL engine and the SQL engine. This feature is useful for data manipulation commands like INSERT, UPDATE, and DELETE. Bulk binding can be implemented using a command similar to the following in your PL/SQL block:

```
FORALL i IN 1..num_of_invoice_recs LOOP
```

Tuning the Interface Programs

This section provides recommendations for tuning your feeder as well as custom interface programs.

1. Review new features and functionality and check whether any of them can be leveraged to improve performance. For example, if you are using PL/SQL, consider using the bulk binding feature because that will improve performance of large loads.

2. Trace all programs and identify areas to tune using statistics such as

   ■ Number of parses/number of executions (use array functionality)

   ■ Buffer gets/executions (check whether query can be rewritten to improve performance)

- Disk reads/executions (check extents, high water mark, etc.)

- Check whether proper indexes are being used

3. Review initialization parameters and tune specific parameters like SORT_AREA_SIZE, SHARED_POOL_SIZE, and BUFFER_POOL.KEEP parameters. Tuning is discussed in more detail in Chapter 12.

4. Consider using temporary tables for staging area tables. Temporary tables can be created for a session or a transaction and do not need as much administration like normal tables.

5. Appropriately size the rollback segments based on the number of transactions. Also consider creating rollback segments in a locally managed tablespace.

6. Use parallel query options wherever appropriate. Make sure you have sufficient free memory and available CPU capacity. Also set the minimum and maximum server processes in the init.ora file and set automatic_parallel_tuning to True.

Summary

The objective of this chapter was to review open interfaces both in the context of what Oracle provides as well as recommendations for techniques for custom development of interfaces. Oracle provides the open interface option for various tables in the Financials arena. Concurrent programs can be used to import data to Financials tables. However, in some situations, you may have to build your own interface programs. The chapter described various techniques you can use, such as PL/SQL and SQL Loader and also discussed specific useful features like autonomous transactions, invoker's rights, and the bulk binding features. Depending on the nature of the load and criticality of the load, appropriate tuning methods must be used to ensure that the interface programs run efficiently and utilize available resources.

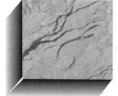

CHAPTER
11

Troubleshooting

- ■ Setting up the printer
- ■ Troubleshooting the cost-based optimizer
- ■ Troubleshooting workflow
- ■ Performance tuning
- ■ Miscellaneous troubleshooting

I n the last few chapters, we reviewed roles and responsibilities of the Financials administrator, discussed features of version 11i, and introduced Oracle technology stack components, installation, configuration, and migration details. As you must have realized, setting up and maintaining version 11i is a fairly complex process that involves knowledge and experience with a number of different related technologies. Oracle's Metalink is an important source of knowledge for information relating to an error or new functionality, or for further exploring a topic. In this chapter, we will review some troubleshooting methods for identifying and fixing common issues.

Setting Up the Printer

In this section of the chapter, we will review the printer setup requirements for the Oracle Application Suite. Printers are used primarily for printing various reports from the application via the Oracle Reports feature. A completed report is sent to the operating system by the Concurrent Manager, which then issues an operating system print command or a custom print command.

The printing process involves

- Identifying the printer to be used

- Identifying the printer type to be used

- Registering printer, printer type, and style

The Concurrent Manager associates a print style and a printer driver with the destination printer's printer type. A printer driver formats the destination printer. An SRW (SQL*ReportWriter) driver formats text and sets page breaks within an Oracle Reports file. SRW drivers are driver files, which are used to define output files of SRW reports into a certain format during the generation of reports. Therefore, SRW drivers only pertain to Oracle Reports output files.

Following are the steps involved in setting up a printer for Oracle applications.

1. Identify print styles. A printer style communicates to the printer the look of a printed output. Print style includes number of lines per page, width of each line, whether the header page should be printed, and other specifications. Print style can be set up by the system administrator via Navigate | Install | Printer | Style, entering the appropriate print style.

2. Create printer drivers. A printer driver uses commands to communicate to the printer how to print using the desired print style. This can be set up by

the system administrator via Navigate | Install | Printer | Driver, entering the
appropriate print driver.

3. Create printer types. A printer type identifies a printer by manufacturer and
model. This can be set up by the system administrator via Navigate | Install
| Printer | Types.

4. Correlate style with drivers in printer types.

5. Register the printer and assign printer type. The system administrator sets
this up via Navigate | Install | Printer | Register.

6. Create SRW drivers, which are required for printing files generated by Oracle
Reports. The drivers are located under $FND_TOP/reports directory.

7. Make changes to concurrent program definitions. This can be set up by
the system administrator via Navigate | Concurrent | Program | Define.

Table 11-1 shows common print styles.

Troubleshooting Printer Setup

The Financials administrator is responsible for setting up the process for configuring
printers so that Oracle application users can print the documents they generate. In
this section, we will discuss some of the common issues with printer setup and also
review how to fix them.

Print Style	Functionality
PORTRAIT	80 characters on a line
DYNAMICPORTRAIT	80 characters on a line with no page break
LANDSCAPE	132 characters on a line
LANDWIDE	180 characters on a line
CHECKS	Standard style for checks
INVOICES	Standard style for invoices

TABLE 11-1. *Common Print Styles*

Report Does Not Print

If your reports are not printing, follow these steps to troubleshoot the issue:

1. Make sure the report file is created and is available.

2. Verify the printer setup.

3. Verify that the Concurrent Report Copies profile option is set to a nonzero number.

4. Verify that the report is printing using standard operating system commands.

Change Printer Driver

If you make changes to the printer driver and then try to print, the driver may not "take effect" and your printer may not print correctly. To fix this issue, you should bounce (shut down and then start up) the Concurrent Manager for the changes to the printer driver to take effect. This is because the Concurrent Manager reads the printing information only when it first starts up.

Pasta Utility

The Pasta utility is shipped with the Oracle Application Suite. This utility helps printing of standard, character-mode reports with English or non-English PostScript printers, which would otherwise not handle UTF8 printing. Make sure your installation has the latest patches available for the Pasta utility. You can download them from the Oracle Metalink site. If the Oracle Application Suite will be installed and used in different languages, then UTF8 is the character set you should pick for creating the database.

Character Set Issues

When you are retrieving report output, your Netscape browser may return question marks (?) instead of national symbols. You can take the following action to troubleshoot this problem:

1. View the report in UNIX and check whether the national characters appear correctly.

2. Check NLS_LANG and your character set. You can do this by using the following command:

   ```
   SELECT * FROM DBA_NATIONAL_CHARACTERSET;
   ```

3. Restart all listeners with the correct environment, and set the character set in Netscape by choosing Netscape | View | Charactersets.

4. The version 11i maintenance scripts can be found in $APPL_TOP/<SID>.env. However, the WebDB 2.5 Listener script adwdbctl.sh references only the environment file in the WebDB (2.5) Home. And the file in <webdb 2.5 home>/<SID>.env doesn't contain an NLS_LANG setting. To solve the problem, edit <webdb 2.5 home>/<SID>.env to include NLS_LANG and restart the WebDB 2.5 Listener. It will show all NLS (natural language support) symbols correctly.

Troubleshooting the Cost-Based Optimizer

In Chapter 9 we discussed details about cost-based optimizer (CBO) and its importance in configuring the 11i environment. Many of the performance issues relating to the 11i application are attributed to improper usage of CBO. In this section, we will cover a checklist of troubleshooting tasks.

To begin, are all the Oracle application init.ora parameters present and correct? Oracle11i requires certain init.ora parameters to be set for CBO use. Check your current settings by running the standard script $FND_TOP/sql/AFCHKCBO.sql. This is supplied in patch 1245516. Alternatively, you can compare your init.ora manually with a correct version. The init.ora file is located in the DBS subdirectory of 8.0.6 $ORACLE_HOME.

You can also check whether statistics on tables and indexes have been gathered. The CBO bases its decisions on the latest statistics gathered by FND_STATS. You must decide carefully how often to run FND_STATS. In the absence of site-specific data to give a more accurate interval, the recommendation is weekly. A longer interval might be recommended for some sites. Transaction tables with high throughput and data volumes require frequent updates. For example, to gather the statistics for all Accounts Receivables tables, run

```
exec fnd_stats.gather_schema_statistics('AR');
```

from sqlplus, or run the concurrent program to gather table statistics. *Always* do this during off hours because of the overhead on resources and performance. You can run FND_STATS.VERIFY_STATS at any time to check when statistics were last gathered. The following query is an alternative to this. It checks the status of individual tables.

```
SELECT table_name, num_rows, blocks,
avg_row_len, to_char(last_analyzed 'MM/DD/YYYY HH24:MI:SS')
FROM dba_tables WHERE table_name IN ('TABLE1', 'TABLE2', ... 'TABLEn');
```

Next, you can modify the WHERE clause according to requirements—for example, use the LIKE clause. Run the FND_STATS package against tables whose

LAST_ANALYZED date is old. A similar query on dba_indexes checks the indexes. The primary concern here is that tables and indexes have *stats*. This document assumes that the stats are present and valid. Database administrators (DBAs) can also ensure that all objects are valid via the AD Administration (adadmin) utility. Statistics cannot be gathered on missing objects. The following query checks indexes on specific tables:

```
SELECT index_name, num_rows, distinct_keys "DISTINCT", leaf_blocks,
clustering_factor "CF", avg_leaf_blocks_per_key "AVG_LB"
FROM dba_indexes WHERE table_name
IN ('TABLE1', 'TABLE2', ... 'TABLEn') ORDER BY index_name;
```

Next, have histograms been created for skewed data? You have skewed data when large differences exist between ranges of values—for example, 10,000 invoices in Q1, 2000 in Q2, 1000 in Q3, and 500 in Q4; or 100 records of type A, 100,000 of type B, and 10 of type C. Run the following query from SQL*Plus:

```
SELECT column_name, num_distinct, num_nulls, num_buckets, density FROM
dba_tab_columns WHERE table_name = ('TABLE1'); ORDER BY column_name;
```

You can run VERIFY_STATS to check that the histograms required have been built. Standard scripts can be used to check histograms by scanning every column. With current releases of the Oracle Server (such as 8.1.x), histograms can be used only with literals. This means you are limited to narrow attribute ranges, such as Yes/No or Open/Close. Developers should use *bind* variables.

Finally, ask yourself these questions:

- Has statistics usage been monitored? Run the package FND_CTL.

- Does your 11i system contain customizations? If so, are you still using the RBO (rule-based optimizer) or the CBO (Cost-based optimizer)? Have the developers used any hints?

If none of these procedures provides acceptable performance, obtain a CBO trace. At this point, the iTAR (Oracle's Technical Assistance Request) should be handed over to a specialist, as reading a CBO trace requires a higher skill level than that needed to read a standard SQL trace.

Troubleshooting Workflow

In Chapters 3 and 4, we discussed Oracle Workflow installation and other issues. Here we will cover some diagnostic issues and tips that can be used if the Workflow

Notification Mailer is not working. Some useful tips for gathering information about your current workflow setup are also included here.

Workflow Support Script (wfsupport.sql)

This script can be downloaded from the Oracle Metalink site. It provides good information about the existing Workflow installation. The script gathers the basic and specific information needed by the Workflow specialists to allow them to expedite resolution of the problem. The script is specifically written for Workflow embedded within Oracle11i. The output of this script is an important document for diagnosing Workflow issues. This script provides the following information:

- Information about WF_WEB_AGENT and WF_ADMIN_ROLE from the WF_RESOURCES table

- Value for APPLICATIONS WEB AGENT system profile

- Workflow version information (status, version, value, owner details) using the wfver.sql script

- Local system name and status information

- Initialization parameter values for AQ_TM_PROCESSES, JOB_QUEUE_PROCESSES, and JOB_QUEUE_INTERVAL

- XML Parser PL/SQL package installation status

- XML Parser Schema Java Class version

- Workflow queue information

- Workflow PL/SQL objects (package) and PL/SQL version information

- Workflow View version information

Workflow Mailer Notification Diagnostics

You can download a script for detecting issues with your Workflow Notification Mailer setup. The script is available as a Zip file called wfdebug.tar.Z from **ftp://oracle-ftp.oracle.com/apps/patchsets/AOL/WORKFLOW/WF_DEBUG/11i/ UNIX/**. Make sure that you download the latest version when troubleshooting a Workflow issue, because this script is constantly updated and improved by Oracle to incorporate latest patch set levels.

The output will check for needed entities and proper configurations for the Workflow Notification Mailer. When it detects an anomaly, it will offer a solution and/or a note on how to remedy the situation. You should run this script for all

Notification Mailer issues prior to logging an iTAR. If this script does not provide a solution, include the output along with the output of the wfsupport.sql script in your iTAR.

To execute this script, follow these steps:

1. Create a staging directory in $OA_HTML/bin called **supp** to download and extract the contents of the Zip file.

2. Copy wfdebug.tar.Z to the $OA_HTML/bin/supp directory.

3. Use WinZip for Win95 or NT to extract the contents of wfdebug.tar.Z into the $OA_HTML/bin/supp directory created in step 1.

4. Substitute the actual APPS user and password in appropriate places.
   Substitute *<PathToAppsEnv>* with the path to the apps env file.
   Substitute *<PathToAppsDbEnv>* with the path to the 8.0.6 env file.
   Substitute *<PathToDbEnv>* with the path to 8.1.6 or 8.1.7 env file.
   Substitute *<PathToApacheTop>* with the path to $APACHE_TOP.

5. Grant read and execute permission on supp_wf_01:

   ```
   #Example:  # chmod 755 supp_wf_01
   ```

   On a Web browser, point your URL to
   http://<hostname>.<domain>:<apacheport#>/OA_CGI/supp/supp_wf_01.

6. Suggestions are provided if discrepancies are observed. You can review the suggestions to resolve the issues.

7. The output of the wfdebug script can be copied to supp_wf_01.html and uploaded as an attachment to your iTar if you are required to send it to Oracle.

Performance Tuning

Performance tuning for Oracle11i needs to be both reactive and proactive. This is critical since the 11i application is completely Internet based and is intended to have high availability and more generic usage. The Financials administrator needs to have access to an extended list of tips and techniques to handle the new challenges of tuning and planning for Internet-based applications. In addition to the traditional approach of tuning the CPU, memory structures, I/O, and so on, the iDBA (Internet Database Administrator) now needs to understand various components of the technology stack and how they interact with each other in the application.

Performance tuning issues are covered in more detail in Chapter 12. Here we will provide a checklist of tuning various components of the Oracle technology stack as a measure of troubleshooting application performance issues.

Tuning the Middle Tier

Tuning the middle tier of the application server includes tuning the Forms server, Report server, Web server, and Admin server. A good understanding of the individual layers of the technology stack will greatly help in the tuning process. The idea will be to collect some statistics about each of the components and then tune them individually. Use the following steps to tune the middle tier of the application server:

1. Identify an objective and set up an expectation baseline.

2. Collect statistics using appropriate tools for each layer of the technology stack.

3. Analyze these statistics based on several parameters. Prepare tuning recommendations that will heavily depend on benchmark available/ prototype done on new features.

4. Tune (execute recommendations) and compare results with the baseline.

In this section, we will list several tuning focus areas for the Financials administrator.

Tuning the Web Server

The general objective should be to reduce a user's wait time after the user has submitted a request. Tuning this layer largely depends on the type of the Web server or the number of Web servers deployed. The function of a Web server is to connect a user request to the appropriate application component. Based on a general usage pattern, the following objectives must be met:

1. Configure a sufficient number of listener processes.

2. Watch out for log files and make sure that the sizes are not very large. Also, develop a process to archive or clean up the log files.

3. The application server could be the same server as the database server or it could be a separate server. For a limited number of users, it may be preferable and more manageable to share a common server (with both database and application server components installed). Care should be

taken to ensure that enough free memory and free processor time are available. For a larger number of users, however, distributing the database server and application server on two different machines is recommended.

4. Estimate the average number of users accessing your Web application concurrently. Then set the minimum number of processes existing at startup equal to that number. Estimates could be based on statistics collected from either the data dictionary or from the application usage statistics.

5. Make sure that the middle layer has an ample amount of free memory allocated to it.

6. Monitor CPU utilization, memory, swapping, and paging on the application server using top, glance, ps, or equivalent utilities. Ensure that the Web listeners are top CPU consumers. Watch for throughput (connections/per second and average response time) for connected users.

7. Swap space should not exceed 70 percent of the allocated space. Watch out for excessive swapping, which could be due to excessive processes or memory leaks. Add more memory if necessary or schedule processes, if possible.

8. The log directory for the server should not be on the same disk as the document root for the site. The server reads files from the document root for every request and writes an entry into the log file for every request. Separating the two will make sure that disk write contention is avoided.

9. Cache hot files, such as the startup HTML page, by specifying them in the listener configuration file.

Tuning the Network

Network utilization monitoring is one of first activities to be done when tuning Internet applications. Use the *nettune -h* command to find a list of parameters to tune. Depending on which flavor of UNIX you are using, check and set the TCP parameters to a high/recommended value. Monitor statistics like bytes sent/bytes returned, rows sent/rows returned, packet losses, retransmits, and SQL*Net overheads. Use the *netstat -i* command to get collisions.

Tuning the CPU

Check your application server for processor utilization. For best performance, Web listeners should be top CPU consumers. Use *sar -um* and *vmstat* utilities to collect utilization statistics. The application server should ideally have free CPU available at all times. The flow chart shown in Figure 11-1 could help analyze CPU bottlenecks and take corrective action.

Tuning Memory

Ensure that there is sufficient free memory available in the middle tier. Use *sar* or *perfview* to get memory and swap related statistics and tune on a regular and continuous basis. Refer to the flow chart in Figure 11-2 to detect memory or swap bottlenecks.

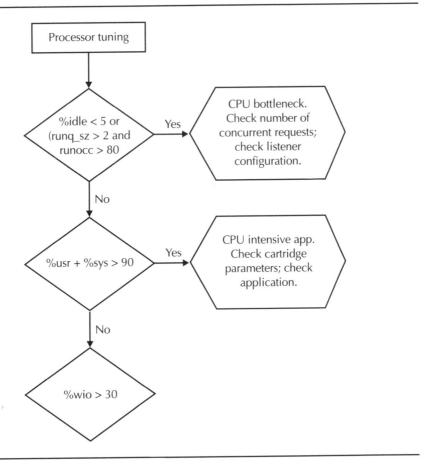

FIGURE 11-1. *Processor tuning flow chart*

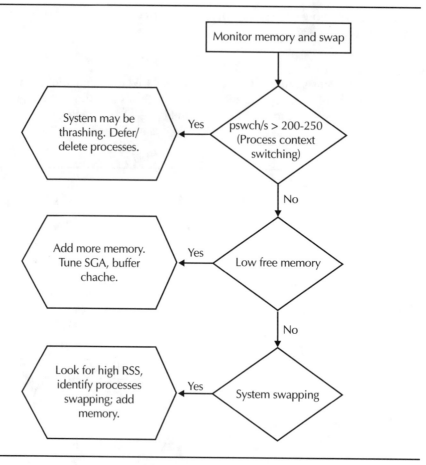

FIGURE 11-2. *Flow chart to monitor memory and swap statistics*

Tuning the Database Tier

Database tuning typically involves performing the following activities:

1. Tune the initialization parameters to reduce waits, increase buffer cache efficiency, and minimize I/O contention.

2. Use multithreaded server implementation to make effective use of memory on the database server.

3. Perform general database tuning including database defragmentation, row chaining removal, hot files identification, and I/O balancing.

4. Review memory, swap utilization on the database server. Use the flow chart shown in Figure 11-2.

5. Consider using a buffer pool for specific tables that are heavily accessed. You can put these tables in the keep pool. Refer to Chapter 18 for more details.

6. Implement the Resource Manager feature in Oracle8i to define a resource plan to limit, restrict, or redirect the processor utilization by specific users. Refer to Chapter 18 for more details on this feature.

7. If your application involves dynamic SQL statement execution, make sure that you are using bind variables to reuse the SQL. This could get you performance benefits, since a hard parse will be avoided if a bind variable is used. Also explore the possibility of setting the new Oracle8i parameter CURSOR_SHARING = FORCE. This will force Oracle to use bind variables for similar SQL statements. Refer to Chapter 18 for more information.

8. Identify expensive SQL statements in the Internet application for possible tuning. You can use Statspack to identify expensive SQLs. Statspack is Oracle's latest package for proactive SQL and database tuning.

Miscellaneous Troubleshooting

If you are using one instance and have other instances on the same box, this section will assist you by providing the 11i load balancing configuration. Complete the following steps:

1. Run RapidWiz to install the first instance on the Database, Apps, and Forms servers.

2. On this first instance, the Forms server will have a metrics server and a metrics client.

3. Create a new Forms server and use the config file or make sure you use the same /mnt points to the first instance.

4. After the second Forms server has been installed, run the following from a prompt:

```
ps -ef |grep
```

You will be looking for the following processes:

- **D2LC60**   The metrics client
- **D2LS60**   The metrics server

5. Navigate to prodcomn/admin/scripts. Find ADFMCCTL.SH, the script for the client. Find ADFMSCTL.SH, the script for the server.

6. Shut both down by using the command:

```
ADFMCCTL.SH STOP -client
ADFMSCTL.SH STOP -server
```

7. Edit the ADFMCCTL.SH script *<client>*.

8. Look for FMS_HOST= *<the server name to first instance>*.

9. Start up the client script by using command *ADFMCCTL.SH START*.

10. Do not bring up the metrics server on the second forms instance.

11. Do not modify the APPSWEB.cfg file, as this already has %LEASTLOADEDHOST% configured.

If you are planning on having multiple instances on one box, you will need to have a metrics server and a metrics client running on different ports for each installed instance. If you do not have a server and a client on each instance, if you shut down the metrics server on the instance running, the server and all the other instances will not be able to load balance.

When Upgrade Fails

This section of the chapter covers a list of things to check after an 11i install or upgrade has failed. Also refer to the *Installing Oracle Applications, Release 11i* and *Upgrading Oracle Applications, Release 11i* manuals for more information on this topic.

NOTE
*The note references are pointers to appropriate document IDs at the Oracle Metalink site. For example, to download note 110372.1, go to the Metalink site (**http://metalink.oracle.com**). Then click Search and enter **110372.1**.*

1. If you have done the install more than once, make sure you follow note 110372.1 (UNIX) or note 107523.1 (NT) before restarting the installer.

2. Make sure that DOMAIN, TERM, and DISPLAY are set prior to the install. On HP, DOMAIN, TERM, and DISPLAY variables must be set within the .login or .profile files of the Oracle and Applmgr users. DISPLAY needs to be set to :0.0 (please see note 2026208.6).

3. On UNIX make sure xhost is set (see note 111161.1 and note 2113863.6).

4. TEMP, TMP, and TMPDIR must be set to :. Most OS requires 650MB; HP requires 1.2GB (11.5.1), and 2.3GB (11.5.2); IBM AIX and Compaq True 64 requires 1.5GB.

5. You must run the installer as root (see Installing Oracle Application 11i pg. 3-18). **Only Exception:** If you are using one user install (where you would use only Oracle to install both $APPL_TOP and $ORACLE_HOME), the user you would be using (such as Oracle) would work.

6. If you are installing on a system that has an existing Oracle installation that has been installed using the Oracle Universal Installer, you might have some permission problems. The Oracle Universal Installer creates a file called oraInst.loc in the /var/opt/oracle or /etc directory that contains the $PATH to your software inventory. The account you are using to install must have *write* permissions in this directory. If it doesn't, the RapidWiz will be unable to start the Oracle Universal Installer without giving any error (refer to note 112659.1). The command to change permission is

```
chmod ### <file name>
```

Where ### represents whether you want the owner, group, or other to have read/write/execute permissions.

7. Make sure you are using the latest software version for 11i:

   ■ Compaq Tru64 UNIX: A85801-01

   ■ Oracle Applications Release 11i CD Pack v3 for Compaq Tru64 UNIX HP-UX: A85807-01

   ■ Oracle Applications Release 11i CD Pack v3 for HP-UX (only available for HP 11)

   ■ IBM AIX: A85802-01; Oracle Applications Release 11i CD Pack v3 for AIX-Based Systems Microsoft Windows NT: A85763-01

   ■ Oracle Applications Release 11i CD Pack v2 for MS Windows NT Sun SPARC Solaris: A85762-01

   ■ Oracle Applications Release 11i CD Pack v2 for Sun SPARC Solaris

8. Oracle and applmgr must belong to the DBA group (this group can be named anything so long as both belong to the same group).

9. If you think your installer is hung, review note 99252.1.

10. Check for any errors in the InstallActions.log, which can be found in the /oraInventory/logs directory or in the config.txt file.

11. If you notice that the application files are not installed when doing a multiuser single node install, and if you also notice that the Installer creates the ORACLE_HOME but does not create the APPL_TOP, review note 113090.1.

12. If this is an upgrade and you receive an error—"ORA 955: *<name>* is already used by an existing object"—review note 113973.1.

13. If you receive a java.lang.NullPointer.Exception error, see note 111324.1.

14. Bug 1527548 is currently open where there may be a corrupt file of disk 8 of 15 for 11.5.2 HP-UX. See note 130204.1.

   ■ Exception thrown from action: copyGroupFromJar

   ■ Exception Name: IOException3_name

   ■ Exception String: I/O error while opening or reading file /tmp/OraInstall/temp454 Exception Severity: 2.

15. If you are on NT and receive the following error during the final stage of 11i installation—"Oracle Universal Installer runs the Configuration Tools which start/create tools"—see note 118521.1.

   ■ CMD.exe Applications Error. The instruction at "0X77f6497f" referenced memory at "0X005c0054."

   ■ The memory could not be "written." Click on OK to terminate the application.

Summary

It is important for the Financials administrator to be able to react to various day-to-day issues in time and minimize downtime due to down production systems. The Oracle Application Suite offers several complex technologies working together, and it is critical that you have sufficient information to troubleshoot various issues and fix them in a timely manner. The Oracle Metalink site is a great source for finding information on various issues and is often the first place to go for troubleshooting a technical issue. Oracle AppsNet (**www.oracle.com/appsnet**) also provides good information on the latest production functionality and availability. This chapter focussed on troubleshooting issues like printer setup, Workflow Notification Mailer setup, and general performance tuning checklists. We will discuss the performance tuning specific to Oracle applications in more detail in the next chapter.

PART

IV

Tuning Your Environment

CHAPTER
12

Application Performance Tuning

- Methods for tuning applications
- Tuning considerations for different applications (DSS, OLTP, Hybrid)
- Oracle server configuration for applications
- SQL tuning
- Optimizer, optimizer modes, using optimizer hints
- Using diagnostic tools
- Data access standards/methods
- DBMS_APPLICATION_INFO package, stored outlines, OUTLN_PKG
- Materialized views

I n the previous chapters, we looked at various features and aspects of the Oracle Application Suite. We also briefly discussed the performance of Oracle applications. In this chapter, we will discuss application performance tuning. This chapter gives an overview of the different components of an application that can be tuned—the client end, the network, the database, and the SQL statements. It also introduces various performance diagnostic tools available in Oracle.

Application *tuning* refers to the process of making changes to the system to best meet the customers' requirements. You need to have a well-planned tuning methodology to ensure optimal performance of any Oracle application. You can use different tuning strategies based on the system that is being used in your organization. For example, the tuning method used for an Online Transaction Processing system is different from the method used for a Decision Support System.

Getting Ready to Tune Performance

The process of application performance tuning involves four steps (including the actual tuning step): collecting information, identifying the problem or bottleneck, verifying the problem, and finally tuning the application. These four phases provide a structured approach that helps in gathering information, identifying the problem, validating it, and iteratively tuning applications until an optimal solution is achieved. Let's look at each of these steps in detail.

Collect Information

This phase involves the following activities:

1. Collect all relevant information pertaining to the problem by meeting with peers and with the client.

2. Verify that all documents to identify system details, including information such as the number of transactions to be executed per minute, the number of users who will be using the system concurrently, the expected response time for transactions, and the acceptable system downtime.

3. Review the existing project documentation.

Identify the Problem or Bottleneck

This phase requires a thorough understanding of the customers' business processes to identify the possible problems. It involves the following activities:

1. Identify a complete list of problems experienced by the customer.

2. Describe and define each and every problem that the customer has faced and document the time, location, and the number of users affected by the problem.

3. Identify any problems that may not have been logged.

4. Identify any other problems that the users perceive might occur in the future.

5. Prioritize the problems and define the critical success factors for solving the problems. This helps to identify and articulate the goals and the customer's expectations.

Verify the Problem

This phase involves further probing and analyzing the problem/bottleneck to check its validity by reproducing the problem at another location. It can involve any of the following activities:

1. Validate the application usage: Address problems related to end user objects, such as forms and reports. You should determine whether user forms are unnecessarily executing queries that result in a heavy load on the server and an increase in the network traffic. You also need to determine whether heavy batch operations are being scheduled at peak time instead of being scheduled at out of peak time.

2. Set benchmarks to best suit the customers' requirements.

3. Identify the most resource-intensive SQL statements by using performance monitoring tools.

4. Check whether the problem/bottleneck is reproducible at another location. This enables you to determine whether the problem is an isolated instance or whether it occurs at other locations in the organization.

Tune the Application

This phase involves creating test cases to improve the application performance, making changes to the system, and measuring the effectiveness of the changes made to the system. It involves the following activities:

1. Identify the test environment where the application will be run. This involves determining which other application should be running on the system at the same time and which other packages will be loaded, and identifying the time of the day when the application should be executed.

2. Define the test cases that will be used. The test cases should clearly represent the problem, be repeatable, and should be run for a sufficient time period to provide valid results.

3. Test each layer of the application to identify the performance bottleneck.

4. Tune the performance bottlenecks.

5. Run the test cases to review and assess the effectiveness of changes.

Tuning Applications

Having looked at the methodology of identifying and defining a problem, let us now look at the components of a system that can be tuned. The process of tuning Oracle applications can be broadly divided into three categories:

- Tuning the client
- Tuning the database and the server
- Tuning SQL

Let's look at each of these components in detail:

Tuning the Client

The process of tuning and optimizing a client computer is a relatively quick and easy task and can improve client performance by better than 50 percent. This step helps in removing the frequently overlooked performance bottlenecks at the client end. Since Oracle clients can be based on multiple operating systems such as Windows 98/NT/2000, the steps to tune these clients varies from one operating system to another. Let's look at some steps that can be used to improve the performance of an operating system and thereby improve the performance of the applications hosted on it:

- Remove/disable screen savers
- Remove wallpapers
- Use service packs

Remove/Disable Screen Savers

Screen savers can use up a lot of system memory—sometimes up to 8MB in a 32MB system. This effectively reduces the amount of memory that is available to applications.

To achieve best levels of performance, it is a good idea to use a screen saver that is less memory intensive or disable the screen saver altogether.

Remove Wallpapers

Just as screen savers use up a lot of system memory, wallpapers also use up memory and monopolize the system bus when the bitmap image has to be refreshed. On certain PCs, you'll notice a delay in starting up applications due to the wallpaper's monopolization of the CPU. It is a good idea to either remove the wallpapers or apply the default system settings for the same.

Use Service Packs

In the Windows NT/2000 environment, service packs contain updates, latest bug fixes, and patches. Service packs help in upgrading the system performance by removing any functional problems that might be encountered. Figure 12-1 shows a System Properties screen that shows the details of the current service pack version.

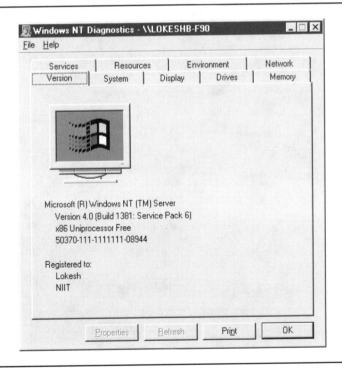

FIGURE 12-1.   *The System Properties display screen showing service pack details*

Improving Application Performance

In the Windows NT/2000 environment, you can boost the performance of foreground or background processes by allocating a larger CPU time slice for the application. Figure 12-2 displays the System Properties Performance screen.

You can set the following values to boost application performance:

- **None** Both the foreground and the background processes are allocated equal amounts of CPU time.

- **Intermediate** Background processes are allocated more CPU time than allocated with None, but the foreground processes still take precedence.

- **Maximum** The foreground processes are allocated the most CPU time.

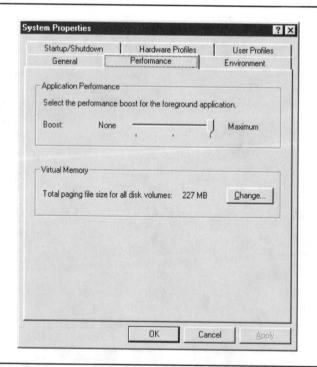

FIGURE 12-2. *The System Properties Performance screen*

TIP
For the Oracle client application, the performance boost for the foreground process should be set to Maximum.

Now let's look at some of the performance monitoring tools. Windows NT/2000 provides a number of tools that help you identify bottlenecks in a system, resources that are being overused, and other performance-related issues. Some of the performance monitoring tools available with Windows NT are

- Performance Monitor

- Task Manager

- Event Viewer

Performance Monitor

The Performance Monitor can be used to monitor performance bottlenecks. It logs the results to a file that can be viewed and analyzed. The following Performance Monitor views can be used to monitor the activities of a network:

- **Chart View**   This is the default view that provides real-time performance data in a graphical format. It can be used to identify resource constraints and bottlenecks in the system. Figure 12-3 shows this view.

- **Log View**   This view is used to write the performance data to a file that can be viewed and analyzed at a later date. It helps you compare the resource usage between peak and off-peak periods.

- **Alert View**   This log alerts you when the performance of a counter exceeds a threshold value.

- **Report View**   This view displays values of key counters in a tabular format.

Task Manager

The Task Manager displays the processes and applications that are active, the amount of CPU and memory that each process is using, and a summary of the CPU and memory statistics for your computer. The Task Manager has the following three tabs:

- **Applications**   Shows all applications that are running and displays the summary statistics of these applications at the bottom of the display.

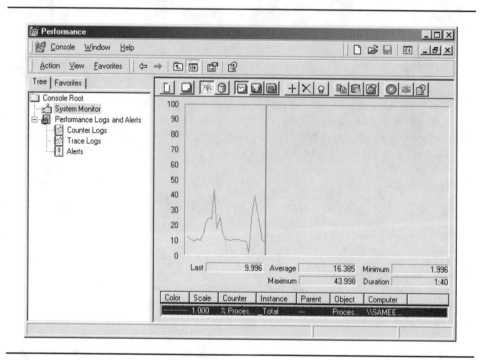

FIGURE 12-3. *Performance Monitor chart view*

The display is divided into two sections, Task and Status. The status of the application can either be Running or Not Responding. This view is also used to terminate unresponsive tasks. Figure 12-4 displays the Applications tab for the Task Manager.

■ **Processes**   Lists the currently running processes, and displays the Image Name, the process ID, the CPU time used, the percentage of CPU time, and the amount of memory used.

■ **Performance**   Displays the overview of the system performance and can be used to detect sudden changes in memory and CPU usage. It is shown in Figure 12-5.

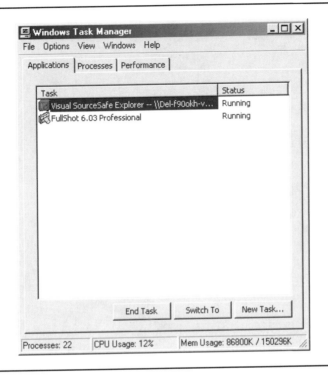

FIGURE 12-4.   *The Applications tab*

Event Viewer

The Event Viewer maintains Application, System, and Security Logs that can be used to monitor the performance of an application. The Application Log is useful for identifying software-related problems. The System Log, shown in Figure 12-6, displays and helps to identify operating system–related events.

Tuning Concurrent Processes and Requests

It is important for the Financials administrator to monitor and tune the concurrent requests to ensure a good balance of online versus batch environments during the normal business cycle. The Financials administrator typically acts as a mediator, or

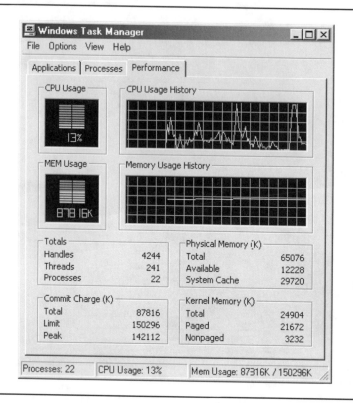

FIGURE 12-5. *The Performance tab*

catalyst, for solving concurrent request issues. The following points can be useful for the administrator in improving the performance of concurrent requests and processes:

- Limit the number of rows in the FND_CONCCURENT_REQUEST table to 5000–10,000. This can be done by regularly purging the Concurrent Manager request either from the SQL prompt or using the Purge Concurrent Request program.

- Regularly analyze the FND tables to ensure that the internal Concurrent Manager uses the appropriate execution plan when manipulating these tables.

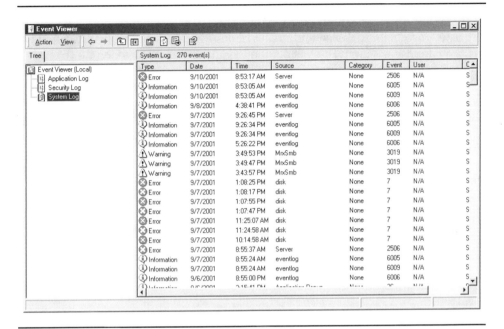

FIGURE 12-6.   *Event Viewer's System Log*

■ Ensure that the FND tables—especially FND_CONCURRENT_REQUEST and FND_CONCURRENT_PROCESSES—do not have chained rows. Chained rows are detrimental to performance.

■ Regularly execute scripts to check how busy various queues are. This will give you an idea of in which part of the day certain queues are busy.

■ Define different queues depending on the nature of the program and the average time taken by programs running in that queue. It is common to define queues—such as SMALL_JOBS, MEDIUM_JOBS, and LARGE_JOBS—as also separate queues for FSG (Financial Statements Generator) or Workflow Background Processes.

■ Keep an eye on the Wait Time, which is the amount of time the requests have to wait before they can be processed. Any wait time greater than 5–10 minutes may indicate scope for refining the process.

■ Some of the performance tuning related to concurrent requests may depend on the way a custom module is designed. It is advisable that such designs are reviewed by the Financials administrator before implementation to avoid issues after deployment.

Tuning the Database and Server

Because your database design and structure must cater to the type of application that you are using, you must consider the type of data that is needed by your application and also identify the structure of the data to get best performance results. To achieve the required performance targets of response time, throughput, availability, and memory utilization, you need to tune application analysis, design, and implementation.

The database server analysis and tuning are critical in an Oracle11i environment, mainly because Oracle8i is a critical component of the Oracle technology stack and a lot of performance gains can be achieved by right-sizing the buffers, I/O limits, and initialization parameters on the server side. The database server tuning involves the following activities:

- Tune the initialization parameters to reduce waits, increase buffer cache efficiency, and minimize I/O contention.

- Use multithreaded server implementation to make effective use of memory on the database server.

- Perform general database tuning, including database defragmentation, remove row chaining, identify hot files, and balance I/O.

- Review memory and swap utilization on the database server.

- Consider using buffer pool for specific tables that are heavily accessed. You can put these tables in the keep pool.

- Implement the Resource Manager feature in Oracle8i to define a resource plan to limit, restrict, or redirect the processor utilization by specific users.

- If your application involves dynamic SQL statement execution, make sure that you are using bind variables to reuse the SQL. This could get you performance benefits since a hard parse will be avoided if a bind variable is used. Also, explore the possibility of setting the new Oracle8i parameter CURSOR_SHARING = FORCE. This will force Oracle to use bind variables for similar SQL statements.

- Identify expensive SQL statements in the Internet application for possible tuning. You can use Statspack to identify expensive SQL statements. Statspack is Oracle's latest package for proactive SQL and database tuning. Refer to Chapter 13 for a complete discussion on Statspack and its implementation details.

Tuning Considerations for Various Applications

Selecting the correct tuning methodology is the key to success. Often, different tuning strategies offer little results; therefore, it becomes essential that you use strategies that offer maximum gains first. Moreover, systems with different purposes such as Online Transaction Processing Systems and Decision Support Systems require different approaches.

The types of applications that use information from a database can be grouped into the following categories:

- Online Transaction Processing Systems (OLTP)

- Decision Support Systems (DSS)

- Hybrid applications

Online Transaction Processing (OLTP)   OLTP applications are high-throughput, insert/update-intensive systems. These systems contain large volumes of data that grow at a rapid pace with thousands of users accessing the system continuously. Airline reservation systems, large order-entry applications, and banking applications fall under this category. High availability, speed, concurrency, and minimum recovery time are the key requirements of such applications.

Following are some key points that should be kept in mind for OLTP applications:

- To avoid performance bottlenecks in dynamically allocating space, explicit space allocation should be made for objects like tables, clusters, and indexes.

- The space allocation for these applications should be planned by checking the growth pattern.

- The index strategy must be carefully designed to avoid index maintenance overheads due to DML (Data Manipulation Language) statements in OLTP applications.

- In these applications, indexing a foreign key helps to modify the child data without locking the parent table.

- For these applications, B-Tree indexes are preferred over bitmap indexes because of locking issues in DML statements. A single B-Tree index entry is locked for a single row; however, when a bitmap entry is locked, it locks a whole range of rows.

- A reverse-key index helps in avoiding frequent B-Tree block splits for sequentially increasing columns.

- Using clusters speeds access on equality queries.

- Code should be shared as much as possible through stored procedures, functions, and packages.

- Variables should be bound rather than using literals to keep parsing to a minimum.

- Constraints are less expensive to process; therefore, constraints should be used instead of application code. The two main constraints that can be considered are referential integrity and CHECK.

- Online transactions are normally short and as such are unlikely to run out of rollback segment space. However, they need enough rollback segments to prevent contention. To identify the number of rollback segments required, you must understand the transaction pattern. For example, for OLTP transactions, the MINEXTENTS value must be at least 10 for small databases and 20 for large databases.

Decision Support System (DSS)   DSS applications are used to prepare user-defined reports from a large collection of data. The data gathered from OLTP systems is fed into a DSS application. DSS applications are data-read–intensive applications. The organization's decision makers can determine the strategies for the organization based on a variety of reports generated by DSS. For example, a marketing tool that captures the buying patterns of consumers can be used by marketing to determine which item sells the most. The key requirements of DSS applications are response time, data accuracy, and high availability.

Some key points that should be kept in mind for DSS applications are listed here:

- Indexes should be used after evaluating their need.

- It is recommended that bitmap indexes with low cardinality columns be used, because they offer faster retrieval of data. For bulk inserts and updates, the init.ora parameters such as SORT_AREA_SIZE, BITMAP_MERGE_AREA_SIZE, and CREATE_BITMAP_AREA_SIZE must be appropriately set.

- Index-organized tables should be used for data access through a primary key or any other key that is prefixed to the primary key. These tables should also be used for queries involving an exact match and complete row retrieval.

- Histograms should be generated regularly for non-uniformly distributed data.

- Clustering must be used wherever possible. For tables that are frequently used in joins, clustering is recommended. Hash clustering gives the best access performance except for tables in which the data is dynamic.

- Partitioning must be used for large amounts of data for which queries usually require recently generated data. It helps in data access with partition scan rather than full table scans.

- Bind variables are problematic in DSS. The optimizer is unable to identify the number of rows returned by the SQL statement when using bind variables. Also, in the case of a DSS application, the same statement might not be used again—unlike in an OLTP environment, in which the statement is repeated several times. In a DSS environment, SELECT statements are used most widely. Generally, the time taken to execute a query is more than the time taken to parse the statement. Hence, there is a much lesser scope for tuning the library cache.

- The execution plan is of utmost importance and must be optimal. The access path chosen is of a high priority and a small variation might cost hours or minutes.

- Parallelized queries, which make the processor work simultaneously to process a single SQL statement, should be used. An SMP (Symmetric Multiprocessor) or MPP (Massive parallel processing) configuration gives the best performance benefits, because the operation can be split across processors on a single system.

The critical tuning elements for a DSS application are

- Data access method
- Parallel executions
- Query optimizer
- Materialized views

These elements are discussed in detail in the next section, "Data Access Methods."

Hybrid Systems   Hybrid systems have both OLTP and DSS applications. Sometimes the data from an OLTP application goes into a DSS application. Therefore, keeping both of these applications separate might involve huge costs and additional infrastructure. Applications such as marketing tools are a combination of both OLTP and DSS applications. In such cases, both applications use the same database. However, different tuning requirements for OLTP and DSS applications can cause performance problems. As a result, you need to make certain compromises to achieve respectable performance.

Although Oracle recommends separate databases for both types of applications, it's possible that customers want to use a single instance for both purposes as data remains the same. In such cases, tuning for both application types becomes difficult, and the contention for resources will be a problem. Some major differences between OLTP and DSS applications that can lead to this contention are listed here:

- OLTP requires more indexes than DSS. In addition, the type of indexes required in both cases might be different.

- OLTP requires a large number of small rollback segments as compared to DSS, which needs larger rollback segments for read consistency.

- For OLTP, a PCTFREE value of 0 will lead to row chaining as rows are updated. However, for DSS applications, the PCTFREE value should be set to 0, as rows are generally not updated.

- OLTP does not require parallel queries, as compared to DSS, which does require them.

- OLTP requires bind variables, as the same SQL statement will be repeated several times. However, for DSS applications, bind variables must not be used, because the optimizer does not know the number of rows returned.

More differences between OLTP and DSS are summarized in Table 12-1.

Now let's look at some of the critical application tuning elements that are used by different applications.

Data Access Methods

To enhance performance of applications, you can use the following data access methods:

- Indexes
- Index-organized tables
- Clusters
- Materialized views
- Histograms

OLTP	DSS
More indexes are needed.	Indexes are not used frequently due to requirements for full table scans.
B-Tree indexes are preferred.	Bitmap indexes are preferred.
Usage of parallel query not required.	Parallel queries are recommended.
Index clusters are recommended.	Hash clusters and partitions are recommended.
PCTFREE should be set, as high update activity is expected.	PCTFREE is not required, as no updates are expected.
Large number of small rollback segments is required.	Less large rollback segments are required.
Usage of shared code with bind variables is recommended.	Usage of bind variables is not recommended.

TABLE 12-1.   *Differences Between OLTP and DSS*

Index-organized tables and clusters are logical structures that are created by the database administrator when necessary. Histograms are statistics that are generated by the *ANALYZE* command, stored in the data dictionary, and used by the optimizer to tune the SQL statement execution.

Indexes

You use indexes to enhance the performance of queries that select only a small number of rows from a table. Indexes come in several types:

- B-Tree
- Bitmap
- Reverse-key
- Function-based

B-Tree Indexes   Balanced tree, or B-Tree, indexes are the default type of index implementations used in Oracle. They are the most common index types found in modern-day relational databases. B-Tree indexes sort the column data of the base tables in an ascending order. They also store a row ID that indicates the position in the indexed table where the remaining data of the row is stored. All these values—the column data and the row IDs—are stored by the index in a tree-structure format.

Let's look at how a B-Tree index works. Consider this example, where the PO_HEADERS_ALL table of your application consists of the following data:

```
SQL> SELECT *
FROM po_header_all;
```

By using various performance tuning tools, you can determine the column on which indexing can improve the performance of the queries. For our example, if a B-Tree index on the LAST_NAME column helps in improving the performance of querying the PO_HEADERS_ALL table, we can create the index on the LAST_NAME column. The following code listing creates an index on the LAST_NAME column of the PO_HEADERS_ALL table.

```
SQL> CREATE INDEX po_header_index
ON po_header_all (po_header_id)
STORAGE (INITIAL 200K NEXT 200K PCTINCREASE 0)
TABLESPACE APPL_IDX;

Index created
```

You should always build your B-Tree indexes on columns whose data is highly *cardinal*. B-Tree indexes are best suited when executing queries that return only a few rows (about 5 percent of the total number of rows) from the table. B-Tree indexes allow you to avoid full table scans and enhance the performance of your queries. While querying a table, you can first search for the index and then access the required data by using the row ID.

Oracle maintains the *balance* in B-Tree indexes. This means that the Oracle server splits the B-Tree index at regular intervals as new data is added to the table. However, whenever a table undergoes an insert or delete activity, the corresponding indexes might build up many levels. The greater the depth of the index, the less its efficiency, because the time taken to reach the level that contains the required index increases.

To find the depth of an index, use the following command:

```
SQL> SELECT index_name, blevel
FROM dba_indexes
WHERE blevel >= 4;
```

This query displays all the indexes that have four or more index levels. As discussed, the deeper the index, the less efficient it is. To avoid this, you need to rebuild the index regularly and improve its performance. You can rebuild an index using the following command:

```
SQL> ALTER INDEX index_name REBUILD;
```

Bitmap Indexes   Unlike B-Tree indexes, bitmap indexes are intended for low-cardinality columns (which generally contain a limited number of values) and queries with multiple WHERE clauses. Bitmap indexes create a binary mapping of the table rows and then store these maps in index *blocks*. Thus, they use minimal storage space as only the binary maps are stored in the index, and the retrieval of the rows is also faster.

Look at the following example to understand how bitmap indexes work. As noted, bitmap indexes are best suited for low cardinality tables. Therefore, from our PO_HEADER_ALL table we can build the bitmap index on the TYPE_LOOKUP_CODE column as it has low cardinality. (In the TYPE_LOOKUP_CODE column only two values are allowed, BLANKET or STANDARD.)

To create the bitmap index on the TYPE_LOOKUP_CODE column, you can use the following command:

```
SQL> SELECT *
FROM po_header_all;
SQL> CREATE BITMAP INDEX type_lookup_code index
ON purchase_order (type_lookup_code)
STORAGE (INITIAL 50K NEXT 50K PCTINCREASE 0)
TABLESPACE APPL_IDX;

Index created
```

In this example, the bitmap index will store two values with the binary mapping for each value. It stores 1 if the value for that column is true and 0 if the value is not true.

The following init.ora parameters associated with bitmap indexes can be used to increase the speed of modifying and creating the indexes:

- **SORT_AREA_SIZE**   Gives the size (in bytes) of the buffer where the row ID and sorted bitmap column information is stored until the batch is committed.

- **CREATE_BITMAP_AREA_SIZE**   Gives the size (in bytes) of the memory that has been allocated to create a bitmap.

- **BITMAP_MERGE_AREA_SIZE**   Gives the amount of memory that has been allocated for the bitmap merges after an index range scan.

TIP
*A bitmap is updated only once per DML activity,
despite any modifications to a number of rows.
Therefore, you should avoid using bitmap indexes
on those tables in which data is frequently inserted,
updated, or deleted.*

Reverse-Key Indexes   Reverse-key indexes are an extension of B-Tree indexes.
They are generally built on columns whose data consists of sequential numbers.
The B-Tree indexes might result in a number of levels if they are built on sequential
data and hence their performance might degrade. The reverse-key index reverses
the data of the indexed column, and then indexes the reversed data. Let's look
at the following example to understand reverse-key indexes.

Because the PO_HEADER_ID column in the PO_HEADER_ALL table contains
sequential data, we can apply reverse-key indexing on this column.

```
SQL> SELECT * FROM po_header_all;
```

After selecting all the records from the PO_HEADER_ALL table, you can create
the index the reverse-key index in the following way:

```
SQL> CREATE INDEX po_header_id_index
ON po_header_all (po_header_id)
REVERSE
STORAGE (INITIAL 200K NEXT 200K PCTINCREASE 0)
TABLESPACE APPL_IDX;

Index created
```

Function-Based Indexes   When a column is frequently used in an expression in
the WHERE clause, there is a high probability that the index built on that column is
not used even though it is available. You can use function-based indexes in such
instances. The advantage of a function-based index is that it creates an index on the
computed value of the expression or function. It can be implemented as a B-Tree or
a bitmap index.

A function-based index can be created for columns involved in arithmetic
expression, SQL functions, and package functions. However, this index cannot be
used with aggregate functions. This index is very useful because Oracle does not
need to recompute the values when it executes queries.

TIP
Rule-based optimization does not support
function-based indexes; therefore, you must
use cost-based optimization in this situation.

Index-Organized Tables

An index-organized table is like a regular table that maintains only one segment for
both the table and the B-Tree index. The database maintains only a single B-tree
index, which contains all the columns values along with the primary-key value.
Index-organized tables offer faster key-based access for queries and also occupy
less space. These tables are suitable for frequent data access through the primary
key or any other key that is a prefix to the primary key. The unique identifier for an
index-organized table is the primary key as against accessing the key using row ID.

Clusters

A *cluster* denotes a group of one or more tables that share the same data block,
because these tables have common columns and are often used together in joins.
This leads to a reduction in the disk input/output (I/O) operations. In addition, the
access time for joins that involve clustered tables improves. The cluster-key value
is stored only once for all rows containing the same key value, which occupies less
storage space. You should not use clusters for tables that are joined occasionally or
are modified frequently. Full table scans on clustered tables are slower than those
on nonclustered tables. Clusters can be categorized into two types:

- Index clusters

- Hash clusters

Index clusters use an index to maintain the data of the clustered tables. This
index contains an entry for each cluster-key value. To locate a row in a cluster,
you use the cluster index. This cluster index is used to find the cluster-key value,
which in turn points to the data block associated with that cluster-key value.

Hash clusters use a function to determine the location of a row. Oracle uses a
function to generate *hash values*, which are based on specific-cluster key values.
The key of a hash cluster can be based on a single column or on multiple columns.
To find or store a row in a hash cluster, Oracle applies the hash function to the
cluster-key value of the row. The resulting hash value corresponds to a data block
in the cluster, which is then read or written on behalf of the issuing statement.

Materialized Views

Materialized views are views with data of their own. Unlike normal views that get data from the underlying tables, materialized views store data just once unless the data needs to be refreshed. This view provides a snapshot of the data at a given point of time.

Materialized views are useful in DSS and hybrid environments, where users are presented with data at a particular point of time. The data in this view is not affected by constant modifications to the database. This view can also be used for queries that involve complex calculations, so that you can avoid executing the complex queries multiple number of times.

In case of cost-based optimization, you can use materialized views to improve the performance wherever possible instead of using the query. Normal queries can be redirected by the optimizer to use materialized views and thus improve the performance drastically.

Materialized views can also be used in distributed databases and can refresh the view in case of updates to master tables. Note that materialized views occupy a larger storage space, because they need to be refreshed to reflect changes to underlying tables, as opposed to normal views.

Creating Materialized Views   Before creating the materialized views, you need to perform the following configuration steps.

1. Determine the statements for which you want to create materialized views. These statements can be JOIN statements and can include summary functions, such as *SUM, MIN,* or *COUNT*.

2. Decide whether the data in the view will be refreshed with the base tables or not. To refresh the data with the base tables, you specify the *FORCE* option while creating the view. However, if you do not want the data to be refreshed with the base tables, you specify the *NEVER* option while creating the view.

   The *FORCE* option allows you to refresh the data in any of the following two ways:

   ■ **Fast**   Populates the materialized view with the data from only those tables that have been modified since the last re-sync. You can use the view's log data or row ID to refresh the data. Oracle uses this option first, and if this option is not available, it uses the other options.

   ■ **Complete**   Completely truncates the materialized view and then populates the data from the base tables.

3. After you have determined which *FORCE* option to use, you need to determine when you want to refresh the data. You can choose from the following two options:

■ **By Time** Allows you to refresh the data at a specified time and date. To enable this option, you use the *START WITH* and *NEXT* options while creating the view.

■ **On Commit** Allows you to refresh the data whenever a committed transaction takes place on the base table.

4. Finally, you need to set the init.ora parameters associated with the materialized views:

■ **QUERY_REWRITE_ENABLED** When set to TRUE, allows the optimizer to rewrite queries dynamically.

■ **QUERY_REWRITE_INTEGRITY** Gives three query options— *STALE_TOLERATED*, *ENFORCED*, and *TRUSTED*—for determining the extent of data consistency when you access materialized views. The *STALE_TOLERATED* query rewrite can transpire even when the base table data and the data in the view is not current. The *ENFORCED* query rewrite transpires only when Oracle ensures that the base table and the data in the views is current. This is the default option. The *TRUSTED* query rewrite takes place with the existence of declared relationships. However, the data in the base table and the view might not be current.

■ **OPTIMIZER_MODE** Set this parameter equal to one of the current cost-based optimizer modes.

■ **JOB_QUEUE_PROCESSES** Gives the Oracle job queue processes that are to be started.

■ **JOB_QUEUE_INTERVAL** Determines how frequently the job queue processes start and verifies the jobs that are pending.

After you have performed these configuration steps, you can create materialized views. Let's now look at an example on how to create a materialized view. To create a materialized view on the PO_HEADER_ALL and PO_LINE_TYPES tables, you can use the following code:

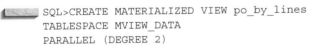

```
SQL>CREATE MATERIALIZED VIEW po_by_lines
TABLESPACE MVIEW_DATA
PARALLEL (DEGREE 2)
```

```
REFRESH FAST
ENABLE QUERY REWRITE
AS
SELECT po_line_types.line_type_id, COUNT (po_header_all.po_header_id)
FROM line_type l, item i, location loc
WHERE po_header_all.po_header_id = i.item_id
AND po_line_types.line_type_id = i.agent_id
GROUP BY po_line_types.line_type_id;

Materialized view created
```

Working with Materialized Views   While working with materialized views, you might often be required to disable, refresh, or drop them.

You can disable materialized views at session, instance, and statement levels. To disable materialized views, use any of the following processes:

- Use the *ALTER SESSION* command at the session level, and set *QUERY_REWRITE_ENABLED = FALSE*.

- Set the *QUERY_REWRITE_ENABLED* init.ora parameter and restart the instance.

- Use the *ALTER SYSTEM* command and dynamically set the value of *COMMAND QUERY_REWRITE_ENABLED*.

- Use the *NOREWRITE* hint in a query. This is used at the statement level.

You can refresh materialized views either automatically or manually. To automatically refresh materialized views, you need to create materialized views with the *COMMIT* option or set the schedule for refreshing the data by using the DBMS_MVIEW package. To manually refresh materialized views, you use the DBMS_MVIEW package.

If you have created a materialized view by using the *REFRESH FAST ON COMMIT* or *REFRESH COMPLETE ON COMMIT* commands, after every commit the materialized view is automatically refreshed. However, this option is not feasible for situations in which the data in the base tables undergoes frequent updates.

You can also use the DBMS_MVIEW and DBMS_JOB packages for automatically refreshing views. However, to use these packages, you must first create the views with the *REFRESH FAST ON DEMAND* and *REFRESH COMPLETE ON DEMAND* options. After you have used these options, you can then use the DBMS_MVIEW and DBMS_JOB packages. The following example will help you understand automatic refresh of materialized views.

Suppose you want a materialized view, PO_BY_LINES, to be refreshed every Monday at 6:00 A.M. Use the following procedure to submit the job for refresh:

```
CREATE OR REPLACE PROCEDURE refresh_po_by_lines
IS
v_job_num NUMBER;
BEGIN DBMS_JOB.SUBMIT(
v_job_num,
'DBMS_MVIEW.REFRESH (''po_by_lines ''); ',
SYSDATE,
'NEXT_DAY(TRUNC(SYSDATE), ''MONDAY'') + 6/24'
);
END;
/
```

To manually refresh materialized views, you can use the DBMS_MVIEW package.
It consists of the following three procedures:

- **REFRESH**   Refresh the specified materialized view. For example, to refresh the materialized view PO_BY_LINES, you can use the following procedure:

```
SQL>EXECUTE DBMS_MVIEW.REFRESH ('PO_BY_LINES');
PL/SQL procedure successfully completed
```

- **REFRESH_DEPENDENT**   Refresh all the materialized views that use this table. For example, to refresh all the materialized views that use the PURCHASE_ORDER table, you can use the following procedure:

```
SQL>EXECUTE DBMS_MVIEW.REFRESH_DEPENDENT ('purchase_order');
PL/SQL procedure successfully completed
```

- **REFRESH_ALL_MVIEWS**   Refresh all materialized views. For example,

```
SQL>EXECUTE DBMS_MVIEW.REFRESH_ALL_MVIEWS;
PL/SQL procedure successfully completed
```

You can drop a materialized view by using the *DROP MATERIALIZED VIEW* command. For example, to drop the materialized view PO_BY_LINE, use the following syntax:

```
SQL> DROP MATERIALIZED VIEW po_by_lines;
Materialized view dropped
```

The data in the base tables does not get affected when you drop a materialized view.

Histograms

Whenever data is uniformly distributed, the optimizer can accurately calculate the cost involved in executing a particular statement. In such a case, histograms can be used to find out the distribution of a particular column. Histograms can be used on frequently used columns in the WHERE clause or on an indexed column.

Tuning the Server

In addition to tuning the database, you need to tune the server for optimizing the performance of your application. Tuning the server involves tuning various components that form the server architecture:

- Memory
- Disk I/O
- Central processing units (CPUs)

If not tuned properly, any of these components can severely impact the function of your applications or servers, resulting in a fall in the performance of these applications or servers. For example, lack of physical memory allocation for some critical applications on the server can drastically degrade the performance of both the CPU and the disk I/O. Tuning the server involves tuning each component that makes up the server architecture. However, before tuning the server, you need to identify the *start point*, which is the component that has a maximum affect on other components. By tuning this component first, you might rectify some part of the problem.

One component that has an affect on other components is memory. The amount of memory allocated on a server impacts both the CPU and disk I/O.

Tuning Memory

All information in Oracle is stored automatically on the hard disk. However, for better performance of your system, it's recommended that you store data in the memory rather than on the disk, because the time taken to access memory is much faster than the time taken to access the disk. In such a situation, tuning memory becomes all the more important, as your operating system might have only a limited amount of available memory.

When you tune memory, you allocate it to the Program Global Area (PGA) and System Global Area (SGA) memory structures of Oracle.

Program Global Area

PGA is the memory structure used by a single Oracle user process. Each process is allocated its own PGA, which contains information for users and background processes.

A *process* consists of a sequence of tasks that a user performs and can be of two types: user processes and Oracle processes. User processes help in executing an application program code, while Oracle processes are invoked to perform some specific function. You can also categorize Oracle processes into Server processes and Background processes. Server processes act as a link between the user processes and the information in memory, while Background processes perform certain specified functions on behalf of the user processes.

The following Background processes are used by Oracle:

- **Process Monitory (PMON)** In case a user process fails, PMON clears theB cache and releases the locks.

- **System Monitor (SMON)** During startup, this process provides instance recovery. Further, it compresses free space, provides CPU recovery in case of a failure, and clears temporary segments.

- **Log Writer (LGWR)** This process manages the redo log buffer.

- **Database Writer (DBWR)** This process writes database buffers to the disk from the cache.

- **The Archiver (ARCH)** This process archives the log. When the logs become full, it copies the online redo log files to other storage devices.

- **The Recover (RECO)** This process resolves failures in any distributed transactions automatically.

System Global Area

SGA consists of shared memory structures that Oracle allocates for controlling information and containing data. Whenever an Oracle instance is started, SGA is automatically allocated, and when the instance shuts down, SGA is deallocated. Since memory structures in SGA are shared, the information in SGA can be shared among multiple users.

The following memory structures make up the SGA:

- Database buffer cache

- Redo buffer cache

- Shared pool

Database Buffer Cache

The database buffer cache caches database blocks of the most recently accessed database objects, such as tables, indexes, clusters, and rollback or temporary segments. The size and content of each buffer is the same as the data block it caches. There are three types of buffers in the database buffer cache:

- **Free** A buffer that is not being used currently. Database blocks stored in free buffers are stored as copies of the database blocks on the disk. This means that the copies in the free buffer and the database blocks on the disk are identical.

- **Pinned** The buffer that is being used by a server process currently.

- **Dirty** A buffer that is not being used currently, but contains data that has not been written to the disk. The copies of database blocks in the dirty buffer are different from those on the disk.

Tuning the Database Buffer Cache   To measure the performance of the database buffer cache, you use the *cache hit ratio*. If the cache hit ratio is high, it shows that the frequency with which you are able to find the required database buffers in the memory is also high. The cache hit ratio information can be obtained by using the V$SYSSTAT dynamic performance table.

NOTE
You can also get hit ratio information from V$SESS_IO and V$SESSION dynamic performance views, the OEM performance manager tool, and UTLBSTAT.SQL and UTLESTSAT.SQL (REPORT.TXT).

The V$SYSSTAT dynamic performance table contains statistics about data access. The following statistics in V$SYSSTAT are used to calculate the buffer cache hit ratio:

- **Physical reads** Provides the number of database blocks read from the disk to the buffer cache.

- **DB block gets**   Provides the total number of data requests answered by using the segment block. Add to consistent gets for the total number of data requests.

- **Consistent gets**   Provides the total number of data requests answered by using a rollback segment. Add to DB block gets for the total number of data requests.

The following example shows how you can use these statistics to calculate the buffer cache hit ratio:

```
Select name, value from v$sysstat
where name In
('db block gets', 'consistent gets', 'physical reads');


NAME                                    VALUE
----------------------------------------
b block gets                            86596
consistent gets                         281047
physical reads                          24165
```

On the basis of these statistics, you can calculate the buffer cache hit ratio using the following formula:

Buffer cache hit ratio = 1 − {(physical reads)/(db block gets + consistent gets)}

From the result of the query we find

- physical reads = 24165

- db block gets = 86596

- consistent gets = 281047

Therefore, the buffer cache hit ratio = 1 − (24165) / (86596 + 281047), or 0.9342704743. Or, in other words, the buffer cache hit ratio is 93 percent.

NOTE
You can also determine the database buffer cache hit ratio by using the OEM Diagnostics Pack component, Performance Manager.

You can improve the performance of the buffer cache by increasing the cache hit ratio using any of the following methods:

■ Increasing the size of the buffer cache

■ Caching tables in memory

■ Bypassing the buffer cache

■ Using multiple buffer pools

The following sections discuss in detail how each of these methods can be used to improve the performance of the buffer cache.

Increasing the Size of the Buffer Cache   Increasing the size of the buffer cache is one of the easiest ways of enhancing the performance of the buffer cache. The buffers in the cache can be retained in the cache for a longer period of time; thus the cache hit ratio also improves. This is because if the size of the buffer cache is small the *Least Recently Used (LRU)* algorithm, which manages the buffer cache, moves the buffer to other storage devices if there is no space in the cache.

NOTE
The LRU algorithm is used by the Oracle server to determine the objects that should be replaced by newer objects in the SGA.

You can determine the size of the buffer cache by using the init.ora parameters DB_BLOCK_SIZE and DB_BLOCK_BUFFERS. The size of the database block is determined by the DB_BLOCK_SIZE and it varies from platform to platform. For example, the default database block size for UNIX-based systems is from 2K to 8K, while for Windows NT–based systems the default data block size is 2K. The number of DB_BLOCK_BUFFER parameters determines the number of database buffers to be created in the SGA. Together the product of DB_BLOCK_SIZE and DB_BLOCK_BUFFERS gives the size of the database buffer cache.

By increasing the value for DB_BLOCK_BUFFERS, you can increase the size of the database buffer cache. However, you should not keep on increasing the size of the DB_BLOCK_BUFFERS if there is no difference in the performance from the last increase. You should increase the size of the DB_BLOCK_BUFFER in the following conditions:

- The cache hit ratio is less than 90 percent.

- A considerable increase in the performance buffer cache occurs since the last increase.

- No undue paging or swapping occurs.

NOTE
Paging *refers to the movement of a process in the form of memory pages, which is a memory block of size 48K or greater.* Swapping *refers to the temporary movement of a process to a disk due to shortage of free memory.*

Oracle provides a table called X$KCBRBH that contains statistics to help you calculate the enhancement in performance of the buffer cache after you have increased the size of the cache. By using these statistics, you can also calculate the number of buffers that you can add to your cache.

Statistics in the SYS.X$KCBRBH table can be used to estimate the performance of a larger cache. Each row in this table shows the change in performance whenever a buffer is added to the cache. Only the SYS user can access this table.

Two columns appear in X$KCBRBH:

- **INDX** Contains a value that is one less than the number of buffers that would be added to the cache.

- **COUNT** Contains a value that is the number of additional cache hits obtained by adding the value of INDX+1 to the cache.

In the first row of the X$KCBRBH table, the value in the INDX column is 0 and the value in the COUNT column is the number of additional cache hits that would be registered after a buffer has been added.

The number of rows in the X$KCBRBH table is determined by the initialization parameter DB_BLOCK_LRU_EXTENDED_STATISTICS. You can set the value of this parameter according to your particular requirements. For example, if you set the value to 50, this table will have 50 rows and each row will have statistics that will show the changes in performance until the addition of the fiftieth buffer.

On the basis of these statistics, you can also estimate the gains in performance by increasing the size of the buffer cache. For example, if you want to determine the number of cache hits that would occur if you were to add 10 buffers to the cache, you can query the X$KCBRBH table as follows:

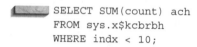

```
SELECT SUM(count) ach
FROM sys.x$kcbrbh
WHERE indx < 10;
```

NOTE
You can also determine the affect of these additional cache hits on the hit ratio by using this formula:
Hit Ratio = 1 – (physical reads – ACH / (db block gets + consistent gets))

Caching Tables in Memory   Caching tables in memory is important especially for tables that are accessed by using a full table scan. This is because tables that are accessed by full table scans place their data blocks at the least recently used part of the LRU list. The data block at the least recently used part of the LRU list tends to be frequently removed from the cache. Therefore, if you want to access the data block again, the data block has to be reread from the memory. To avoid this, you need to cache the tables.

When cached tables are accessed using full table scans, they place their buffers in the most recently used part of the LRU list. Buffers in the most recently used part stay in the cache for a longer period of time.

You can cache tables using the following three methods:

- By creating the table
- By altering the table
- Using hints

First, let's discuss caching by creating the table. You can cache a table by including the keyword *CACHE* while creating the table. However, by default all tables that you create are NOCACHE tables unless you specify the *CACHE* option. Here's an example:

```
CREATE TABLE purchase_order
(po_id        number,
vendor_id     number,
freight_terms_ lookup_code    varchar2(25),
currency_code     varchar2(15),
approved_flag     varchar2(1))
TABLESPACE appl_tab
```

```
STORAGE (INITIAL 50K NEXT 50K PCTINCREASE 0)
CACHE;
```

Next, you can cache by altering the table. You can change a NOCACHE table to a CACHE table by using the *ALTER TABLE* command with the keyword *CACHE*. Similarly, you can convert a cache table to a NOCACHE table by using the keyword *NOCACHE*. Here's an example:

```
ALTER TABLE purchase_order CACHE;
```

You can also use the appropriate hint to cache or nocache a table. The hint that you provide is applicable only to that query and not the complete table. Here's an example:

```
SELECT /*+ CACHE */ item_id, item_description
FROM item;
```

To view which tables are cached in the DBA_TABLES view, you can use the CACHE column. Here's an example:

```
SELECT table_name
FROM dba_tables WHERE LTRIM(cache) = 'Y';

TABLE_NAME
ITEM
PURCHASE_ORDER
```

Bypassing Buffer Cache   To improve the performance of the buffer cache and increase the cache ratio, you can bypass the buffer cache for a few particular requests. When you bypass the buffer cache, buffers that exist in the cache do not move out of the LRU list. One buffer request that lets you bypass buffer requests is a *parallel DML*. Parallel DML results in multiple processes that perform numerous updates, inserts, and deletes simultaneously. Parallel DML results in an increased load on the CPU and thus should be used only when you have many CPUs that are not being utilized to their full potential.

Using Multiple Buffer Pools   Because database buffer cache buffers are used by all database segments, it might happen that the tables that are frequently used are pushed out of the memory by tables that are infrequently used. To avoid such a situation, you can segregate the database buffer cache in a number of areas referred to as *buffer pools*. The following are the three types of buffer pools that you can use:

- **Keep Pool**   Used to cache those database segments that you use frequently and want to retain in the database buffer cache for a long period of time.

- **Recycle Pool**   Used to cache those database segments that you use rarely and do not want to retain in the database buffer cache.

- **Default Pool**   Used to cache database segments other than those cached in the keep pool or the recycle pool.

You need to determine which database segments should be cached and in which particular pool they should be cached. Oracle provides two views—namely, V$BH and DBA_SEGMENTS—that can help you in determining the segments that are to be cached. The V$BH view is created by the CATPARR.SQL script and shows the number of the file and the blocks that exist in the SGA. After you have determined the segments that you want to cache, you should determine the size of each pool. You can use the BLOCKS column of DBA_TABLES and DBA_INDEXES to determine the size of each pool. After determining the size of each buffer pool, you need to create the buffer pools. The init.ora parameters shown in Table 12-2 are associated with the configuration of buffer pools.

NOTE
A latch is a process used to protect access to the shared memory structures of Oracle.

Initialization Parameter	Description
DB_BLOCK_BUFFERS	Provides the total number of database buffers that are to be created in the database buffer cache.
DB_BLOCK_LRU_LATCHES	Provides the total number of *latches* that are to be created to access the database buffer cache. By default, it has a value of 1 or half the number of CPUs, whichever is greater.
BUFFER_POOL_KEEP	Provides the number of DB_BLOCK_BUFFERS and DB_BLOCK_LRU_LATCHES that are allocated to the keep pool.
BUFFER_POOL_RECYCLE	Provides the number of DB_BLOCK_BUFFERS and DB_BLOCK_LRU_LATCHES that are allocated to the recycle pool.

TABLE 12-2.   *init.ora Parameters Associated with the Configuration of Buffer Pools*

To assign database segments to their respective pools, you can use the *ALTER* command:

```
ALTER TABLE po_header_all.po_header_id
STORAGE (BUFFER_POOL KEEP);

ALTER TABLE po_header_all.agent_id
STORAGE (BUFFER_POOL KEEP);

ALTER TABLE po_header_all.vendor_id
STORAGE (BUFFER_POOL KEEP);

ALTER TABLE po_header_all.vendor_site_id
STORAGE (BUFFER_POOL RECYCLE);
```

After you have assigned database segments to their respective non-default buffer pools, you can view these segments and their pools by querying DBA_SEGMENTS:

```
SELECT owner, segment_name,
buffer_pool
FROM dba_segments
WHERE buffer_pool != 'DEFAULT';
```

OWNER	SEGMENT_NAME	BUFFER_POOL
PO_HEADER_ALL	PO_ID	KEEP
PO_HEADER_ALL	AGENT ID	KEEP
PO_HEADER_ALL	VENDOR ID	KEEP
PO_HEADER_ALL	VENDOR CITY ID	RECYCLE

NOTE
If the cache hit ratio for the keep pool is high and that of the recycle pool is low, the multiple buffer pools have been tuned properly.

Redo Log Buffer

The *redo log buffer*, as the name suggests, stores the information necessary to redo a transaction in case of its failure due to a media or user error. This redo information is stored in the redo log buffer by the server process of the application user. The redo log buffer is managed by the Log Writer (LGWR) background process. LGWR empties the contents of the redo log buffer in any one of the following situations:

■ A *COMMIT* command is issued by a user

- Redo log buffer becomes one-third full

- Every 3 seconds

- Occurrence of a *database checkpoint*

NOTE
A database checkpoint is a time when the database is in a steady state. When a checkpoint occurs, all buffers containing committed transactions in the database buffer cache are moved to the disk and all contents of the redo log buffer are moved to the redo log.

Tuning the Redo Log Buffer   You can measure the performance of the redo log buffer using the V$SYSSTAT and V$SYSSTAT_WAIT dynamic performance views. These views show the number and length of waits that the server processes undergo when they are adding entries on the redo log buffer.

V$SYSSTAT contains certain statistics you can use to tune the performance of the redo log buffer. These statistics are redo buffer allocation retries, redo entries, and redo log space requests.

V$SYSSTAT Redo Log Buffer Statistics	Description
Redo buffer allocation retries	The number of times that the server processes retries to place the entries in the redo log buffer.
Redo entries	Provides the number of entries that the server process has placed in the redo log buffer.
Redo log space requests	Measures the number of times a LGWR waits for the occurrence of a redo log switch.

You can use the redo buffer allocation retries and redo entries to calculate the redo log buffer retry ratio. It is recommended that the value of this redo log buffer retry ratio should be less than 1 percent. Here's an example:

```
SELECT retries.value/entries.value
"Redo Log Buffer Retry Ratio"
FROM retries.name = 'redo buffer allocation retries'
AND entries.name = 'redo entries';
```

```
Redo Log Buffer Retry Ratio
---------------------------
000415
```

The next parameter, V$SYSSTAT_WAIT, is used to determine the events and the time for which the user sessions have waited. Here's an example:

```
SELECT username, wait_time, seconds_waited
FROM v$session_wait, v$session
WHERE v$session_wait.sid = v$session.sid
AND event LIKE 'log buffer space';
```

USERNAME	SECONDS_WAITED	STATE
PAUL	10	WAITING
CHARLIE	180	WAITED SHORT TIME

NOTE
You can also use the Performance Manager to monitor the performance of the redo log buffer.

Improving the Performance of the Redo Log Buffer   You need to tune the redo log buffer to ensure that the server processes do not have to wait for placing entries in the buffer. To improve the performance of the redo log buffer, you can use any one of the following methods:

- Increase the redo log buffer size
- Increase the speed of archiving
- Decrease the amount of redo information generated
- Enhance checkpoint efficiency

Like the database buffer cache, you can improve the performance of the redo log buffer by increasing its size. When its size is increased, the server process does not have to wait to place the redo entries in the buffer as it gets enough space in the buffer to place the redo entries immediately.

You can use the init.ora parameter, LOG_BUFFER to specify the size of the redo log buffer. However, the size of the redo log buffer differs from platform to platform.

NOTE
If you reduce its size to a very low value, Oracle overrides your settings and restores the redo log buffer to its default value.

When your database is operating in the archive log mode, the archive background process, ARC0, copies the information of the redo log files to the archive files. This archiving process can hamper the performance of the redo log buffer because if LGWR has to write some data into the redo log files then it has to first wait until ARC0 has completed copying redo log files to the archive files. To avoid this, you can configure the LGWR to archive redo log files by initiating additional archive background processes, such as ARC1 and ARC2. You can also use the init.ora parameter LOG_ARCHIVE_MAX_PROCESSES to set the number of archive background processes. The LOG_ARCHIVE_MAX_PROCESSES can have a value ranging from 1 to 10.

You can use the following options to reduce the amount of redo information generated:

- NOLOGGING

- UNRECOVERABLE

The NOLOGGING option allows you to specify the tables that would not generate any redo entries when acted upon by certain DML statements. You can use this option while creating a table or with the *ALTER TABLE* command.

You use the UNRECOVERABLE option when you are creating a table by using the *CREATE TABLE AS SELECT* command. Here's an example:

```
CREATE TABLE po_release_info
AS
SELECT *
FROM po_release
UNRECOVERABLE
```

When you create tables in this way, the tables do not generate any redo information for the *CREATE TABLE AS SELECT* command. However, if some other DML statements act upon the table, the table will generate some redo information.

You need to manage the activity of the checkpoint to avoid the unnecessary I/O events. This is because once started, a checkpoint event causes useless I/O events by initiating DBWR and LGWR to clear the database buffer cache and redo log buffer.

You can use the init.ora parameter LOG_CHECK_POINT_TIMEOUT and LOG_CHECKPOINT_INTERVAL for managing checkpoints. For Oracle8i, the LOG_CHECK_POINT_TIMEOUT has a default value of 900 seconds, while for Oracle8i Enterprise Edition this value is 1800. The default value for LOG_CHECKPOINT_INTERVAL varies from operating system to operating system, but is generally from 1 to unlimited.

Shared Pool

Shared pool is the final memory structure in the SGA, which caches the recently used PL/SQL statements. Just like database buffer cache, a shared pool is managed by the LRU algorithm. The shared pool enhances the performance of the memory by keeping the most used PL/SQL statements in memory and phasing out the least used statements.

The following three components make up the shared pool:

- Library cache

- Data dictionary cache

- User global area

The library cache in the shared pool is the area where the recently used PL/SQL statements are cached by Oracle. You can use the V$LIBRARYCACHE dynamic performance table to examine the performance of the library cache. Each row of the V$LIBRARYCACHE table contains statistics that correspond to an object in the library cache. You can use the NAMESPACE column in the table to identify the objects corresponding to each row. The library cache activities for SQL statements and PL/SQL blocks can be viewed in the rows with these NAMESPACE column values. You can query the V$LIBRARYCACHE as follows:

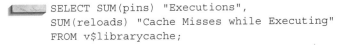

```
SELECT SUM(pins) "Executions",
SUM(reloads) "Cache Misses while Executing"
FROM v$librarycache;
```

The result of this query is as follows:

```
Executions          Cache Misses while Executing
-----------         ----------------------------
31982               579
```

NOTE
The PINS column in the V$LIBRARYCACHE table depicts how many times an object of the library cache was executed. The RELOADS column in the V$LIBRARYCACHE table depicts how many times library cache misses occurred during the execution of the query.

NOTE

To monitor the library cache hit ratios, you can also use the Performance Manager from the OEM Diagnostics Pack.

When you execute an SQL or PL/SQL statement, you should check the data dictionary to ensure that the tables, columns, and datatypes that you have used in your query are correct. All this information is cached in the data dictionary cache. You can monitor the performance of the data dictionary cache by using the V$ROWCACHE table. You can use the GETS and GETMISSES columns of this table to calculate the data dictionary cache hit ratio. Here's an example:

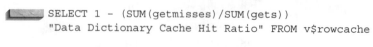

```
SELECT 1 - (SUM(getmisses)/SUM(gets))
"Data Dictionary Cache Hit Ratio" FROM v$rowcache

Data Dictionary Cache Hit Ratio
---------------------------------
95432059
```

This means that the required information in the data dictionary cache can be accessed by an application 95.4 percent of the time.

NOTE

To monitor the data dictionary cache hit ratios, you can also use the Performance Manager from the OEM Diagnostics Pack.

User Global Area   The User Global Area or UGA is the memory allocated for users. In case of MTS or multithreaded server configurations, UGA is part of the SGA. The following script can be used to check the amount of UGA used up in your instance.

```
set linesize 100
col name format a25
col value format 999,999,999,999
spool ugacheck.rep
select * from v$sysstat where name like '%uga%'
order by statistic#;

spool off;
```

As the RDBMS allocates more shared memory for the MTS session memory, the amount of shared pool memory available for the shared SQL cache decreases. By configuring the large pool, you can use session memory from another area of shared memory, and the RDBMS can use the shared pool memory primarily for caching shared SQL and not incur performance overheads from shrinking the shared SQL cache.

Tuning the Shared Pool   You can improve the performance of the shared pool by increasing the hit ratios of the library cache and data dictionary cache. You can use any of the following methods to increase library cache and data dictionary cache hit ratios:

- **Increase the size of the shared pool**   Use the init.ora parameter SHARED_POOL_SIZE to specify the size of the shared pool. By default, the size of the shared pool is 64MB for a 64-bit operating system and 16MB for a 32-bit operating system.

- **Allow large PL/SQL statements to be cached separately**   Create a *shared pool reserved area* for large PL/SQL statements using the SHARED_POOL_RESERVED_SIZE init.ora parameter. By default, the size of this area is 5 percent of the size of the shared pool. To monitor the performance of the shared pool, use the V$SHARED_POOL_RESERVE dynamic performance view.

- **Store critical PL/SQL code in the memory**   Frequently used PL/SQL code should be cached permanently in the memory. This is called *pinning*. You can perform pinning by using the DBMS_SHARED_POOL PL/SQL package. Caching frequently used PL/SQL statements also results in an increase in the shared pool hit ratios.

- **Reuse code**   Use the code that already exists in the shared pool to improve the shared pool hit ratio. If the hash value of the cached statement corresponds to that of a newly executed statement, both the statements are considered equivalent.

Tuning I/O

The performance of many software applications is inherently limited by disk input/output (I/O). Disk I/O can adversely affect the performance of a large number of software applications. Often, CPU activity must be suspended while I/O activity completes. Such an application is said to be *I/O bound*. Oracle is designed so that performance is not limited by I/O.

Tuning I/O can enhance performance if a disk containing database files is operating at its capacity. However, tuning I/O cannot help performance in CPU bound cases, or cases in which your computer's CPUs are operating at their capacity. When your servers are dealing with huge loads, tuning the memory and disk I/O might not be helpful in increasing the performance of your applications. You also need to tune the CPU and monitor its utilization.

Tuning the CPU

The performance of your system might vary with the amount of CPU that is available. You need to monitor the CPU utilization to determine whether your system is using too much CPU or the CPU is underutilized.

You can monitor CPU utilization when the workload is normal, heavy, or idle. Monitoring the workload is important when you are determining CPU utilization. For example, when the workload is heavy, a CPU utilization of up to 90 percent is acceptable. However, when the workload is light, a CPU utilization of 40 percent is not acceptable, because the CPU might not be able to perform when the workload becomes heavy.

While monitoring CPU utilization, you need to examine all the processes that are using the CPU. When you use Oracle statistics to view the amount of CPU utilization, they return results for only the Oracle processes, not for non-Oracle processes that might also be utilizing the CPU. Tuning these non-Oracle processes can also improve the performance of your Oracle applications.

NOTE
To monitor CPU utilization for the complete system, you can use various tools, such as sar –u for UNIX and Performance Monitor for NT-based systems.

To view the amount of CPU utilization for all Oracle sessions, you can use the dynamic performance view, V$SYSSTAT.

Tuning SQL

Application design and tuning provide a great number of performance benefits. The method and the amount of data that is selected have a direct impact on the performance of a database. Typically, a DBA is not directly involved in tuning SQL statements, but she must be familiar with the performance impact caused by poorly written statements.

The DBA must use various tools to diagnose the performance of SQL statements and identify alternative methods to rewrite the SQL statements for performance enhancements. You can use a number of approaches to tune SQL statements. Some of these approaches are discussed in the following sections.

Reframing an SQL Statement

You can diagnose the performance problem with SQL statements and reframe these statements to provide a better performance. Once the objectives of a statement are clear, you can rewrite the statement to get an optimal performance.

Data can be extracted from a database in a number of ways. You can choose the best method by comparing the performance of each method. To compare the performance, you can use various diagnostic tools provided by Oracle, such as SQL Trace and EXPLAIN PLAN. In some situations, despite the availability of an index, Oracle might not use it. You can look at the execution plan of the statement with the help of the EXPLAIN PLAN utility and diagnose the access path. You can also use explicit hints that can be provided in the statements to use the index or the statement can be rewritten so that it uses the index. You should avoid full table scans whenever possible. Using index scans can also degrade performance if your query returns more than 30 to 40 percent of the rows from the table. You should use EQUIJOINS to gain better performance, as these statements are easy to tune.

The JOIN order of tables also significantly affects performance. It is important to identify the base table in case of joins. It is recommended that a table with few rows be the base table, because it is always easy to perform the lookup from a table that contains only a few rows. Consider the following example for illustration purposes:

TableA – 10 Rows
TableB – 10,000 Rows

It's easy to choose one row from TableA and look for corresponding rows in TableB rather than choosing one row from TableB and looking for a corresponding row in TableA.

In addition, if additional WHERE conditions appear on any single table, it is recommended that these conditions should be executed first to eliminate rows that are not required for the JOIN to go ahead. The following code will clarify this point:

```
Select * from po_header_all
where po_header_all.type_lookup_code = po_lookup_codes.type_lookup_code
and
po_header_all.vendor_id = (Select vendor_id from po_vendor
where vendor_site_id = 'vs004');
```

Here, the vendor_id rows will be eliminated first and then the join between po_header_all and po_look_up_codes tables will be executed.

You should avoid using SQL functions in JOIN conditions. If the column used in the WHERE clause is a part of an expression, the optimizer will ignore any indexes on that column. It's recommended that you not use columns with different data types in the WHERE clause, because Oracle does an implicit conversion before using the column values, which definitely causes overhead on the system. Whenever such need arises, it is a good idea to do an explicit conversion.

Index Strategy

Using indexes does not necessarily improve performance. You should remove unnecessary indexes to improve performance. The DML statements are most affected in case of a high number of indexes. You should use cluster indexes, hash indexes, and function-based indexes wherever possible. It is a good idea to use function-based indexes for columns involved in expressions in the WHERE clause. If required, you can rebuild and restructure indexes for better performance.

Data Distribution

Data distribution is as important as index restructuring. To reorganize data, you can move it to a newer location or partition the table. Partitioning improves performance so that SQL statements access only a part of the database rather than the entire database. Partitions are helpful in a DSS environment as well as for hybrid systems. You can use various types of partitioning options for different applications. You can also use distributed databases to hold the data to improve the performance of distributed queries.

Database Triggers

The excessive use of database triggers not only slows down the performance of the database but also slows down the DML statements. Whenever a DML statement is executed, a trigger is fired that in turn can fire several other triggers, leading to a cascading effect. Oracle recommends using triggers only in conditions where the data integrity or business rule cannot be enforced with the help of available constraints, and when you need to perform some cascading effect in case of distributed databases. It is a good idea to disable some triggers if possible.

Parallel Queries/DML

For queries that take a long time in executing or statements that process huge amounts of data, you can go for parallel query methods for faster response. A parallel query allows you to split a single job to multiple processes, thus giving a faster response. It also allows you to use the available system resources more effectively.

The parallel option can be used for queries, DMLs, and DDLs as well. Parallel execution can improve performance in DSS applications.

Optimization

Optimization is the process of choosing the most cost-efficient way to execute an SQL statement. This is an important step in processing any DML statement. There may be many different ways to execute a SQL statement—for example, the order in which tables or indexes are accessed. The plan Oracle adopts to execute a statement can vastly affect how quickly the statement executes.

Optimizer is a part of Oracle, and it chooses the most efficient way to execute SQL statements. The optimizer takes into consideration a number of factors to select among alternative access paths. At times, the application designer, who has a greater amount of information about a particular application's data than is available to the optimizer, can choose a more effective way to execute an SQL statement. The application designer can use hints in SQL statements to specify how the statement should be executed.

In Oracle, two types of optimizer modes can be chosen:

- Rule-based

- Cost-based

Rule-Based Optimization

In rule-based optimization, the server determines the execution plan from among the available access paths by examining the query. The optimizer uses a set of predefined rules for choosing the access path. Rule-based optimization does not require any statistics. It is syntax driven and uses the syntax of the statement to determine the access path.

The rule-based optimization approach consists of the following steps.

The optimizer first evaluates the statement and conditions in the statement. Here, Oracle might transform certain constructs to equivalent syntactic constructs. The constants used in statements are evaluated only once and are subsequently used in each execution of the statement.

The following examples show how Oracle evaluates a statement and if needed converts them into equivalent constructs.

Using the Like Operator Without Wildcards   Here's an example:

```
Select * From po_lines_all
Where po_line_all_id like 'po001';
```

Here is the equivalent construct as converted by the optimizer:

```
Select * From po_lines_all
Where po_line_all_id = 'po001';
```

Using the IN Operator   This example uses the IN operator:

```
Select * From po_lines_all
Where po_line_all_id In ('po001', 'po002', 'po003', 'po004');
```

The equivalent construct as converted by the optimizer is next:

```
Select * From po_lines_all
Where po_line_all_id = 'po001' or po_line_all_id = 'po002' or
po_line_all_id = 'po003' or po_line_all_id = 'po004';
```

Using the ANY and ALL Operators   Here's an example:

```
Select * From po_line_locations_all
Where quantity_received > ANY (:qty1,:qty2,:qty3);
```

The equivalent construct as converted by the optimizer in this example:

```
Select * From po_line_locations_all
Where quantity_received > :qty1 or quantity_received > :qty2 or
quantity_received > :qty3;

Select * From po_line_locations_all
Where quantity_received > ALL (:qty1,:qty2,:qty3);supposed to be only one semicolon
```

The equivalent construct as converted by the optimizer is shown here:

```
Select * From po_line_locations_all
Where quantity_received > :qty1 and quantity_received > :qty2 and quantity_received > :qty3;
```

Using the BETWEEN AND Operator   Here's an example:

```
Select * From po_line_locations_all
Where quantity_accepted Between 500 and 600;
```

Here's the equivalent construct as converted by the optimizer:

```
Select * From po_line_locations_all
Where quantity_accepted >= 500 and quantity_accepted <=600;
```

Using Subqueries   For complex statements like subqueries, the optimizer will convert statements into equivalent join statements, like so:

```
Select * From po_line_locations_all
Where quantity_received='500' or quantity_accepted= '300';
```

Here's the equivalent construct as converted by the optimizer if indexes are available for the respective columns:

```
Select * From po_line_locations_all Where quantity_received='500';

Union All

Select * From po_line_locations_all
Where quantity_accepted = '300'
And quantity_received <>'500';
```

For every table accessed by the statements, the optimizer chooses a particular access path to retrieve the data.

There may be a different access path by which data can be retrieved, but the optimizer chooses one of them. The basic methods by which data can be accessed by Oracle are

- Full table scan

- Access on the basis of ROWID

- Cluster scan

- Hash scan

- Index scan

In case of a Join statement, the optimizer decides which pair of tables should be joined first and which table should be joined to the result of the first join.

Cost-Based Optimization

The optimizer determines the execution plan that will incur the least cost by evaluating all available access paths based on the statistics present in the data dictionary. The optimizer also considers the optimization hints included in the comment of a statement.

The cost-based optimization approach consists of the following steps:

1. The optimizer generates a set of possible execution plans for the statement based on the available access paths using hints provided, if any.

2. The optimizer estimates the cost involved for each execution plan based on the available statistics in the data dictionary and data distribution. The cost reflects value proportional to the expected resource use needed to execute the statement using the execution plan.

3. The optimizer calculates the cost based on the estimated computer resources, including I/O, CPU time, and memory required to execute the statement in a particular execution plan.

4. The optimizer then compares the cost involved in each of the execution plans and chooses the one with the least cost (see Figure 12-7).

It's important to note that a cost-based optimization needs statistics to estimate the cost of each execution plan. These statistics are generated using the *ANALYZE* command and they reflect the way the data is distributed and storage characteristics for each type of object. Once these statistics are generated, they can be viewed using the following data dictionary tables/views:

■ USER_TABLES / DBA_TABLES

■ USER_TAB_COLUMNS / DBA_TAB_COLUMNS

■ USER_TAB_PARTITIONS / DBA_TAB_PARTITIONS

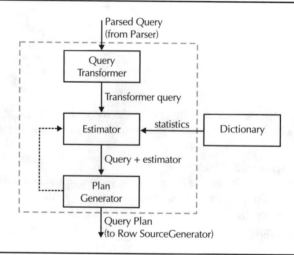

FIGURE 12-7. *Cost-based optimizer*

- USER_INDEXES / DBA_INDEXES

- USER_IND_PARTITIONS / DBA_IND_PARTITIONS

- USER_PART_COL_STATISTICS / DBA_PART_COL_STATISTICS

- USER_CLUSTERS / DBA_CLUSTERS

In case of non-uniform data distribution, *histograms* provide improved estimation in the presence of data skew, which results in generating optimal execution plans. One of the basic abilities of cost-based optimization is to determine the select values appearing in a query. These estimates are used to determine when to use an index and the order in which tables are joined.

Consider, for example, a column with values between 1 and 100 and a histogram with 10 units. If the data in the column is uniformly distributed, the histogram would appear as shown in Figure 12-8.

If the data is not distributed uniformly, the histogram will appear as shown in Figure 12-9.

Most of the time, Oracle uses height-balanced histograms rather than width-balanced histograms. Height-balanced histograms place the same number of values into each range so that the endpoints of the range are determined by how many values are in that range. The advantage of height-balanced histograms is in situations when the data is non-uniformly distributed. Width-balanced histograms divide the data into a fixed number of equal-width ranges and then count the number of values falling into each range.

It is appropriate to create the histogram on the indexed column, because columns most often used in the WHERE clause are indexed. The following tables can be used to view histograms:

- USER_HISTOGRAMS / DBA_HISTOGRAMS

- USER_PART_HISTOGRAMS / DBA_PART_HISTOGRAMS

- TAB_COLUMNS

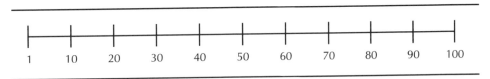

FIGURE 12-8. *Histogram showing uniformly distributed data*

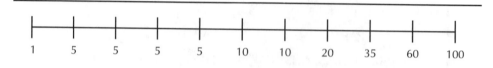

FIGURE 12-9. *Histogram showing non-uniformly distributed data*

The following factors determine an optimizer's behavior in choosing a specific approach in executing a SQL statement:

- OPTIMIZER_MODE parameter
- Statistics available in the data dictionary
- OPTIMIZER_GOAL parameter
- Hints in SQL statements

OPTIMIZER_MODE Parameter   This parameter in the initialization parameter file decides the default behavior for choosing the optimization approach. The parameter can have one of the following values:

- **CHOOSE**   Indicates that the optimizer will choose the cost-based optimization if statistics are available in the data dictionary. If the data dictionary does not contain statistics for at least one of the tables being accessed, the optimizer will choose the rule-based approach. By default the OPTIMZER_MODE has a value of CHOOSE.

- **ALL_ROWS**   Makes the optimizer choose cost-based optimization irrespective of statistics being available. In this case, the optimizer examines all the available access paths and chooses the one that takes the minimum resources to complete the statements.

- **FIRST_ROWS**   Forces the optimizer to choose a cost-based approach even if statistics are not available. It examines all the available access paths and chooses the one with best throughput to process the first row of the result set.

- **RULE**   The optimizer will choose the rule-based approach for all SQL statements regardless of the presence of statistics.

OPTIMIZER_GOAL Parameter   This parameter can be set in the session only. The value will override the value of the OPTIMIZER_MODE parameter in the initialization parameter file for the session.

This parameter can have the following values:

- CHOOSE
- FIRST_ROWS
- ALL_ROWS
- RULE

Here's an example of using the parameter:

```
SQL > ALTER SESSION SET OPTIMIZER_GOAL=CHOOSE;
```

Using Hints in the SQL Statement   By specifying a hint in a SQL statement, you can override the values of the OPTIMIZER_MODE and OPTIMZER_GOAL parameter.

The values are the same as for OPTIMIZER_MODE, OPTIMIZER_GOAL parameters.

```
SQL> Select /*+ FIRST_ROWS */ *
From po_header_all
Where enabled_flag = 'Y';
```

Here, the OPTIMIZER_MODE parameter value is overwritten by the hint in the SQL statement.

The hints for access methods are shown here:

- **FULL** Instructs the optimizer to go for a full table scan. So even if there is an index on a specified column, Oracle will perform a full table scan.

- **CLUSTER** Explicitly uses a cluster scan to access a specified table. This will apply only to tables in a cluster.

- **HASH** Explicitly uses a hash scan to access the specified table. This option also is available only to tables present in a cluster.

- **INDEX** Goes for an index scan for the specified table. You can use this hint to explicitly use a particular index. Other index hints are INDEX_ASC,

INDEX_DESC, INDEX_JOIN, INDEX_COMBINE, NO_INDEX, and INDEX_FFS.

- **ROWID**   Explicitly chooses a table scan by ROWID for the specified table. Here's an example:

```
Select /*+ROWID(po_header_all)*/ *
From po_header_all
where po_header_id= 10;
```

- **ORDERED (Hint for Join)**   Instructs the optimizer to join the tables in the same order in which they appear in the FROM clause, like so:

```
Select /*+ ORDERED */ po_header_id, po_lines_all.po_line_id,
segment1,
po_vendor_sites.vendor_site_id
From po_header_all, po_lines_all, po_vendor_sites
Where po_header_all.vendor_site_id=
po_vemdor_sites.vendor_site_id
And (segment1 Between Loseg and Hiseg);
```

- **PARALLEL**   Specifies the number of concurrent processes used for parallel processing of the statement. This hint takes in two arguments, the table name and degree of parallelism.

```
Select /*+ PARALLEL(po_header_all,4) */ *
From po_header_all;
```

- **NOPARALLEL**   Specifies PARALLEL specifications in the table clause.

```
Select /*+ NOPARALLEL(po_header_all) */ *
From po_header_all;
```

Tuning the Network

Networks form the backbone of any communication. As networks continue to grow more complex and dependable, tuning a network becomes all the more critical. Even so, network tuning generally takes a back seat to application tuning. However, network tuning is a crucial step in improving overall performance. Too much traffic on a network can seriously impact the performance of your applications.

You can use the following system tools and utilities to manage and monitor your network:

- NetStat

- PING

- Traceroute

- ntop

- Windows NT Performance Monitor

- SymbEL

NetStat

You use NetStat to display network information. The syntax of NetStat is operating system dependent. The following table lists some of the command line options that you can use with NetStat:

NetStat Command Line Option	Description
-n	Shows port numbers and IP addresses
-a	Shows all listening ports and connections
-s	Shows network protocol statistics since last boot of the system
-l	Shows the status of all network interfaces; not supported by Windows NT
-e	Shows statistics relating to network interfaces

The following example shows the results of the *netstat –s* command:

```
C:\WINNT>netstat -s
IP Statistics
Packet Received                        = 15491
Received Header Errors                 = 0
Received Address Errors                = 282
Datagrams Forwarded                    = 0
Unknown Protocols Received             = 0
Received Packets Discarded             = 0
Received Packets Delivered             = 15443
Output Requests                        = 8938
Output Packets No Route                = 0
Reassembly Required                    = 24
Reassembly Successful                  = 12
Datagrams Successfully Fragmented      = 12
Datagrams Failing Fragmentation        = 0
Fragments Created                      = 24
```

```
ICMP Statistics

                              Received           Sent
Messages                      63                 336
Errors                        0                  0
Destination Unreachable       15                 288
Time Exceeded                 0                  0
Parameter Problems            0                  0
Source Quenches               0                  0
Redirects                     0                  0
Echos                         0                  0
Echo Replies                  48                 48
Timestamps                    0                  0
Timestamps Replies            0                  0
Address Masks                 0                  0
Address Masks Replies         0                  0


TCP Statistics
Active Opens                              = 273
Passive Opens                             = 372
Failed Connection Attempts                = 23
Reset Connections                         = 44
Current Connections                       = 3
Segments Received                         = 8438
Segments Sent                             = 7483
Segments Retransmitted                    = 77


UDP Statistics
Datagrams Received                        = 10118
No Ports                                  = 1030
Receive Errors                            = 0
Datagrams Sent                            = 2176
```

PING

You use the PING command to test network connectivity between two nodes. Based on the ICMP protocol, PING sends an ICMP echo request to a remote node. If the remote node is connected to the network, it replies with an ICMP echo reply. If PINGing is not successful, you receive a timed-out message.

Traceroute

You use the *traceroute* command to trace the route of an IP packet from its host to its destination. Traceroute uses UDP packets to trace the route of the IP packets. You use the *tracert* command in Windows NT instead of *Traceroute.Nslookup.*

You can also use this command to resolve names to IP addresses and query DNS servers.

ntop

This command is specific to UNIX and displays the use of network the by the top ten nodes.

Windows NT Performance Monitor

You can use the Windows NT Performance Monitor to manage and monitor counters from several systems. You can also set alert levels for the counters that you are monitoring.

SymbEL

SymbEL is a toolkit for Solaris that can be used for building performance tools and utilities. Some of the commands it uses in addition to the standard command are listed here:

- netmonitor.se

- netstatx.se

- net.se

Oracle Performance Diagnostic Tools

The four main performance diagnostic tools used by Oracle to tune the applications are

- EXPLAIN PLAN

- Statspack

- SQL Trace

- TKPROF

These tools are discussed in the following sections.

Using EXPLAIN PLAN

By using the *EXPLAIN PLAN* command, you can determine how Oracle would execute a given SQL statement. The *EXPLAIN PLAN* command displays the execution plan and shows the sequence in which Oracle executes different steps of the statement.

The various components of the execution plan are

- Ordering of tables referenced by the statement
- Access path for each table in the statement
- Join methods chosen for tables in the statement

Before you use the *EXPLAIN PLAN* command, you need to create a table for the explain plan output.

Run the UTLXPLAN.SQL script present in the $ORACLE_HOME/rdbms/admin directory to create the PLAN_TABLE in your schema. PLAN_TABLE is the default table where EXPLAIN PLAN redirects the execution plan output. Otherwise you can create your own table and while issuing the EXPLAIN PLAN command, redirect the output to the desired table. The default structure of the plan table is as follows:

```
STATEMENT_ID       VARCHAR2 (30)
TIMESTAMP          DATE
REMARKS            VARCHAR2 (80)
OPERATION          VARCHAR2 (30)
OPTIONS            VARCHAR2 (30)
OBJECT_NODE        VARCHAR2 (128)
OBJECT_OWNER       VARCHAR2 (30)
OBJECT_NAME        VARCHAR2 (30)
OBJECT_INSTANCE    NUMBER (38)
OBJECT_TYPE        VARCHAR2 (30)
OPTIMIZER          VARCHAR2 (255)
SEARCH_COLUMNS     NUMBER (38)
ID                 NUMBER (38)
PARENT_ID          NUMBER (38)
POSITION           NUMBER (38)
COST               NUMBER (38)
CARDINALITY        NUMBER (38)
BYTES              NUMBER (38)
OTHER_TAG          VARCHAR2 (255)
PARTITION_START    VARCHAR2 (255)
PARTITION_STOP     VARCHAR2 (255)
PARTITION_ID       NUMBER (38)
OTHER              LONG
DISTRIBUTION       VARCHAR2 (30)
```

Table 12-3 describes the columns contained in the plan table.

Column	Description
STATEMENT_ID	The value of the STATEMENT_ID parameter specified in the EXPLAIN PLAN statement.
TIMESTAMP	The date and time of issuance of the EXPLAIN PLAN statement.
REMARKS	Comments you want to associate with each step of the explained plan. To add or change a remark on any row of the PLAN_TABLE, use the UPDATE statement to modify the rows of the PLAN_TABLE.
OPERATION	In the first row generated for a statement, the column contains one of the following values: –Delete statement –Insert statement –Select statement –Update statement
OPTIONS	A variation on the operation described in the OPERATION column.
OBJECT_NODE	The database link used to reference an object.
OBJECT_OWNER	A user who is owner of the schema containing the table or index.
OBJECT_NAME	The table or index name.
OBJECT_INSTANCE	The position of the object as it appears in the original statement.
OBJECT_TYPE	A modifier that provides information about the object—for example, NON-UNIQUE for indexes.
OPTIMIZER	The current optimizer mode.
SEARCH_COLUMNS	Columns that are not used currently.
ID	A number assigned to each step in the execution plan.
PARENT_ID	The ID of the next execution step that operates on the output of the ID step.

TABLE 12-3. *Description of the Columns in PLAN_TABLE*

Column	Description
POSITION	The processing order for steps with the same PARENT_ID.
COST	The cost of the operation as estimated by the cost-based optimizer. For rule statements that use rule-based optimization, this column is null.
CARDINALITY	The estimate of the number of rows accessed by the operation.
BYTES	The estimate of the number of bytes accessed by the operation.
OTHER_TAG	Describes the contents of the OTHER column.
PARTITION_START	Provides the start partition of a range of partitions that have been accessed partitions. It can have the following values: −*n* indicates that the start partition has been identified by the SQL compiler. −*KEY* indicates that the start partition will be identified at execution time. −*ROW LOCATION* indicates that the start partition will be computed at execution time from the location of each record being retrieved. −*INVALID* indicates that the range of partitions that have been accessed is empty.
PARTITION_STOP	The stop partition of a range of accessed partitions. It can have one of the following values: −*n* indicates that the stop partition has been identified by the SQL compiler. −*KEY* indicates that the stop partition will be identified at time of execution. −*ROW LOCATION* indicates that the stop partition will be computed at execution time from the location of each record being retrieved. −*INVALID* indicates that the range of accessed partitions is empty.

TABLE 12-3. *Description of the Columns in PLAN_TABLE* (continued)

Column	Description
PARTITION_ID	The step that has computed the pair of values of the PARTITION_START and PARTITION_STOP columns.
OTHER	Miscellaneous information specific to the execution step and might be of some use to a user.
DISTRIBUTION	Stores the method used to distribute rows from producer query servers to consumer query servers.

TABLE 12-3.   *Description of the Columns in PLAN_TABLE* (continued)

Some examples of the EXPLAIN PLAN command are shown here:

```
SQL> Explain Plan for Select po_header_id, po_line_id,
type_lookup_code
From po_header_all ph1, po_lines_all a1here ph1.po_line_id= a1.po_line_id;
SQL> Select OBJECT_NAME, OPERATION, OPTIONS From Plan_Table;
OBJECT_NAME      OPERATION                        OPTIONS
-----------   ----------------               ----------------
NESTED LOOPS     SELECT STATEMENT po_header_all   TABLE ACCESS
FULL             po_lines_all                     TABLE ACCESS
BY INDEX ROWID   pk_vendor     INDEX              UNIQUE SCAN
```

In case of a table having a bitmap index, the EXPLAIN PLAN might look like this:

```
OPERATION                OPTIONS              OBJECT_NAME
----------            ----------           ----------
SELECT STATEMENT      INLIST ITERATOR      TABLE ACCESS
BY INDEX ROWID        po_header_all         BITMAP CONVERSION
TO ROWIDS                BITMAP INDEX        SINGLE VALUEpo_header_name
```

In case of a partition column, the EXPLAIN PLAN output will look like this:

```
OPERATION      OPTIONS   OBJECT_NAME   PARTITION_START   PARTITION_STOP
------------  --------  -----------   ---------------   --------------
SELECT STATEMENT    PARTITION      KEY(INLIST)       KEY(INLIST)
TABLE ACCESS   BY ROWID    po_header_all       KEY(INLIST)       KEY(INLIST)
INDEX          RANGE SCAN  po_header_name KEY(INLIST)       KEY(INLIST)
EXPLAIN PLAN can be used to derive user-defined CPU and I/O costs for indexes.
EXPLAIN PLAN displays these statistics in the OTHER column of PLAN_TABLE.
OBJECT_NAME       OPERATION          OPTIONS          OTHER
-----------     ----------------   ------------    ----------------
SELECT STATEMENT   po_header_all    TABLE ACCESS      BY ROWID
po_issue_date      DOMAIN INDEX     CPU: 300, I/O:      4
```

The EXPLAIN PLAN statement explains the way Oracle executes the statement, but it cannot find differences between a well-tuned statement and a poor statement. It shows the access path and usage of the index.

Oracle does not support EXPLAIN PLAN for statements performing implicit type conversion of date bind variables. With bind variables in general, the EXPLAIN PLAN output may not represent the real execution plan.

Using Statspack

Oracle uses the UtlBstat and UtlEstat database statistics report to collect and examine statistics relating to performance tuning. In earlier versions of Oracle, this report was known as BSTAT/ESTAT. However, Oracle8i introduced an improved version of UtlBstat known as *statspack*. In addition to providing functionalities the same as in UtlBstat/UtlEstat, statspack offers some additional features:

■ Comprises additional data in terms of SQL statements

■ Stores data in database tables and not as text files

■ Runs continuously in the background if required

The UtlBstat and UtlEstat database statistics reports are based on two standard SQL scripts, namely UtlBstat.sql and UtlEstat.sql. These two scripts are stored in the $ORACLE_HOME/rdbms/admin directory. The UtlBstat.sql script is used to create a set of tables and views. These tables and views are then populated with the initial database performance statistics. The UtlEstat.sql scripts populate the tables with the end database performance statistics and then create a new set of tables that contain the differences of the initial statistics and final statistics. You use these statistics to create the UtlEstat reports.

To create UtlEstat reports, perform the following steps:

1. Ensure that timed_statistics are enabled. To check whether timed_statistics are enabled you can use the command

   ```
   show parameter timed_statistics
   ```

   in the server manager. If the timed_statistics are not enabled, you need to issue the following command:

   ```
   Alter system set timed_statistics=true;
   ```

2. In the server manager, run UtlBstat.sql by issuing the command

   ```
   @$ORACLE_HOME/rdbms/admin/utlbstat
   ```

3. After running the UtlBstat.sql script, you need to run the batch job or report that is facing the problem.

4. In the server manager, run UtlEstat.sql by issuing the command

```
@$ORACLE_HOME/rdbms/admin/utlestat
```

After you have performed all these steps a file called report.txt is created, which contains statistics relating to performance tuning. The main sections of the UtlEstat report are:

- Library Cache [LC]
- General Statistics [GS]
- Average Write Queue [WQ]
- Wait Events [EV]
- Latches [LA]
- Buffer Busy Waits [BW]
- Rollback Segments [RS]
- Initialization Parameters [IP]
- Rowcache Statistics [RW]
- Tablespace and File I/O Statistics [IO]

Using SQL Trace

The SQL Trace utility can provide information on the performance of the SQL statements. This utility can be enabled for an instance or a session. Once enabled, it generates statistics for all the executed SQL statements. The SQL Trace utility writes the performance statistics to a trace file in the USER_DUMP_DEST directory. If the SQL Trace is enabled at session, it creates a trace file for all the statements in the session; whereas if it is enabled for a session, it creates one trace file for each process.

SQL Trace can generate the following statistics for each statement:

- Parse, execute, and fetch counts
- CPU usage and elapsed time
- The number of logical and disk reads
- Library cache misses
- Number of rows processed

To use the SQL Trace command, set the following initialization parameters in the init.ora file. In addition, the DBMS_APPLICATION_INFO package provides more parameters for use with SQL Trace.

- **USER_DUMP_DEST** Specifies the destination directory where Oracle will create the trace file to write the statistics generated by the SQL Trace utility. This parameter can be set both in the initialization parameter file and at the session level.

- **TIMED_STATISTICS** Enables collection of timed statistics such as CPU time, elapsed time, and collection of some statistics in the data dictionary for the SQL Trace utility. This parameter can be set both in the initialization parameter file and at session level.

- **MAX_DUMP_FILE_SIZE** Controls the maximum size of trace files. The default value for this parameter is 500. This parameter can be set both in the initialization parameter file and also at the session level.

- **SQL_TRACE** Enables SQL Trace. This parameter can be set both in the initialization parameter file and at the session level. The default value for this parameter is False.

To enable SQL Trace for a session, enter the following command:

```
SQL> Alter Session Set SQL_TRACE = True;
```

Alternatively you can use the following procedure to enable SQL Trace for a session:

```
DBMS_SESSION.SET_SQL_TRACE
```

To enable SQL Trace for an instance, include the following parameter in the initialization parameter file:

```
SQL_TRACE = True
```

To enable SQL Trace for all the sessions once the server is started, use the following command:

```
SQL> Alter System Set SQL_TRACE = True;
```

DBMS_APPLICATION_INFO Parameter Package

This package is used with SQL Trace for tracking transactions in the database to collect their performance statistics. This package allows you to register a module or application so that its performance can be tracked for further tuning. The module or application can be a Developer2000 Form or a Pro*C program.

Once you have registered the module or application with the help of this package, the system starts tracking performance by monitoring the resource usage by each registered module or application. One must have access to DBMS_APPLICATION_INFO package to use it; this can be created by running the dbmsutl.sql script present in the $ORACLE_HOME/rdbms/admin directory. You can query the dynamic performance views V$SQLAREA and V$SESSION to find out the registered modules.

The following are some important procedures within the DBMS_APPLICATION_INFO package:

- **SET_MODULE**   Registers the name of the application or module.

- **SET_ACTION**   Sets the current action within the module.

- **SET_CLIENT_INFO**   Sets additional information about the client.

Using TKPROF

After the SQL Trace generates statistics for statements, you can format the output of the trace file into a readable output file by using TKPROF. You can also use TKPROF to determine the execution plan of a statement. TKPROF reports the resources consumed by each statement and the number of times the statement was called. By looking at the statistics generated, you can easily figure out the statements that use the maximum resources.

To use TKPROF, you must have statistics gathered in the trace file by the SQL Trace utility. TKPROF takes this trace file as an input and produces a readable output file. TKPROF must be run on each individual trace file. Following are some examples of TKPROF syntax.

In this example, the first parameter is the name of trace file and the second parameter is the output trace file:

```
C:\> TKPROF ora53269.trc ora53269.txt
```

Now look at the following example:

```
SELECT *
FROM po_header_all, po_lookup_codes
WHERE po_header_all.type_lookup_code = po_lookup_code.type_lookup_code;
call     count       cpu     elapsed       disk      query current       rows
---- -------  -------  ---------  --------  -------- -------  ------
Parse      1      0.16       0.29          3         13       0          0
Execute    1      0.00       0.00          0          0       0          0
```

```
Fetch      1     0.03      0.26       2        2       4       14
Misses in library cache during parse: 1
Parsing user id: (8) SCOTT
Rows       Execution Plan
-------    -----------------------------------------------------
14         MERGE JOIN
4          SORT JOIN
4          TABLE ACCESS (FULL) OF 'po_lookup_codes'
14         SORT JOIN
14         TABLE ACCESS (FULL) OF 'po_header_all'
```

Statistics for a SQL statement is indicated by the value of the CALL column:

- PARSE column translates the SQL statement into an execution plan, including checks for proper security authorization and checks for the existence of tables, columns, and other referenced objects.

- EXECUTE is the actual execution of the statement by Oracle. For INSERT, UPDATE, and DELETE statements, this modifies the data. For SELECT statements, this identifies the selected rows.

- FETCH column retrieves rows returned by a query. Fetches are performed for select statements only.

- COUNT column counts the number of times a statement was parsed, executed, or fetched.

- CPU column keeps track of the total CPU time in seconds for all parse, execute, or fetch calls for the statement. This value is zero (0) if TIMED_STATISTICS is not turned on.

- ELAPSED column keeps track of the total time elapsed in seconds for all parse, execute, or fetch calls for the statement. This value is zero (0) if TIME_STATISTICS is not turned on.

- DISK keeps track of the total number of data blocks physically read from the datafiles on disk for all parse, execute, or fetch calls.

- QUERY keeps track of the total number of buffers retrieved in consistent mode for all parse, execute, or fetch calls. Buffers are usually retrieved in consistent mode for queries.

- CURRENT keeps track of the total number of buffers retrieved in current mode. Buffers are retrieved in current mode for statements such as INSERT, UPDATE, and DELETE.

■ ROWS keeps track of the total number of rows processed by the SQL statement. This total does not include rows processed by subqueries of the SQL statements.

Using Stored Outlines to Store Performance Parameters

In Oracle, you can use stored outlines to store performance parameters and ensure constant performance parameters to an application. It can overlook changes to the database memory structure, optimizer mode settings, and initialize parameters so that applications are not affected.

Stored outlines are nothing but the execution plans generated by Oracle Optimizer. These execution plans are preserved in the stored outlines so that you can use the same execution plan for all the subsequent calls of the statement without being affected by the database environment and system configuration changes. Stored outlines can be created for all SQL statements, and the optimizer starts using them once stored outlines are enabled.

For every SQL statement, a stored outline will be generated, and reuse of the stored outline for subsequent execution of the same statement will depend on whether both the statements match exactly or not. It does exact statement matching before the optimizer can decide to use the same outline for the statement. Hence for statements that have some attributes that change frequently, stored outlines might degrade the performance. As a result, stored outlines can be used for statements that require Oracle to use a constant execution plan, irrespective of the environment.

You can use stored outlines effectively while upgrading the system from one optimizer mode to the other. If some applications have been designed to use rule-based optimization and you have measured the performance to be very good in rule-based optimization, you can preserve the execution plan designed while moving the rest of the application to cost-based optimization. Also, while upgrading Oracle, the optimizer might behave differently. To preserve the same execution plan over the Oracle releases, you can use stored outlines.

Create an Outline Based on CREATE_STORED_OUTLINE

Stored outline creation and usage is dependent upon the parameter CREATE_STORED_OUTLINE in the parameter file. If this parameter is set to True, Oracle creates and uses the stored outlines. However, enabling the CREATE_STORED_OUTLINE parameter does not allow creation of stored outlines. You must grant the CREATE ANY OUTLINE privilege to the user in which outlines need to be created.

Apart from the CREATE_STORED_OUTLINE parameter, the following parameters may also need to be set for the outline to work properly:

- QUERY_REWRITE_ENABLED
- STAR_TRANSFORMATION_ENABLED
- OPTIMZER_FEATURE_ENABLED

You can use the following command to create a stored outline for any statement:

```
Create or Replace OUTLINE dss_outline
On Select po_header_id,agent_id,type_lookup_code from po_header_all;
```

You can create outlines for the following SQL statements:

- SELECT
- DMLs
- INSERT INTO...SELECT * FROM
- CREATE TABLE...AS SELECT

While creating an outline, you can specify the category in which the outline will be stored. If not specified, it is stored in the DEFAULT category.

To use the execution plans that are kept in the stored outline, you need to set the USE_STORED_OUTLINES parameter to True or to a category name depending on the statement.

The information about the stored outlines can be found from the following data dictionary tables:

- USER/ALL/DBA_OUTLINES
- USER/ALL/DBA_OUTLINE_HINTS
- OL$
- OL$HINTS

Using the OUTLN_PKG   The OUTLN_PKG provides a set of procedures to manage the stored outlines. Some of these procedures are

- **DROP_UNUSED**   Drops all unused outlines since they were created.

- **DROP_BY_CAT**   Drops all outlines belonging to a category.

- **UPDATE_BY_CAT**   Assigns a new outline category to all outlines in a category.

Using DBMS_STATS Package

To use cost-based optimization, Oracle needs some statistics in the data dictionary. DBMS_STATS package allows you to generate and manage statistics required for cost-based optimizer to work. It can gather statistics for the following objects:

- Tables

- Partitions

- Columns

- Indexes

It cannot generate statistics for clusters. The following is a list of some important procedures in the DBMS_STATS package:

- **GATHER_INDEX_STATS**   Collects index statistics.

- **GATHER_TABLE_STATS**   Collects statistics for tables including statistics for columns and indexes.

- **GATHER_SCHEMA_STATS**   Collects statistics for all objects in a schema.

- **GATHER_DATABASE_STATS**   Collects statistics for all objects in the database.

- **DELETE_INDEX_STATS**   Deletes all index-related statistics.

- **DELETE_TABLE_STATS**   Deletes all table-related statistics.

- **DELETE_SCHEMA_STATS**   Deletes all statistics in the schema.

- **DELETE_DATABASE_STATS**   Deletes all statistics in the database.

- **CREATE_STAT_TABLE**   Creates a table with the name "stattab" to hold statistics for the current user.

- **DROP_STATS_TABLE**   Removes the "stattab" table from the current user.

Oracle can gather statistics automatically whenever you specify the COMPUTE STATISTICS option while creating or rebuilding indexes.

Summary

In this chapter, you learned that you need to have a well-planned tuning methodology to ensure optimal performance of any Oracle application. You can use different tuning strategies based on the system that is being used in your organization. Application tuning refers to the process of making changes to the system to best meet the customers' requirements. The process of application performance tuning starts with collecting information, identifying problems/bottlenecks, verifying the problem, and finally tuning the application. Since Oracle clients can be based on multiple operating systems such as Windows 98/NT/2000, the steps to tune these clients varies from one operating system to another.

You learned about the different types of applications that use information from a database. You learned that you can enhance performance of applications by using any of the following data access methods:

- Indexes
- Index-organized tables
- Clusters
- Materialized views
- Histograms

You learned about tuning the network and various system tools and utilities that can be used to manage and monitor your network. You also learned that optimization is the process of choosing the most cost efficient way to execute an SQL statement.

Finally, you learned about the three main performance diagnostic tools used by Oracle to tune the applications.

CHAPTER
13

Collecting Statistics
Using Statspack

- What is Statspack?
- Benefits of using Statspack vs. utlbstat/utlestat
- Using snapshots in Statspack
- Statspack installation and setup
- Purging and archiving Statspack tables
- Setting up a process for analyzing Statspack tables
- Statspack reports
- Custom reporting examples

A s DBAs, one of the critical items in our To Do list is to understand and
know our system environment. It is critical for a DBA not only to
understand the types of applications and access methods used but
also to be able to analyze database statistics at different times of the
day and take proactive corrective action. Knowledge about utilization
of memory, I/O, waits, and the like can help the DBA to tune the Financials
environment proactively.

Statspack is Oracle's new diagnostic tool that helps the administrator collect
statistics about database usage. Statspack scripts are written mainly using SQL,
SQL*Plus, and PL/SQL. Statspack is the successor to the UTLBSTAT.SQL and
UTLESTAT.SQL scripts (also known as BSTAT/ESTAT), but Statspack includes many
new features.

Unlike utlbstat/utlestat, Statspack provides a robust and complete set of tuning
statistics. A plethora of tools are available for collecting performance statistics about
the operating system, database, network, and application. The primary objective of
these diagnostic tools is to help the DBA better understand the system environment.

This chapter provides detailed information to help you, as the DBA, understand
the installation and setup of Statspack. It highlights the use of Statspack in the
Oracle Financials environment administration context and evaluates the benefits of
implementing Statspack. More detailed discussion about tuning the application,
database, and other parts of the financials technology stack is covered in Chapter 12.

This chapter also provides a comparison of Statspack with its predecessor
utlbstat and utlestat scripts and defines important terminology. A step-by-step
method for installing Statspack is provided for using it in the context of Oracle
Financials. Because Statspack involves storing database statistics in Oracle tables,
the chapter also provides information and sample scripts for implementing a purge
process for deleting old, unwanted statistics.

After Statspack has been set up and is ready to collect statistics at regular
intervals, you'll need to analyze the statistics tables at every interval so that the
standard Statspack report, as well as any custom reports built using the Statspack
tables, can be efficiently executed. Statspack is a relatively new tool, and we can
expect Oracle to provide many more standard reports with subsequent versions of
Statspack. With this version, you can write your own custom scripts using the
STATS$ tables, as discussed here.

What Is Statspack?

Statspack is an Oracle-provided set of scripts that can be used for collecting, storing,
and viewing database-related statistics. Statspack can be particularly useful when
migrating from one application release to the next. In this case, you can take
snapshots at various points in time before the migration and after the migration and

then compare them. This process is critical in that it can help you conduct impact analyses and iron out issues proactively before they become show stoppers.

Statspack is intended to be used with Oracle versions 8.1.6 and later. However, an unsupported 8.0.x- and 8.1.5-compatible version can be downloaded from Oracle's Web site. The older version works just as well as the new one and can be installed in a production environment with minimal risk.

Benefits of Using Statspack vs. utlbstat/utlestat

Prior to Statspack's release, the utlestat/utlbstat tool (available in versions prior to Oracle 8.0) was the only diagnostic tool that let you see database statistics as a report for a single window of time. The utlbstat/utlestat report does provide a reasonably good overall knowledge about the database; however, it has become archaic because it does not provide good information for Oracle's newer features—for example, large buffers, locally managed tablespaces, and so on. Also, utlbstat/utlestat provides information for a single window of time only. This information could be insufficient, particularly if you wanted to track the performance hourly or perform some trend analysis and comparisons. In addition, utlbstat/utlestat reports are hard to interpret and read. Comparing reports for two different periods can be a difficult exercise. Further, utlbstat/utlestat reports include a lot of statistics and numbers that are undocumented and may not always help with tuning.

Statspack provides a better alternative for Oracle instances. Statspack provides for a solid method of collecting statistics relating to Oracle database server. Following are some of Statpack's benefits:

- Statspack allows you to take statistics at regular intervals and provides reporting to compare two different section evaluations of the database, called *snapshots*. Refer to the "Custom Reporting Examples" section of this chapter to see how you can use this feature to perform trending analysis.

- Statspack identifies high resource SQL statements.

- Statspack is easier to work with than its predecessors because the statistics collection process is different from the reporting process.

- Statspack helps you establish baselines timings. Comparison of current statistics with baseline statistics can help you identify performance issues. After the initial baseline has been set and some performance data captured, Statspack can be used as a tool for regularly monitoring the health of the database side of the Oracle Financials environment. The report can reveal information about various activity levels, changes in number of users, and other areas of tuning.

- Statspack can be run in an Oracle Parallel Server (OPS) environment, where you can connect and collect statistics on specific instances and keep a central repository of all statistics.

- Statspack's database statistics are stored permanently in tables and can be used for custom reporting. This means that you can develop many different reports for trending and proactive tuning.

- Statspack lets you collect snapshots at more frequent intervals and still maintain the regular collection process.

Using Snapshots in Statspack

Statspack allows you to *snap* a *snapshot* of a particular section of data. A snapshot is a single collection of performance data collected at a single period of time. A snapshot of database statistics is collected using a procedure called *snap*. Both standard and custom reporting can be performed at any time from the snapshots that have been collected separately.

You can collect snapshots at frequent intervals and still maintain the regular data collection process. For example, under normal circumstances, you can set up a process that collects statistics every hour, but when working on a specific production performance issue, snapshots can be taken every half hour or even for a single session.

NOTE
Performance impacts' actual execution time for running the snap package on a large production machine running 8.1.5 is about 10 to 20 seconds. The response from a user's perspective is minimal. The execution time can be further reduced by adjusting the SQL statement thresholds to capture only the most critical statistics. The effect of the snapshot in a reasonably large hardware environment running Oracle applications should be minimal. After the basic data capture has been completed and baselines have been established, the frequency of Statspack can be further reduced. Statspack can help identify whether the resources are being used optimally.

A snapshot is collected using the following command:

```
execute statspack.snap;
```

Oracle generates a SNAP_ID for every snapshot and stores more information about the snapshot in a table called STATS$SNAPSHOT.

Table 13-1 shows the 25 Statspack tables included in version 8.1.5, with brief descriptions.

The PERFSTAT schema in 8.1.7 includes changes from the previous versions. Table 13-2 shows the tables in the version 8.1.7 schema.

Table Name	Contents
STATS$BG_EVENT_SUMMARY	Summary of waits and timeouts
STATS$BUFFER_POOL_STATISTICS	Buffer pool statistics information
STATS$DATABASE_INSTANCE	Initialization parameters
STATS$ENQUEUESTAT	Enqueue statistics for various snapshots
STATS$FILESTATXS	File I/O statistics
STATS$IDLE_EVENT	Idle Event statistics
STATS$LATCH	Latch information
STATS$LATCH_CHILDREN	Supporting latch information
STATS$LATCH_MISSES_SUMMARY	Contains a summary of latch misses
STATS$LEVEL_DESCRIPTION	Stores a description of various Statspack levels (level 0, 5 and 10)
STATS$LIBRARYCACHE	Library cache statistics for each snapshot
STATS$PARAMETER	Statspack parameters information
STATS$ROLLSTAT	Rollback segment statistics
STATS$ROWCACHE_SUMMARY	Provides a summary of usage of row cache
STATS$SESSION_EVENT	Session event information
STATS$SESSTAT	Session statistics
STATS$SGASTAT_SUMMARY	SGA Usages Statistics
STATS$SGAXS	SGA Usages Statistics
STATS$SNAPSHOT	Information about the snapshot, such as start time

TABLE 13-1. *Statspack Tables in Version 8.1.5*

Table Name	Contents
STATS$SQL_SUMMARY	Information about SQL statements
STATS$STATSPACK_PARAMETER	Current level and threshold values for various parameters
STATS$SYSSTAT	System statistics
STATS$SYSTEM_EVENT	System events for various snapshots
STATS$WAITSTAT	Wait statistics for various snapshots

TABLE 13-1.   *Statspack Tables in Version 8.1.5* (continued)

Table Name	Contents
STATS$BG_EVENT_SUMMARY	Summary of waits and timeouts
STATS$BUFFER_POOL_STATISTICS	Buffer pool statistics information
STATS$DATABASE_INSTANCE	Initialization parameters
STATS$ENQUEUESTAT	Enqueue statistics for various snapshots
STATS$FILESTATXS	File I/O statistics
STATS$IDLE_EVENT	Idle Event statistics
STATS$LATCH	Latch information
STATS$LATCH_CHILDREN	Supporting latch information
STATS$LATCH_MISSES_SUMMARY	SGA Usages Statistics
STATS$LEVEL_DESCRIPTION	Stores a description of various level Statpack levels (level 0, 5 and 10)
STATS$LIBRARYCACHE	Library cache statistics for each snapshot
STATS$PARAMETER	Statspack parameters information
STATS$ROLLSTAT	Rollback segment statistics
STATS$ROWCACHE_SUMMARY	Provides a summary of usage of row cache

TABLE 13-2.   *Statspack Tables in Version 8.1.7.*

Table Name	Contents
STATS$SESSION_EVENT	Session event information
STATS$SESSTAT	Session statistics
STATS$SGA	SGA Usages Statistics
STATS$SGASTAT	SGA Usages Statistics
STATS$SNAPSHOT	Information about the snapshot, such as start time
STATS$SQLTEXT	New table in 8.1.7
STATS$SQL_STATISTICS	New table in 8.1.7
STATS$SQL_SUMMARY	Information about SQL statements
STATS$STATSPACK_PARAMETER	Current level and threshold values for various parameters
STATS$SYSSTAT	System statistics
STATS$SYSTEM_EVENT	System events for various snapshots
STATS$TEMPSTATXS	New table in 8.1.7
STATS$WAITSTAT	Wait statistics for various snapshots

TABLE 13-2.   *Statspack Tables in Version 8.1.7.* (continued)

TIP
When comparing two snapshots, make sure that they reflect the same type of activity. This helps ensure that you are comparing like variables. You may need to collect more snapshots for accurately determining a performance problem. Many times, there are different types of activities happening on the instance at different times. For example, there could be many batch programs and fewer transactions during the off-business hours and the converse may be the case during business hours. It may be helpful to work with multiple snapshots (probably every hour) to more accurately determine the cause of the performance issue.

TIP
When taking a Statspack report to compare two snapshots, make sure that the instance was not shut down between the two snapshots. This may give misleading results.

Snapshot Levels

Statspack can be executed at three snapshot levels:

- **Level 0** Statspack collects overall statistics about the database, including wait statistics, library cache, rollback segment, and I/O.

- **Level 5** The default level for Statspack. In addition to level 0 statistics, Statspack gathers resource-intensive SQL statements. The thresholds for identifying a resource-intensive SQL statement can be tuned. This is helpful in restricting your list and avoiding collection of huge amounts of statistics. The idea here is to tune only the top offenders. The following thresholds can be changed:

  - Number of executions: default value is 100

  - Number of disk reads: default value is 1000

  - Number of parse calls: default value is 1000

  - Number of buffer gets: default value is 10000

- **Level 10** Takes longer to execute and should be used only on advice from Oracle support technicians. Running Statspack with level 10 could cause performance impacts (which we won't go into here).

i_ucomment

The i_ucomment text line can be stored along with the snapshot information. This comment line could be used for storing details about the snapshot itself—information such as identification of the snapshot: for example, "Baseline Snapshot" or "Snapshot after changing the Buffer values."

Statspack Installation and Setup

As discussed earlier, Statspack is designed to be used starting with Oracle version 8.1.6. However, 8.0.x- and 8.1.5-compatible Statspack versions can be downloaded from the Oracle Web page and can also be executed successfully. Figure 13-1 shows the scripts that are installed as part of the Statspack and their functions.

Starting with version 8.1.6, Statspack scripts are installed automatically along with Oracle server installation. If you are planning to use Statspack with either version 8.0.x or 8.1.5, make sure you download the scripts and copy them to $ORACLE_HOME/rdbms/admin. Figure 13-2 shows a list of Statspack scripts in 8.1.6 along with their purposes.

Following is a step-by-step procedure for installing Statspack in your Oracle Financials environment. These steps assume that the Statspack scripts are available under $ORACLE_HOME/rdbms/admin.

Step 1   Create a new tablespace to store the schema created by Statspack.

```
CREATE TABLESPACE STATSPACK DATAFILE
'/u01/oradata/finp11i/statspack1.dbf' SIZE 1024M
DEFAULT STORAGE- (INITIAL 1M NEXT 1M PCTINCREASE 0);
```

It's a good idea to create a separate tablespace for Statspack so you can have better control of the tables. You should also keep your initial extent and next extent

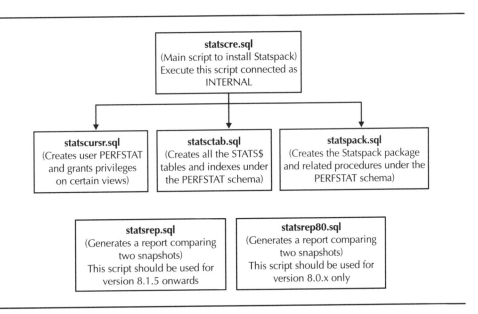

FIGURE 13-1.   *Statspack scripts in version 8.1.5 and their functions*

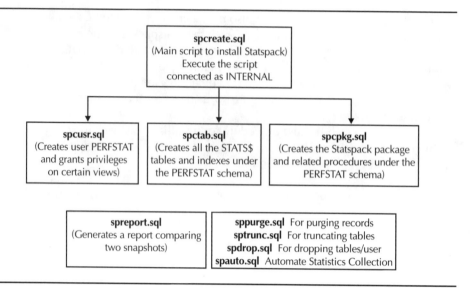

FIGURE 13-2. *Statspack scripts in version 8.1.6 and their purpose*

small, because some of the create index statements do not have storage parameters assigned to them.

Step 2   If you are planning to install Statspack on either version 8.0.x or 8.1.5, execute the script to create the v$buffer_pool_statistics view. This script needs to be run because Statspack makes use of this view, and this view does not exist on either 8.0.x or 8.1.5. If you are running on version 8.1.6, this step is not necessary, and you can proceed to step 3.

```
sqlplus internal
sql>@$ORACLE_HOME/rdbms/admin/statscbps
```

Step 3   Execute the script to install Statspack. For version 8.1.5, use this:

```
sqlplus internal
sql>$ORACLE_HOME/rdbms/admin/statscre
```

For version 8.1.6 and later, use this:

```
sqlplus internal
sql>$ORACLE_HOME/rdbms/admin/spcreate
```

This script creates a user called PERFSTAT and creates all the STATS$ tables and indexes under PERFSTAT. The script also creates the Statspack package under PERFSTAT. Make sure that you specify the default tablespace for PERFSTAT, as the PERFSTAT tablespace created in step 1 is also an appropriate temporary tablespace.

TIP
The statscre.sql or spcreate.sql script does not define storage parameters for some indexes. Also, tables and indexes are created in the same tablespace. Make sure that you create your tablespace with small initial and next extents to avoid overallocation of extents. You may also consider using locally managed tablespaces for storing Statspack tables.

Step 4   Now you are ready to take snapshots of database statistics and save them to various tables under the PERFSTAT schema. You can either execute a snapshot from the SQL prompt or set up a cron job or a batch process to execute the snapshot periodically. A cron job helps schedule a batch job at a particular time or at specific time intervals. Cron jobs are set up in the crontab file in UNIX. Refer to the section "Automating the Process of Gathering Snapshots" for a discussion on setting up a cron job. To take a snapshot, execute the following command:

```
execute statspack.snap;
```

Step 5   To execute the standard report that is available with Statspack, use the following scripts.
For version 8.1.6 and later:

```
sqlplus perfstat/perfstat
sql>@$ORACLE_HOME/rdbms/admin/spreport
```

For version 8.1.5 and later:

```
sqlplus perfstat/perfstat
sql>@$ORACLE_HOME/rdbms/admin/statsrep
```

For version 8.0.x:

```
sqlplus perfstat/perfstat
sql>@$ORACLE_HOME/rdbms/admin/statsrep80
```

The script displays all the available snapshots (SNAP_ID and SNAP_TIME are displayed). It accepts two snapshots and proceeds to print a comparative report for that window of time. The script also displays a report file name that can be modified. The default for the report name is st_<*starting-snap-id*>-<*ending-snap_id*>.lst.

The statsrep report is a detailed report similar to utlbstat/utlestat. The first page of the report provides a summary of the database and includes sections on cache sizes, load profiles, instance efficiency percentages, and the top five wait statistics. This first page can be used to analyze specific causes of contention, such as buffer waits and extended waits on database file scattered read. The rest of the report provides details on aspects such as library cache, rollback segment, I/O statistics, and wait statistics, as well as resource-intensive SQL statements individually listed and ordered by executions, parse calls, buffer gets, and disk reads.

Changing Statspack Levels and Thresholds

The default level at which Statspack runs is 5, which means that, by default, snapshots will capture overall database statistics as well as resource-intensive SQL statements. However, you can execute Statspack to take a snapshot at a different level by using the following command:

```
sqlplus internal
sql>execute statspack.snap(I_snap_level=>0);
```

You can also use the snap procedure to change the four SQL statements thresholds. Thresholds are valid for the current run of the snapshot only. To make changes permanent for all snapshots, use the modify_statspack_parameter procedure, shown next. This script will change the thresholds for all snapshots taken after executing this statement.

```
begin
    statspack.modify_statspack_parameter(i_executions_th => 1000,
    i_disk_reads_th => 10000,
    i_parse_calls_th => 10000,
    i_buffer_gets_th => 100000);
end;
/
```

Automating the Process of Gathering Snapshots

Snapshots can be collected at periodic intervals—say every hour—by executing the snap procedure. The process can be automated either by using a cron job (in UNIX) or AT (on Windows), or by using DBMS_JOB script that is part of the Statspack scripts. Statspack includes a script called statsauto.sql that helps with the Statspack setup.

Here's how to automate this process using a cron job. You will develop a wrapper program called *snap.ksh* that will execute the statspack.snap procedure. The snap.ksh script will then be set up as a cron job to be run periodically.

The following script (snap.ksh) illustrates a way of collecting database statistics using Statspack. The script connects to the appropriate database instance and executes the snap procedure to collect statistics and store it in database tables under the PERFSTAT schema. The script can be executed at regular intervals for getting trending information.

```
##################################################################
#   snap.ksh
#   Shankaran Iyer   Sept, 2000
#   This script executes the snapshot procedure for collecting
#   database statistics using Statspack
#   This script can be executed using cron to run at regular times
##################################################################
echo 'Snapshot Started at '`date`
ORACLE_HOME=/u01/app/oracle/8.1.5
ORACLE_SID=finp11I
export ORACLE_HOME
export ORACLE_SID
$ORACLE_HOME/bin/sqlplus -s <<EOF
perfstat/perfstat
execute statspack.snap;
exit;
EOF
echo 'Snapshot Completed at '`date`
```

The following code shows the crontab entry to execute the previous code every hour to collect performance statistics.

```
# The following entry will execute the snap.ksh every hour to collect snapshot
00 0-23 * * * $ORACLE_BASE/admin/scripts/snap.ksh > /dev/null 2>&1
```

Using Statspack Tables

In addition to processing the standard report for a given range of snapshots, the STATS$ tables can be used in the following ways:

- To help you write custom scripts to compare a particular statistic for every snapshot to perform trend analysis.

- To provide analytical information to help you dig into specific areas, such as wait statistics or I/O analysis.

Sending a Statspack Report via E-mail

After setting up a process for collecting Statspack information, you can initiate a process to e-mail the Statspack reports to the Oracle administration team. Whether this is necessary depends on the size of the application and the number of administrators involved in the tuning process. In any case, sending an e-mail of the one-page overall statistics to critical project folks—such as the project lead, architect, and the functional lead—could be a useful way of communicating the health of the Oracle environment.

You can set up status report (statsrep) to run periodically as a cron job (or a similar scheduling mechanism) and use a command similar to the following for e-mailing the report to the team:

```
mailx -s "Statspack Report" <E-Mail-ID> </u04/logs/DBA/statsrep.log
```

NOTE
The structures of the STATS$ scripts are likely to change in later versions of Oracle Financials, and there is no guarantee of upward compatibility. This means that you may need to develop a process for mapping out the old tables when you upgrade to new ones.

Purging and Archiving Statspack Tables

Beginning with version 8.1.7, the script sppurge.sql can be used to delete snapshots from the Statspack tables. Although no standard script for deleting old snapshot information existed prior to version 8.1.7, it is a good idea to delete old data to make room for new data. For example, you can build a process for deleting snapshot information that is more than three months old, based on the SNAP_TIME field in the STATS$SNAPSHOT table. A good workaround is to delete corresponding records from the STATS$SNAPSHOT table, and because of the DELETE CASCADE referential integrity that exists with other tables, corresponding rows from other tables are deleted as well.

The following script can be used for deleting snapshot data that was collected during a specific period of time. This script can be executed periodically to purge unwanted statistics and make room for new statistics.

This script can be used for periodically purging the data collected by STATSPACK. It accepts a start and end STARTUP_TIME and deletes records from STATS$SNAPSHOT. Corresponding records from other tables are deleted automatically because of the DELETE CASCADE RI. This script can be executed using cron to run at regular times:

```
##################################################################
#  delete_snap.ksh
#  Shankaran Iyer    Sept, 2000

##################################################################
echo 'Starting to purge STATSPACK tables at '`date`
ORACLE_HOME=/u01/app/oracle/8.1.5
ORACLE_SID=finp11I
export ORACLE_HOME
export ORACLE_SID
$ORACLE_HOME/bin/sqlplus -s <<EOF
perfstat/perfstat
delete from stats$snapshot where startup_date between $1 and $2;
exit;
EOF
echo 'Purge of Statspack tables complete at  '`date`
```

Analyzing Statspack Tables

All the Statspack tables should be analyzed periodically to make sure that the Oracle optimizer will use an appropriate execution plan when using these tables. Following is a suggested script that could be used for analyzing Statspack tables:

```
execute dbms_utility.analyze_schema('PERFSTAT','ESTIMATE',null,20);
```

Custom Reporting Examples

The STATS$ table can be used for custom reporting in a number of ways. A plethora of scripts can be developed to help with trending and to help you understand the behavior of the environment at specific points—for example, you may want to determine whether you need to tune the environment differently for your batch runs during the evening as compared to the daytime, when many Internet-based users expect fast response times. By comparing specific statistics over a period of time, you can not only establish your requirements in terms of capacity, but you can also pinpoint which parameters need to be changed for optimal performance. This section includes two examples of how STATS$ tables can be used for custom reporting.

Comparing Hourly Average Instance Efficient Percentages

This script picks up the overall percentage information from various snapshots (on an hourly basis) and tabulates the results. The report uses a temporary table called IEP to store the various ratios. The structure of the IEP table is as follows:

```
CREATE TABLE IEP
   (BSID              NUMBER(7),
    ESID              NUMBER(7),
    SDT                      DATE,
    EDT                      DATE,
    BUFFER_NOWAITS           NUMBER(5,2),
    BUFFER_HIT               NUMBER(5,2),
    LIBRARY_HIT              NUMBER(5,2),
    REDO_NOWAIT              NUMBER(5,2),
    IN_MEMORY_SORT           NUMBER(5,2),
    SOFT_PARSE               NUMBER(5,2),
    LATCH_HIT                NUMBER(5,2)
   );
```

The following script populates the IEP table with various ratios from the Statspack snapshot information:

```
declare
cursor c1 is
select snap_id,
       snap_time
 from stats$snapshot order by 1;

 bid  number  := '';
 bdt  date;
 eid  number  := '';
 edt  date;
 lhtr number;
 bfwt number;
 tran number;
 chng number;
 ucal number;
 urol number;
 rsiz number;
 phyr number;
 phyw number;
 prse number;
 hprs number;
```

```
    recr number;
    gets number;
    rlsr number;
    rent number;
    srtm number;
    srtd number;
    srtr number;
    strn number;
    call number;
    lhr  number;
    sp   varchar2(512);
    bc   varchar2(512);
    lb   varchar2(512);
    bs   varchar2(512);
    twt  number;

begin
  for c1rec in c1 LOOP
    if bid is null then bid := c1rec.snap_id; bdt := c1rec.snap_time;
                        eid := c1rec.snap_id; edt := c1rec.snap_time;
    else bid := eid; bdt := edt;
         eid:= c1rec.snap_id; edt := c1rec.snap_time;
           STATSPACK.STAT_CHANGES
    ( bid,  eid      -- IN arguments
    , lhtr, bfwt, tran, chng, ucal, urol, rsiz, phyr, phyw
    , prse, hprs
    , recr, gets, rlsr, rent, srtm, srtd, srtr, strn
    , lhr, bc, sp, lb, bs,   twt
    );
    call := ucal + recr;
    insert into iep values
    (bid,eid,bdt,edt,
       round(100*(1-bfwt/gets),2),
       round(100*(1-phyr/gets),2),
       round(100*lhtr,2),
       decode(rent,0,to_number(null),
           round(100*(1-rlsr/rent),2)),
       decode((srtm+srtd),0,to_number(null),
           round(100*srtm/(srtd+srtm),2)),
       round(100*(1-hprs/prse),2),
       round(100*(1-lhr),2)
      );
     commit;
    --dbms_output.put_line('bid '||bid||' '||to_char(bdt,'hh24:mi')||' '||' eid '||
    --           eid||' '||to_char(edt,'hh24:mi'));
    end if;
  end loop;
end;
/
```

Here is the script for printing the average percentages:

```
SET LINESIZE 100 SET PAGESIZE 60 NEWPAGE 0
COLUMN buffer_nowaits FORMAT 999.99 HEADING 'BUF|NOWAIT|RATIO'
COLUMN buffer_hit FORMAT 999.99 HEADING 'BUF|HIT|RATIO'
COLUMN library_hit FORMAT 999.99 HEADING 'LIB|HIT|RATIO'
COLUMN redo_nowait FORMAT 999.99 HEADING 'REDO|NOWAIT|RATIO'
COLUMN in_memory_sort FORMAT 999.99 HEADING 'IN MEM|SORT|RATIO'
COLUMN soft_parse FORMAT 999.99 HEADING 'SOFT|PARSE|RATIO'
COLUMN latch_hit FORMAT 999.99 HEADING 'LATCH|HIT|RATIO'

TTITLE 'Report compares Average Hourly Instance Efficiency %ages across
all snapshots'

SPOOL rep2.rep

SELECT TO_CHAR(sdt,'hh24:mi') ||' to '||TO_CHAR(edt,'hh24:mi') dt
 ,AVG(buffer_nowaits)    buffer_nowaits,
  AVG(buffer_hit)        buffer_hit,
  AVG(library_hit)       library_hit,
  AVG(redo_nowait)       redo_nowait,
  AVG(in_memory_sort)    in_memory_sort,
  AVG(soft_parse)        soft_parse,
  AVG(latch_hit)   latch_hit
FROM iep  GROUP BY
        TO_CHAR(sdt,'hh24:mi') ||' to '||TO_CHAR(edt,'hh24:mi');

SPOOL OFF;
```

The output of this customized report looks like this:

```
Report compares Average Hourly Instance Efficiency %ages across all snapshots
                BUF      BUF     LIB    REDO     IN MEM  SOFT    LATCH
                NOWAIT   HIT     HIT    NOWAIT   SORT    PARSE   HIT
DT              RATIO    RATIO   RATIO  RATIO    RATIO   RATIO   RATIO
-----------------------------------------------------------------------------
00:00 to 01:00   99.97   93.45   99.91  100.00   99.40   99.83   99.93
01:00 to 02:00  100.00   99.02   99.98  100.00   97.36   99.95   99.95
02:00 to 03:00  100.00   97.14   98.85  100.00   99.38   95.19   99.98
03:00 to 04:00  100.00   91.55   99.87  100.00   98.30   99.64   99.91
04:00 to 05:00   99.95   96.07   99.92  100.00   99.96   99.73   99.70
05:00 to 06:00   99.97   96.06   99.94  100.00   99.70   99.84   99.84
06:00 to 07:00   99.94   93.37   98.51  100.00   99.94   96.30   99.77
07:00 to 08:00   99.95   91.03   98.34  100.00   99.90   95.78   99.67
08:00 to 09:00   99.95   87.91   98.01  100.00   99.87   95.07   99.77
09:00 to 10:00   99.98   88.96   97.92  100.00   99.82   94.65   99.05
10:00 to 11:00  100.00   90.35   97.70  100.00   99.68   93.80   99.54
11:00 to 12:00   99.97   86.95   97.63  100.00   99.83   94.25   99.80
12:00 to 13:00  100.00   94.27   97.57  100.00   99.84   94.49   99.88
```

```
13:00 to 14:00   100.00    93.18    97.77   100.00    99.85    93.11    99.84
13:09 to 13:14    99.99    89.89    98.33   100.00    99.56    91.97    99.78
13:14 to 14:00    99.98    91.07    97.92   100.00    99.83    93.35    99.65
14:00 to 15:00    99.97    92.41    97.75   100.00    99.86    93.71    99.85
15:00 to 16:00    99.97    94.63    97.89   100.00    99.84    94.05    99.84
16:00 to 17:00    99.94    89.92    97.86   100.00    99.82    94.28    99.88
17:00 to 18:00    99.91    88.71    97.65   100.00    99.72    93.69    99.91
18:00 to 19:00    99.99    81.32    97.28   100.00    99.80    94.52    99.92
19:00 to 20:00    99.98    82.42    97.76   100.00    99.96    95.16    99.93
20:00 to 21:00   100.00    86.16    96.16   100.00    99.95    89.01    99.85
21:00 to 22:00   100.00    89.67    96.97   100.00    99.99    92.11    99.91
22:00 to 23:00   100.00    92.16    76.09   100.00    99.99    34.76    99.57
23:00 to 00:00   100.00    91.57    88.71   100.00    99.96    67.79    99.91
```

This report can be used to obtain information about the health of the application at different points during the day. It is critical to analyze this information from the Oracle application point of view. It can help you establish capacity planning to ensure that the concurrent users get consistent response from the environment.

Analyzing Hot Data Files in the Production Environment

This example illustrates a method for identifying consistent hot data files. The temporary table called HOT_FILES stores information about the data files that are consistently hot. Here is the structure of HOT_FILES table:

```
-----------------------------------------------------------------------
-- hot_files.sql
-- Shankaran Iyer    Sept, 2000
-- This script creates a temporary table called HOT_FILES
-- After it is populated HOT_FILES can be used for further analysis
-- of I/O related statistics
-----------------------------------------------------------------------

CREATE        TABLE HOT_FILES
   ( SID      NUMBER(7),
     SDT      DATE,
     TSNAME   VARCHAR2(30),
     FILENAME VARCHAR2(257),
     NUM_OF_IOS NUMBER
   );
```

The HOT_FILES table is populated based on the information from the STATS$FILESTATXS table that stores physical reads and writes information on various datafiles. The following script calculates the I/O performed by various datafiles for a period of 60 minutes (the snapshot is executed every hour). The identified files are populated in the HOT_FILES table.

Analyze File I/O Statistics from STATSPACK repository. This script reads through the I/O Statistics, identifies the hot datafiles having > 40 I/Os per sec. The script creates a temporary table called HOT_FILES. This table can be used for further analysis of the hot datafiles.

```
-----------------------------------------------------------------------
--   Shankaran Iyer   Sept, 2000

-----------------------------------------------------------------------
SET SERVEROUTPUT ON SIZE 300000

DECLARE
CURSOR c1 IS
   SELECT DISTINCT tsname,filename FROM stats$filestatxs;
  c1rec c1%ROWTYPE;

CURSOR c2 IS
  SELECT rownum rn, a.snap_id,snap_time,
  tsname,filename,
  phyrds+phywrts i_o
  FROM stats$filestatxs a ,stats$snapshot b
  WHERE    a.snap_id = b.snap_id
    AND filename = c1rec.filename;
  c2rec c2%ROWTYPE;

  prev_io    number;
  hrly_io    number;
  firstrec  boolean :=TRUE;

BEGIN
  DELETE FROM hot_files;
  COMMIT;
  OPEN c1;
  LOOP
  FETCH c1 INTO c1rec;
  EXIT WHEN c1%NOTFOUND;
  firstrec := TRUE;
    OPEN c2;
    LOOP
    FETCH c2 INTO c2rec;
    EXIT WHEN c2%NOTFOUND;
    IF firstrec THEN firstrec := FALSE; prev_io := c2rec.i_o;
    ELSE
      IF c2rec.i_o - prev_io > 2400 THEN
         hrly_io := c2rec.i_o - prev_io;
      INSERT INTO HOT_FILES VALUES
      (c2rec.snap_id,c2rec.snap_time,c1rec.tsname,c1rec.filename,hrly_io);
      END IF;
      prev_io := c2rec.i_o;
    END IF;
    END LOOP;
```

```
      COMMIT;
      CLOSE c2;
    END LOOP;
   CLOSE c1;
 END;
 /
```

The HOT_FILES table can now be used for reporting various proactive statistics:

- Marking consistently hot datafiles that need to be redistributed

- Identifying patterns during specific times of the day

- Exploring tuning of the background processes to improve I/O

Here is an example of a script that identifies hot datafiles based on their physical reads and writes:

```
SET LINESIZE 80 PAGESIZE 60 NEWPAGE 0
COLUMN filename FORMAT A60 HEADING 'FILENAME'
COLUMN avg_io FORMAT 9999999.99 HEADING 'AVG I/O'

TTITLE 'Consistently Hot Data Files '

SPOOL hot_files.rep
SELECT filename,avg(num_of_ios) Avg_IO from hot_files
   group by filename
   order by 2 DESC;

SPOOL OFF;
```

Summary

Starting with version 8.1.6, Oracle has provided a new way to collect statistics: Statspack is implemented using PL/SQL. Statspack is the next level of utlbstat/utlestat that provides a much superior solution in terms of a way to collect database statistics. In Statspack, the process of collecting statistics and reporting statistics are different. This makes Statspack easier to use as well as more useful, since you can continue to collect statistics for a continuous period and process reports whenever you are working on a performance issue. In addition, Statspack can help you track down expensive SQL statements and database statistics. The statistics collected using Statspack are valuable for performance tuning Oracle applications Tuning is discussed in more detail in Chapter 12. Statspack also provides valuable information for making sizing and capacity planning decisions, which is the focus of the next chapter.

CHAPTER 14

Capacity Planning and Sizing

- Benefits of capacity planning
- Methodology for capacity planning
- Benchmarking and sizing applications
- Capacity planning tools

ne of the critical responsibilities of a systems administrator or a Financials administrator of Oracle applications is to provide a variety of projections and extrapolations about the application and the database environment. This information is essential to the people who make capacity planning decisions. Critical sizing of the environment in terms of disk allocation, CPU speed, and number and memory available as well as choice of the hardware platforms are dependent on capacity planning and sizing. In this chapter, we will review the benefits of capacity planning and discuss a methodology for collecting information from various contributing layers. We will also discuss sizing methods and discuss tools that help with capacity planning, such as Oracle Capacity Planner and Statspack.

Benefits of Capacity Planning

Capacity planning is an essential component of any Oracle application environment. Capacity planning and sizing are required to allow the DBA to make authoritative decisions about implementing additional modules, adding more functionality, and even creating a business intelligence component to an existing Oracle applications environment. Capacity planning is an essential component for sustaining day-to-day growth and uptime.

Most e-businesses, large or small, need some kind of capacity planning. Essential to this planning activity are identifying and procuring appropriate hardware, which can take several weeks to months, and planning and forecasting capacity and growth. Collecting, analyzing, and understanding the capacity and performance data also helps the DBA to implement related technology and plan realistically for various resources. For instance, capacity data for an Oracle customer's implementation could be used as a starting point for planning the Oracle purchasing module.

Following are some of the questions that capacity data can help to answer:

- How many Web users can we add to our application before the server peaks?

- What factors must be considered when planning a large Web deployment?

- What kind of open architecture is necessary to plan a Web-based deployment?

- What are the appropriate tuning steps to use for improving performance of Oracle Web applications?

- What additional challenges, such as the need for stress testing, does our system require?

The overall objective of any capacity planning and sizing exercise should be the following:

■ To minimize downtime for the end users due to unavailable resources

■ To ensure that the project implementation deadlines do not suffer for lack of environmental resources

Capacity planning can be accomplished successfully only when an organization collects historical and performance data about various components or layers of the environment. The following components need to be tracked from the capacity planning point of view:

■ Network statistics

■ Operating system statistics (for both application tier and database tier)

■ Database statistics

■ Application volumetrics

■ Web server use

■ Forms/reports server use

Needless to say, to collect statistics, additional processes need to be run—not only on the production systems but sometimes also on the test environments. This leads to additional costs and could create performance concerns to the end users of the production systems. In most cases, the organization should be able to weigh the importance of costs vs. performance.

Procuring the appropriate hardware components is a complex task, especially in the Oracle Financials environment and is certainly worth foregoing a bit of performance to ensure that you collect important growth statistics from the production systems. The other important factor to consider, however, is ensuring that the method adopted for capacity planning has low overhead and does not hamper normal business processing. You must choose a methodology that can be configured so that it can either collect overall statistics of growth and performance data or, if required, can be set to collect more detailed statistics over certain periods of time. By ensuring adequate performance, you can reduce the additional overhead of collected detailed statistics when all you really need is the summary. The next section discusses a methodology for capacity planning and sizing.

Methodology for Capacity Planning

Capacity planning is a detailed exercise, and your success largely depends on the periodicity, accuracy, and reliability of the data you collect. Capacity planning involves reviewing each of the components that contribute to the running of the application, including the database tier, application or middle tier, and the desktop tier. A good methodology should include the following steps:

■ Identify each of the layers, including operating system (UNIX and Windows NT), database (different versions), and application (different versions) and classify them into distinct groups for the purpose of collecting and analyzing the statistics.

■ Collect compatible statistics for similar periodicity. If you are running Statspack on the database every hour, for example, make sure you are also collecting UNIX statistics using sar (system activity report), MeasureWare, or similar utilities during the same time periods. This makes your data easier to analyze and correlate.

■ Review your statistics periodically and make sure that your thresholds are set to appropriate values. This will ensure that you are not collecting too many unnecessary statistics. The crux of capacity planning is to weed out much of the information, while still ensuring that you can make accurate decisions based on critical statistics.

■ Make sure that you periodically publish results about how the environment is doing. This will not only help management understand the application health, but it will help establish the importance of capacity planning and improve your processes. It is always a good idea to perform capacity planning on a continuous basis rather than as a one time exercise, which may lead to inconsistent processes, which in turn lead to inaccurate estimations.

■ If you are not using a particular measurement tool, you may need to use statistical techniques such as an extrapolation formula, sampling techniques, or operational research methodology to apply to the available data to get an idea of your future needs. It is critical to choose the appropriate formula that will apply to your situation, but you need to make sure it is realistic and statistically appropriate to your system.

■ As they say in statistics, do not draw conclusions from one or two discrete values. Instead, look for continuous patterns before making conclusions about CPU usage, memory contention, and other issues.

Capacity Planning Example

Following is an example of how capacity planning can work. We begin with Table 14-1, which shows the number of employees and transactions needed for implementing an Oracle expenses implementation. Table 14-2 shows the company growth in terms of disk space. Here is a list of several important factors that should be considered.

1. The most critical parameter to monitor in an Oracle Web-based application is "number of concurrent users"—not the total number of users who can access the application. Accordingly, you can set up your environment to ensure that enough resources are available for all the concurrent users.

2. The three important resources to monitor closely and tune, in order, are network usage (bandwidth), memory, and CPU.

3. Typically, Web-based applications require a variable memory of about 5 to 15MBs per user, and about 250MB per 100 users. In addition, Oracle Web-based applications require a fixed memory of about 20 to 25MB. The CPU is heavily used only when database activities are performed and not for the time the user is connected into the application.

	Q2-2000 No. of Employees	Q2-2000 No. of Transactions	Q2-2001 No. of Employees	Q2-2001 No. of Transactions
Business Unit A	2500	40,000	2500	40,000
Business Units B & C			40,000	400,000
Disk Space (See Point 1)		21 GB		205 GB
Application Server (See Point 2)		Separate app server with minimum configuration of 3+ CPUs 1 GB memory		

TABLE 14-1. *Expense Reporting Volumetrics*

	Unit Size (bytes) (2)	Estimate 2000 (3)	Estimate 2001
HR Information	400	1 GB	15 GB
Expense History	250	10 GB	95 GB
AP	250	10 GB	95 GB
Setup	Calculate based on the module to be installed	Calculate based on the module to be installed	

TABLE 14-2. *Disk Space Requirement*

4. From the scalability point of view, you need to consider two alternatives:

   ■ Add more processor, memory, and other extensions to the existing server.

   ■ Separate certain components from the middle tier into another application server. By separating the application server and database server, you can balance I/O and get better performance, because both servers will not compete for the same system resources. The Oracle9i Application Server has several new features, such as caching, which can help optimize performance of the middle tier.

5. For a very large capacity of concurrent users, using stress testing tools such as LoadRunner by Mercury Interactive is recommended to make sure that you get the desired performance for your application.

6. Typically, an application server with four CPUs and 1 GB of memory can handle about 500 to 600 concurrent users if using the Oracle8i application server and Apache listener.

You can scale Web applications in two ways:

■ By adding more resources (memory, CPU) to a given server

■ By adding application servers as necessary

Configuring multiple application servers helps balance the load and also avoids competition for system resources by database and application servers. (Figure-14-1 illustrates two application configurations.)

The application server can have the following installed components:

■ Web request broker (Web listeners)

■ Cartridges (such as PL/SQL, NCA, or Java)

■ SQL*Net (for communication with the database server)

Figure 14-1 shows an example of a middle-tier configuration with two different servers. In this case, the total load is balanced between the two available servers.

Analyzing the Capacity Data

Three major resources must be monitored and controlled with Oracle Web applications: network utilization, memory consumption, and CPU utilization. In general, it is recommended that you tune the network before monitoring memory or CPU. This section provides more information on the resource requirements for increasing the number of concurrent users. The section is designed to help you make capacity planning and sizing decisions.

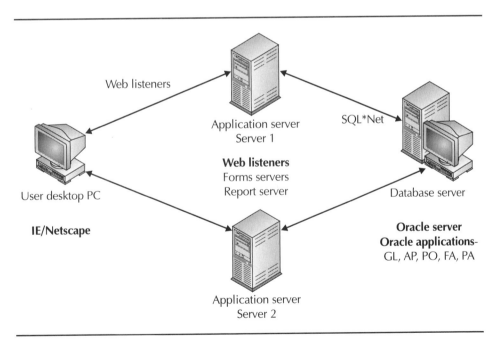

FIGURE 14-1. *Middle-tier spread across two different servers for load balancing*

Network Utilization   Network traffic is measured in megabits per second per user. Obviously, network utilization increases with an increasing number of users, so the higher the network traffic, the higher the CPU consumption and the greater the network utilization. Hence, the number of packets transmitted over the network determines the network utilization. A 100 Mbps Ethernet connection for both the database server and the application server is recommended for best performance. Adding more listeners on different distributed servers can ease network bandwidth issues.

Typically, an application server with four CPUs and 1GB of memory can handle about 500 concurrent users under an Oracle8i application server with Apache listener. This number may need to be revisited when you upgrade to the Oracle9i Application Server (which is expected to be better).

The following table shows estimated sizes.

No. of Users	No. of App Servers	Memory (MB)	No. of CPUs
100	0 or 1	250	2
500	1	700	3
1000	2	2000 (1 Gig each)	4 (2 each)
2000	4	7500	8
4000	8	9000	24

Memory Utilization   Memory utilization can be broken down into two parts: variable memory and fixed memory. The variable memory portion scales linearly based on the number of concurrent users. The fixed memory is fixed for a given application server at about 20 to 25MB (based on average memory consumption by the Web request broker [WRB] processes and listener process).

The following table and Figure 14-2 show actual and extrapolated memory utilization for different user loads. The memory consumption figure includes variable costs only.

No. of Users	Conservative Est. Memory Consumption
1	5MB
5	15MB
20	45MB
100	250MB
500	700MB
1000	2000MB

No. of Users	Conservative Est. Memory Consumption
2000	3750MB
4000	7500MB

Figure 14-2 shows a graph of memory utilization for various user levels. These consumption levels are indicative only and can be used for planning purposes.

CPU Utilization   In general, CPU utilization on Hewlett-Packard servers scale linearly, just as it does for memory consumption. CPU consumption can be optimized by reducing (that is, attempting to reduce) unnecessary communication from the browser to the application server. The following table provides a general guideline for planning the number of CPUs on the application server (for Web listeners only). In general, Windows NT uses more CPUs than HP or Sun Solaris. Still, Windows NT should probably be the preferred platform for the application server.

No. of Users	No. of CPUs
100	2
500	3
1000	4
2000	6
4000	10

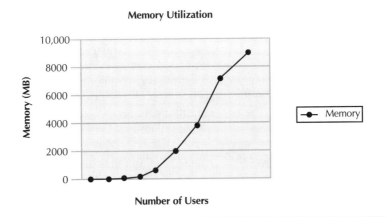

FIGURE 14-2.   *Memory utilization for various user levels*

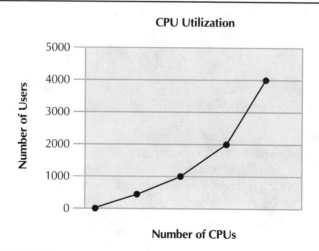

FIGURE 14-3. *Number of CPUs versus concurrent users*

Figure 14-3 shows a graph of the typical number of CPUs versus concurrent users accessing the application. These consumption levels are indicative only and can be used for planning purposes.

Benchmarking and Sizing Applications

When using Oracle applications, it is important that you review the speed of various operations, such as response on the Internet, screen-to-screen navigation, transaction processing speed, and data retrieval speed. This information is not only helpful for tackling day-to-day application upkeep issues but also provides useful insight and complements capacity planning studies. Performance testing can ensure that the Oracle application performance is acceptable after deployment. Testing is typically conducted by simulating a production type user load of various transactions and then making observations about system performance. Some of the testing tools also provide recommendations about various bottlenecks and how to avoid them. The testing includes stress testing the application; database; and hardware components such as PCs, servers, storage devices, and peripherals; and network components such as routers and communication servers.

If the production implementation is completed after performing a detailed stress test, the project obviously has better chances of succeeding and will have less performance issues after implementation. More and more large Oracle application implementations follow the pattern of stress testing before production deployment.

Performance Testing Tools

Many third-party testing tools are available. These tools have automatic, repeatable testing procedures for setting up, managing, and analyzing the environment. A testing tool should be selected based on its merits of testing on the Internet and its suitability to test a vast suite such as Oracle applications.

Mercury Interactive's LoadRunner provides several toolsets that conduct performance testing on the Oracle applications environment. For a small user base, you can also have users perform documented test cases on your test environment and then document the results.

Standard Benchmark for Oracle Applications

The Oracle Application Standard Benchmark (OASB) provides a common standard metric to evaluate and compare the performance of the suite on various hardware components. OASB has been available with Oracle Financials version 10.7 NCA as also Oracle Financials version 11.0 suites. The newer version of OASB provides a method for comparing actual performance with the standard and is a step up from the point of view of sizing the application.

OASB works on a typical workload scenario and has representative online transaction processing (OLTP) users as well as batch programs. This workload is executed on different hardware platforms to evaluate performance, such as the detailed definition of a workload's runtime characteristics. OASB is designed to provide additional information for making sizing decisions—especially those used to ensure that a high number of concurrent users can be successfully implemented on your platform of choice. OASB setup involves configuring the entire three-tiered architecture—the database tier, middle or application tier, and desktop tier.

For more information on OASB you can visit the Web site at **www.oracle.com/ apps_benchmark**. You can also download "The Oracle Applications Standard Benchmark: A Users Guide" to get a detailed description of how to use the product. The document is also available on Oracle Metalink.

Capacity Planning Tools

In this section, we will review some tools that could be helpful for collecting capacity planning data.

Oracle Capacity Planner

Oracle Capacity Planner is an Oracle Enterprise Manager application that allows you to collect different types of performance statistics and record that data in an historical database. Oracle Capacity Planner can be used to analyze historical data and extrapolate future capacity. Oracle Capacity Planner uses Oracle Data Gatherer to collect historical data. Oracle Data Gatherer must be installed on all the systems for which the data needs to be gathered.

NOTE
If historical data was captured for Capacity Planning using a newer version of Oracle Data Gatherer, it is not possible for an older version of Oracle Data Gatherer to store data in that database. However, if the Oracle Data Gatherer was created using an older version, all later version data can be stored in that database.

Oracle Data Gatherer works along with Oracle Intelligent Agent as part of the Oracle Enterprise Manager suite. Oracle Capacity Planner is a part of the Performance Pack for Oracle Applications that is available with Oracle Enterprise Manager.

Oracle Enterprise Manager provides a low-overhead data collection mechanism that gathers performance and system data for use by Oracle Applications Management Pack's Capacity Planner and Performance Manager. The same data collection mechanism used by the Performance Manager is used to collect historical performance and resource consumption data for capacity planning. The Management Pack uses Capacity Planner to analyze concurrent processing server performance data to help administrators configure systems appropriately and project future capacity needs.

NOTE
If the Oracle database and the application has to be taken down for some reason, make sure that Oracle Data Gatherer is first shut down before taking the application down. Similarly, start up the Oracle Data Gatherer after bringing up the application. This will avoid the chance of Data Gatherer failing to connect again after the application is brought back up.

Features of Oracle Capacity Planner   The Oracle Capacity Planner features

- Automated data collection

- Automated management of historical data

- Graphical analysis of historical data

Capacity Planner provides the administrator with a comprehensive set of Oracle applications and collectable operating system statistics. The same data points collected for Performance Manager are used by Capacity Planner. The collections themselves are completely customizable, allowing administrators to select any subset of statistics and the interval at which they should be sampled. In conjunction with Oracle Diagnostics Pack, Capacity Planner allows administrators to collect historical data for Oracle databases as well as third-party databases such as SQL Server. An administrator can then use a single tool to collect and analyze data for all major systems: the operating system, the concurrent processing servers, the forms servers, and the databases.

To control the amount of data that is stored over time, Oracle Capacity Planner allows administrators to establish management policies for the collected data. Administrators can specify how often collected data should be loaded into the historical database. This allows administrators to schedule the load when extra network and system resources are available. Capacity Planner also aggregates and rolls up data automatically. For example, at the end of each hour, minute data is rolled up to hourly data. This gives administrators both a detailed and a high-level view of the system's performance data. Administrators can also set policies for how long data should be stored before it is aged out, thus providing control over how much storage is needed for the historical data.

In addition to browsing the collected historical data, Capacity Planner provides graphical analyses that allow administrators to predict resource needs over time. Capacity Planner can identify trends and predict future hardware requirements by analyzing historical information about performance and resource use. Administrators can also extrapolate to a particular point in time to find out when a particular event will occur; for example, DBAs can predict what their disk requirements will be at the end of the year or predict when they will need an additional disk.

Oracle Capacity Planner works in the following ways:

■ The Intelligent Agent collects the data at an interval that can be configured using the Capacity Planner software. The data is stored in binary form.

■ At a specified loader interval, the binary data is stored in a historical database by the Oracle Capacity Planner.

■ The Agent can be configured to provide aggregations and summaries of various statistics periodically, such as hourly, weekly, and monthly.

■ The historical data can be purged periodically using the options provided by Oracle Capacity Planner. You can specify how much you want to purge to avoid excessive disk space usage.

Oracle Capacity Planner can be used to perform event management activities such as

■ Tracking space on various datafiles and setting up an event when a disk system is 90 percent full.

■ Tracking, estimating, and extrapolating the total I/O rate for the server as a whole at a future date. This information can help with hardware procurement decisions and can also drive decisions to split applications across additional servers.

■ Determining the number of user sessions per application to extrapolate the changing user pattern.

NOTE
For more information on using and configuring Oracle Capacity Planner, please refer to "Oracle Enterprise Manager: Getting Started with the Oracle Management Pack for Oracle Applications" (Part # A85229-01) from Oracle Corporation.

Setting Up a Collection   To set up a collection, use the following steps:

1. Define the collection frequency (typically every hour).

2. Define the frequency of loading class data.

3. Define the frequency of retention of data.

4. Specify the service to collect data (system, processor, memory, cache).

5. Specify the classes to collect data.

NOTE
Oracle Capacity Planner uses data sets to plot various charts for performing analysis. The data sets are collected by Oracle Data Gatherer which is part of the Oracle Intelligent Agent process. The maximum number of data sets that can be included in a chart is 50 for a single analysis. This includes selected sources/items and their extrapolations.

General Tools for Capacity Planning

In addition to Oracle Capacity Planner, several third-party tools can be used for the purposes of collecting, analyzing, and trending growth and performance data. Table 14-3 shows commands and tools that can be used to collect similar information. These tools could be invaluable for collecting one-time statistics and can also be customized to fit your environment.

Performance Layer	Capacity Planning Component	Command Set	Notes
Operating system (UNIX)	CPU	sar -uM, vmstat, runocc, runq_sz	Track %usr+%sys and %idle time every hour
	I/O	sar -d	Track reads+writes > 40/sec for each datafile
	Memory	sar -gw;	Track used memory, free memory and swap
	Network	netstat -i; ping	Perform trend analysis for bandwidth utilization, latency
Database	Overall wait statistics; session level waits	v$waitstat, v$sesstat	
	Hot datafiles	v$filestat	Identify hot data files
	Latch contention	v$latch	Identifying latch contention
Application	Expensive SQL statements	Use Statspack tables	Identify based on number of executions, buffer gets, disk reads, and parse calls; look for patterns during the day

TABLE 14-3. *Capacity Planning Tools*

Performance Layer	Capacity Planning Component	Command Set	Notes
	Session profiles for users	v$session	Identify users consuming maximum resources based on their profile/ resource group
	Top resource consuming users	Use v$sesstat, v$session	
	Number of sessions per user	v$session	Monitor multiple sessions per user
	Concurrent Manager process utilization	Use Oracle Management Pack for Oracle Applications	
	Number of hits per hour	Use Statspack tables	Calculate average and maximum hits per hour for each module over a period of time

TABLE 14-3.   *Capacity Planning Tools* (continued)

Summary

Capacity planning and sizing Oracle applications is critical for ensuring smooth and seamless operation. Capacity planning includes collecting historical data for various components of the environment, such as operating system, database, and application, and then analyzing them to make deployment decisions. Capacity planning is a detailed and complicated task, but a methodology is essential to make it repeatable and reliable.

Performance testing is critical for an added level of confidence in production deployment. The Oracle Application Standard Benchmark provides a common metric with which to judge performance of Oracle applications on various platforms and should be considered when making capacity planning decisions or first-time implementations.

These tuning steps should be followed to ensure that the Web environment performs at its best and uses all available resources:

1. Tune network bandwidth before CPU and memory.

2. Separate the application server from the database server to balance I/O.

3. Tune the operating system parameters—for example, TCP/IP parameters should be set to maximum values.

4. Watch out and fix Web listener log files and keep the file sizes small.

5. Configure multiple listeners based on additional loads.

6. Tune listener level parameters to appropriate values.

7. Try to get various snapshots of listener loads.

8. Cache reference tables and pin Web packages in the SGA.

9. Provide for adequate swap space.

10. Ensure that sufficient memory is available in the middle tier.

This chapter discussed the importance of performing capacity planning and sizing exercises on a regular basis. Several tools are available to help you with performance testing and capacity planning. In the next chapter, we will review some of the tools in a Financials administrator's toolkit.

PART

V

DBA Tools
and Processes

CHAPTER
15

Financials
Administrator's Toolkit

- Financials administrator's toolkit: a closer look
- Oracle Enterprise Manager: an introduction to the management pack features
- Features of Oracle Tuning Pack
- Features of Oracle Change Management Pack
- Features of Concurrent Processing Tuning Assistant

F
rom our discussions in the previous chapters, it is clear that the
Financials administrator is a key player in keeping the increasingly
complex technology-centric environment up and running and
supportable. To continue to be productive, the Financials administrator
has to be up to speed on a variety of technology components related
to software, hardware, networking, and application. She (or he) also needs to be
an expert at problem identification and fixing them. This seemingly easy step of
problem identification and fixing get increasingly complex when a new technology
component is added to the application environment—for example, when a business
decides to add a standby database for Oracle applications. It is important for the
Financials administrator to have a set of useful tools to manage this type of a
complex environment.

In this chapter, we will review tools such as Oracle Enterprise Manager and others
that help the building and managing process. We will also discuss a wish list of tools
that will be useful for managing the Oracle application environment and provide
some additional scripts to add to any administrator's toolkit.

Financials Administrator's Toolkit: A Closer Look

The Oracle technology stack comprises several complex technologies working together.
Oracle E-Business Suite is established on this foundation. To effectively manage such
an environment, several third-party tools and Oracle tools are available. These tools
perform maintenance, monitoring, migration, and tuning activities. The Financials
administrator has to evaluate the tools he needs based on a wish list created by
everyone in the team. An evaluation of available tools in relation to the wish list
can help the organization come to a good decision about which tool to invest in.
Compatibility and availability, both for the database and application version,
should be a critical factor considered during tools selection.

Tools help the administrator by automating repetitive tasks that are prone to errors
and are time consuming. On the other hand, depending on the tool, some tools need
initial setup and configuration time as well as training for the administrator.

Availability of the environment (database and application) is another issue that
needs to be considered in choosing a toolkit. In this section, we will evaluate the typical
tasks of a Financials administrator and recommend tools she can use to perform them.

Administration and Management Tasks

In Chapter 2, we reviewed the broad areas of tasks for the Financials administrator.
The Financials administrator can make use of different tools that help in performing
these tasks. This section has some details on these tasks and a list of tools for
performing those tasks.

The Financials administrator is involved with installing and configuring the Oracle Application Suite environment and installing various components of the technology stack. The administrator ensures that the components of the Database tier, Middle tier and the Desktop tier are properly installed. The administrator is also responsible for applying the latest available patches for each of the components. Often, the DBA is called in to recommend a feasible technical architecture based on available hardware resources and other site-specific requirements. Tools like Visio can help the administrator lay out recommended architecture. Microsoft Project can be used for planning installation tasks, keeping track of them, and communicating the progress. Refer to Chapter 3 for more information and an introduction to various components of the technology stack.

The administrator also plays a major role in Oracle applications upgrades or migration. The administrator is responsible for ensuring compatibility of the database and application version as also any third-party tools installed in the environment. Based on the compatibility, the administrator prepares a plan to upgrade the database and the application. The administrators also prepare a detailed list of patches to be applied for migration and ensures that the database and application are backed up before the upgrades. The administrator is also responsible for highlighting any application or database functionality that may be used to improve existing processes. The administrator makes decisions about upgrade or migration architecture in terms of number of application servers, server partitioning implementation, and other considerations. For a more detailed discussion on upgrading the Financials environment, refer to Chapter 4. From the tools point of view, Microsoft Office Suite, like Excel, Word, and Visio, can be of real help with these tasks.

After the upgrade or the installation has been performed and the environment has been prepared and deployed to production, the administrator is responsible for activities around the upkeep of the environment and implementing best practices. The administrator is responsible for setting processes or scripts for automating repetitive tasks such as creating instances based on standard Oracle Financial Analyzer (OFA) principles and site-specific sizes for production, testing, development, sand-box, and training environments. The administrator is also responsible for defining refresh procedures to refresh either entire instances or specific schema from production instance to test or development. The administrator utilizes the AD utilities for applying patches, re-linking executables, and performing other functions. More details on managing the Financials environment is available in Chapter 5. Several third-party tools can help rebuild an Oracle instance with minimal keystrokes. Tools are also available to migrate program code and replicate patches into different environments. Tools by Kintana (previously Chain Link Technologies) can help migrate application and database objects into different environments quickly and easily.

The administrator has the responsibility of managing and controlling the Concurrent Manager programs, processes, and requests. She is in charge of setting best practices, tuning, maintaining history, and scheduling decisions about which batch program can execute during which time for a particular module. She does this based on her overall knowledge about concurrent requests and how busy the system is during a particular time of the day. You can refer to Chapter 6 for a discussion about the administrative tasks involved with the Concurrent Manager. For managing the Concurrent Manager, the administrator should ideally use a combination of home-grown scripts and Oracle Enterprise Manager's Management Pack module, called Concurrent Processing Tuning Assistant. The last section of this chapter has some useful scripts for managing and monitoring the Concurrent Manager queues and requests.

The administrator also has the responsibility of analyzing, monitoring, and tuning the growth of various tables within the application area and proactively sizing them. When performing this activity, the administrator recommends better indexing strategy, index rebuild options, and other sizing functions, and he also keeps an eye on fragmentation. The Oracle Enterprise Manager (OEM) Management Pack module called Capacity Planner can help the administrator with the managing effort. OEM events to track and store database growth statistics should be collected every week (or month) so that the growth can be compared over a period of time.

In a typical busy Oracle application environment, at least five environments must be maintained. The administrator is responsible for implementing the change control process for the application so that changes are tracked for application enhancements and customizations. The administrator is also responsible for patch management. PVCS (a suite of Change Management tools from Merant Inc. (**http://www.merant.com**) is a fairly standard tool for version control.

Starting with 11i, Oracle makes use of cost-based optimization (CBO) as compared to rule-based optimization (RBO). The application tables and indexes need to be periodically analyzed so that the application can effectively utilize CBO. The administrator has the responsibility of ensuring this by implementing a process to gather statistics using either the Concurrent Manager process or using the FND_STATS package. For completing this task, the main thing is to be able to track the SQL statements currently running and identify the expensive ones. The second part of the activity is to tweak the SQL statements so that the code uses the best possible execution plan. Precise/SQL by Precise Software Solutions (**http://www. precise.com**) is useful in tracking down expensive SQL and also drilldowns to explain plans, usage statistics, and other information. The tool also has options for collecting statistics on different SQL statements and much more.

Open Interfaces

Open Interfaces are procedures for feeding data from an external source into Oracle application tables. Depending on the customizations in your environment, you may have the need to define custom open interface programs using techniques like PL/SQL, SQL*Loader, and Java. The administrator could help out with building and implementation of open interfaces. When choosing an appropriate tool for this activity, one of the options to be considered may be a rule-based extraction, transformation, and loading (ETL) tool like PowerMart (by Informatica—**http://www.informatica.com**). PowerMart provides a fast and easy way of loading data from a source database to a target database with several transformation options. It reduces the efforts of coding and makes the environment more tools based.

Troubleshooting

The Financials DBA or the administrator is the first point of contact for all developers and end users of the application in case they have a problem. The administrator is involved in understanding and resolving the problem. The resolution in many cases involves talking to Oracle Support, and in this sense the administrator serves as a liaison with Oracle Support folks. The administrator also prepares the environment for reproducing the error in the testing environment. The troubleshooting tools obviously depend on the nature of the problem. The obvious choice for getting information about the database and application is the Oracle Enterprise Manager. If alerts have been set up for various events and if a problem is found, the OEM repository will contain more information about the type of the error. From the Concurrent Manager side, looking at the log file will provide more details.

Performance Tuning

The Financials administrator is responsible for monitoring, analyzing, and tuning the environment and implementing tuning recommendations. The Financials administrator typically implements a process to collect performance or utilization statistics for various components like the Database and middle tier components and then analyzes them. The Financials administrator also reviews expensive SQL statements for performance improvement and makes recommendations for improvement, like adding a new index or changing some initialization parameter. Several tools options are available to the administrator in this task category:

- Oracle Enterprise Manager, Management Pack

- Precise suite of tools including Precise/SQL, Precise/Pulse!, and Precise/Interpoint

- Workbench of home-grown scripts

Capacity Planning and Sizing

The Administrator is responsible for providing statistics related to utilization of various hardware resources like CPU, memory, network, and disk space and also makes projects and extrapolations to evaluate whether there is sufficient capacity to sustain projected growth or even for adding new modules, customizations, or other functionality. The administrator plays a key role in evaluating the advantages and disadvantages of various possible architectures as well. Refer to Chapter 14 for a more detailed discussion on sizing and capacity planning.

For database capacity planning, the administrator can use sizing information collected using an event in Oracle Enterprise Manager. For application capacity, the Management Pack module called Capacity Planner can help. It should be noted that these tools can provide information related to sizing only. Actual interpretation and architecture decisions should be made based on individual situations. It is here that the Financials administrator's experience comes in handy!

Backup and Recovery

A Financials administrator is responsible for implementing a backup and recovery methodology for the Oracle Financials environment. In most cases, the Financials administrator has to work with other DBAs to evaluate various options for backup and recovery. The Financials administrator has to provide for both file-level backup and options for object-level backups. The object-level backups are useful for refreshing specific tables or schema. The Financials administrator is a critical resource for planning a maintenance window for doing a database recovery or for restoring archived data for a special project.

Several third-party backup and recovery tools are available. Backup solutions from Veritas and Legato offer fairly sophisticated and high availability solutions. This can be combined with Oracle's RMAN (Recovery Manager) to define a fairly complete backup and recovery strategy. The administrator can centrally control the backup status by defining RMAN catalogs in a central Oracle instance dedicated to the RMAN instance.

Oracle Enterprise Manager: An Introduction to the Management Pack Features

The Oracle Enterprise Manager architecture consists of a three-tier framework. Unlike a two-tier client/server structure, a three-tier architecture provides reliability, scalability, and fault tolerance for enterprise environments. Oracle Enterprise Manager tiers are listed next.

■ **Console and Management Applications—First Tier**
   This tier maintains the GUI management applications such as

   ■ Consoles (GUI-based management applications)

   ■ Administrative tools for all management tasks

   ■ Oracle Management Pack applications

■ **Oracle Management Server(s)—Second Tier** This tier processes system management tasks sent by the console. It provides centralized intelligence and distributed control between the console (first tier) and the managed nodes (third tier). Specifically, the second tier maintains the following:

   ■ One or more Oracle management servers

   ■ A repository that stores system data, application data, information about the state of the managed nodes, and information about any system management packs

■ **Managed nodes containing databases and other services—Third Tier** A managed node is any machine on your network that has a database or other services that you want to administer. Specifically a managed node can have

   ■ Databases

   ■ Services (such as the Oracle Intelligent Agent and data collection service)

The flexibility of a three-tier architecture enables you to install the tiers on the same machine or on separate machines—whatever makes sense for your environment.

The Oracle Enterprise Manager has a new tool called the Management Pack for Oracle Applications. This tool has the following modules:

■ Oracle Change Management Pack

■ Oracle Diagnostics Pack

■ Oracle Tuning Pack

The Oracle Change Management, Diagnostics, and Tuning Packs work with the 7.3.4, 8.0.X, 8.1.X versions of the Oracle database. Following is a discussion about the features and functionality of these tools.

Oracle Change Management Pack

The Oracle Change Management Pack is essentially a version control tool for managing and migration of Oracle application code. The Oracle Change Management Pack simplifies the management of complex changes to the Oracle server and database objects. It has several new features:

■ **Comparison of index and table statistics** Used to compare index and table statistics. When the Compare Statistics option is enabled, the statistics for tables and indexes are compared. All the statistics that are displayed on the Statistics property page for tables and indexes are used in the comparison. Time stamps are not included in the statistics comparison for tables and indexes.

■ **Logging capabilities in command line interface**   The *-l* option is used to enable logging for the capture, compare, generate, and execute commands. When logging is enabled, the same messages that would be displayed on the GUI during the operation are displayed in the DOS window. By default, the messages are not displayed in the DOS window while the operation progresses.

Issues and Workarounds

Following is a list if issues and workarounds for using the Oracle Change Management Pack, in no particular order.

Propagating a Tablespace to a Different Database   When you propagate a tablespace to a different database, Change Manager does not verify the existence of the directory specified for the tablespace's datafile(s), nor does it check whether any datafile in the tablespace is already in use by another tablespace. If the directory does not exist, the script will fail. If a specified datafile is already in use by another database, including the destination database, the script may corrupt that database. Therefore, use extreme caution when propagating tablespaces. There is no way to change a datafile specification in a tablespace exemplar.

Drop Column Operation   The Drop Column operation available in Oracle8i has no effect when creating a directive. The table column context menu contains both a Drop Column and a Delete entry when editing a table directive. Only the Delete choice is effective. The Oracle Change Manager operation, which deletes the column by dropping and re-creating the table, should not be confused with the Drop Column operation, which hides the column and marks it for later clean-up.

Malformed Object Names   If the name of an object starts with a *0* or *1*, a directive on the object is created as a *scoped* directive, and the scope spec shows the name of the object without its leading character. This does not appear as a translation error during script generation. You might miss the fact that no script step was generated for the change. The workaround is to edit the scope spec, removing the malformed name and adding the correct name with the leading numeral.

Histories with Thousands of Entries   For histories with several thousand entries, the History dialog box might take considerable time before it gets launched. To improve the performance of the query that retrieves the history records, an index can be added on the object_type, object_owner, and object_name of the VBZ$HISTORY table in the repository schema.

Snapshots and Refresh Groups   Snapshots will be removed from the source refresh group as they are inserted in the destination refresh group, if you propagate a refresh group from one schema to another within a database. Snapshots can exist in at most one refresh group, so this is the correct behavior; however, it may be unexpected and no warning is issued. To avoid this situation, propagate the snapshots along with the refresh group if that is your intention.

Changing Script Option   If you generate a script, change a script option (such as mapping or temporary tablespace), and then execute the script, the application does not prompt you to regenerate the script. This means you could run the script without realizing the script option changes you requested were not in effect. Be sure to regenerate the script after changing script options.

ARCHIVELOG Mode and the RECOVERABLE Keyword   Script generation does not check for the ARCHIVELOG mode when the RECOVERABLE keyword is specified. The generation will not report an error, but the script will fail unless the destination is in ARCHIVELOG mode. To fix the problem, turn on ARCHIVELOG mode (if available) or edit the script to remove the RECOVERABLE keyword.

Script Execution and Interruptions   During script execution, if the destination database crashes or the user interrupts execution at the wrong time, Change Manager may lose track of the last step completed. If this occurs, an attempt to Undo the execution will not start with the last completed step. The following procedure will correct the problem:

1. Obtain the script ID by editing the script and copying the long number in the line *set SCRIPTID nnnnnnnn.*

2. At the destination database, in the schema of the user executing the script (that is, the user in the destination's preferred credentials), find the table VBZ$JOB_TABLE_SID and examine the row whose script_id equals the script ID obtained in step 1.

3. If the problem occurred while executing in the forward direction, decrement the value of last_step by 1. If the problem occurred while executing in the reverse direction (Undo), increment last_step by 1. Commit the change. It should now be possible to continue with script execution or Undo.

Dropping and Re-creating Cluster Objects   Operations that cause the cluster objects to be dropped and re-created may result in scripts that do not execute properly. In general, it might be better to avoid such operations, although it may be possible to continue the script execution in some cases, like an ORA-955 error.

ASCII Characters   Make sure that the database login credentials use only ASCII characters to avoid tripping over the NLS issues in the generated TCL script.

Schema Objects, ALTER Statements, and the Scratch Tablespace   For schema objects that are rebuilt using the ALTER statements, if the scratch tablespace happens to be locally-managed, then the NEXT_EXTENT parameter of the object may not be preserved when the object is moved back to the original tablespace.

Currently Unsupported Features
The Oracle Change Management Pack currently (up to version 2.2), does not support the following features. Future versions will have many of them.

- Unsupported object-oriented features, such as object tables, nested tables, index only tables, and object views

- Snapshots that are not read-only

- Consumer groups (belonging to users and to roles)

- Hash partitions and subpartitions

- Partitioned tables that contain a LOB column are not currently supported when the plan drops and then creates an existing table

- The FLOAT datatype (but its equivalent, NUMBER(n,n), is supported)

NOTE
If you create a change plan that references an object with unsupported features, a diagnostic message will be displayed when you generate a script to alert you to the unsupported feature.

An object with unsupported features can become part of a plan when you

- Create an exemplar for an object with any of the unsupported features

- Request an operation that forces the dropping and/or creation of such an object (for example, ask to rename a schema that contains an object table)

■   Create a directive for an object with any of the unsupported features or that attempts to modify the object to have any of the unsupported features

Create Baseline and Compare Database Objects applications will capture objects and compare them, but some attributes of the unsupported features, such as nested tables, are ignored.

Partially Supported Database Features

Oracle Change Management Pack supports certain database features only partially. This section contains a list of the partially supported features.

Some attributes are supported, except that you cannot compose a directive that refers to these attributes. Thus, you can use Create Baseline and Compare Database Objects applications to capture and compare these attributes, and you can use exemplars to reproduce these attributes elsewhere. However, you cannot modify these attributes using a directive.

Partially supported database attributes are listed here:

■   **Index key compression**   Can be captured and reproduced, but differences are not detected in Compare Database Objects application and you cannot change the setting using a directive

■   **Column-level grants**   For example, granting the SELECT privilege on a single column in a table

■   **Attributes for a table constraint**   *[NOT] DEFERRABLE EXCEPTIONS INTO <table>*

Unsupported Database Attributes

Here is a list of attributes that are unsupported by Oracle Change Management Pack. These attributes are not captured by the Create Baseline application. The Compare Database Objects application does not detect differences between objects that include these attributes. In addition, when reproducing an object that includes these attributes, the new object will not include these attributes. Finally, when dropping and re-creating an object that includes these attributes (for example, to eliminate a table column), the object will not be properly re-created.

The unsupported database attributes are

■   For a database link—*SHARED* and *AUTHENTICATED BY*

■   *STORAGE* clause—*BUFFER_POOL*

■   *CREATE SNAPSHOT* statement—*CLUSTER* clause and table partitioning information

- *CREATE SNAPSHOT LOG* statement—table partitioning information

- *NOLOGGING* attribute on snapshot logs

Oracle Diagnostics Pack

Oracle Diagnostics Pack provides monitoring and troubleshooting abilities and provides the administrator with a health overview of the database's at-a-glance performance. It provides tools for monitoring the health of the system, diagnosing problems, detecting problems automatically, and planning for the future.

In this section, we will review the features of this tool. We will review the following modules of Oracle Diagnostics Pack:

- Performance Manager

- Capacity Planner

- Oracle Trace Manager

- Oracle Data Viewer

- E-Business Management Tools

Oracle Diagnostics Pack has the following new features:

- Improved real-time performance monitoring and troubleshooting

- More integrated SQL tuning through the diagnostics launch-in-context of Tuning Pack's SQL Analyze application

- Apache Web server monitoring support, including service discovery, real-time performance monitoring, event testing, and server usage reporting

- New event tests for the Solaris, HP-UX, and NT operating systems; expanded diagnostics reports

Performance Manager Issues

Oracle Performance Manager is an Oracle Enterprise Manager application that allows you to monitor different types of real-time performance data. Oracle Performance Manager uses the Agent data gathering service (also called the Oracle Data Gatherer) to collect performance data. To monitor some types of data, you must install the Oracle Data Gatherer on the system (or systems) where you want to monitor data. See the *Oracle Intelligent Agent User's Guide* for information on managing the Agent data gathering service on a system. In addition, see the *Oracle Management Pack for Oracle Applications Installation* booklet for information on installing the Intelligent Agent Extensions from the Management Pack for Oracle Applications CD-ROM.

If you are using Oracle Performance Manager to monitor Concurrent Manager performance, the Agent data gathering service can be installed on another system. The types of performance data that Oracle Performance Manager can monitor on a system depend on the products that are installed. The number of services that appear in the Performance Manager navigator tree will also vary, depending on the number of applications you have installed.

The Oracle Performance Manager can be used for the following activities:

- Monitor one or more services concurrently.

- View the monitored data in various chart formats, including strip (line), pie, bar, table, and hierarchical.

- Set the refresh rate for a chart's data.

- View multiple charts concurrently for each monitored service.

- View multiple charts in a single window.

- Drill down from one chart to another related chart.

- Drill down from real-time chart data to historical chart data.

- Choose the collected data and data sources to display in a chart.

- Print a chart.

- Generate an HTML report for a chart.

- Display context-sensitive help for a chart, if help is available for the chart.

- Play a recording of a chart, with fast-forward and pause features.

Performance Manager Workarounds

This section contains some issues and workarounds related to implementation of Performance Manager.

- If the chart window is not large enough to display the chart, only the legend will appear in the chart. Resize the window to view the data.

- To collect disk statistics for a Windows NT host, you must enable disk statistics collection on Windows NT before using Performance Manager or Capacity Planner. This is done by typing the ***diskperf -Y*** command on the host to be monitored. Disk statistics will then be enabled the next time the system is restarted.

- User-defined charts do not support a drilldown to another chart.

- A memory leak occurs each time a chart is displayed and dismissed, which requires a restart of the tool to release memory used by the monitor.

- If the create-like feature is used to copy a user-defined chart from one database to another, the query uses *select* * and the target database has a different number of columns that an unhandled ArrayIndexOutOfBoundsException will occur.

- A chart will be unviewable if the chart name includes apostrophes.

- When killing a session from the lock chart, no confirmation dialog is displayed, but the session is killed immediately.

Capacity Planner Issues and Workarounds

This section contains some issues and workarounds related to implementation of Capacity Planner.

- Upgrading to the Oracle 8.1.7 Agent will disable any User-Defined Classes added under a previous release of the Capacity Planner. The definitions for these user-defined classes must be re-entered and the collections must be restarted.

- The maximum number of data sets (lines) that can be included in a chart is 50. It is not possible to display more than 50 data sets in a single analysis. This includes selected sources/items and their extrapolation fits.

- The Capacity Planner user has the option of setting the data collection and load intervals. Given that the Capacity Planner data is being collected to support longer term operations such as trend analysis (as opposed to the Performance Manager real-time monitoring model), high-frequency collections and loads are likely to be unnecessary. Be aware that setting these intervals to high frequencies (i.e., sample collections every 10 seconds and data loads every 60 seconds) may overload the Agent Data Gatherer.

- A memory leak occurs for each analysis chart shown. Therefore, you should exit and restart Capacity Planner from time to time, if a large number of analyses are shown in a single session.

- No automatic refresh of analysis data occurs during load passes. Once attached to a Capacity Planner data repository, no automatic refresh of the data is available in the navigator once loads have occurred. It is necessary to disconnect and reconnect to the Capacity Planner data repository to refresh this view.

■ Services added at runtime are not saved. Any service added to the navigator at runtime is visible in the navigator only during that session. To make the service available for future sessions, it must be added to the Oracle Enterprise Manager discovery cache through the console.

■ The removal of lines or exclusion of points from a Capacity Planner Analysis is not saved as part of that analysis.

■ A memory leak occurs when connecting and then disconnecting from a target. It is necessary to exit and restart Capacity Planner from time to time if a large number of connections have been made in a single session.

■ For a pre-defined analysis, the default date selection of one month of hourly data cannot be changed.

■ If a chart contains multiple data sources and you remove a line for one of the data sources, the line for that data item is removed from all other data sources included in the chart.

■ Two modes are available in Capacity Planner: Collection mode and Analysis mode. When creating or viewing charts in Capacity Planner Analysis mode, descriptions of the chart items are not available. This is because the descriptions are obtained from the Agent Data Gatherer and there is no connection to the Agent Data Gatherer when in Analysis mode.

■ If a Capacity Planning data repository was initially created by a later Data Gatherer version, it will not be possible for an earlier Data Gatherer version to store data in that repository. If, however, the repository was initially created by an earlier Data Gatherer, all later Data Gatherer versions may store data in that repository.

Oracle Trace Manager Issues and Workarounds
This section contains some issues and workarounds related to implementation of Oracle Trace Manager.

■ To use the Oracle Trace Manager application to collect data for an Oracle 7.3.3 server, the Oracle Tcl job scripts located in the 7.3.3 Oracle home must be replaced. If you want to use Oracle Trace Manager for this configuration, please contact Oracle support to receive an updated set of Oracle Trace Tcl job scripts to replace those located in $ORACLE_HOME/network/agent/jobs/oracle/otrace/general.

■ If using Oracle Trace Manager to discover products in an Oracle8 or Oracle8i oracle_home, note that the SQL*Net product definition file (the file describing what to collect) has been removed for Oracle 8.0.3

(and higher) server releases. Therefore, the Oracle Trace Manager does not discover SQL*Net products for Oracle8 or higher releases.

■ If a database appears in the dropdown list of formatter databases in the form host:port:sid (and the database is not version 8.1.6 or greater), discover the database through the Enterprise Manager console. The database will then be discovered with its normal service name.

■ The following problem exists for collections against 8.1.6 databases. If you collect data for any of the following events—Connect_Disconnect, CACHEIO, SQL_Text_Only, SUMMARY, or Wait_Events—and then try to format this data to a schema that does NOT contain data from any of the following events—SQL_Txns_and_Stats, ALL, DEFAULT, EXPERT, SQL_and_Wait_Stats, SQL_Stats_and_Plan—the formatting will appear to fail and you will see an error dialog in Trace Manager. However, the format has failed only in a post-processing step. Therefore, the workaround is to launch Trace Dataviewer in standalone mode and connect to that formatted schema. Trace Dataviewer will correctly complete the post-processing step in the format.

■ It is recommended that you start Oracle Trace from the console instead of from the Start menu. Problems with multi-byte characters or fatal errors such as "epc.exe Exception: Access violation (0x0000005)" may occur if Trace is not launched from the Console.

■ An Oracle Trace collection must be formatted to a database of the same version. For example, a Trace collection for Oracle 8.1.7 must be formatted to an Oracle 8.1.7 database schema.

■ Formatted data collected from Oracle 8.1.7 databases that has been viewed from the Oracle Trace Data Viewer 2.x cannot be deleted using the Oracle Trace Manager (Bug 1361074). If necessary, the formatted collection can be deleted using the following SQL command while connected to the format database:

```
DELETE FROM epc_collection WHERE collection_id = <coll_id>
```

■ Oracle Trace Manager discovery of UNIX nodes running the Oracle 8.1.7 Intelligent Agent may fail if there is also a monitored Oracle 8.1.5 home present on the Agent node. This problem can be corrected by modifying certain Oracle Trace TCL scripts. Contact Support for information regarding these modifications should this be necessary.

Oracle Trace Data Viewer Issues and Workarounds

This section contains some issues and workarounds related to implementation of Oracle Trace Data Viewer.

■ As noted earlier, to collect and view Oracle Trace data for Oracle8 or Oracle8i databases, you must set the value of the *ORACLE_TRACE_ ENABLE* parameter in your *init<sid>.ora* to TRUE.

■ For WAIT event time statistics to be collected and presented in the Oracle Trace Data Viewer, you must enable the *timed_statistics* parameter for your instance. This is a dynamic parameter that can be enabled from Oracle Enterprise Manager Instance Manager without re-starting the instance.

■ The Oracle Trace Data Viewer user must have database privileges to create tables, indexes, stored procedures, and functions.

■ CPU statistics may not be present in Oracle Server 7.3.3 collections on SUN OS databases.

■ As of version 2.0.4, the Trace Data Viewer requires the SELECT_ANY_ TABLE SYSTEM privilege in addition to the privileges listed in Appendix C of the *Oracle Trace User's Guide.*

■ If you have both versions 1.x and 2.x of Trace Data Viewer installed in separate homes on the same system, you cannot create both 1.x and 2.x repositories in the same schema. If you attempt to create a 1.x repository in a 2.x repository schema, you will encounter errors.

■ Invalid statistics can usually be detected by either negative values or seemingly random very large values. Note that if you use a Data View that sorts by one of the invalid statistics, the results are misleading. If you believe that the statistics you are viewing are not good, either choose a different data view that sorts by a non-corrupt statistic or modify the selected data view to display and sort by valid statistics.

■ The CPU statistics for Oracle 8.0.5 that are collected in the Oracle Trace binary data file are valid. The values are corrupted during Trace formatting. Note that you can view the valid CPU values with the Oracle Trace Statistics Reporting utility. Options and information on the reporting utility are available in Appendix A of the *Oracle Trace User's Guide.* Replacing the 8.0.5 formatter ($ORACLE_HOME\bin\otrcfmt.exe for target database) with an 8.0.4 formatter fixes the problem.

■ The following resource utilization statistical values are not initialized and not set for Oracle 8.0.5 on an NT platform; therefore, they are random values: CPU, both user mode and system mode CPU statistics; Input_IO; Output_IO; Pagefaults; Pagefault_IO; and Max_resident_set_size. Note that using Data Viewer data views that sort by invalid resource utilization statistics (i.e., CPU consumption) will produce misleading results. Data views can be modified to display and/or sort by other statistics. Modified data views are saved to the Custom data view folder.

■ When a record is not written to the EPC_FACILITY_REGISTRATION table in the collection's formatted data, the user may see an error similar to the one listed here. Removing the Filtering By User option on collections targeting Oracle Server release 8.0.4 databases will correct this problem for future collections.

XP-21016: A database error has occurred:
SELECT DISTINCT FACILITY_NUMBER, FACILITY_VERSION, VENDOR
FROM EPC_FACILITY_REGISTRATION WHERE COLLECTION_ID - :1
ORA-00942: table or view does not exist

■ See the *Oracle Trace User's Guide*, Appendix C, for information on how to manually add an EPC_FACILITY_REGISTRATION record for the collection. Details are in the Trace Data Viewer section under the "Table or View Does Not Exist (or No Data in Collection)" topic.

■ If you get this error when Viewing Formatted Data from the Trace manager—XP-21162: Database connection attempt failed, ORA-12154: TNS could not resolve service name— in the Enterprise Manager Console, choose Add Services to tnsnames.ora from the System menu. Previous versions of Enterprise Manager updated your tnsnames.ora file automatically upon discovery of a node. Now you must update the file manually by selecting this command.

■ SQL Statements executed from within a stored procedure may not be visible from the Trace Data Viewer. The statements are in the collection; however, you must uncheck the Exclude SQL Executed As User SYS checkbox. This bug was fixed for collections on Oracle Server 8.1+ databases.

■ Oracle Forms Data Views supplied by the Data Viewer are considered to be beta and are not translated.

■ Oracle Trace Manager SQL_text_only event set does not collect SQL statement text. To collect SQL statement text, choose the SQL_and_Stats, Default, or any other event set that collects query text as well as other statistics.

E-Business Management Tools Issues and Workarounds

This section contains some issues and workarounds related to implementation of E-Business Management Tools.

■ In Windows NT, the Total Servers metric that is displayed in the Server Utilization Chart may appear as a constant value. This will interfere with an event that is registered to trigger if the Total Servers metric exceeds a designated level since NT sees this value as always having been exceeded.

■ PERL version 5 or higher is required to use the reporting features of the E-Business Management Tools. For configuration information, see the *Installation Guide for Oracle Enterprise Manager with Change Management, Diagnostics and Tuning Packs.*

■ When monitoring Web servers on Solaris, in Performance Manager, when the customer navigates to the Server Utilization/Idle Servers chart and hovers the mouse pointer over the Description data item in the right pane, the Data Gatherer disconnects. The client gets an Error dialog box with an ArrayOutofBound Exception. The workaround is to disconnect from the Web server and reconnect.

■ When setting the Log Analysis report Output Directory parameter, for any path name that normally ends in a single backslash (\), end the path name in a double backslash (\\) or no backslash instead.

Oracle Tuning Pack

Oracle Tuning Pack provides the necessary tools for performance monitoring and tuning. It provides the ability to compare multiple explain plans as also ability to analyze and manipulate SQL statements. The Oracle Tuning Pack addresses particular tuning needs and activities that ensure that database and applications run at peak efficiency. In this section, we will cover the following modules and wizards:

■ SQL Analyze

■ Oracle Expert

■ Tablespace Map and Reorg Wizard

Following are some new features of Oracle Tuning Pack:

■ Performance profile comparison—Statistics for multiple explain plans can be brought together in a single performance profile window for comparison.

■ A SQL Analyze user can now change their SQL Analyze session's operating environment from within SQL Analyze—This allows the user to issue SQL or PL/SQL to change variables, call stored procedures, or manipulate other factors before viewing explain plans.

- Tablespace Map "Zoom Out and Zoom In"—Allows the user to change the map resolution: zoom out provides a view of the entire tablespace within the map window, and zoom in increases the size of map objects and provides a scroll bar for navigating the map.

- Automatic selection of segments by the Tablespace Map that are candidates for reorganization based upon the Tablespace Analysis Report.

- Launch of the Reorg Wizard from the Tablespace Map in the context of selected segments or the entire tablespace.

- A consolidated Tablespace Map Analysis Report that lists all segment problems detected for the tablespace. The report can be saved as an HTML file.

- Tablespace Map Analysis options can be set by the user, such as detecting segments that exceed a user-specified number of extents.

- Chained rows can be repaired by the Reorg Wizard without rebuilding the entire object.

SQL Analyze Issues and Workarounds

Oracle SQL Analyze identifies inefficient SQL statements and provides a workbench for identifying and tuning problematic SQL statements that are causing the greatest impact on database performance. SQL Analyze identifies the SQL statements executing on the database and evaluates the statements based on user-selected criteria, such as resource usage and I/Os per statement. Once a problem SQL statement is identified, it can be dragged and dropped from the database library cache to the SQL Analyze tuning window for evaluation and tuning. This section contains some issues and workarounds related to implementation of SQL Analyze.

- SQL Analyze uses a data repository that is shared with other Oracle Tuning Pack applications, and multiple users can read the repository from multiple Tuning Pack applications. The last user who saves to the repository will override previous data. Because of this, you must be careful about performing repository operations from concurrently open Tuning Pack applications. A known problem related to this (Bug 778225) involves the following series of steps:

  1. Open a SQL Analyze repository that contains a database service with SQL nodes.

  2. Before expanding the list of SQL nodes, delete the same database service from the Oracle Expert navigator.

  3. If you then try to expand the SQL node list for the database service in SQL Analyze, an application error will occur.

■   The user account logged into SQL Analyze requires certain object privileges. You can create a database role (SQLADMIN), which can be used to grant SQL Analyze users privileges required for SQL monitoring and tuning. Create this role by running VMQROLE.SQL, found in the oracle_home\sysman\ admin directory.

■   If the user does not have a plan-table named PLAN_TABLE in his schema, SQL Analyze will create a PLAN_TABLE for the user. For this to work, the user must have permissions to create the plan table. If the user does not have these permissions, SQL Analyze will attempt to create this table and fail. The user will have to exit the application and obtain privileges to create a table or create the PLAN_TABLE and then run SQL Analyze.

■   SQL Analyze is multi-threaded. The maximum number of threads allowed per session is three by default. If you wish to increase or decrease this number, in SQL Analyze choose View | Preferences, and set the number of Database Sessions per User. The minimum allowable value is one and the maximum is ten.

■   The SQL History feature is a repository of SQL statements associated with a specific database service that have been collected from the SQL cache. The SQL History is shared between SQL Analyze and Oracle Expert. If you have saved a SQL History from Oracle Expert, that SQL History will be available to SQL Analyze. If you open a SQL History container in SQL Analyze for a database service that does not have a previously saved SQL History, SQL Analyze will create a SQL History for that database service. The default setting for the SQL History option is to exclude recursive SQL (SQL generated by Oracle). Therefore, if you do not have any application SQL in the SQL cache and you have elected to exclude recursive SQL, then the new SQL History will be blank.

■   If you change schema objects (i.e., adding an index from EM Schema Manager) while SQL Analyze is running, SQL Analyze will automatically use these changes in any subsequent operations. However, to view these changes in the SQL Analyze–Object Properties, you must refresh the Object Properties view using the Refresh button.

■   The data results set retrieved by queries run from SQL Analyze can be viewed by using the Execution Results toolbar button. To provide fast access to this data, the results sets are cached in local memory by SQL Analyze. The number of rows cached can be controlled by the user in SQL Analyze by choosing View | Preferences | Execution Results. You should check this setting to ensure that you have limited the number of rows to be displayed. Be aware that a high number of cached rows may cause the program to run out of memory.

■ SQL Analyze's File | Open SQL command has restrictions: SQL statements contained in SQL files opened with the Open SQL command can be imported into SQL Analyze only if each statement begins on a new line and is terminated with a semicolon. SQL files cannot contain SQL comments beginning with REM.

■ If you load SQL statements from a file and an error in parsing one of the SQL statements occurs, SQL Analyze will show only the statements that were successfully parsed prior to the error. It will not show any statements that followed the incorrect SQL statement.

■ In TopSQL, you have the option to filter out recursive SQL statements. However, if you log in as user SYS, TopSQL will filter out your non-recursive SQL statements too. So if you log in as SYS, do not select the option to filter out recursive SQL statements.

■ SQL Analyze allows users to create an explain plan for a SQL statement run by any user. It does this by validating a schema name with an object name. If an object belongs to multiple schemas, it interacts with the user to resolve the schema name. However, public synonyms cannot be qualified. So if you are trying to get an explain plan containing a public synonym and you also have a table, view, or a private synonym in your schema, the explain plan you get may not be the same as the one seen by other users.

■ The View definition dialog can be used to display only view names selected from a syntactically valid SQL statement.

■ The SQL Tuning Wizard rule of thumb for tuning queries containing MINUS and UNION does not support statements containing the asterisk (*) in the column list. The workaround is to list the column names in the query.

■ Regarding SQL statements using the Oracle8i Plan Stability feature, SQL statements brought into SQL Analyze from either the TopSQL feature, through the launch of SQL Analyze tuning from the Diagnostics Pack Performance Manager application, or exported from a SQL file will automatically be checked for the use of the Plan Stability feature. If a stabilized plan outline is detected for the SQL statement, the user will receive an information notice and will not be allowed to work on the statement in SQL Analyze. Note that this automatic check excludes stabilized SQL statements that are copied into or created by hand in the SQL edit window.

Oracle Expert Issues and Workarounds
This section contains some issues and workarounds related to implementation of Oracle Expert.

■   Oracle Expert expects the following tables to exist in the target database
    being tuned to perform collection. If any of these tables do not exist during
    collection, errors may result:

dba_tab_column	dba_constraints	dba_users	dba_data_files
dba_objects	dba_indexes	dba_segments	dba_ind_columns
dba_tables	dba_rollback_segs	dba_sequences	dba_views
dba_tablespaces	dba_synonyms	dba_ts_quotas	dba_clusters

■   It is currently possible to run more than one Oracle Expert session against
    the same repository. Oracle Expert does not have integral support for
    avoiding data conflicts between sessions. Do not run more than one session
    against the repository at any one time. However, if this is required, each PC
    session should access a different tuning session.

■   To use the Oracle Expert Autotune feature, you must first select a database
    from the Oracle Expert Navigator window. Once started, Autotune will
    continue to run until the Autotune menu's Stop function is invoked for the
    selected database or the system is rebooted. Note that to use the Autotune
    feature, Oracle Expert must be started connected to the Oracle Management
    Server (Bug 1359935).

■   Do not attempt to use Oracle Expert to tune the SYS or System schema.

■   A schema collection will halt before completion if a table and cluster in
    the same schema have the same name (Bug 604088).

■   If a SQL statement is greater than 8K, an error occurs when attempting to
    edit the request that contains the statement. The error reads "Error while
    attempting to load attribute for display." The Request property sheet is still
    displayed, but the SQL text is not visible.

■   Oracle Expert does not currently support tuning of tables that use the Oracle8
    partitioning feature. Partitioned tables will be ignored during data collection.

■   Any workload request containing SQL that utilizes a *dblink* to attach to a
    database is not validated against the database referenced by the *dblink*.

■   Importing an Oracle Expert tuning session (.xdl file) that contains extremely
    large (pages long) SQL statements can cause Oracle Expert to appear to
    hang and subsequently accessing these SQL statements from the view/edit
    window may not be possible (ref. 651722).

■   Source lines greater than 1024 bytes in import files may cause a syntax error.

■ Due to a change in parameter syntax, Oracle Expert may make inaccurate recommendations for the *BUFFER_POOL_KEEP* and *BUFFER_POOL_RECYCLE* parameter settings for an 8.1.6 database (Bug 1357057). If you want tuning advice for these two parameters you can avoid the potential error by using the 8.1.5 parameter syntax in your 8.1.6 initialization file. The 8.1.5 parameter syntax statements for these two parameters are

BUFFER_POOL_KEEP=(buffers:nnn, lru_latches:nnn)
BUFFER_POOL_RECYCLE=(buffers:nnn, lru_latches:nnn)

Tablespace Map and Reorg Wizard Issues and Workarounds

This section contains some issues and workarounds related to implementation of Tablespace Map and Reorg Wizard.

Note that the Oracle Tablespace Manager application that existed in Tuning Pack releases prior to version 2.1 has been replaced with two new applications: Tablespace Map and Reorg Wizard.

■ The Reorg Wizard does not currently support reorganization for the following objects: Index-organized tables, hash and composite partitions, tables that contain columns of user-defined types, indexes on columns of user-defined types, function-based indexes, and domain indexes. Partitioned tables that contain a LOB column can be reorganized on a per-partition basis, but operations that require reorganization of the entire partitioned object (such as the reorganization of a complete tablespace) cannot be performed if the partitioned object contains a LOB column. Note that if you perform a reorganization that includes an object from this unsupported list, a diagnostics message will be displayed in the Impact Summary Report and reorg script alerting you of the unsupported object.

■ Under certain circumstances, canceling the generation of the Impact Summary and reorg script may take a while, during which time the application may appear unresponsive.

■ Reorg job execution may fail if the script includes the reorganization of a table that has constraints that are in the NOVALIDATE state.

■ Using the Reorg Wizard to reorganize database objects containing long or long raw datatypes that exceed 32KB requires using the Oracle Agent version 8.1.6 on the server where the object resides.

■ Note that if a reorg job fails while in process, the reorg operation can be recovered. See the documentation for details.

■   If using a scratch tablespace to hold the temporary objects used in the
     reorganization, the scratch tablespace and production tablespace should be
     of the same management type; both should be either dictionary-managed or
     locally-managed.

Concurrent Processing Tuning Assistant

The Concurrent Processing Tuning Assistant is a reporting mechanism that allows
you to examine historical processing information about Oracle Concurrent Processing
requests and Concurrent Managers. The Tuning Assistant provides information that
assists you in achieving better concurrent processing throughput by adjusting
Concurrent Manager assignments and request scheduling. The Tuning Assistant
provides several predefined reports that identify problem areas in Concurrent
Manager processing. The Tuning Assistant generates reports directly against the
information stored in the Oracle Application Object Library tables.

Because the Tuning Assistant generates reports directly from information stored
in the Application Object Library tables, the amount of concurrent processing request
data has a direct impact on performance. A large amount of data can cause delays in
gathering the information necessary to display report data. One method for improving
Tuning Assistant performance in retrieving data is to periodically use the SQL language
ANALYZE command to compute statistics on tables that the Tuning Assistant accesses.
These tables include the following:

■   FND_APPLICATION_TL

■   FND_LOOKUPS

■   FND_CONCURRENT_PROCESSES

■   FND_CONCURRENT_PROGRAMS

■   FND_CONCURRENT_PROGRAMS_TL

■   FND_CONCURRENT_QUEUES

■   FND_CONCURRENT_QUEUES_TL

■   FND_CONCURRENT_REQUESTS

■   FND_USER

■   FND_CONC_PP_ACTIONS (for Apps 11.x)

■   FND_CONC_RELEASE_CLASSES (for Apps 11.x)

■   FND_CONC_RELEASE_CLASSES_TL (for Apps 11.x)

If the concurrent processing tables are purged frequently or if Concurrent Manager and request data are purged at different intervals, the usefulness of the data displayed in the reports could be limited. This requirement contradicts the fact that the general recommendation is not to have 5000–10000 rows in the FND_CONCURRENT_ REQUESTS table to reduce performance issues.

When looking at information presented by the Concurrent Processing Tuning Assistant, be aware of the data purge policies of your system administration and the effect these policies may have on the data reported.

NOTE
Tuning Assistant reports do not include currently running requests. Only completed requests are included in reports.

Concurrent Manager Balancing

To determine Concurrent Manager balancing, view the Waiting Requests by Hour (24×7) report and look for the time periods with the greatest wait times. If you find a time period that seems to have a relatively great number of backups, examine which requests were run and which requests were waiting during this time period. For selected time periods, drill down to the Requests that Waited report to identify the requests that waited. It may be necessary to schedule these requests during periods with excess Concurrent Manager capacity.

To find time periods with excess Concurrent Manager capacity, examine the Concurrent Managers by Hour (24×7) report and look for underutilized time periods. For details about activity during selected time periods, drill down to the Requests that Ran report. To reduce wait time, consider rescheduling a program to run when the Concurrent Managers have capacity to spare. Use these reports to identify requests whose schedules can be adjusted to distribute load more evenly.

If all Concurrent Managers are running at near or maximum capacity, it may be necessary to add more Concurrent Managers. If system resources are also fully utilized, it may be necessary to add additional hardware to support processing demands.

Summary

Managing a complex technical environment like the Oracle technology stack is no doubt time consuming and challenging at the same time. A plethora of third-party and Oracle provided tools are available to help perform various functions easily, quickly, and without mistakes. Oracle Enterprise Manager, Management Pack, and Precise tools provide many necessary tools to help the Financials administrator perform her day-to-day activities of migration and upkeep and tuning. In this chapter, we reviewed the tasks versus tools recommendation for the Financials administrator. We also reviewed various modules of the Oracle Enterprise Manager to get an overview of the tool and its strengths.

The choice of the right tool is indeed a difficult one. Several tools perform the same or similar function with additional features and different price tags. Evaluating and picking up the right tool is a critical exercise for any administrator. More often than not, a single tool seldom caters to all the requirements. In addition, it is fairly common for experienced administrators to have their own home-grown library of management scripts. Efforts to create a toolkit with a combination of different tools and home grown scripts can help administrators perform specific functions. Also it is critical to build a consolidated script library so that uniform scripts are used by everyone.

CHAPTER
16

Backup and Recovery

- Backup requirements of an e-business site
- Backup and recovery processes and the application administrator
- Application availability
- Standby recovery database
- Oracle8i backup features to leverage with applications
- Introduction to Oracle Recovery Manager

his chapter discusses the nature of e-business applications and their specific backup requirements. The chapter also reviews various file-level backup and recovery processes as well as object-level backup mechanisms that an administrator will need defined to manage the Oracle Financials environment. The chapter discusses availability issues, Oracle Parallel Server architecture concepts, as also some of the Oracle8i features related to backup that can be leveraged in the applications area. The objective of this chapter is to help the administrator decide which backup and recovery processes he needs and also help him understand specific needs of backing up the middle tier and the Database tier in the three-tiered architecture. With this objective, the chapter does not focus on the actual procedure of doing the backup and recovery but lays out a methodology for backup, discusses the backup processes, and reviews best practices relating to backup and recovery systems.

Backup Requirements of an E-Business Site

Every business needs ample planning, sound technical expertise, and scalable and reliable tools for building a solid backup process for a critical e-business–based application like the Oracle Application Suite. The backup procedure and process for an Internet-based application is different and more challenging than a client/server-based application, because Internet-based applications have complicated requirements in respect to availability and performance.

Table 16-1 shows some of the distinguishing features of Oracle-based Internet applications.

A typical Oracle Application Suite environment could include several of the following hardware components that may need backup:

- Database server

- Application server

- Web servers

- Load balancers

The software component corresponding to this could include the following:

- Database software—binaries and data

- Application server—binaries and data

Feature	Explanation
Maximum uptime	Based on the type of modules you have implemented, your users/customers may be expecting the system to be available to them at any time. This means that maintenance or downtime windows have to be carefully planned and seamlessly executed.
Maximum concurrent usage of the application	It is difficult to predict the number of concurrent users/customers who will access the application. The system needs to be tuned for handling excess capacity and growth.
Overall application performance	Satisfactory application performance is critical for the end users. The most important objective of tuning is to reduce client-side wait time for users.
Technical complexity	Several components in the technology stack must work and interact for the application to work. It is critical to plan a sound backup process.

TABLE 16-1.   *Features of Internet Applications*

- Operating system files
- Middle tier application components including Web server

Backup and Recovery Processes and the Application Administrator

As an administrator of a relatively complex application environment, you should plan the type of backup you are going to use in addition to the recovery procedures. An administrator is the users' first point of contact for backup and recovery issues. The administrator must back up both the Database tier and the middle tier as well as specific components of the Desktop tier. From the database backup point of view, the administrator needs to define processes to back up the following three components:

- Database binaries, administration scripts, init.ora parameters
- File backup of all datafiles, control files, and redo logs, and archived log files

■ Object-level backup of certain critical application tables

Another critical administration decision is choosing the periodicity of the backup. The administrator should come up with a daily, weekly, and monthly schedule for backup of various types in consultation with the functional team. These backup decisions are dependent on the size of the application, service level agreement, and availability issues.

The administrator has several options for implementing backup procedures. Many third-party tools can help with these procedures. For example, a combination of Veritas and RMAN can be a reliable and manageable option for backing up moderately large volumes. For smaller applications, the administrator can also develop a home-grown script using either shell programming or PERL script. Again, the main objective should be to reduce the overall burden of the administrator and to make backup reliable, easy, and scalable.

Application Availability

Availability and uptime of business-critical applications like Enterprise Resource Planning (ERP) is critical in an e-business environment. With the emergence of the Internet, business tends to operate in the "anytime, anywhere" paradigm. If the production system is down, it results not only in loss of productivity but it could impact the overall goals of the organization. In this section of the chapter, we will review various availability options that administrators should consider for improving uptime of an environment.

The following guidelines can help you in planning for a high-availability Oracle Application environment.

■ *Develop a scalable architecture.* The hardware, software, and network infrastructure should be proportional or derived from critical statistics, such as number of users and size of your application. The architecture should be easily scalable to add more components if the number of users, modules, and complexities of the application are increased.

■ *Design an architecture for high availability.* Build some amount of hardware redundancy into your architecture. Plan ahead and choose solutions and tools that are flexible and that work in heterogeneous environments before deploying it as part of your application.

■ *Maximize performance.* When planning for availability, make sure that the hardware and software components in your architecture can be tuned to a high degree. This will ensure that you will be able to run performance tests and tune your environment so that these resources are properly utilized. This step will also help you in making capacity planning decisions.

Administrators should provide the following to ensure high availability:

1. A latest copy of the production environment should always be available to use for reporting and ad-hoc usage.

2. Any availability techniques, such as a Standby Recovery Database, should not have an adverse impact on the availability or response of the primary production database.

3. A failover mechanism must be built in, so that when the primary fails, seamless rollover to a secondary database occurs without loss of transactions.

4. A quick, smooth, and relatively easy administration method for switching back to the primary environment should be defined.

5. Document the failover and switch-back procedure, always assign a primary and secondary administrator, and rehearse various failover scenarios in a sand-box or production-like environment before implementing.

Evaluating the Need for High Availability

The uptime of your application environment depends on the Service Level Agreement (SLA) that you have with your business community. These business folks should require good reason for 24×7 support and should understand that high availability requires more administration and more planning and is in general more expensive. The SLA can be based on parameters like these:

- Nature of business
- Type of the application
- Number of users
- Size of the application
- Countries implemented

Consider the following questions to help you decide whether 24×7 availability is necessary.

1. *What is the cost of downtime?* The business community needs to work out this cost. Both tangible and intangible benefits should be considered for evaluation.

2. *Which modules are required more during off hours?* For example, a payroll application may be required during the pay-period weekends.

Certain long reports may have to be run every night, and uptime becomes necessary just for that. Based on an evaluation of need, the technical folks can work out their backup and availability schedules.

3. *How can we handle migrations, upgrades, and production patch updates?* A discussion about the amount of downtime necessary for upgrading to newer application releases as well as the application of critical production patches should be done at the SLA meeting. The resulting downtime should be communicated and evaluated to determine availability.

4. *Do we need a separate reporting instance?* If your environment has two distinct types of users—one using long batch jobs and reporting and the other using the core modules—you can consider implementing a reporting instance that is separate from the primary instance.

High Availability Solutions

Several solutions are available to ensure high availability in any Oracle Financials system. These solutions are outlined in this section.

Standby Recovery Database

The standby recovery database solution involves maintaining another database instance as a standby instance—a copy of the primary production database. The copy is kept current by periodically applying an archived redo log from the primary to the standby environment.

Replication

Oracle's replication functionality can be used to provide the ability to replicate the production database on another server, which can be used for reporting and as a standby in case of a disaster. Oracle provides the Replication Manager to help you with this task.

The first release of Replication Manager support began with Oracle8i release 2.1. Before deploying any new version, you should use Metalink to verify that it is supported on your environment. The initialization parameters shown in Table 16-2 should be set for replication.

Oracle8i Enhancements to Replication   Starting with version 8i, Oracle introduced several new features and functionality for replication. These features improve performance, increase ease of use with the Replication Manager, and provide security enhancements. We will evaluate some of these features in this section.

Parameter	Recommended Value/Explanation
COMPATIBLE	8.1.6
SHARED_POOL_SIZE	Increase by at least 25–50MB
GLOBAL_NAMES	TRUE
DISTRIBUTED_TRANSACTIONS	Add two per additional master
REPLICATION_DEPENDENCY_TRACKING	TRUE
JOB_QUEUE_INTERVAL	Ten
JOB_QUEUE_PROCESSES	Three (add one per additional master)
PARALLEL_MAX_SERVERS	Ten
PARALLEL_MINIMUM_SERVERS	Two

TABLE 16-2. *Initialization Parameters for Replication*

- **System generated replication packages** Executes from within the database PL/SQL engine and performs much better. The internal triggers are written in C and compiled in the database engine, which makes them faster.

- **Single snapshot refresh** This can contain up to 400 snapshots. The performance of snapshot refresh is considerably improved.

- **Snapshot deployment templates** Creates a centralized environment for distribution to multiple sites, which can be instantiated online and offline.

- **Privileges** The proxy-snapshot administrator has a way of accessing objects in object groups without being granted excessive privileges. Also, EXECUTE ANY PROCEDURE privileges need not be granted to the receiver in Oracle8i. This is managed automatically.

- **Oracle Enterprise Manager** Allows Replication Manager to run from anywhere in the network.

- **Advanced Replication option** Supports separate links for each replication group, allowing for independent scheduling of groups and reducing the round trips.

■ **Parallel Propagation** Makes use of the pool of available parallel server processes. This follows the same pattern as parallel query technology. A parallel coordinator controls the server processes by tracking dependencies, allocating work, and tracking progress.

Figure 16-1 shows a multiple master replication situation implemented using Oracle8i replication features.

Remote Disk Mirroring

Remote disk mirroring provides disk mirror to a remote location, in a synchronous or asynchronous fashion. In case of asynchronous mirroring, the primary database does not wait for the data to be committed to the remote site. In case of synchronous mirroring, the application waits for commit acknowledgement from the remote site.

Performance is the primary concern for this type of availability solution. Also, in the context of Oracle Financials, it is preferable to implement a synchronous method of mirroring to ensure consistent status of the instance when a failure occurs. Many third-party tools can help with remote disk mirroring, such as EMC

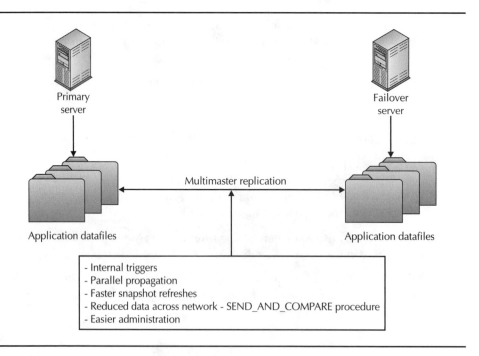

FIGURE 16-1. *Oracle replication features*

solutions. The choice of the solution or the tool depends on how much you want to spend and how much availability you really need.

Oracle Parallel Server

Oracle Parallel Server (OPS) offers another solid option for high availability solutions. Oracle Application Suite 11i is certified for use with OPS technology. In case of OPS, many different instances running Oracle on different hardware environments can share the same database on shared disks. OPS is better than Standby Recovery Database in the sense that the instance is actively being used and at the same time failover is provided. OPS provides a reasonably feasible solution for small as well as moderately large Oracle applications environments.

Oracle Parallel Server Architecture   Figure 16-2 shows an example of Oracle Parallel Server architecture.

The Oracle Parallel Server architecture consists of a single database containing datafiles, log files, and control files. These files are serviced by two or more

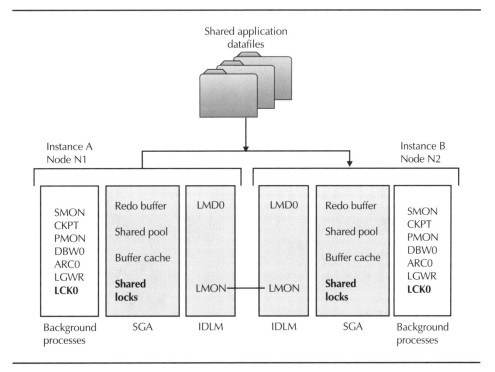

FIGURE 16-2.   *Oracle Parallel Server architecture*

instances running on different computer servers or nodes. In addition to the standard background processes like PMON, SMON, ARCH, DBWR, and LGWR, these instances also have certain lock processes defined called LCK1, LCK2, and so on, and an area in the SGA called the *shared lock area*. The shared lock area maintains the current status of the Parallel Cache Management (PCM) locks. The instances use these locks for ensuring that blocks are accessed in a consistent mode.

The LCK*n* processes work along with Integrated Distributed Lock Manager (IDLM) to maintain lock ownership and status between two nodes. In OPS, cluster management software works in conjunction with the IDLM to establish internode and shared-disk access.

Application failover provides the following features:

- Connection is not lost when an instance is up and running.

- SELECT statements can be executed before the instance fails.

- Transactions have to be re-executed after the backup instance takes over.

The salient features of OPS from the administrator's perspective are

- Reconnection time can be improved by using prespawn connections.

- Better control on the application run on various instances and the failover order.

- Maintenance and scheduled outages can be implemented with minimum inconvenience to the users.

In Oracle Parallel Server implementation, you can control some of the functionality of failover. These failover functionality options are as described here:

- **SELECT** Allows users with open cursors to continue to fetch

- **SESSION** Failover sessions do not attempt to recover SELECTS

- **NONE** This is the default

There are two ways to improve the performance of failover connect:

- **BASIC** Requires work on the backup instance.

- **PRECONNECT** Faster than basic. Requires that the backup instance be able to support all connections from every instance in the backup.

Note that some columns have been added to V$SESSION view for reviewing failover options:

- **FAILED_OVER**   Yes or no
- **FAILOVER_TYPE**   Select, session, or none
- **FAILOVER_METHOD**   Basic or preconnect

Local Disk Mirroring

This option involves preserving local mirrors of datafiles. This method protects against disk failures of various forms. If a disk fails, a resync operation involving performing a complete copy of the mirror is performed. This process may take time depending on the size of the datafiles. Tools such as Veritas provide better and faster techniques of refreshing.

NOTE
Local mirroring does not provide for local disaster or problems with the Oracle instance itself.

Standby Recovery Database

The standby recovery database is a feature available starting with Oracle7, which enables you to shadow a copy of your production database. In case of a breakdown, the standby database can take over and the application is up and running in a matter of minutes. A standby database is more refined and has several enhancements in Oracle8i.

In creating a standby recovery database, some activities take place on the primary server and some on the standby server.

1. Make a cold backup of the primary system.

2. Create a control file for the standby database using the following command:

   ```
   ALTER DATABASE CREATE STANDBY CONTROLFILE AS <ctlfilename>
   ```

3. To ensure consistency in backup, control files and log files issue the following command:

   ```
   ALTER SYSTEM ARCHIVE LOG CURRENT
   ```

4. Copy all the duplicate files to the standby system.

5. Use the same names for both the instances.

6. Set the following initialization parameters in the standby system:

```
DB_FILE_NAME_CONVERT and LOG_FILE_NAME_CONVERT
```

You can also set the new 8i parameter called STANDBY_ARCHIVE_DEST. This parameter defines the standby database destination for the archive redo log file group.

7. Add the instance in standby mode:

```
SVRMGR> startup nomount
SVRMGR> alter database mount standby database;
SVRMGR> alter database recover standby database;
```

8. Apply archive logs as appropriate.

9. With the new remote archival feature, archive logs can be automatically created on the remote (standby) host. To fully automate the process of recovering (rolling forward) the standby database, you can put the database into sustained recovery mode:

```
SVRMGR> recover managed standby database
```

The server process applies the archive logs as they are generated on the standby host. The server process wakes itself internally every 15 seconds to check for archival of the next required log. The DBA can also specify a timeout period (minutes) for sustained recovery. If no new logs are generated within this period, the recovery session is cancelled.

```
SVRMGR> recover managed standby database timeout 10
```

10. To cancel a sustained recovery session, from another server manager session issue the following command:

```
SVRMGR> alter database recover managed standby database cancel;
```

11. The standby database is always kept in the recovery mode until it is required. To keep it current, the archived redo logs have to be copied from primary to secondary. To do this, execute a cron job on UNIX or schedule a batch program (say every hour) on the primary server that will identify the log file generated over the last period and post it to the standby system.

Accessing the Standby Database

Oracle8i provides a way to open the standby database in read-only mode. This means that the standby database can be used as a reporting repository. This is a useful feature because it can help reduce the number of users signing on to the primary database. The database can subsequently be shut down and recovery restarted *without* having to be refreshed (regenerate the standby datafiles and control files from the primary). The extended syntax for this operation is shown here:

```
SVRMGR> alter database open read only;
```

Performing Disk-Based Sorts in the Standby System

Disk-based sorts create sort segments on disk that traditionally incurs DML operations on certain dictionary tables. Thus, disk sorts that are managed in this way are prohibited on read-only databases. If a session attempts a disk sort, the following error occurs:

ORA-01647: tablespace 'TEMP' is read-only, cannot allocate space in it.

To perform disk sorts on the read-only databases, use locally-managed temporary tablespaces. See Chapter 18 for more details on using locally managed tablespaces. In case of locally managed tablespaces, extent information is stored as part of the datafile. This is different from the regular dictionary managed tablespaces, where the data dictionary manages the extents.

Temporary tablespaces can be created as locally managed by using a special syntax:

```
CREATE TEMPORARY TABLESPACE  lm_temp TEMPFILE
'/u02/oradata/11iprod/temp01.dbf' SIZE 200M EXTENT MANAGEMENT LOCAL
UNIFORM EXTENT 1M;
```

Following is a list of notes about TEMPFILEs:

■ TEMPFILEs are recorded only in the control file.

■ No redo operations are generated for operations on the TEMPFILEs.

■ TEMPFILEs are set to NOLOGGING MODE.

■ TEMPFILEs cannot be made read-only.

■ TEMPFILEs cannot be renamed. They have to be dropped and re-created in the new location.

■ ALTER DATABASE BACKUP CONTROLFILE TO TRACE command does not generate information about TEMPFILEs.

To do disk-based sorts, execute the following steps:

1. Create a locally managed temporary tablespace.

2. Change the temporary tablespaces for all users performing reporting operation on the standby system to TEMP using the command

```
SQL> alter user report_user temporary tablespace lm_temp;
```

3. Recover and open the standby instance in read-only mode:

```
SQL> alter database open read only;
```

4. Add a datafile to the lm_temp tablespace:

```
ALTER  TABLESPACE  lm_temp ADD TEMPFILE
'/u02/oradata/11iprod/temp02.dbf' SIZE 100M;
```

These steps are necessary because TEMPFILE definitions are not stored in the SYS.FILE$ dictionary table. Because adding a TEMPFILE on the primary does not update SYS.FILE$, there is no redo generated, so recovery on the standby cannot create the file.

Creating a Warehouse Instance from the Standby Recovery Instance

As you saw in the previous section, a method implements a standby recovery instance. Also with Oracle version 8.1.7, the instance can be used in read-only mode. This is different from earlier versions, in which the standby database was always in the recover mode. You can consider using this method for creating a staging area or a reporting repository of your main application.

The staging area or the standby instance can be used for servicing ad-hoc users and standard reporting requirements. The primary instance can still continue to run the core modules in read-write mode. The other advantage of this approach is that because you are maintaining a standby recovery database, in case the primary instance goes down for any reason, you can still be up and running in minutes by transporting the newly created archive log files to the standby server and applying them to the standby instance. Note that this is only the first phase of creating a reporting system. Based on your specific reporting requirements, you could also create aggregates and summary tables for quicker reporting.

Refer to Figure 16-3 for an illustration of this scenario.

NOTE
It is possible to direct an SMR server session to delete archived redo logs once they have been backed up. This option should obviously be used with extreme caution! Delete archive logs only if you are 100 percent satisfied that you have good copies and backups elsewhere.

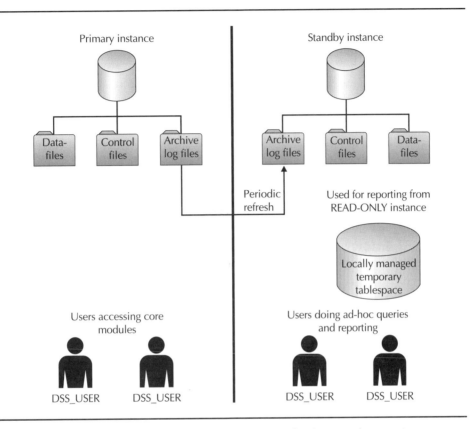

FIGURE 16-3.   *Implementing a standby recovery database with reporting*
functionality

Oracle8i Backup Features to Leverage with Applications

This section of the chapter is dedicated to reviewing some features available in
Oracle8i for improving the backup process.

Enhancements to Archiving

The following changes have been made to the archiving process with a view to
prevent archive logs from becoming the point of recovery.

You can specify multiple archive destinations for your instance. The destination
could be local or remote and could be specified as required or desirable. If a remote

archiving is specified, a remote file server (RFS) is responsible for receiving the file on the remote site and storing it in the specified location.

You can also specify multiple archive processes by specifying the init.ora parameter LOG_ARCHIVE_DEST_1, LOG_ARCHIVE_DEST_2, and so on. This parameter can be modified at session level and up to five destinations can be specified.

LOG_ARCHIVE_DUPLEX_DEST can be specified in addition to LOG_ARCHIVE_DEST in the init.ora file. LOG_ARCHIVE_DUPLEX_DEST provides a backup destination.

When specifying a destination for LOG_ARCHIVE_DEST_*n* parameters, you can define them either as MANDATORY or OPTIONAL. Specifying a parameter as MANDATORY means that the system will not allow the redo file to be overwritten until *all* mandatory files are successfully written.

Archiving Information

You can get archiving information from the following data dictionary views:

View Name	Explanation
V$ARCHIVE_DEST	Column BINDING could be optional or mandatory; STATUS field could be valid, inactive, deferred, in error, or disabled; ERROR field gives an error text.
V$ARCHIVE_PROCESS	STATUS field has stopped, scheduled, starting, active, stopping or terminated; LOG_SEQUENCE field contains sequence number of the current log archived.

LogMiner Utility for Analyzing Redo Log Files

Log files contain lots of useful information about the Oracle database. LogMiner is a PL/SQL-based utility provided by Oracle for reading, analyzing, and interpreting redo log files. With LogMiner

- Changes can be tracked without the need for auditing.

- Logical recovery can be done without the need for performing a point-in-time recovery.

- This information can be useful for planning and trending analysis.

LogMiner provides several features in the form of PL/SQL procedures to extract the data dictionary information into a text file. The main package is called

DBMS_LOGMNR_D. LogMiner generates its analysis information in the data dictionary table called V$LOGMNR_CONTENTS. The information can be used to roll back changes or undo certain activities without a need to go through the recovery procedures. Following are some of the other views that contain important information about logs analyzed.

- V$LOGMNR_DICTIONARY
- V$LOGMNR_LOGS
- V$LOGMNR_PARAMETERS

Corrupt Block Detection and Repair

Oracle8i provides a method by which an administrator can detect and report block corruptions proactively and make them usable again. This is achieved through an Oracle provided package called DBMS_REPAIR. In addition, a new init.ora parameter called DB_BLOCK_CHECKING can be set to TRUE to check data and index blocks whenever they are changed.

Introduction to Oracle Recovery Manager

Recovery Manager (RMAN) can be used to back up and restore database files, archive logs, and control files. RMAN can also be used for different database recovery situations. RMAN starts Oracle server processes on the database to be backed up or restored. The backup, restore, and recovery is driven through these processes, hence the term "server-managed recovery." RMAN can be controlled using the Oracle Enterprise Manager module called Backup Manager. This section provides a brief introduction to RMAN.

Backup Sets

An RMAN backup set has the following components:

- Contains one or more datafiles or archive logs
- Stored in an Oracle proprietary format
- Comprises a complete set of backup pieces
- Constitutes a full or incremental backup

Each backup piece in the set is a single output file. The size of a backup piece can be restricted to no larger than the maximum file size that your file system will support. If the size is not restricted, the backup set will comprise one backup piece.

RMAN can be used to take different types of backups of Oracle instances. One of them is called an image copy. Image copy is a copy of a single file (datafile, archive log or control file); it is similar to an Operating System copy of the file in the sense that no compression of the data is performed. A full backup set is a backup of one or more datafiles that contains all used blocks in the datafile. Blocks that have never been used are not backup. Oracle performs backup set compression in case of a full backup set.

The other type of backup that can be performed using RMAN is called an incremental backup. An incremental backup is a backup of one or more datafiles that contains only those blocks that have been modified since a previous backup at the same or lower level. As with full backups, compression is performed.

The Snapshot Control File

When RMAN needs to resynchronize from a read-consistent version of the control file, it creates a temporary snapshot control file. The default name for the snapshot control file is port-specific. From the command line, use the following command to change the name of the snapshot control file:

```
set snapshot control file name to file_name
```

Subsequent snapshot control files that RMAN creates use the name specified in the command.

The snapshot control file name can also be set to a *raw* device. This operation is important for OPS databases in which more than one instance in the cluster use RMAN, because server sessions on each node must be able to create a snapshot control file with the same name and location.

RESETLOGS Option

Whenever you open the database with the RESETLOGS option, all datafiles get a new RESETLOGS SCN and timestamp. Archived redo logs also have these two values in their header. Because Oracle will not apply an archived redo log to a datafile unless the RESETLOGS SCN and timestamps match, the RESETLOGS operations prevents you from corrupting your datafiles with old archived logs.

Database Incarnation

Whenever you perform incomplete recovery or perform recovery using a backup control file, you must reset the online redo logs when you open the database. The new version of the reset database is called a *new incarnation*. All archived redo logs generated after the point of the RESETLOGS on the old incarnation are invalid in the new incarnation.

RMAN's Recovery Catalog

The *recovery catalog* is a repository of information that is used and maintained by RMAN to determine how to execute requested backup and restore actions. The recovery catalog can be in a schema of an existing Oracle8 database. However, if RMAN is being used to back up multiple databases, it is probably worth creating a dedicated recovery catalog database.

NOTE
The recovery catalog database cannot be used to catalog backups of itself.

Ensure that catalog and catproc have been run, and make sure that catproc has been run on the target database as SYS (do not use SYSTEM) to set up the recovery catalog. Then execute the following:

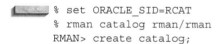
```
SVRMGR> spool create_rman.log
SVRMGR> connect internal
SVRMGR> create user rman identified by rman
temporary tablespace temp
default tablespace rcvcat quota unlimited on rcvcat;
SVRMGR> grant recovery_catalog_owner to rman;
SVRMGR> grant connect, resource to rman;
```

From the UNIX shell, run the following code to generate the recovery catalog schema in the default tablespace for RMAN:

```
% set ORACLE_SID=RCAT
% rman catalog rman/rman
RMAN> create catalog;
```

NOTE
It is important that the recovery catalog database is backed up regularly and frequently.

Connecting to RMAN with a Recovery Catalog
To connect RMAN with a recovery catalog, set ORACLE_SID to be the target database, and issue the following command:

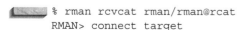
```
% rman rcvcat rman/rman@rcat
RMAN> connect target
```

```
or if the target database uses a password file,
% rman rcvcat rman/rman@rcat target targdba/<password>@targdb
```

Once connected to the target database, you can specify RMAN commands either interactively or by using stored scripts.

Here's an example of using RMAN interactively:

```
RMAN> resync catalog;
```

The target database must be registered with the recovery catalog before using RMAN against the database for the first time. To do so, use this code:

```
RMAN> register database;
```

Connecting to RMAN Without a Recovery Catalog

To connect to RMAN without a recovery catalog, set ORACLE_SID to be the target database, and issue the following command:

```
% rman nocatalog
RMAN> connect target
or if the target database uses a password file,
RMAN> connect target targdba/<password>@targdb
```

Resetting the Recovery Catalog

Before you can use RMAN again with a target database that you have opened with the RESETLOGS option, notify RMAN that you have reset the database incarnation. The reset database command directs RMAN to create a new database incarnation record in the recovery catalog. This new incarnation record indicates the current incarnation.

RMAN associates all subsequent backups and log archiving done by the target database with the new database incarnation. If you issue the ALTER DATABASE OPEN RESETLOGS statement but do not reset the database, RMAN cannot access the recovery catalog because it cannot distinguish between a RESETLOGS command and an accidental restore of an old control file. By resetting the database, you inform RMAN that the database has been opened with the RESETLOGS option.

In the rare situation in which you wish to undo the effects of opening with the RESETLOGS option by restoring backups of a prior incarnation of the database, use this command to change the current incarnation to an older incarnation:

```
reset database to incarnation key.
```

Resyncing the Recovery Catalog

The recovery catalog should be kept as up to date as possible. This means that it should reflect the status of the target database. This can be achieved by resyncing the catalog, which can be a full or partial operation. A full resync updates the catalog with *all* control file information that has changed since the last resync. This includes changes to the physical structure of the database. A manual (explicit) resync performs a full resync, while full (implicit) resyncs are performed after an SMR backup. A partial resync updates only the catalog with redo log, backup set, and datafile copy information—i.e. physical structure changes are *not* refreshed. A partial (implicit) resync is performed before an SMR backup. At a *minimum*, you should resync the recovery catalog at intervals less than the init.ora parameter CONTROL_FILE_RECORD_KEEP_TIME. After this number of days, control file information will be overwritten. Because resyncing is a relatively cheap operation, it is advisable to resync as often as possible, especially if the database switches logs frequently.

The following sample shell script could be scheduled to run hourly:

```
rman target un/pw@<target alias> rcvcat un/pw@<rcvcat alias> << EOF
resync catalog;
exit;
EOF
```

Resyncing the recovery catalog involves synchronizing the recovery catalog with the target database control file. Certain operations perform this implicitly. To resync manually, issue the *resync catalog;* command from RMAN.

The catalog should be resync'd frequently, especially if the target database generates many archive logs. It should also be resync'd after making any structural changes to the target database. Although the target database's control file is automatically updated whenever new control file records are created (for example, creation of new archived logs or new datafiles), if the target is not resync'd and a backup control file is restored, the new records must be cataloged manually:

```
catalog archivelog '<logname>';
```

Examples of Using RMAN

This section contains some examples of backing up a database, a tablespace, individual datafiles etc. using RMAN scripts.

Backing Up a Complete Database

```
RMAN> run {
2> # back up the complete database to disk
3> allocate channel dev1 type disk;
4> backup
5> full
6> tag full_db_sunday_night
```

```
7> format '/oracle/backups/db_t%t_s%s_p%p'
8> (database);
9> release channel dev1;
10> }
Line#
2: Comment line (anything after the '#' is a comment)
3&9: See section 15 - Channels
5: Full backup (default if full or incremental not specified)
6: Meaningful string (<=30 chars)
7: Filename to use for backup pieces, including substitution variables.
8: Indicates all files including control files are to be backed up
```

To view this backup in the catalog, use the following command:

```
RMAN> list backupset of database;
```

Backing Up a Tablespace

```
RMAN> run {
2> allocate channel dev1 type disk;
3> backup
4> tag tbs_users_read_only
5> format '/oracle/backups/tbs_users_t%t_s%s'
6> (tablespace users);
7> release channel dev1;
10> }

Line#
6: Specifying only the USERS tablespace for backup
```

To view this tablespace backup in the catalog, use the following command:

```
RMAN> list backupset of tablespace users;
```

If, for example, the USERS tablespace is going to be READ ONLY after being backed up, subsequent full database backups would not need to back up this tablespace. To cater to this, specify the *skip read only* option in subsequent backups.

Backing Up Individual Datafiles

```
RMAN> run {
2> allocate channel dev1 type 'SBT_TAPE';
3> backup
4> format '%d_%u'
5> (datafile '/oracle/dbs/sysbigdb.dbf');
```

```
6> release channel dev1;
7> }
```

Line 2 of this code allocates a tape drive using the media manager layer (MML). Note that no tag was specified and the tag value is therefore set to null.

To view this tablespace backup in the catalog, use the following command:

```
RMAN> list backupset of datafile 1;
```

Backing Up the Control File

```
RMAN> run {
2> allocate channel dev1 type 'SBT_TAPE';
3> backup
4> format 'cf_t%t_s%s_p%p'
5> tag cf_monday_night
6> (current controlfile);
7> release channel dev1;
8> }
```

NOTE
*A database backup will automatically
back up the control file.*

Recovery Scenarios Using RMAN

This section discusses a few recovery situations and how they can be handled using RMAN.

Database Open, Datafile Deleted

The datafile has been deleted from a running database. There are two methods of open database recovery: restore the datafile and recover either the datafile or the tablespace. The next two examples show both methods:

Here's the datafile recovery method:

```
RMAN> run {
2> allocate channel dev1 type disk;
3> sql "alter tablespace users offline immediate";
4> restore datafile 4;
5> recover datafile 4;
6> sql "alter tablespace users online";
7> release channel dev1;
8> }
```

Here's the tablespace recovery method

```
RMAN> run {
2> allocate channel dev1 type disk;
3> sql "alter tablespace users offline immediate";
4> restore tablespace users;
5> recover tablespace users;
6> sql "alter tablespace users online";
7> release channel dev1;
8> }
```

Complete Restore (Lost Online Redo) and Rollforward–Database Closed

```
RMAN> run {
2> allocate channel dev1 type disk;
3> set until logseq=105 thread=1;
4> restore controlfile to '/oracle/dbs/ctrltargdb.ctl';
5> replicate controlfile from '/oracle/dbs/ctrltargdb.ctl';
6> restore database;
7> sql "alter database mount";
8> recover database;
9> sql "alter database open resetlogs";
10> release channel dev1;
11> }
RMAN> reset database;
```

Restore of a Subset of Datafiles, Complete Recovery

```
RMAN> run {
2> allocate channel dev1 type disk;
3> sql "alter database mount";
4> restore datafile 2;
5> restore datafile 3;
6> restore archivelog all;
7> recover database;
8> sql "alter database open";
9> release channel dev1;
10> }
```

Summary

Backup and availability are critical to a successful deployment of any successful three-tier implementation of an Oracle Financials application. This is more important because Internet-based applications typically have more visibility and higher expectation levels from users. An administrator should plan the different types of backup that are required to service her users and then define the tools and scripts to implement them. Application availability is a critical issue and should be discussed as part of the SLA between the business and technical teams. There are several solutions to implement high availability like Oracle Parallel Server, standby recovery database, replication, and local and remote disk mirroring. Several sound third-party solutions are available to implement both backup and availability. Oracle8i provides several new features that can help the administrator improve her backup and recovery processes. This chapter discussed the overall backup, recovery, and available options for the applications administrator. In the next chapter, we will review security.

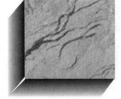

CHAPTER
17

Security

- Securing the Oracle e-business environment
- Managing security in Oracle applications
- Implementing security in custom modules
- Implementing a Virtual Private Network using fine grained access control
- Oracle advanced security

ecurity is defined as the ability of the organization to identify and enforce confidentiality, integrity, and availability of its critical data. Security policies and methods have become critical to an organization and are now considered an important part of the information technology (IT) infrastructure. This is because an organization's data is considered a valuable assets, and there is a need to protect it just like other assets, such as land and buildings.

Managing security has become more and more complex over the years. Gone are the days when security was restricted to mainframes and users could access them using dumb terminals. Now there is more and more cheap hardware, network backbones, and several client applications that are part of the corporate IT architecture backbone. They have to be supported as well as secured from both internal and external hackers. The advent of the Internet has enhanced the need to create a solid security methodology for all the hardware, software, and application fragments of an organization's infrastructure. In today's security paradigm, the focus is not only on keeping external hackers from accessing data, but internal hackers must be kept from trying to access sensitive corporate data for malicious purposes.

The objective of this chapter is to review the security requirements for the Oracle E-Business Suite implementation. We also discuss steps for building a solid security model and discuss various building blocks for implementing security.

Securing the Oracle E-Business Environment

Setting up a security solution for a complex environment like Oracle Financials not only involves meticulous planning and execution but also solid background information on networking, system administration, and available security options. In this section, we will review the steps required to secure the Oracle Application Suite.

Risk Assessment

A Financials administrator or a database administrator (DBA) typically performs risk assessment on a network. A risk assessment is a review of security risks that need to be guarded against by the business community and management. A formal risk assessment is recommended since it provides a good mechanism for communicating risks to management and also to suggest methods for guarding against them.

When writing the risk assessment document, the DBA should consider the following factors:

- Document each situation and the chance of that situation happening.

- Provide examples of previous situations when a mishap occurred and how it could have been averted.

- Review the impact and downtime of each of the situations and also the type of resources that will be required. Also include the effect of these situations on other currently running projects.

- Discuss legal and financial restrictions because of possible data loss.

- Provide recommendations based on what has been identified.

Following are some of the areas that need to be reviewed for setting up good security for an Oracle environment.

- Network security

- Operating system security

- Web server security

- Database security

- Password and account management

- Backup and recovery

- Software development security

Network Security

Network security is a critical part of securing your 11i applications. Because Oracle11i is an Internet-based application, it is critical to secure the Web server and the database server and also keep them separate. The team implementing network security should be knowledgeable in various networking techniques, firewall implementation, and operating system internals.

A firewall between the application server and the database server is often recommended in the architecture. If an application needs to be integrated to some of your internal custom applications, it is recommended that a firewall be placed between the Oracle application and the custom application.

Following are additional implementation tips that relate to network security:

- Password protect the routers and firewall servers.

- Limit access to the firewall server to the team responsible for security.

- Choose well-trained personnel for implementing and supporting the firewall and make sure that the implications of each of the setups are properly discussed and authenticated by the technical team before implementing.

- For all problems encountered, fixes should be appropriately documented. This may reveal hidden risks in the form of short-term production fixes that may have opened a security risk.

- Implement a regular security audit (more on audit in the next section).

- Restrict remote dial-ins to folks who need to have them. Implement additional verification for remote dial-in.

- Hire or mentor a network administrator who is knowledgeable in the field and provide him or her sufficient authority to maintain network security.

Operating System Security

The operating system is yet another critical component of the overall Oracle Financials environment. No security can be complete without security access to the operating system prompts. It is critical that access is provided only to specific users who need to use the application. In addition, the users should have only the permissions necessary to perform their roles and tasks. Here are more recommendations for securing the operating system:

- Implement a log of all changes along with reason for and dates of the changes.

- Ensure that the operating system is at appropriate patch levels. Implement operating system patches in time on an ongoing basis.

- Important login ID information, including oracle and applmgr, should be regularly monitored for access. Develop a procedure for regularly changing the operating system passwords. This should definitely occur when a team member leaves the organization.

- Implement a login banner, warning unauthorized logins about the inappropriate usage of the system.

- All log files should be reviewed periodically for any abnormal security errors.

- Set up a procedure to trap and audit certain commands at the operating system level.

Database Security

The Financial administrator has most control of this layer of security. This layer is important since much sensitive information is stored at this level. Here are some tips for implementing database security:

- SYS, SYSTEM, and oracle should be regularly changed. This should be done especially when a technical member leaves the team.

- Make sure that all unnecessary user accounts are deleted. Implementing password aging is highly recommended. Users should be encouraged to change their application and database passwords often.

- Use special encryption for sensitive data like credit card information. You can also implement fine-grained access control for highly sensitive tables.

- Password and account security should be implemented for the application server (middle tier) as well as database tier.

- The Financials administrator should work closely with the development team working on custom development. She should ensure that no security rules are violated as a result of any custom implementation. If any program requires special privileges, it should be agreed to be treated separately by granting execute access to specific users.

- The Financial administrator should implement some change management process to keep track of custom program code and should also be able to track down changes to specific schema objects. For example, by using the event level trigger, the administrator can track any changes to any object in the production instance. This will help him keep track of unplanned changes as well as analyze a complex downtime situation.

- Database system privileges should be limited. The administrator should verify that no user has SELECT ANY TABLE privilege or DBA role.

- Indirect access to stored procedures and triggers should be controlled.

Managing Security in Oracle Applications

This section of the chapter provides an overview of the security requirements of Oracle Financials. The key component of security in Oracle is responsibility, which defines the following:

- Application database privileges
- An accessible applications functionality
- The available concurrent programs and reports

Implementing Security

A Financials administrator defines a user and then assigns one or more responsibilities to that user. Application privileges depend on these responsibilities. An administrator can assign standard responsibilities available with the Oracle Application Suite or define custom responsibilities. For example, the administrator can define a responsibility for viewing Financials reports.

Responsibilities can be attached to a data group, a request security group (optional), and menu. An administrator can request security to specify the report, request sets, and set concurrent programs that your users run by using a standard submission form known as the *Submit Request Form*. The request group is then referred to as a *request security group*. You can define a request group to contain single requests, request sets, or all the requests and request sets in an application.

Implementing Security in Custom Modules

Oracle applications provide several packages and application programming interfaces (APIs) to help implement basic functionality of the application in the custom modules. Most of these packages are PL/SQL based and implement such functionality as messaging, security, user profiles, concurrent processing, and file I/O. In this section, we will discuss the security functionality in the Oracle Application Suite that is provided by a function called FND_FUNCTION.

The FND_FUNCTION Package

The FND_FUNCTION package is designed to verify that the currently logged in user has sufficient permissions to execute code and also ensures that the program fragment is executed within the boundaries of such permission. FND_FUNCTION is written in PL/SQL and can either be used in a stored program (stored procedure or package) or can be called from a form. Following is a description of various procedures and their functionality.

TEST

TEST is a function and returns a boolean value. It is used to determine whether a given function is accessible. This function can be used in a form to decide which functions to enable and disable based on the user's responsibility.

The following table shows aspects of the TEST parameter.

Parameters	IN or OUT	Data Type	Notes
FUNCTION_NAME	IN	VARCHAR2	The function name to be tested

TEST_ID

TEST_ID is also a function and returns a boolean value. It is similar to TEST but accepts a FUNCTION_ID instead of a FUNCTION_NAME. This function can be used in a form to decide which functions to enable and disable based on the user's responsibility.

The following table shows aspects of the TEST_ID parameter.

Parameters	IN or OUT	Data Type	Notes
FUNCTION_ID	IN	NUMBER	The function ID to be tested

EXECUTE

EXECUTE is a stored procedure that executes the specified form function. The form function must be defined in Oracle Application Object Library (AOL) and must be in the menu for that responsibility.

Here is a list of various parameters and their meanings for EXECUTE.

Parameters	IN or OUT	Data Type	Notes
FUNCTION_NAME	IN	VARCHAR2	Name of the function to be executed
OPEN_FLAG	IN	VARCHAR2	'Y' indicates open form as OPEN_FORM; 'N' indicates open form as NEW_FORM
SESSION_FLAG	IN	VARCHAR2	'Y' indicates open form in a new session; 'N' indicates open form in the same session
OTHER_PARAMS	IN	VARCHAR2	Additional parameters
ACTIVE_FLAG	IN	VARCHAR2	ACTIVATE for making the new form ACTIVE; NO_ACTIVATE will invoke the new form but returns to the calling form or code after exiting the new form

QUERY

QUERY is used to check whether a given function is accessible and returns information about the function. If the function is not accessible, the OUT parameters are set to empty strings.

Here is a list of various parameters and their meanings for QUERY.

Parameters	IN or OUT	Data Type	Notes
FUNCTION_NAME	IN	VARCHAR2	Name of the function to be executed
ACCESSIBLE	OUT	VARCHAR2	Set to 'Y' if accessible; otherwise set to 'N'
FUNCTION_TYPE	OUT	VARCHAR2	This string contains the type of function as specified in the Form Functions
FORM_PATH	OUT	VARCHAR2	This string contains the entire path name of the form; NULL if function is not accessible
ARGUMENTS	OUT	VARCHAR2	List of function arguments

USER_FUNCTION_NAME

This function returns the user name of the function defined for the specified function.

Parameters	IN or OUT	Data Type	Notes
FUNCTION_NAME	IN	VARCHAR2	Name of the function to be executed

CURRENT_FORM_FUNCTION

This function returns the function name with which the current form was called.

Implementing a Virtual Private Network Using Fine Grained Access Control

In this section, we will cover details about fine grained access control (FGAC), a feature available in Oracle8i for implementing added security at the table or view level.

FGAC provides an additional layer of security for Oracle applications as well as sensitive custom tables and views. Using FGAC, a Financials administrator can ensure that the end user can access only certain rows. This is critical in situations with a single production instance and different types of users (like batch users, online users, and reporting users) access the application and the database throughout the day. FGAC can also be beneficial for situations in which the DBA has to build additional layers of security in addition to the application-level security provided by Oracle. FGAC is also relevant in self-service Web applications, in which tables are frequently accessed by different tools and by different user groups. In such cases, FGAC may help provide a common layer of security on the database side.

Overview of FGAC

FGAC provides a method of implementing security policy for a table or view. We can also build additional logic; for example, a department supervisor can query and update all employees for that department. Internally, a *context package* (coded by the Technical Support team) sets up context attributes for the user. After connecting to the application panel, whenever User1 queries a table, Oracle internally checks if a SELECT POLICY is defined for that table and attaches a PREDICATE to the SELECT statement usually in the form of a WHERE statement. This statement is then executed on the database.

Some of the important terms to know in FGAC are listed here:

- **Application Context**   Any information about the user that we may want to use for deciding what his or her access should be. The predicate as well as application context is defined using PL/SQL, and we can take advantage of the language features and functionality. Application context is implemented by creating a CONTEXT.

- **Predicate**   A security policy for a table or view is implemented using a Policy Function. This function returns a string of characters, which is transparently appended to the SQL statement at execution time. This string is called the PREDICATE. Using various application contexts, we can return different values for the PREDICATES. Predicates need to be less than 4000 bytes long. This restriction comes from the fact that predicate is actually a VARCHAR2 field in PL/SQL.

Benefits of FGAC

Some of the benefits of implementing fine grained access control are as follows:

- Handle data at table/view level regardless of what front-end or application is used. This provides an additional server-side security layer. This functionality can be complemented with the application-level security to build robust applications.

■ Hide sensitive data from people who should not see it, even through SQL*Plus, Access, Excel, or any other tools.

■ An application can be customized to behave in different ways based on the user requirement for security. This will again help in situations where a single instance serves as an OLAP database, a batch, and a Data Warehouse repository.

■ Useful for Web-based applications since they allow public access to critical data. Restrict access of sensitive information like payroll data, credit card information, and human-resources-related data.

Implementing FGAC

Five steps are required to set up FGAC:

	Description	Notes	Command Reference
1	Create a CONTEXT.	Creates a namespace for the context and associates it to a package.	CREATE CONTEXT hr_category USING hr_ctx;
2	Write the context package and grant execute permission to those who need it.	A PL/SQL program that sets values for different context attributes. Values can be used in Step 3 for determining the predicate string.	CREATE PACKAGE CREATE PACKAGE BODY Usual Oracle Package commands and syntax
3	Write the policy function.	A PL/SQL program that returns predicates corresponding to the values of the context attributes.	CREATE PACKAGE CREATE PACKAGE BODY Usual Oracle Package commands and syntax
4	Associate policy function with the table or view.	Same policy can be used for multiple tables, *or* multiple policy can be used for a given table (for SELECT, UPDATE, etc.)	Use the DBMS_RLS .ADD_POLICY package and supply actual parameters to it.
5	Define logon trigger to set context.	This trigger is executed when any user logs on to the instance.	CREATE OR REPLACE TRIGGER <t.name> AFTER LOGON ON DATABASE BEGIN...END;

Implementation Recommendations

Here are some recommendations to help you implement FGAC.

- Performance is not likely to be an issue with a large volume of data since the PREDICATE part of the query is replaced before the query is optimized. Since the policy function as well as the context package are PL/SQL programs, we can make sure that these routines are properly tuned and use appropriate indexes so that performance is sustained for any table size.

- Add FGAC only to tables or views where it is needed.

- FGAC can be implemented without a lot of customization or changes to the application level. If used effectively, it can leverage application security and help the process of sharing application data with other third-party applications and interfacing with data warehousing tools as well.

- Some of the areas for implementation in addition to the application tables could be to restrict access to the table and still provide the ability to maintain a common sign-on from all applications. FGAC can also be used to restrict a panel for a group of operator IDs.

Issues and Workarounds

When writing the policy function, we need to write the entire predicate without syntax errors. The following policy function compiles fine in spite of the syntax error in the predicate (since at that stage predicate is only a string of characters and is not executed yet). However, when a user tries to sign on, he or she gets an error: "ORA-28113 Policy predicate has error."

This points to a syntax error in the predicate. To find out what it is, you may have to either inspect your PREDICATE string manually (could be tricky) or trace your program using ALTER SESSION SET SQL_TRACE=TRUE. The trace file will have to extract the error, which you can easily fix.

Also, when coding the AFTER LOGON ON DATABASE, if you get a compilation error, you will keep getting errors when trying to log in with any schema. To fix this problem, you need to go to the Server Manager or connect to SQL*Plus using the internal account and then either drop the trigger or disable the trigger.

Oracle Advanced Security

Oracle Advanced Security provides a comprehensive suite of security services for the Oracle Database Cache, Oracle8i JVM (Java Virtual Machine), and Oracle8i PL/SQL. Its functionality is twofold:

- Protects enterprise networks and securely extends corporate networks to the Internet.

■ Integrates security and directory services, combining to provide enterprise user management and single sign-on.

Network Security in a Distributed Environment

Organizations around the world are deploying distributed databases and client/server applications in record numbers, often on a national or global scale based on Net8 and Oracle8i. This proliferation of distributed computing has been matched by an increase in the amount of information that organizations now place on computers. Employee records, financial records, product testing information, and other sensitive or critical data have moved from filing cabinets into file structures. The volume of critical or sensitive information on computers has increased the value of data that may be compromised.

The increased distribution of data in these environments brings with it some serious security threats:

■ **Data tampering**   Distributed environments bring with them the possibility that a malicious third party can execute a computer crime by actually tampering with data as it moves between sites.

■ **Eavesdropping and data theft**   Over the Internet and in wide area network (WAN) environments, both public carriers and private network owners often route portions of their network through insecure land lines, extremely vulnerable microwave and satellite links, or a number of servers, leaving valuable data open to view for any interested party. In local area network (LAN) environments within a building or campus, the potential exists for insiders with access to the physical wiring to view data not intended for them.

■ **Falsifying user identities**   In a distributed environment, it becomes more feasible for a user to falsify an identity to gain access to sensitive and important information.

■ **Administering too many passwords**   In a distributed system, users may need to remember multiple passwords for the different applications and services that they use. For example, a developer may have access to an application in development on a workstation, a production system on a mini-computer, a PC for creating documents, and several mini-computers or workstations for testing, reporting bugs, configuration management, and so on. Administration of all these accounts and passwords is complex and time-consuming.

Users generally respond to multiple accounts in one of two ways:

■   If they can choose their own passwords, they may standardize them so that they are the same on all machines. This results in a potentially large exposure in the event of a compromised password. Or they may use passwords with slight variations that can be easily guessed from knowing one password.

■   Users with complex passwords may simply write them down or forget them.

Either strategy severely compromises password secrecy and service availability. The Oracle Advanced Security option protects against these threats to the security of distributed environments. Specifically, the Oracle Advanced Security option provides the following features, each of which is described in the next few pages.

■   **Data Privacy**   To ensure that data is not disclosed during transmission

■   **Data Integrity**   To ensure that data is not modified during transmission

■   **Authentication**   To ensure that users', hosts', and clients' identities are correctly known, and to provide for single sign-on capability in place of using multiple passwords

■   **Authorization**   To ensure that a user, program, or process receives the appropriate privileges to access an object or set of objects

Data Privacy

The Oracle Advanced Security option ensures data privacy through both RSA and DES (Data Encryption Standard) encryption.

■   **RSA Encryption**   An encryption module that uses the RSA Data Security RC4 encryption algorithm. Using a secret, randomly-generated key for every session, all network traffic is fully safeguarded—including all data values, SQL statements, and stored procedure calls and results. The client, server, or both can request or require the use of the encryption module to guarantee that data is protected. Oracle's optimized implementation provides a high degree of security for a minimal performance penalty. For the RC4 algorithm, Oracle provides encryption key lengths of 40 bits, 56 bits, and 128 bits.

Because the Oracle Advanced Security option RSA RC4 40-bit implementation meets the U.S. government export guidelines for encryption products, Oracle provides an export version of the media and exports it to all but a few countries, allowing most companies to safeguard their entire worldwide operations with this software.

■ **DES Encryption** The U.S. Data Encryption Standard required for financial and many other institutions. The Oracle Advanced Security option for domestic use offers a standard, optimized 56-bit key DES encryption algorithm. Due to current U.S. government export restrictions, standard DES is initially available only to customers located in the U.S. and Canada. For customers located outside the U.S. and Canada, the Oracle Advanced Security option for export use also offers DES40, a version of DES that combines the standard DES encryption algorithm with the international availability of a 40-bit key. Selecting the algorithm to use for network encryption is a user configuration option, allowing varying levels of security and performance for different types of data transfers.

Data Integrity

To ensure that data has not been modified, deleted, or replayed during transmission, the Oracle Advanced Security option optionally generates a cryptographically secure message digest—through cryptographic checksums using the MD5 algorithm (MD5 was developed by Professor Ronald L. Rivest of MIT. The MD5 alogirthm takes as input a message of arbitrary length and produces as output a 128-bit "fingerprint" or "message digest" of the input. It is conjectured that it is computationally infeasible to produce two messages having the same message digest, or to produce any message having a given prespecified target message digest. The MD5 algorithm is intended for digital signature applications, where a large file must be "compressed" in a secure manner before being encrypted with a private [secret] key under a public-key cryptosystem)—and includes it with each packet sent across the network. Moreover, the Secure Sockets Layer (SSL) feature of the Oracle Advanced Security option allows the use of the Secure Hash Algorithm (SHA). SHA is slightly slower than MD5, but it produces a larger message digest to make it more secure against brute-force collision and inversion attacks.

Oracle Advanced Security makes it virtually impossible for an intruder to modify, delete, or replay packets without detection. The secure message digest is included with each packet sent across the network.

Authentication

The Oracle Advanced Security option (formerly Secure Network Services and Oracle Advanced Networking option) provides a comprehensive suite of security features to protect enterprise networks and securely extend corporate networks to the Internet. The Oracle Advanced Security option provides a single source of integration with network encryption and authentication solutions, single sign-on services, and security protocols. By integrating industry standards, it delivers unparalleled security to the Oracle network and beyond.

Oracle Advanced Security provides strong authentication of Oracle users' support for third-party authentication services. The following authentication methods are supported:

- SSL with X.509v3 certificates

- RADIUS

- Kerberos and CyberSafe

- Smart cards (RADIUS compliant)

- Token cards (SecurID or RADIUS compliant)

- Biometrics (Identix or RADIUS compliant)

- DCE (Distributed Computing Environment)

Authorization

Once users are authenticated, they are authorized to access only those services permitted by a corporate or business policy as found in a policy repository. Authorizations are provided with some of the third-party authentication solutions, such as DCE, as well as with the enterprise user security functionality in Oracle Advanced Security.

Enterprise User Security

Oracle Advanced Security integrates with LDAP v3-compliant (Lightweight Directory Access Protocol) directory services, such as Oracle Internet Directory, for enterprise user management, enterprise role management, and single sign-on.

Single Sign-on

Oracle Advanced Security provides the single sign-on feature whereby the user authenticates once and from that point authentication occurs transparently. This also means that users can use a single password to connect to multiple databases and services. Oracle Advanced Security supports many forms of single sign-on, including Kerberos and CyberSafe, as well as SSL-based single sign-on.

Oracle Advanced Security provides SSL-based single sign-on for Oracle users by virtue of integration with LDAP v3-compliant directory services. Integrated security and directory services and Oracle PKI (Public Key Infrastructure) implementation in Oracle Advanced Security enable SSL-based single sign-on to Oracle8i databases. Single sign-on enables users to authenticate once at the initial connection and subsequent connections authenticate the user transparently based on his or her

X.509 certificate. This brings ease of use to the users and single-station administration for the administrator with centralized management of users and authorizations.

Enterprise User Management

Oracle Advanced Security provides enterprise user management, allowing administrators to manage users on a central directory service, rather than repeatedly managing the same users on individual databases. Using Oracle Enterprise Security Manager, a tool accessible through Oracle Enterprise Manager, enterprise users and their authorizations are managed in Oracle Internet Directory or other LDAP v3-compliant directory services. Enterprise users can be assigned enterprise roles that determine their access privileges in a database, and enterprise roles can be granted to one or more enterprise users.

Schema-Independent Users

Oracle Advanced Security allows the separation of users from schemas so that many enterprise users can access a single, shared application schema. Instead of creating a user account in each database that a user needs to access, administrators need to create only an enterprise user in the directory and point the user at a shared schema, which many other enterprise users can also access. This allows administrators to create an enterprise user once in the directory. Then that enterprise user can access multiple databases using only the privileges he or she needs, thus lowering the overhead of managing users in an enterprise.

PKI Credential Management

Oracle Wallet Manager provides secure management of PKI user credentials. It issues certificate requests to Certificate Authorities (CA), manages the X.509 certificates and trusted certificates, and creates a private and public key pair for users. In most cases, a user never needs to access a wallet once it has been configured, but the user can easily access a wallet using Oracle Enterprise Login Assistant, a login tool that hides the complexity of a private key and certificates from users. Users can then connect to multiple services over SSL without providing additional passwords. This provides the benefit of strong, certificate-based authentication as well as single sign-on.

Directory Integration

An Oracle Advanced Security license provides the use of Oracle Internet Directory to store and manage users and their authorizations. It supports enterprise user management with Oracle Internet Directory, which is fully integrated with Oracle8i. Additionally, Oracle Advanced Security supports other leading LDAP-compliant directories.

For more information about Oracle Advanced Security refer to *Oracle Advanced Security Administrator's Guide.*

Authentication Methods Supported

The Oracle Advanced Security option supports the following authentication methods:

Secure Sockets Layer (SSL)

SSL is an industry-standard protocol for securing network connections. SSL provides for authentication, encryption, and data integrity. You can use the SSL feature of the Oracle Advanced Security option to secure communications between any client and any server. Specifically, you can use SSL to authenticate

- Any client or server to one or more Oracle servers

- An Oracle server to any client

You can use SSL features by themselves or in combination with other authentication methods supported by the Oracle Advanced Security option. For example, you can use SSL along with Kerberos, using the encryption provided by SSL in combination with the Kerberos authentication method. You can configure SSL to require server authentication only or both client and server authentication.

RADIUS

RADIUS (Remote Authentication Dial-In User Service), a client-server security protocol, is most widely known for enabling remote authentication and access. The Oracle Advanced Security option uses this emerging standard in a client-server network environment to enable use of any authentication method that supports the RADIUS protocol. You can use RADIUS with a variety of authentication methods, including token cards and smart cards.

Kerberos and CyberSafe

The Oracle Advanced Security option support for Kerberos and CyberSafe provides the benefits of single sign-on and centralized authentication in an Oracle environment. Kerberos is a trusted third-party authentication system that relies on shared secrets. It assumes that the third party is secure. It provides single sign-on capabilities, centralized password storage, database link authentication, and enhanced PC security. It does this through Kerberos authentication and through the CyberSafe TrustBroker, a Kerberos-based authentication server.

Smart Cards (RADIUS Compliant)

This authentication method uses a hardware device that looks much like a credit card. It has memory and a processor and is read by a smart card reader located at the client workstation. Smart cards offer the following benefits:

- **Increased security**   The smart card relies on two-factor authentication. The smart card can be locked, and only the user possessing the card and knowing the correct PIN can unlock it.

- **Improved performance**   Some sophisticated smart cards contain hardware-based encryption chips that can provide better throughput than software-based implementations. A smart card can store a user name.

- **Accessibility from any workstation**   The user logs in simply by inserting the smart card in a hardware device that reads the card and prompts the user for whatever authentication information the card requires—for example, a PIN. Once the user enters the correct authentication information, the smart card generates and enters whatever other authentication information is required.

Token Cards (SecurID and RADIUS Compliant)

Token cards can provide improved ease-of-use through several different mechanisms. Some token cards dynamically display one-time passwords that are synchronized with an authentication service. The server can verify the password provided by the token card at any given time by contacting the authentication service. Other token cards have a keypad and operate on a challenge-response basis. In this case, the server offers a challenge (a number) that the user types into a token card. The token card provides a response, namely another number cryptographically-derived from the challenge, which the user then offers to the server.

Token cards provide the following benefits:

- **Ease of use**   Users need only remember, at most, a personal identification number (PIN) instead of multiple passwords.

- **Ease of password management**   One token card rather than multiple passwords.

- **Enhanced password security**   To masquerade as a user, a malefactor would have to have the token card as well as the PIN required to operate it.

- **Enhanced accountability**   Token cards provide a stronger authentication mechanism.

You can use SecurID tokens through either SecurID or through RADIUS.

Bull ISM

ISM (Integrated System Management) is an offering of Bull Worldwide Information Systems that provides system administrators with a variety of management tools. This authentication method is available on the AIX (Advanced Interactive Executive) platform only. See your AIX-specific documentation for more information.

Biometric Authentication (Identix)

Identix Biometric Authentication is used on both the clients and Oracle servers to communicate biometric authentication data between the authentication server and the clients.

Summary

To implement security you must work through all layers of the organization. Some of the layers we reviewed in the chapter included network, operating system, database, application server, and Web server. It is necessary that you ensure that the security policy is balanced and is not skewed to a particular type of risk. Audits are important activities in security implementation because the best and most secure plan is worthless if it has not been actually practiced. Also the security requirements should be reexamined to make them relevant to dynamically changing situations. A carefully crafted and well balanced security policy that takes into consideration most of the important risk factors along with a solid and strict implementation and audit schedule normally goes a long way in building a highly secure Oracle Application environment. Needless to say, it is critical to involve highly technical resources for achieving this complex yet important objective.

CHAPTER
18

Using Oracle8i
Features

- Fine grained access control (FGAC)
- Partitioning
- Locally managed tablespace
- Resource manager
- Oracle Management Pack for Oracle Applications
- Buffer pools
- Temporary tables
- Function-based indexes
- Invoker's rights
- Cursor sharing initialization parameter

racle11i has several features and enhancements and is built to use a solid technology stack consisting of a Desktop tier, Application or Middle tier, and the Database tier. Each of the components within the stack contribute to making 11i a flexible, manageable, and easy-to-use Internet-based application suite. Release 11i leverages powerful features from each of the components of the technology stack and Oracle8i, in particular by making use of features to optimize application performance and reduce network round trips.

In this chapter, we will discuss some features of Oracle8i that are used by the Oracle11i Application Suite. Many of these features can also be enabled after migration to make improvements to an existing environment. Some of these features can be used in developing custom modules and enhancements to work along with the core modules. It is critical that you have a good understanding of some of these Oracle8i features.

Because the number of Oracle8i features included in the new release are many, this chapter will cover only the most important ones from the point of view of Oracle Financials. Other features have been discussed in other chapters as well.

Fine Grained Access Control

Fine grained access control (FGAC) provides a method for implementing security policy for a table or view. For example, using FGAC for an HR (human resources) application, we can implement a policy whereby

- Every employee can query and update *only* his employee information.

- A department supervisor can query and update all employees for that department.

Prior to Oracle8i, there was no elegant way of implementing such security policies, except for creating a view based on the current user and taking care of this in the application.

FGAC is an important component of the Oracle technology stack. By providing a security layer around the objects, it opens several areas within the scope of applications where it can be used, including reporting, business intelligence reports, and with third-party analysis tools. The following sections take a peek at FGAC and provide implementation tips, workarounds, and recommendations. The last part of the section includes an example script to implement FGAC that you can use as a starting point for building your own VPN (virtual private network).

Some of the benefits of FGAC include the following:

- *Handles data at table/view level* regardless of what front-end or application is used. This provides an additional server-side security layer. This functionality can be complemented with application-level security to make for more robust and flexible security.

■ *Hide sensitive data from the people who should not see it*, even through SQL*Plus, desktop tools, Internet-based tools, and so on.

■ *The same application can be customized to behave in different ways* based on the user requirement for security. In the Enterprise Resource Planning (ERP) suite applications context, FGAC can help implement a security layer without impacting application-level security that may have already been defined or without having to perform clumsy customizations.

■ *Useful for Internet applications* because profile and security are critical components for allowing public access to critical data. Using FGAC, we can restrict access of unwanted information and build a "virtual private database."

■ *You can use FGAC without a defined application context*. For example, we can define a security policy on an employee table where every employee can query only his or her own record. This does not require any user-defined context and requires only a predefined context, *SYS_CONTEXT('USERENV','SESSION_USER')*. However, if we define application context, we get much more flexibility when we are coding the predicate logic.

FGAC Terminology

Following is a list of FGAC terms and their definitions.

■ **Application Context** Any information about the user that we may want to use for deciding what his or her access should be. For example, we may want to check whether an employee is a manager (from one or more tables). We can define MANAGER as one application context and then decide what *predicate* (defined next) will be used if the context is MANAGER. By relating the application context with the predicate, we can implement any complex security policy. The predicate as well as application context is defined using PL/SQL, and we can take advantage of PL/SQL's features and functionality. Application context is implemented by creating a context.

■ **Predicate** A security policy for a table or view is implemented using a policy function. This function returns a string of characters that is transparently appended to the SQL statement at execution time. This string is called the *predicate*. Using various application contexts, we can return different values for the predicates. Predicates need to be less than 4000 bytes long. This restriction comes from the fact that a predicate is actually a VARCHAR2 field in PL/SQL.

■ **Extensible Security**   Refers to the added security that can be implemented with FGAC in addition to the usual control mechanisms (grants, object privileges, and roles) already available on the Oracle server.

■ **Dynamically modified queries**   FGAC is implemented for a table or view. A security policy is implemented using a function (PL/SQL block). Any user accessing the table or view invokes the server to return the access control condition known as the predicate. The query is dynamically rewritten using a WHERE clause transparent to the user. We can code the predicate based on the application context.

FGAC: The User Layer

Let's review FGAC implementation from a user's perspective. Every user connects to the database instance in the normal way. However, the SELECT, UPDATE, DELETE, and INSERT statements (on particular tables or views) return values based on the predicate that has been defined. The predicate is dynamically created and attached to the statement at the time of execution.

Figure 18-1 shows the user's view of a FGAC implementation.

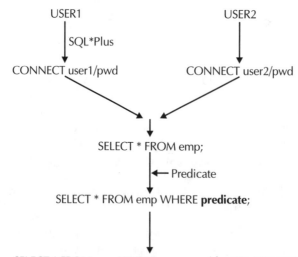

FIGURE 18-1.   *User perspective of FGAC*

Implementing FGAC

The following five steps implement FGAC along with the application context. The notes section following the table contains more information about each of the five steps.

	Step Description	Notes	Command Reference
1.	Create a CONTEXT.	Creates a namespace for the context and associates it to a package. *(see "Step 1 Notes")*	CREATE CONTEXT hr_category USING hr_ctx;
2.	Write the context package and grant execute permission to everyone who needs to use it.	A PL/SQL program that sets up values for different context attributes. These values can be used in Step 3 for deciding the predicate string. *(see "Step 2 Notes")*	CREATE PACKAGE CREATE PACKAGE BODY Usual Oracle package commands and syntax
3.	Write the policy function.	A PL/SQL program that returns predicates corresponding to the values of the context attributes. *(see "Step 3 Notes")*	CREATE PACKAGE CREATE PACKAGE BODY Usual Oracle package commands and syntax
4.	Associate policy function with the table or view.	Same policy can be used for multiple tables, OR multiple policy can be used for a given table (for SELECT, UPDATE, etc.) *(see "Step 4 Notes")*	Use the DBMS_RLS .ADD_POLICY package and supply actual parameters to it
5.	Define logon trigger to set context.	This trigger is executed when any user logs on the instance. *(see "Step 5 Notes")*	CREATE OR REPLACE TRIGGER <t.name> AFTER LOGON ON DATABASE BEGIN...END;

Step 1 Notes

Make sure that you carefully plan your context and the predicates to take care of all your access scenarios.

```
Create or replace context hr_category using fgac.hr_ctx;
```

Note that the package *hr_ctx* does not need to exist before you execute this statement.

Step 2 Notes

Here is an example of a context package. We define three contexts based on various scenarios:

- **mgr_role** could take the value DBA, MGR, or EMP based on whether the signed on user is a DBA, a manager, or a regular employee.

- If the employee is a manager, we also define a context to store his **GROUP_ID** and **COUNTRY_ID**.

- Finally, for a regular employee we are creating a context called **emp_name**.

Here is an example of a procedure from the context package:

```
PROCEDURE set_ctx IS
    countrec number;
    vuser_id   varchar2(8);
    vgroup_id varchar2(5);
    vcountry_id   varchar2(5);

BEGIN
-- Define your contexts that will be useful when deciding the predicates
-- We define mgr_role as 'DBA' (full access),
--'MGR' (access for his division) and 'EMP' (only
-- his own records.
  IF sys_context('userenv','session_user') =  'SYS' OR
    sys_context('userenv','session_user') =  'SYSTEM'
    THEN
      dbms_session.set_context('hr_category','mgr_role','DBA');
    ELSE
      -- Check if the current employee is a Manager
      countrec := 0;
      SELECT user_id,group_id, country_cd, nvl(COUNT(*),0) INTO
        vuser_id, vgroup_id,vcountry_id, countrec
        FROM fgac.hr_users WHERE
        user_id = sys_context('userenv','session_user') AND
        mgr_code = 'Y'
        GROUP BY user_id,group_id,country_id;
      IF countrec > 0 THEN
-- If MGR then we are defining two more contexts with
-- group_id and country_id of the MGR
-- This will be useful in coding the predicate where
-- we will restrict the records
--only to this sector and division
        DBMS_SESSION.SET_CONTEXT('hr_category','mgr_role','MGR');
        DBMS_SESSION.SET_CONTEXT ('hr_category','group_id',vgroup_id);
        DBMS_SESSION.SET_CONTEXT ('hr_category','country_id',vcountry_id);
      ELSE
-- for regular employee, we define emp_name to compare with his username
--
        DBMS_SESSION.SET_CONTEXT ('hr_category','emp_name',vuser_id);
      END IF;
END IF;
  EXCEPTION
    WHEN NO_DATA_FOUND THEN
        NULL;
END set_ctx;
END;
/
```

Step 3 Notes
The policy function returns a predicate string specific to a CONTEXT. In this example, we are setting three different predicates based on whether the currently logged in user is a DBA (logged in as SYS or SYSTEM), a MGR, or a regular user.

```
FUNCTION emp_sec_sel (obj_schema varchar2, obj_name varchar2)
RETURN varchar2 is d_predicate varchar2(2000);
BEGIN
-- First check if the employee is a manager
    IF SYS_CONTEXT('hr_category','mgr_role') = 'MGR'   THEN
       d_predicate :=
          'emp_v.group_id = sys_context('||''''||'hr_category'||
          ''''||','||''''||'group_id'||''''||') and '||
          'emp_v.country_id = sys_context('||''''||'hr_category'||
          ''''||','||''''||'country_id'||''''||')';
-- If DBA then he/she has access to all records
    ELSIF SYS_CONTEXT('hr_category','mgr_role') = 'DBA'   THEN
       d_predicate := '1=1';
    ELSE
-- If 'normal' employee, just give him access to his own records
       d_predicate :=
          'emp_v.emp_name = sys_context('||''''||
          'userenv'||''''||','||''''||'session_user'||''''||')';
    END IF;
    RETURN d_predicate;
END emp_sec_sel;
```

Step 4 Notes
Here is an example. This association is used to identify the package and function to be executed when a user enters a SQL Statement for a particular table:

```
BEGIN
   DBMS_RLS_ADD_POLICY(object_schema => 'PROD',
        object_name => 'emp_v',
        policy_name => 'emp_sel_policy',
        function_schema => 'hr_sec',
        policy_function => 'hr_security.emp_sec_sel',
        statement_types => 'select');
   DBMS_RLS.ADD_POLICY(object_schema => 'PROD',
        object_name => 'emp_v',
        policy_name => 'emp_upd_policy',
        function_schema => 'hr_sec',
        policy_function => 'hr_security.emp_sec_upd',
        statement_types => 'update');
END;
/
```

Step 5 Notes

Define logon trigger to set context. We create this trigger to make sure that everyone who connects to the database goes through the process of FGAC.

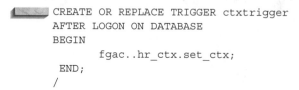

```
CREATE OR REPLACE TRIGGER ctxtrigger
AFTER LOGON ON DATABASE
BEGIN
        fgac..hr_ctx.set_ctx;
 END;
/
```

How Does FGAC Work?

Using the previous example, this section traces through the various steps to help you understand how the pieces fit together. Assume that the preceding five steps are successfully executed.

1. User SCOTT connects to the database instance with the command

   ```
   sqlplus scott/tiger@prod
   ```

   DEFINE LOGON TO DATABASE trigger (ctxtrigger) is executed and context is defined (Step 5). This executes the Context Package fgac.hr_ctx.set_ctx. (See Step 1 for CONTEXT definition; see Step 2 for the package source.)

Context Name	Context Attribute Name	Value
hr_category	mgr_role	MGR
hr_category	group_id	AA
hr_category	country_id	USA

2. After connecting, user SCOTT chooses to type a SQL statement:

   ```
   SELECT * FROM emp_view;
   ```

   Oracle checks to see whether a SELECT POLICY is defined for EMP_VIEW (defined in Step 4).

   Internally a query like the following is executed:

   ```
   SELECT POLICY_NAME,PACKAGE,FUNCTION from DBA_POLICIES
   WHERE OBJECT_NAME='EMP_VIEW' and SEL='YES';
   ```

   In this case, PACKAGE=hr_security and FUNCTION=emp_sec_sel, so that function is executed (see Step 3 for the package/function source).

   If mgr_role for SCOTT is MGR, the predicate that is returned is emp_view.sector_id = 'AA' and emp_view.div_cd = 'USA'. This predicate gets automatically attached to the SELECT statement that SCOTT entered, and the resulting statement looks like this:

```
SELECT * FROM EMP_VIEW
WHERE emp_view.sector_id = 'AA' and emp_view.div_cd = 'USA';
```

Data Dictionary Views, Stored Package, and Other References
The following sections contain references about data dictionary views and stored packages that will help you identify and manipulate the various contexts that have been defined.

Context   For displaying all the contexts defined for an instance, use the command

```
SELECT * FROM DBA_OBJECTS  WHERE OBJECT_TYPE='CONTEXT';
```

To get a list of all the context with the schema and package information, use the command

```
SELECT * FROM DBA_CONTEXT;
```

To get a list of context for which you have access, use the command

```
SELECT * FROM ALL_CONTEXT;
```

Logon Trigger   For displaying all the logon set context triggers, use the command

```
SELECT * FROM DBA_TRIGGERS WHERE
TRIGGER_TYPE='AFTER EVENT' and
TRIGGERING_EVENT='LOGON';
```

Policies Associated to a User   For a list of all policies accessible to a given user, use the command

```
SELECT * FROM ALL_POLICIES;
```

(DBA_POLICIES and USER_POLICIES views can also be referenced.)

Policies Function and Context Package   Use the standard method of displaying stored program code, such as

```
SELECT text FROM DBA_SOURCE WHERE NAME=' ABC';
```

SYS_CONTEXT   Returns the name of the current user. Several other attributes can be used.

```
SELECT SYS_CONTEXT('userenv','session_user') FROM DUAL;
```

Setup Errors, Fixes, and Other Issues

This section contains information that can help you through your installation and use of contexts.

- If you get a compilation error when coding the AFTER LOGON ON DATABASE, you will keep getting errors when trying to log in with any schema. To fix this problem, you need to go to the Server Manager or connect to SQL*Plus using the internal account and then either drop or disable the trigger.

- When writing the Policy function, you need to write the entire predicate without syntax errors. The Policy function compiles fine in spite of the syntax error in the predicate (since at that stage predicate is only a string of characters and is not executed yet). However, when a user tries to sign on, he or she gets this error:

      ORA-28113 Policy predicate has error

  This essentially points to a syntax error in the predicate. To find out what it is, you can either inspect your PREDICATE string manually (could be tricky) or trace your program using ALTER SESSION SET SQL_TRACE=TRUE. Then you get that error again. The trace file will have the exact error, which you can easily fix.

- Make sure that you have granted appropriate privileges to the objects. Sometimes basic object privilege issue (like EXECUTE on the context package) may be mistaken as a FGAC issue. Make sure you grant execute privilege on the context package to all the users or to PUBLIC. Note that the DBAs can still have access to all information. We can implement this by creating a context for SYS and SYSTEM user name. Also make sure that the user has appropriate (SELECT, UPDATE, DELETE, INSERT) privilege on the table or view for which you have implemented FGAC.

Recommendations

This section contains recommendations for implementing FGAC and application context for Internet-based applications.

- FGAC is a good method of implementing security policies in applications like Finance, HR, and Manufacturing without introducing too many complexities.

- Performance is not likely to be an issue with large volumes of data because the PREDICATE part of the query is replaced before the query is optimized. Because the policy function as well as context package are PL/SQL programs, we can make sure that these routines are properly tuned and use appropriate indexes so that performance is sustained for any table size.

- FGAC can complement Oracle-based purchased applications since FGAC can be implemented without any customization. We can also implement different policies for different business units. In case of application version upgrade, the FGAC needs to be re-examined and appropriate corrections made. It is important to note that FGAC assumes that every user that accesses the application has a schema (user name) defined in the instance.

  Some of the purchased applications use a single login to sign on to the database, and the users are managed by the application. In such cases, FGAC can be implemented in a more elaborate method. For example, we can use the OSUSER field in the v$session view to identify the current user (equivalent to SYS_CONTEXT('userenv','session_user') and compare it with the user name stored in the application. Various contexts can be set up based on this setup.

- FGAC can be used in a data warehouse as well. For example, consider a central data warehouse that stores sales information for multiple products by multiple brands. In this case, we may want to provide access only to a particular brand of products to certain users or we may want to add another brand at a later date with a different security policy. FGAC may be useful in this type of situation. In addition, the end user queries will be easier because all the security policies are built into the package. If FGAC is implemented, setting up Discoverer (or other query tools) will be much easier.

- Application context for a user is defined when he or she connects to the database. Sometimes the users are logged into their schema for a long time. If any change is implemented to the tables that changes their application context (such as adding a new employee or changing department number for an employee), that change is visible only when the user signs off and signs back in again. To prevent this, make sure that if you are making any changes to the security tables, inform the affected users about the change and tell them to sign off and re-enter the application.

Partitioning

The partitioning option first made its presence in Oracle8 and has been enhanced in Oracle8i. The partitioning allows a table and/or index to be placed on two or more partitions. In the earlier Oracle versions, we used partition views that were created using UNION ALL of several similar tables. Indexes and constraints were created for each table and partition elimination was enforced at table level. With Oracle 8.1.7, partition views still work but are no longer supported. Partitioning of tables and indexes are a solid option for moving away from partition views. In case of table partition, rows are assigned to a particular partition based on a range of values, using a hash algorithm or both.

This section of the chapter is devoted to discussion on using partitions as part of the Oracle Application Suite rollout for both core and custom modules. A table can be partitioned for various reasons, including the following:

- Partitioning can break a table into multiple segments, which means we can use parallel processing for operations like loading, inserts, updates, and queries. This could result in significant performance improvement. Also, full-table scans can be done in parallel in partitioned tables.

- Partitioning provides a way of easy manipulation of large tables. For example, old partitioned data can either be truncated or exported and then dropped. Since each partition is like a separate table, DBAs and administrators have better control.

- Partition pruning is a process by which the cost-based optimizer (CBO) is able to eliminate the partitions not required by the where clause of a query. This results in savings since all parts of a table do not have to be scanned to get a final answer.

To use partitions, the following must occur:

1. Install the partitioning option. This option can be chosen when installing the software from the Oracle distribution CD. When installing Oracle software, choose the option that will install Oracle with the partitioning option. For more information, refer to the relevant Oracle Server Installation Guide for your appropriate Oracle version and your operating system.

2. Set the initialization parameter to **COMPATIBLE = 8.1.6**. This can be done by editing the initORACLE_SID.ora file to modify the COMPATIBLE parameter and shutting down and restarting the Oracle instance.

Selecting, Inserting, Updating, and Deleting from a Partition: Examples

SQL has been enhanced to SELECT, INSERT, UPDATE, and DELETE from a partition. For example, the following SQL statement illustrates an example of querying total order quantity for March, 2000, by selecting from a single partition MAR00 of table ORDER_HISTORY:

```
SELECT PART_NO,VENDOR_NO,
       SUM(ORDER_QUANTITY)
       FROM ORDER_HISTORY PARTITION (mar00);
```

In this example, *mar00* is the actual partition name for the partitioned table called ORDER_HISTORY. The query could have also been written like this:

```
SELECT PART_NO,VENDOR_NO,
        SUM(ORDER_QUANTITY)
        FROM ORDER_HISTORY;
```

This statement will work as well and return the same number of rows. The Optimizer will do the partition elimination automatically.

The following example can be used for deleting from a partition:

```
DELETE FROM ORDER_HISTORY PARTITION (mar99)
        WHERE VENDOR_NO < '12345';
```

A partition can be moved from one tablespace to another using this command:

```
ALTER TABLE ORDER_HISTORY MOVE
        PARTITION mar99 TABLESPACE ts_mar99_new;
```

A partition can be split into two partitions using the SPLIT PARTITION command:

```
ALTER TABLE ORDER_HISTORY SPLIT
        PARTITION mar00
            AT ('3/15/2000') INTO
                ( PARTITION mar00_1 TABLESPACE ts_mar00,
                    PARTITION mar00_2 TABLESPACE ts_mar00
                );
```

Table partitions can be exported and imported specifically by name as well. Partitions can be dropped, added, and truncated just like tables. Here are some more examples:

```
ALTER TABLE ORDER_HISTORY TRUNCATE
        PARTITION mar99;
ALTER TABLE ORDER_HISTORY DROP
        PARTITION mar99;
ALTER TABLE ORDER_HISTORY ADD
        PARTITION apr00 TABLESPACE ts_apr00;
```

Two partitions can be merged into one using the following command:

```
ALTER TABLE ORDER_HISTORY MERGE
        PARTITIONS mar99, apr99 INTO
        PARTITION mar_apr99;
```

Rows between a partition and a table can be swapped using the EXCHANGE PARTITION command. Here is an example:

```
ALTER TABLE ORDER_HISTORY EXCHANGE
            PARTITION mar00 WITH TABLE
            ORDERS_FOR_MAR_2000;
```

After execution of this command, the rows in partition *mar00* of the ORDER_ HISTORY table are swapped with the rows in the ORDERS_FOR_MAR_2000 table.

Range Partitioning

Range partitioning is the basic form of partitioning that has been available since Oracle8. In a range partition, one or more partition columns are specified as the partition *key* (a column or group of columns that determine the partition a row belongs to), and a range of values for those columns are specified for each partition.

A table is initially created with various partitions. Each partition has a maximum key value that a row can have. Each partition stores records which have key values less than the stated maximum key value. The last partition for a table can be created optionally with a maximum key value of MAXVALUE indicating it can accommodate all rows that cannot be put in any other partition.

Here is an example of range partitioning:

```
CREATE TABLE ORDER_HISTORY
     (part_no     NUMBER(5),
      vendor_no  NUMBER(5),
      order_quantity     NUMBER(10,2),
      order_date     DATE)
    PARTITION BY RANGE (order_date)
  (PARTITION mar01 VALUES LESS THAN ('04/01/2001') TABLESPACE ts_mar01,
   PARTITION apr01 VALUES LESS THAN ('05/01/2001') TABLESPACE ts_apr01,
   PARTITION may01 VALUES LESS THAN ('06/01/2001') TABLESPACE ts_may01,
   ...
   PARTITION mar02 VALUES LESS THAN (MAXVALUE) TABLESPACE ts_mar02
     );
```

All values that evaluate below the first range specified are assigned to the first partition. The last partition has a key value called MAXVALUE. The last partition is the catch-all partition.

Hash Partitioning

Hash partitioning was new with Oracle 8.1.5. Hash partitioning is useful in cases where ranges cannot be specified. Oracle assigns a hash function to the value of the partition key that results in a partition. Unlike range partitioning, you do not know the partition where your record resides. We rely on Oracle to manage our partitioning scheme using a representative hash algorithm. Following is an example of hash partitioning:

```
CREATE TABLE ORDER_HISTORY
     (part_no     NUMBER(5),
      vendor_no  NUMBER(5),
```

```
     order_quantity    NUMBER(10,2),
     order_date    DATE)
  PARTITION BY HASH (order_date)
 (PARTITION mar01 TABLESPACE ts_mar01,
 PARTITION apr01 TABLESPACE ts_apr01,
 PARTITION may01 TABLESPACE ts_may01,
   ...
 PARTITION mar02 TABLESPACE ts_mar02
   );
```

Partition split, drop, merge syntax does not apply to hash partitioning because we do not know the actual contents of a particular partition (unlike range partitioning).

The ALTER TABLE ORDER_HISTORY COALESCE PARTITION command can be used for hash partitioning. Starting with Oracle 8.1.5, rows can be moved from one partition to another using the following command:

```
ALTER TABLE ENABLE ROW MOVEMENT;
```

Composite Partitioning

A *composite* partition is a mix of both range and hash partitioning techniques. In case of composite partitioning, you first apply range partitioning and then hash partitioning for each of the ranges to create subpartitions. This approach is useful for large tables with uneven partitions. Here is an example of a composite partition:

```
CREATE TABLE ORDER_HISTORY
     (part_no    NUMBER(5),
      vendor_no  NUMBER(5),
      order_quantity    NUMBER(10,2),
      order_date    DATE)
PARTITION BY RANGE (order_date)
    SUBPARTITION BY HASH (vendor_no) SUBPARTITIONS 3
    STORE IN (TS_MAR01, TS_APR01, TS_MAY01)
  (PARTITION mar01 VALUES LESS THAN ('04/01/2001'),
   PARTITION apr01 VALUES LESS THAN ('05/01/2001'),
   PARTITION may01 VALUES LESS THAN ('06/01/2001'),
   PARTITION mar02 VALUES LESS THAN (MAXVALUE)
     );
```

In this example, a total of 12 partitions will be created: 4 range partitions, each divided into 3 subpartitions.

Partition-Wise Joins

A partition-wise join is a join when two or more tables are equi-partitioned and joined using partitioned columns. Equi-partitioned tables have the same partition columns, number of partitions, and range of values.

Index Partitioning

Like tables, indexes can be partitioned. Partitioned tables may or may not include partitioned indexes.

Prefixed vs. Nonprefixed

In a *prefixed* partitioned index, the leftmost columns of the index are the same columns that appear in the partition columns of the table. The CBO takes advantage of this when identifying the execution plan for the query. A *nonprefixed* partitioned index is a partitioned index in which the leftmost columns of the index do not correspond to the table partition columns.

Global vs. Local Indexes

A *global* index is built on the entire table. A *local* index is built for every partition. A global index must be rebuilt whenever a new partition is added or a partition is truncated or dropped, and this can be more time consuming than dropping, truncating, and re-creating a local index.

Here is an example of a local index corresponding to a partitioned table named PO. Notice that for every partitioned table, a corresponding local index is created.

```
CREATE INDEX po_index ON  PO (po_no, po_dt)
LOCAL
(PARTITION P_L_PO_INDEX_1 TABLESPACE POC1,
 PARTITION P_L_PO_INDEX_2 TABLESPACE POC2);
```

Global Prefixed Index   A *global prefixed* partitioned index is a global partitioned index whose leftmost columns match the partition columns of the table. The CBO takes advantage of partition pruning when accessing the table. Here is an example of a global prefixed index (partitioned on PO_DT):

```
CREATE INDEX po_index ON  PO (po_no, po_dt)
GLOBAL PARTITION BY RANGE(PO_NO)
(PARTITION P_L_PO_INDEX_1 VALUES LESS THAN (10000),
 PARTITION P_L_PO_INDEX_2 VALUES LESS THAN (MAXVALUE));
```

Local Prefixed Index   A *local prefixed* index is built at the partition level and its leftmost columns are included in the table partition columns. Here is an example of a local prefixed index (partitioned on PO_DT):

```
CREATE INDEX po_index ON  PO (po_dt, po_no)
LOCAL
(PARTITION P_L_PO_INDEX_1 TABLESPACE POC1,
 PARTITION P_L_PO_INDEX_2 TABLESPACE POC2);
```

Local Nonprefixed   A *local nonprefixed* index is built at the partition level, and its leftmost columns are not included in the table partition columns. This can be useful in cases when one portion of the where clause can drive partition pruning and a second portion of the where clause can use the nonprefixed index. Here is an example of a local nonprefixed index:

```
CREATE INDEX po_index ON  PO (po_no)
LOCAL
(PARTITION P_L_PO_INDEX_1 TABLESPACE POC1,
 PARTITION P_L_PO_INDEX_2 TABLESPACE POC2);
```

Data Dictionary Views for Partitioning

Table 18-1 shows the most commonly used data dictionary views related to partitioning. Note that other similar view names, such as USER_TAB_PARTITIONS and ALL_IND_PARTITIONS, are also available and can be used.

Locally Managed Tablespaces

Tablespaces are made up of multiple datafiles. Space within a datafile is allocated from one or more Oracle blocks called *extents*. Prior to Oracle8i, only one method was available for managing extents: the dictionary-managed method, which manages extents at the data-dictionary level. Oracle8i provides another way of managing extents within a tablespace called the locally managed method, which manages extents locally using bitmaps to keep track of free or used status of the blocks in the datafile.

View Name	Purpose
DBA_PART_TABLES	Information about partitioned tables
DBA_IND_SUBPARTITIONS	Information on index subpartitions
DBA_PART_COL_STATISTICS	Column statistics for partitioned tables
DBA_ PART_KEY_COLUMNS	Information about partitioned key columns
DBA_ TAB_PARTITIONS	Information about table partitions
DBA_SUBPART_HISTOGRAMS	Histogram information for subpartitions
DBA_SUBPART_COL_STATISTICS	Column statistics for subpartitions

TABLE 18-1.   *Commonly Used Data Dictionary Views*

Each of the bits in the bitmap for a locally managed tablespace corresponds to a block or group of blocks. When an extent is allocated or deallocated, Oracle changes the bitmap values to reflect the new status of the blocks. These changes do not generate rollback information because they do not update the data dictionary with as much information as dictionary managed tablespace.

Locally Managed tablespaces have several solid advantages over dictionary managed tablespaces:

- If extents are locally managed, recursive space management operations can be avoided.

- Locally managed tablespaces automatically track adjacent free space, eliminating the need to coalesce free extents.

- Locally managed tablespaces ensure that the data dictionary is freed up to a large degree.

- Locally managed tablespaces manage space more efficiently.

- By using the concept of standard size extents along with locally managed tablespaces, you can avoid defragmenting your instance and increase reliability and availability.

- In case of a dictionary managed tablespace, ST (Space transaction enqueues) lock is used to control space management operations to avoid deadlocks. Since only a single ST latch exists, only one space management can occur at a given time. This performance bottleneck can be alleviated using locally managed tablespaces.

A locally managed temporary tablespace is similar to a regular tablespace, with the following exceptions:

- Tempfiles are set to NOLOGGING mode.

- Tempfiles cannot be made read-only.

- Tempfiles cannot be renamed. You must drop and re-create them to copy to a different location.

- The ALTER DATABASE BACKUP CONTROLFILE TO TRACE command does not generate information about tempfiles.

Examples

When creating a locally managed tablespace, you can specify the extent allocation in two ways. The extents can be automatically allocated using the AUTOALLOCATE feature or UNIFORM extents of a specific size can be allocated. In the AUTOALLOCATE method, users cannot specify extent size when creating their tables and indexes. In the UNIFORM method, however, users can specify the SIZE of their choices for creating extents.

Here are two examples of creating a locally managed tablespace using the two methods of extent management:

```
CREATE TABLESPACE RBS DATAFILE '/u01/oradata/11iprod/rbs01.dbf'
SIZE 200M EXTENT MANAGEMENT LOCAL AUTOALLOCATE;

CREATE TABLESPACE RBS DATAFILE '/u01/oradata/11iprod/rbs01.dbf'
SIZE 200M EXTENT MANAGEMENT LOCAL UNIFORM SIZE 1M;
```

An Oracle instance can have a combination of locally managed and dictionary managed tablespaces. However, if the SYSTEM tablespace is created as locally managed, all rollback segments must be created in a locally managed tablespace.

A temporary tablespace can be created as locally managed as well. CREATE TABLESPACE system privilege is required for creating locally managed tablespaces. Here is an example of creating a temporary locally managed tablespace:

```
CREATE TEMPORARY TABLESPACE temp
TEMPFILE '/u02/oradata/11iprod/temp01.dbf'
SIZE 200M EXTENT MANAGEMENT LOCAL UNIFORM SIZE 1M;
```

Here, the TEMPFILE clause causes the temporary tablespace to be recorded only in the control file. Since temporary segments will not be stored in the data dictionary, no redo operations need to be generated to protect against data dictionary transaction failure.

Sizing the Datafiles for a Locally Managed Tablespace

The sizing of datafiles for a locally managed tablespace may pose some challenges. You need to ensure that the tablespace has enough space for its internal bookkeeping in addition to other data requirements. Following are some of the things you need to provide for:

■ One database block for the recovery header

■ A space file header that provides information including whether or not the datafile can be resized, its maximum size, and the amount to increment by one each resize

■ Bitmap space representing the usage of blocks belonging to that datafile

A reasonable formula for arriving at the size for a locally managed tablespace could look like this:

Size = Datafile required + one database block for recovery header + x$ktfbhc.ktfbhchz for the space file header + bitmap space requirement

Data Dictionary Views for a Locally Managed Tablespace

The following data dictionary views can be used for managing a locally managed tablespace:

View Name	Notes
V$TEMPFILE	Information about all the tempfiles from the control file
V$TEMP_EXTENT_MAP	Information about chunks of space in the temporary tablespace
V$TEMP_SPACE_HEADER	Information about file level space management for tempfiles
V$TEMP_EXTENT_POOL	Summary of information about each file's extent map
V$SORT_USAGE	Information about sort usage

To see a list of all the locally managed tablespaces, execute the following command:

```
select tablespace_name from dba_tablespaces where
extent_management = 'LOCAL';
The extent_management for normal tablespaces is 'DICTIONARY'.
```

The DBMS_SPACE_ADMIN package is used to provide management functionality for locally managed tablespaces. This package is created using $ORACLE_HOME/ rdbms/admin/dbmsspace.sql. The package runs with SYS privileges, allowing any user who has the privilege to execute the package to be able to manipulate the locally managed tablespace bitmaps. The DBMS_SPACE_ADMIN package contains a number of useful procedures. The package can be used by the DBA for checking bitmap corruption and rebuilding the bitmaps.

Further Recommendations

■ *Implement locally managed tablespace in the Oracle application environment gradually.* The first candidates can be the rollback segment tablespace and the temp tablespace. These tablespaces can be easily re-created and rebuilt. You can then proceed to convert some of the other high-activity tablespaces to locally managed.

■ *Use the UNIFORM extent method of extent allocation.* It gives you the flexibility not only to specify the extent size based on the size of the table but also retains equal size extents in the tablespace.

■ *Use Statspack statistics or an equivalent tool to trend and understand the impact of converting from dictionary to locally managed.* Refer to Chapter 13 for details about how to install and collect performance statistics using Statspack. By performing a trend analysis, you will understand and prove the overall performance improvements because of locally managed tablespace implementation for the application.

■ *Consider implementing locally managed tablespaces when first migrating Oracle Applications to 11i.* The initial testing can be done on a smaller non production instance. Production implementation of converting a specific tablespace can be done after this effort is completed. It is always a good idea to test on development or a smaller environment first before deploying to production.

■ *Build an administrative procedure to check bitmap corruption periodically.* This is more for the purpose of proactive problem fixing than anything else. This can be done by executing the following procedure

  1. Get the block information using this SQL command:

     ```
     SELECT SEGMENT_NAME,RELATIVE_FNO,HEADER_BLOCK
     FROM DBA_SEGMENTS WHERE SEGMENT_NAME='RBS_01'AND
     TABLESPACE_NAME = 'RBS';
     ```

  2. Verify the segment using the following command:

     ```
     sql>EXECUTE DBMS_SPACE_ADMIN.SEGMENT_VERIFY('RBS',-
     vrelative_fno,vheader_block);
     ```

     This command generates a trace file that contains information about corruption, such as data block address changes, bitmap block ranges, and so on. If no trace is generated, no further action needs to be taken. If segment corruption is detected, further action needs to be taken.

3. You can verify that the bitmaps and extent maps for objects in a tablespace are synchronized using the following command:

```
sql>EXECUTE DBMS_SPACE_ADMIN.TABLESPACE_VERIFY('RBS');
```

Database Resource Manager

Oracle8i has a Database Resource Manager feature that lets you control and manage the amount of CPU time and resources and degree of parallelism that Oracle instances can acquire from the operating system. This feature is of major importance to Internet-based applications such as the Oracle Application Suite to ensure the following:

- CPU time is always available for normal users of the application.
- Any one user or a group of users do not hog all the CPU resources.
- Internet applications have adequate resources for running efficiently.

The Database Resource Manager feature can also help reporting and business intelligence types of applications by ensuring that resources are allocated for each query and that CPU time is distributed between batch jobs and queries.

This section of the chapter has details about setting up and using the Database Resource Manager.

Resource Manager Terminology

Following are a few terms that you need to understand before we go further.

Resources   CPU and degree of parallelism are the only two resources that can be controlled.

Resource Consumer Groups or Resource Groups   You should group all sessions or users having similar resource needs under resource groups. Each user can be assigned to multiple user groups but only one group can be active at a time. Further resource groups can be assigned dynamically by DBAs to a user or a session. The data dictionary view DBA_RSRC_CONSUMER_GROUPS contains all the resource consumer groups. Each user has a default consumer group called DEFAULT_CONSUMER_GROUP. Users can use PL/SQL package/procedures to switch from one consumer group to the other.

Resource Plan   A named plan shows how the resources will be allocated among the resource consuming groups or resource groups. You can query the view, V$DBA_RSRC_PLANS, to see all the resource plans.

You can define multiple plans (such as daytime and nighttime plan or a weekday and weekend plan), but only one plan is active for each instance. A resource plan can be activated from init.ora at startup time or it can be altered using a command:

```
ALTER SYSTEM SET RESOURCE_MANAGER_PLAN=AFTERHOUR_PLAN;
```

Resource groups are not related to resource plans. Resource plan directives (defined a bit later) bring the resource plan and resource consumer groups together.

Oracle provides a default resource plan called SYSTEM_PLAN, which includes three consumer groups: SYS_GROUP (CPU level 1—100%), OTHER_GROUPS (CPU level 2—100%) and LOW_GROUP (CPU level 3—100%). These consumer groups can be used to implement priority so that all users assigned to SYS_GROUP get top priority, and then users assigned to OTHER_GROUPS get priority, and so on. SYS and SYSTEM belong to SYS_GROUP but this can be changed. (If you want to implement this default plan, you need to execute Steps 6 and 7 in the section "The Seven Steps of Implementing Resource Management.")

Special Consumer Groups   There are two special groups to be noted: OTHER_GROUPS is assigned to all sessions that do not belong to a consumer group that is not part of the active plan schema, but those sessions belong to some other plan. DEFAULT_CONSUMER_GROUP is assigned to all sessions that do not belong to any group. These two groups should always be defined and CANNOT be modified or deleted. View DBA_RSRC_PLANS for details on resource plans and their attributes.

Resource Allocation Method   This method is policy to be used when allocating a particular resource. For checking the available CPU allocation method use the command

```
SELECT * FROM V$RSRC_PLAN_CPU_MTH;
```

EMPHASIS is the only method available currently. For checking allocation methods for limiting the degree of parallelism use the command

```
SELECT * FROM V$PARALLEL_DEGREE_LIMIT_MTH
```

PARALLEL_DEGREE_LIMIT_ABSOULUTE is the only method available currently.

In the EMPHASIS method of CPU resource allocation, Oracle provides for eight levels of CPU usage, 1 being the highest. The usage is specified as a percentage. Sessions in resource consumer groups with lower level non-zero percentages get the first opportunity to run. If a consumer group does not consume all its resources, the remaining CPU resources are passed on to the next lower level and not to the other consumer group at the same level. The sum of percentages at any given level is always less than or equal to 100. Unused CPU time gets recycled—the retry starts with level 1.

Resource Plan Directives   Using plan directives, you can assign a consumer group to a resource plan. This is where you specify actual values for consumption. For example, using a plan directive, you can specify that all OLTP users get 75 percent of the CPU time. Query V$DBA_RSRC_PLAN_DIRECTIVES. There is one resource plan directive for each entry in the plan.

Resource Plan, Consumer Groups, and Plan Directives are all created using two PL/SQL based packages provided by Oracle: DBMS_RESOURCE_MANAGER and DBMS_RESOURCE_MANAGER_PRIVS.

Pending Area   This is used to store new resource manager plans, consumer groups, and resource plan directives and changes before they are committed. The pending area helps to validate the plan before committing it to the database. It is created using the procedure CREATE_PENDING_AREA. During validation, if errors occur, they are pointed out as PL/SQL errors and need to be fixed to apply the changes to the database. SUBMIT_PENDING_AREA is used for committing the changes. If the commit is successful, the pending area is automatically cleared. If an error is returned a CLEAR_PENDING_AREA is required before making further changes.

Relationship Between Resource Plan, Resource Consumer Group, and Resource Plan Directive   Plan Directive refers to the plan name and consumer group names and links the two. In addition, it also defines CPU levels and degree of parallelism. See Figure 18-2.

How Resource Manager Works

Figure 18-3 shows the components that need to be defined for implementing a successful resource plan in an Oracle environment.

The Seven Steps of Implementing Resource Management

This section discusses a step-by-step approach to implementing resource management. For the purpose of this discussion, the following simple example is used:

Resource Plan–WEEKDAY_PLAN

Per this resource plan, users could be assigned to either the OLTP consumer group or DSS consumer group. Accordingly, this plan will limit CPU usage based on the following chart.

Resource Consumer Group	Allocation Method Parameters
OLTP	CPU–75%
DSS	CPU–25%

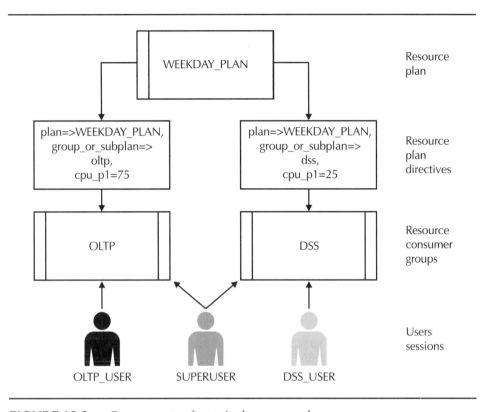

FIGURE 18-2. *Components of a typical resource plan*

Note that we can define many resource plans, but at any one time only one plan is effective (this can be controlled by modifying the init.ora parameter

```
RESOURCE_MANAGER_PLAN= xxx
```

or by using

```
ALTER SYSTEM SET RESOURCE_MANAGER_PLAN=xxx;
```

Step 1: Create a Pending Area
As mentioned previously, changes to the resource manager objects can only occur using a "scatch" area called the pending area. We make the changes in the pending area, validate them, submit them before the changes take effect, and clear the pending area.

```
DBMS_RESOURCE_MANAGER.CREATE_PENDING_AREA;
```

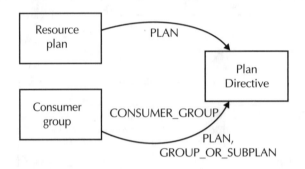

FIGURE 18-3. *Relationship between resource plan, consumer group, and Plan Directive*

(Similarly, we can use procedures like CLEAR_PENDING_AREA and DELETE_PENDING_AREA.)

Step 2: Create a Resource Plan

When a resource plan is defined, it is stored in the pending area. The administrator can specify the name and a comment while defining a plan. Similarly, procedures are available to delete or modify a plan. A SYSTEM_PLAN is created by default when the database is created.

```
DBMS_RESOURCE_MANAGER.CREATE_PLAN
(plan => 'WEEKDAY_PLAN', comment => 'Plan for Normal WeekDay Activities');
```

(Similarly, we can use procedures like UPDATE_PLAN, DELETE_PLAN, and DELETE_PLAN_CASCADE.)

Step 3: Create Resource Consumer Groups

```
DBMS_RESOURCE_MANAGER.CREATE_CONSUMER_GROUP('OLTP',
'Resource Consumer Group for OLTP Users');
DBMS_RESOURCE_MANAGER.CREATE_CONSUMER_GROUP('DSS',
'Resource Consumer Group for DSS Users');
```

(Similarly, we can use procedures like UPDATE_CONSUMER_GROUP and DELETE_CONSUMER_GROUP.)

Step 4: Create Resource Plan Directive

```
DBMS_RESOURCE_MANAGER.CREATE_PLAN_DIRECTIVE(
plan => 'WEEKDAY_PLAN',
group_or_subplan => 'OLTP',
comment => 'Plan Directive for OLTP Users',
cpu_p1 => 75);
DBMS_RESOURCE_MANAGER.CREATE_PLAN_DIRECTIVE(
plan => 'WEEKDAY_PLAN',
group_or_subplan => 'DSS',
comment => 'Plan Directive for DSS Users',
cpu_p1 => 25);
```

To avoid getting errors, define a group called OTHER_GROUPS when you create the plan directive. This is to take care of users who are not assigned to any of the predefined groups.

```
DBMS_RESOURCE_MANAGER.CREATE_PLAN_DIRECTIVE(
plan => 'WEEKDAY_PLAN',
group_or_subplan => 'OTHER_GROUPS',
comment => 'Plan Directive for other unassigned users');
```

Step 5: Validate and Submit the Pending Area

```
DBMS_RESOURCE_MANAGER.VALIDATE_PENDING_AREA;
DBMS_RESOURCE_MANAGER.SUBMIT_PENDING_AREA;
```

Validation procedure will check consistency of the resource plan and make sure that the rules are followed.

Step 6: Assign Users to Various Consumer Groups

```
DBMS_RESOURCE_MANAGER_PRIVS.GRANT_SWTICH_CONSUMER_GROUP
('DSS_USER','DSS',TRUE);
DBMS_RESOURCE_MANAGER_PRIVS.GRANT_SWITCH_CONSUMER_GROUP
('OLTP_USER','OLTP',TRUE);
DBMS_RESOURCE_MANAGER.SET_INITIAL_CONSUMER_GROUP('DSS_USER','DSS');
DBMS_RESOURCE_MANAGER.SET_INITIAL_CONSUMER_GROUP('OLTP_USER',OLTP');
```

Step 7: Activate the Plan

```
ALTER SYSTEM SET RESOURCE_MANAGER_PLAN = 'WEEKDAY_PLAN';
```

Figure 18-4 shows an example of a Financials Resource Plan containing subplans.

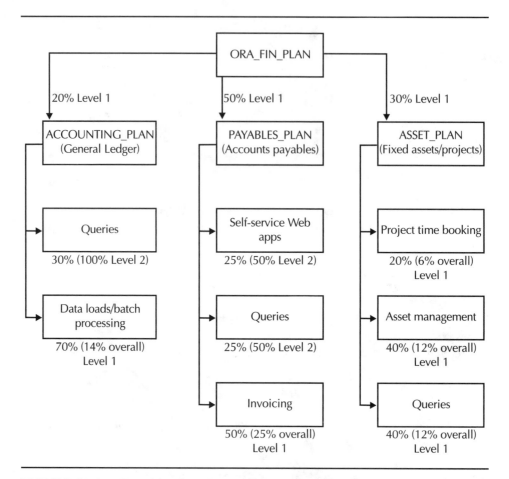

FIGURE 18-4. *Example of a resource plan with subplans*

Here is some additional information to keep in mind:

■ ACCOUNTING_PLAN, PAYABLES_PLAN, and ASSET_PLAN are subplans for the plan ORA_FIN_PLAN.

■ By defining subplans, you can implement multiple plans at the same time and have better control.

■ Remember that for each CPU level (there are eight levels), percentages cannot exceed 100.

Data Dictionary Views, Stored Packages, and Other References

An init.ora parameter called RESOURCE_MANAGER_PLAN can be set to the name of the resource plan to be used. If this parameter is used, Oracle loads the top plan, consumer group, and plan directives.

The following static data dictionary views can be used for getting information about Database Resource Manager:

- To get information about various plans for the given instance

  ```
  SELECT * FROM DBA_RSRC_PLANS;
  ```

  Note the STATUS column. STATUS has to be ACTIVE for your users to use a plan.

- To get information on various consumer groups

  ```
  SELECT * FROM DBA_RSRC_CONSUMER_GROUPS
  FROM DBA_RSRC_PLAN_DIRECTIVES WHERE plan='AFTERHOURS_PLAN';
  ```

- To get information about which user is assigned to which consumer group use the command

  ```
  SELECT * FROM DBA_RSRC_CONSUMER_GROUP_PRIVS;
  ```

  This view also tells us whether the consumer group is the default for that user and whether the user has grant options.

- To get a list of plan directives for a given plan use

  ```
  SELECT * FROM DBA_RSRC_PLAN_DIRECTIVES;
  ```

- The following dynamic data dictionary views are also available:

  V$RSRC_CONSUMER_GROUP, V$RSRC_PLAN

- DBAs can change a consumer group for a given session or all sessions for a given user using

  ```
  DBMS_RESOURCE_MANAGER. -
  SWITCH_CURRENT_CONSUMER_GROUP_FOR_SESS -
  (SID, Serial#, 'OLTP_GRP');
  ```

  or

  ```
  DBMS_RESOURCE_MANAGER.SWITCH_CURRENT_CONSUMER_GROUP_FOR_USER(SID, Serial#,
   'OLTP_GRP');
  ```

  Note that these changes take affect immediately.

- To view all sessions corresponding to a specific consumer group

  ```
  SELECT * FROM V$SESSION WHERE RESOURCE_CONSUMER_GROUP='DSS_GRP';
  ```

Deleting a Resource Plan

In this section, two methods are discussed for deleting a resource plan.

Here's the first method:

```
BEGIN
    DBMS_RESOURCE_MANAGER.CREATE_PENDING_AREA;
    DBMS_RESOURCE_MANAGER.DELETE_PLAN_CASCADE('ORA_FIN_PLAN');
    DBMS_RESOURCE_MANAGER.VALIDATE_PENDING_AREA;
    DBMS_RESOURCE_MANAGER.SUBMIT_PENDING_AREA;
END;
/
```

Note that by using DELETE_PLAN_CASCADE, we can delete the plan definition, plan directive relating to that plan, and corresponding consumer groups.

Here is the second method:

```
BEGIN
    DBMS_RESOURCE_MANAGER.CREATE_PENDING_AREA;
    DBMS_RESOURCE_MANAGER.DELETE_PLAN_DIRECTIVE(
        'ORA_FIN_PLAN','OLTP_GRP');
    DBMS_RESOURCE_MANAGER.DELETE_PLAN_DIRECTIVE(
        'ORA_FIN_PLAN','DSS_GRP');
    DBMS_RESOURCE_MANAGER.DELETE_PLAN_DIRECTIVE(
        'ORA_FIN_PLAN','OTHER_GROUPS');
    DBMS_RESOURCE_MANAGER.DELETE_CONSUMER_GROUP('OLTP_GRP');
    DBMS_RESOURCE_MANAGER.DELETE_CONSUMER_GROUP('DSS_GRP');
    DBMS_RESOURCE_MANAGER.DELETE_PLAN('ORA_FIN_PLAN');
    DBMS_RESOURCE_MANAGER.VALIDATE_PENDING_AREA;
    DBMS_RESOURCE_MANAGER.SUBMIT_PENDING_AREA;
END;
/
```

Assigning Users to a SYSTEM_PLAN

A default resource plan is available for use with three consumer groups. The resource plan is called SYSTEM_PLAN and the consumer groups are SYS_GROUP, OTHER_GROUPS, and LOW_GROUP. This script could be used for assigning the consumer plans to various users.

```
BEGIN
    DBMS_RESOURCE_MANAGER_PRIVS.GRANT_SWITCH_CONSUMER_GROUP
        ('DSS_USER', 'OTHER_GROUPS', true);
    DBMS_RESOURCE_MANAGER_PRIVS.GRANT_SWITCH_CONSUMER_GROUP
        ('OLTP_USER', 'LOW_GROUP', true);
END;
/
```

```
BEGIN
  DBMS_RESOURCE_MANAGER.SET_INITIAL_CONSUMER_GROUP
        ('DSS_USER','OTHER_GROUPS');
  DBMS_RESOURCE_MANAGER.SET_INITIAL_CONSUMER_GROUP
        ('OLTP_USER','LOW_GROUP');
    END;
/
```

Use the following command to find users not assigned to any resource plan:

```
SELECT DISTINCT username FROM dba_users
MINUS
SELECT DISTINCT grantee FROM dba_rsrc_consumer_group_privs;
```

Setup Issues, Workarounds, and Other Notes

Users can be given permission to switch consumer groups. This permission can also be given to a role and all users who are granted that role and have it enabled can switch consumer groups. Here's an example:

```
DBMS_RESOURCE_MANAGER_PRIVS.GRANT_SWITCH_CONSUMER_GROUP(
'OLTP_USER','OLTP_GROUP',TRUE);
```

In this case, TRUE is the grant option that lets OLTP_USER grant access.

Resource Management can either be done using a SYSTEM account or any other schema. Oracle provides for a single system privilege called ADMINSTER_RESOURCE_MANAGER. For example,

```
DBMS_RESOURCE_MANAGER_PRIVS.GRANT_SYSTEM_PRIVILEGE('SIYER','ADMINISTER_
RESOURCE_MANAGER',FALSE);
```

This command grants SIYER privileges to use resource manager packages. However, this is not really required if the schema already has DBA privileges. This feature could be useful in situations where the resource management function and DBA functions are managed separately.

Before making changes or deleting a consumer group, make sure that no plan directives are using it. In this case, Oracle errors with ORA-29383—all leaves of the top plan must be consumer groups. You can check the plan directives by querying the DBA_RSRC_PLAN_DIRECTIVES view.

Some consumer groups should not be dropped. For example, the following command will result in an Oracle error:

```
DBMS_RESOURCE_MANAGER.DELETE_CONSUMER_GROUP('OTHER_GROUPS')
```

OTHER_GROUPS need to be included as part of the top plan. This takes care of all users and sessions that are not assigned to any consumer group.

A user cannot be in more than 32 consumer groups.

Plan and consumer group names should be different. If we assign both the plan name and consumer group name to the same value then we get an "ORA-29357 object *xxx* already exists" error.

The default plan is called SYSTEM_PLAN. This plan is always active.

Restrictions

The target customers for using Database Resource Manager will be Internet-based Oracle applications. We can use the Resource Manager features to create a separate consumer group for Internet users and restrict the amount of resources for that group. Internet applications are network- and CPU-intensive and the nature of transactions depends on the number of concurrent users who are accessing the application and the amount of time that they are online.

To deactivate a resource plan, comment out the RESOURCE_MANAGER_PLAN init.ora and restart the instance. This cannot be done using the ALTER SYSTEM command.

The Resource Manager feature can be beneficial in an Internet-based environment, especially when an instance is shared between different types of users—such as reporting users, Web users, and batch program users.

Oracle Management Pack for Oracle Applications

Oracle Enterprise Manager (OEM) provides a three-tiered architecture to support and proactively manage Oracle databases. OEM provides a Management Pack for Oracle applications to manage the Oracle Application Suite tasks typically done by a DBA.

The three tiers can be installed on a separate server or on one server, depending on the size, nature of the application, and hardware involved. This three-tier architecture provides reliability, scalability, and maintainability:

- **Console and Management Applications**   This tier provides a graphical user interface such as consoles and administrative tools.

- **Oracle Management Server**   The main purpose is to process system management tasks. This tier maintains Oracle Management Server and a repository of application data, nodes, and other management information.

- **Managed Nodes**   This tier includes all the servers that are to be monitored/administered through the network. The services are implemented through Oracle Intelligent Agent and data collection service.

A single repository is usually sufficient for multiple Oracle Management Servers in the middle tier.

NOTE
The Management Pack needs to be separately licensed. Make sure you are licensed to use it before implementing.

Managing a complex environment like the Oracle Application Suite 11i presents a day-to-day challenge for administrators and DBAs. Managing the instances, Concurrent Managers, and performance tuning are more involved now than with earlier versions of both Oracle Servers and Oracle Applications.

The Management Pack for Oracle Applications helps with this challenge. It helps you to monitor your systems from a single console and also monitor and administer Oracle instances and Concurrent Managers. Further, the Management Pack also provides for capacity planning and performance tuning spanning across all the technology stack components.

Following are the features of the Oracle Management Pack:

- **Graphical representation of all services to be monitored.**

- **Centralized Monitoring**   Data collected using Intelligent Agents.

- **Oracle Enterprise Manager Console**   Notifies you if any servers are down as well as discovers Concurrent Manager. Enables you to manage the environment centrally.

- **Oracle Performance Manager**   This module provides database and application monitoring charts for Concurrent Manager and Oracle forms sessions. This can be used for tuning various processes.

- **Oracle Capacity Planner**   Provides trend analysis and resource consumption patterns for a period based on actual usage statistics.

- **Concurrent Processing Tuning Assistant**   This utility helps you to analyze your historical concurrent processing requests.

Installing Management Pack

When you install the Management Pack for Oracle Applications 2.2, the following software is installed:

- Oracle Performance Manager 2.2.0.0.0
- Oracle Capacity Planner 2.2.0.0.0

- Concurrent Processing Tuning Assistant 2.2.0.0.0

- Oracle Applications Manager

- Oracle Applications Advanced Event Tests 2.2.0.0.0

- Oracle Management Pack for Oracle Applications Documentation 2.2.0.0.0

- Agent Extensions for Oracle Applications (Solaris 2.5.1 only) 2.2.0.0.0

Oracle Performance Manager

The Management Pack for Oracle Applications uses Oracle Performance Manager, a tool also available as part of the Oracle Diagnostics Pack. Oracle Performance Manager has been extended to monitor the performance statistics of Concurrent Managers. Oracle Performance Manager displays performance data in real-time graphical views that can be automatically refreshed at user-defined intervals. Multiple charts and tables can be presented in a single monitoring window, affording you a multifaceted view of applications' system performance. For example, an Oracle Applications administrator can monitor

- The number of Oracle Forms sessions

- Pending concurrent requests

- The number of running concurrent requests

Following are some of the predefined chart groups shipped with the Management Pack for Oracle Applications. Most of these charts provide for further drilldown analysis.

- System Activity Overview Chart Group

- Forms Sessions and Concurrent Requests Chart

- Completed Requests by Status Chart

- Pending Requests per Manager Chart

- Running Requests per Manager Chart

- Longest Running Requests Chart

- Top Resource Consumers Chart Group

- Top Form Sessions Chart

- Top Running Requests Chart

Oracle Capacity Planner

The performance data collected by Oracle Performance Manager is also used for trending analysis for making capacity planning decisions. The Management Pack for Oracle Applications uses Oracle Capacity Planner to analyze Concurrent Manager performance data to help you configure your systems appropriately and project your future capacity needs. The data collected can be customized and rolled up, and you can also select samples of the entire data for a period. The collected data can be charted out for trending. These charts can also be customized to enable you to get a unified view of several statistics. For more information on Capacity Planning, see Chapter 14.

Concurrent Processing Tuning Assistant

The Concurrent Processing Tuning Assistant reports historical information about Concurrent Managers, concurrent programs, and concurrent processing requests. You can use these reports to achieve better throughput and performance. Unlike other Management Pack for Oracle Applications tools, the Tuning Assistant does not connect to the Oracle Management Server. Instead, you log in directly to the database schema containing the Oracle Application Object Library tables for the subsystems you want to tune.

The Tuning Assistant provides the following:

- Time periods with greatest wait times
- Requests that waited during those time periods
- Time periods with excess Concurrent Manager capacity

Oracle Applications Manager

Oracle Applications has integrated its Concurrent Manager administrative interface with Oracle Enterprise Manager, enabling administrators to better manage their systems. The Oracle Applications Manager console provides an applications DBA-oriented subset of the current Oracle Applications System Administration functions. These functions include administration of Concurrent Managers, processes, and requests.

The Oracle Applications Manager is available for Releases 11.0 and 11i. This new functionality is in addition to the multiwindow Oracle Applications forms, and administrators can choose which tools to use. Requests submitted within the standard Oracle Applications windows can be viewed from the Oracle Applications Manager console. Likewise, Concurrent Managers defined in the console can be accessed from within the Oracle Applications windows. The Oracle Applications Manager can be found in the Windows Start menu under Oracle Applications, or on the Enterprise Manager Tools menu under Application Management.

The Intelligent Agent

The Intelligent Agent does not get installed with installation of the Management Pack for Oracle Applications. You install Intelligent Agent from Oracle8i version 8.1.7 media using the following steps:

1. Launch the Oracle Universal Installer from the Oracle8i database installation media.

2. Select a new Oracle home for the Intelligent Agent. (Use a different ORACLE_HOME.)

3. Select Oracle8i Enterprise Edition from the list of available products.

4. Select Custom for the installation type.

5. Deselect all components. (You must deselect Oracle Product Options 8.1.7 before you can deselect Oracle8i Server 8.1.7.) Under Product Options, locate Oracle Enterprise Manager Products 8.1.7 and select it. Select Oracle Intelligent Agent 8.1.7 and continue with the installation.

The Oracle Intelligent Agent is an autonomous process running on a remote node in the network. The Intelligent Agent resides on the same node as the service it supports. However, the agent can support more than one service on a particular node. For example, if two databases are installed on one machine, a single agent can support both databases. An Intelligent Agent can be started and stopped using the following command:

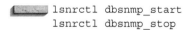

```
lsnrctl dbsnmp_start
lsnrctl dbsnmp_stop
```

The Agent is responsible for

- Providing local services or calling operating system–dependent services to interact locally with the managed targets.

- Accepting jobs or events from the Oracle Management Server or other third-party applications.

- Running Oracle Enterprise Manager jobs, collecting their results and output, and/or queueing the results as required.

- Checking for events, and queueing the resulting event reports for Oracle Enterprise Manager.

■ Canceling jobs or events as directed by the Console or other applications.

■ Handling Simple Network Management Protocol (SNMP) requests, if SNMP is supported on the Agent's platform.

For information on configuring the Agent, see the Oracle server platform-specific installation documentation for your system.

The Data Gathering Service

The data gathering service (also known as Oracle Data Gatherer) is used to collect performance data. The Oracle Data Gatherer is responsible for handling requests from client applications (for example, Oracle Capacity Planner and Oracle Performance Manager) that want to collect data. For each client application, you specify the performance data to collect (for example, file I/O, or CPU usage data) and the time interval between data samples. The Oracle Data Gatherer then collects the requested data for the client at the specified interval.

The Oracle Data Gatherer is part of the Oracle Intelligent Agent, and it is automatically installed when the Agent is installed on a managed host.

The Oracle Data Gatherer collects performance data for databases, operating systems, and other supported sources. Typically, the Data Gatherer should be configured on the host where the database is monitored and is located.

Other Oracle8i Features

This section has some discussion on some of the other important features of Oracle8i that could prove useful in your Oracle Financials implementation.

Buffer Pools

Multiple buffer pools were first introduced in Oracle8. They allow DBAs to allocate schema objects to specific cache buffer pools. By placing all the blocks read from the object in the appropriate buffer pool, Oracle provides a better method of controlling the buffer pool by making more efficient use of caching. Oracle8i provides for the following type of buffer pools.

KEEP Pool

The KEEP buffer pool maintains the objects in the buffer cache. This is more appropriate for small tables that are frequently accessed. Since these objects are never aged out, response time for read operations is quick.

RECYCLE Pool

The RECYCLE pool literally recycles objects to eliminate use of further cache space. This pool is suitable for large tables that are accessed less frequently. A good example could be a large fact table in a data warehouse that is not accessed by many users.

DEFAULT Pool

Oracle assigns the DEFAULT pool to all objects that have not been assigned either to the KEEP pool or RECYCLE pool. It is important to note that the buffer pool configuration is determined by the initialization parameter DB_BLOCK_BUFFERS * DB_BLOCK_SIZE. The KEEP, RECYCLE, and DEFAULT buffer pools are subsets of the Oracle buffer cache.

The buffers are divided into two lists: dirty buffers and LRU (least recently used) list. Dirty buffers are buffers that contain modified data that needs to be written out to disk. The LRU list contains buffers that are either free or pinned. The DB_BLOCK_LRU_LATCHES initialization parameter determines the maximum number of LRU latch sets.

The following parameters are specified for setting the KEEP and RECYCLE buffer pool in the init.ora file:

- BUFFER_POOL_KEEP = (BUFFERS:1000, LRU_LATCHES:5)

- BUFFER_POOL_RECYCLE = (BUFFERS:2000, LRU_LATCHES:10)

Each of the buffer pool definitions has its own set of block buffers and LRU latches. The remaining buffers (from the DB_BLOCK_BUFFERS) are assigned to the DEFAULT pool and the remaining LRU latches (from DB_BLOCK_LRU_LATCHES) are also assigned to it. BUFFER_POOL_KEEP should be sized to store the objects that need to be put in the KEEP pool.

Objects can be assigned to specific buffer pools using a syntax like this:

```
CREATE TABLE or ALTER TABLE ....
...
STORAGE (BUFFER POOL KEEP);
```

Buffer pool statistics can be monitored by trending the cache hit ratio. If you are using Statspack, this statistic is part of the Overall Instance Efficiency page. You can calculate cache-hit ratios for individual buffer pools from a data dictionary view called V$BUFFER_POOL_STATISICS using a command like this:

```
SELECT name, 1 - physical_reads/(db_block_gets+consistent_gets)  HIT_RATIO
FROM v$buffer_pool_statistics;
```

Temporary Tables

Oracle8i has a new feature called *global temporary table.* This permits the DBA to create temporary tables to hold session-specific data by specifying whether the data is specific to a session or a transaction.

The difference between a normal table and a temporary table is that in case of the latter the data exists in the table only for the duration of the session or transaction. In addition, the data in a temporary table is private to the session and only that session can view and modify the data. Indexes can be created on temporary tables, but they are also temporary. Temporary tables can be shared by different sessions or users, but each user gets his own copy of the data.

In the context of Oracle applications, temporary tables can be used by DBAs in implementing customization requirements. Performance improvements can be achieved by caching the values for a complex query in a temporary table and then further work on the temporary table to get the final report. This could reduce batch processing time and time required for processing large reports considerably. Remember that INSERT, UPDATE, and DELETE on temporary tables do not generate redo log information. TRUNCATE TABLE can also be used with temporary tables. Also, data in the temporary tables is dropped automatically when the session terminates or when the user logs off.

The syntax for creating a session-specific temporary table is

```
CREATE GLOBAL TEMPORARY TABLE my_temp ON COMMIT PRESERVE ROWS
```

The syntax for creating a transaction-specific temporary table is

```
CREATE GLOBAL TEMPORARY TABLE yrly_report ON COMMIT DELETE ROWS
```

Function-Based Indexes

In Oracle8i you have the ability to create indexes on functions and use those indexes in a query. A function-based index is an index on an expression or a function. This feature is useful for improving performance of range scans and ORDER BY clauses.

Here is an example of a function-based index:

```
CREATE INDEX vendor_master_index ON
    VENDOR_MASTER(upper(NAME));
```

With this index in place, the following query will perform an indexed search:

```
SELECT VENDOR_NAME FROM vendor_master
    where upper(NAME) = 'MCDONALD';
```

Here is another example of a function-based index. In this case, we are creating an index on an expression:

```
CREATE INDEX order_history_index ON
    ORDER_HISTORY(order_quantity * order_rate);
```

Once we have created this index, the following query will be index based:

```
SELECT * from order_history where
    order_quantity*order_rate < 100.00;
```

The function-based indexes will be beneficial as a tool for application tuning where you are looking to tune a specific batch application for performance. It will also be helpful in case of custom applications where you could create function based indexes before running a long report.

Invoker's Rights

In the pre-Oracle8i versions, stored programs like procedures, packages, and functions were executed with definer's rights. This meant that the object names were resolved and privileges depended on the owner of the PL/SQL code. In Oracle8i, however, stored procedures can also be defined to use what are called *invoker's rights*. With this feature, you can use the privileges and object resolution of the schema executing the object rather than the object owner.

The syntax for using invoker's rights in a PL/SQL block is shown here:

```
PROCEDURE my_proc(mytable_name VARCHAR2)
IS
AUTHID CURRENT_USER
```

Specifying AUTHID CURRENT_USER indicates that the user running the package should be able to perform all the actions required within the body of the package.

The syntax for using definer's rights in a PL/SQL block is shown here:

```
PROCEDURE my_proc(mytable_name VARCHAR2)
IS
AUTHID DEFINER
```

The AUTHID DEFINER is an optional parameter.

By default, when a package or procedure executes, the code is run under the security domain of the schema that owns the compile code. For example, the owner for a package my_package can be found out by running the command

```
    SELECT owner FROM DBA_OBJECTS
    WHERE OBJECT_NAME='MY_PACKAGE' AND
            OBJECT_TYPE='PACKAGE';
```

Other users who use this package cannot perform specific database actions directly but get indirect permission by executing the package. This is useful for performing certain types of tasks, but on some occasions it may be beneficial to provide more security or conditional security to the executor of the package.

The Oracle Application Suite makes use of the invoker's rights feature by implementing the same set of PL/SQL based packages that are used for multiple currency and multiple set of books architectures.

Cursor Sharing Initialization Parameter

Starting with Oracle 8.1.6, an initialization parameter called CURSOR_SHARING can be set to FORCE. Setting this value causes SQL statements that are not using bind variables to be rewritten by Oracle to use bind variables. This parameter can help improve scalability and reduce parsing significantly. This parameter is especially useful in environments where the application needs to be modified to use bind variables but you cannot modify the code.

This parameter can be changed at the session level using the command

```
alter session set cursor_sharing = force;
```

Oracle then internally rewrites similar SQL statements with bind variables.

Summary

In this chapter, we discussed several useful features of Oracle8i. These features help leverage the Oracle Application Suite to make it flexible and scalable. We talked about FGAC as a method for implementing additional security at the object level. We discussed partitioning and reviewed range, hash, and composite partitioning schemes and the situations when they are suitable. We also talked about the newest Management Pack for Oracle Applications that lets you manage your entire application from a single console and covered some features like function-based indexes, temporary tables, and invoker's rights that go a long way toward making the application environment powerful and increases performance. Some features like locally managed tablespaces can be implemented after the migration to 11i as well. When implementing a new feature, always remember to test it on a nonproduction environment first before rolling it out.

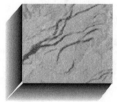

PART

VI

Miscellaneous
Topics

CHAPTER
19

The Oracle Portal Technology

- What is Oracle Portal?
- Oracle Portal terminology
- Oracle Portal as an application customization tool
- Installation and configuration issues
- Examples

his chapter reviews the Oracle Portal (formerly WebDB) layer of the Oracle applications technology stack. The chapter contains details about installing and configuring Oracle Portal and also highlights how the powerful capabilities of Oracle Portal can be used for developing certain customizations and enhancements in the Oracle11i environment.

What Is Oracle Portal?

Oracle Portal provides an easy and efficient way to manage and access information using a Web browser. Oracle Portal allows you to build Web applications with which different users can access content areas, applications, and much more. Oracle Portal can help bring together information from different sources, such as Oracle applications, corporate data warehouses, and so on, and display it in a single place using no special mechanism but a browser.

Oracle Portal does this by creating entities like the following:

- **Page** A single location for accessing data gathered from distinct sources

- **Content areas** Built-in structures for organizing, classifying, and cross-referencing various items

- **Application** Software used for manipulating and displaying data from Oracle Application Server

These entities, along with others, are discussed in the following sections.

Terminology

This section introduces some of the terminology used in working with Oracle Portals.

Page Users see and work with a *page* to interact with the contents of the portal. *Page style* refers to the specific characteristics associated with a page, such as colors, fonts, and so on. A page is divided into square or rectangular parts called *regions*. Within these regions are *portlets*.

Region These are specific areas within a page. Each region has specifications regarding how the portlets placed within it are displayed.

Portlets Portlets are the building blocks of a typical Oracle Portal application. A portlet is a reusable component that provides access to an information source. Each portlet belongs to a *portlet provider*.

Content Area   A *content area* is composed of folders that store one or more items. Content area is a collection of related information used to store content in Oracle Portal. A content area includes all the tools required to manage its content. This is called a *site* in WebDB 2.x and Oracle Portal 3.0. Content areas contain a hierarchy of folders for organizing content.

Folder   A folder can contains files, URLs, images, and other folders. Four types of folders are supported in Oracle Portal: container, PL/SQL, URL, and search.

- A container folder is a repository for related items including files, text, documents, images, application components, and so on.

- PL/SQL folders contain PL/SQL code which generates HTML when the folder is rendered.

- A URL folder provides a route to another Web page, either inside or outside this content area. When a user clicks the folder link, the Web page referenced by the link is displayed.

- A folder based on an Oracle Portal content area search creates different views of the content for different audiences. For example, you can create a search folder for all items belonging to the same category. Search folders are dynamic and are updated each time the folder is rendered.

Item   Items are basic units of content that are placed in the content area folder. Each item is assigned to a category.

Attribute   An *attribute* defines an item. Attributes could include creation date, expiration date, and author information for an item or a folder.

Activity Log   Oracle Portal provides a record of end-user requests in a database table called the *activity log*. The log contains useful information such as time of request, user name, and server information.

Batch Job   An Oracle Portal user could run a *batch job*. A batch job runs in the background and is useful for running large queries that fetch many rows from a database.

Component   A PL/SQL stored procedure or package created by Oracle Portal to build a report, chart, or form is called a *component*.

Database Access Descriptor (DAD)   DAD refers to a set of values that defines connectivity from Oracle Portal to the listener to fulfil an HTTP request. The DAD needs information such as user name, password, and connect string.

Using Oracle Portal for Application Customization

Oracle Portal can be used effectively for building and deploying customized Web database applications. Oracle Portal uses a set of browser-based HTML tools that are easy to deploy, which is particularly important in the context of Oracle11i. This is because it is important to keep the extent of customizations to a minimum and use simple and easy tools for customization. Unlike forms- and reports-based customization projects, portals can be developed, maintained, and enhanced by functional team members and does not require that they have special programming skills. Oracle Portal also detects the browser that is being used and generates the appropriate JavaScript for optimization purposes.

Oracle Portal does not require any special development environment or setups, so the entire development and configuration cycle can be managed using a single browser environment. This is unlike a forms/reports-based customization, which often involved a complicated development setup, depending on the number of developers or customization projects. With Portal, since the installed components reside on the database tier and the application tier, there is no need to install the software on all the developer workstations.

Oracle Portal can leverage the application security built within the self-service application suite. Security can be customized by coding backend PL/SQL-based packages to validate the application user ID and password. Performance tuning can be accomplished to a large extent by tuning and tracing the PL/SQL packages used at the backend for creating dynamic HTML pages. If a particular package is used often, you can pin it to the SGA (System Global Area) so that performance is optimized. Pinning makes a package memory resident and can improve overall application performance.

```
Execute DBMS_SHARED_POOL.KEEP('<Package Name>');
```

Oracle Portal can be used along with such Oracle8i features as fine-grained access control to build a more secure environment. For example, when building a user registration form in Oracle Portal to set up employees as Web users, you can create context on the PER_PEOPLE_F table to ensure that each employee can choose and view only his or her own information.

Oracle Portal could be a good solution in the following situations:

■ When there are multiple simple reporting requirements

■ In creating an application for a specific user community

■ When development time is short

■   In an application for which you are trying to combine information from
two or three different sources, such as Oracle application modules, data
warehouses, and so on, and you are providing a single consolidated view
of the information

NOTE
*Oracle Portal can be used with either Oracle version
8.1.6 or 8.1.7, depending on the version of the
database used by the application. When migrating
from one version to another, you must make sure
that the objects owned by the WebDB schema are
valid. In addition, earlier applications developed
using WebDB 2.1 or 2.2 can be easily upgraded to
be used with Oracle Portal.*

How Does Oracle Portal Work?

Oracle Portal works on a *three-tier architecture* that's similar to the Oracle Applications
Suite architecture, discussed in Chapter 3, as part of the Oracle technology stack.
Oracle Portal fully leverages the Oracle technology stack layers. The *database server*
layer consists of an Oracle instance with procedural option (PL/SQL installed). The
middle or *application* layer includes Apache and Web server components. The
browser is used by end users for viewing database content. Figure 19-1 shows the
Oracle Portal architecture.

Following are the characteristics of Oracle Portal implementation in the context
of Oracle applications. Users can type in a URL or it can be built into and called
from the Oracle Application Suite. No special client installation is necessary.

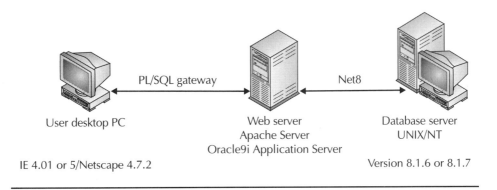

FIGURE 19-1.   *Oracle Portal architecture*

■ Oracle Application Server translates requests from the browser to database calls. Oracle Portal can use the same Web listener that is configured for using self-service Web applications. This helps you take advantages of socket-level security, load balancing, and scalability.

■ The PL/SQL Web toolkit that's installed as part of the Portal installation translates user requests into dynamic HTML and JavaScript from the database and displays it on the browser.

■ The PL/SQL gateway uses database access descriptors (DAD) for capturing the database connection information. The URL maps to DAD to execute the PL/SQL procedure. DAD can be maintained within the Portal itself.

■ The PL/SQL gateway depends on the Oracle Web Agent PL/SQL package, which is part of the Oracle9i Application Server implementation.

■ Oracle Portal does not require heavy SQL knowledge, so it is an ideal platform for functional folks. Oracle Portal does not require the skills of an experienced forms and reports developer.

Installation and Configuration Issues

This section contains a review of the installation and configuration of Oracle Portal. Oracle Portal can be implemented both on the Window NT (Service Pack 3 and above) and the UNIX environments. It can be run on any of the following browser versions:

■ Microsoft Internet Explorer version 4.0.1 or 5.0

■ Netscape version 4.0.8 or 4.7.2

Oracle Portal can also work with Oracle Application Server Enterprise Edition version 8.1.6 or 8.1.7. Before using it, ensure the following:

■ The database on which Oracle Portal is going to be installed should be up and running.

■ A SYS schema should exist in the instance.

■ Oracle Portal should be installed in a separate ORACLE_HOME.

You should also consider the following, with regards to tablespace usage:

- The SYSTEM tablespace should have around 100MB of free space.

- Consider creating a different tablespace for storing various content areas. This will help you keep better control of the size of the content areas.

You should also make sure that the following init.ora parameters are adjusted or set on the target Oracle instance:

```
max_enabled_roles = 25 (minimum)
open_cursors = 50 (minimum)
Compatible = 8.1.0 (or above)
java_pool_size = 20
```

You must ensure that the TNS alias points to the Oracle instance where Oracle Portal is installed. If this is not done, you will not be able to use Oracle Portal successfully.

Finally, make sure that the TNS_ADMIN variable points to the location of the tnsnames.ora file. Add the TNS_ADMIN variable to the following:

```
<ORACLE_HOME>/Apache/Apache/bin/apachectl
```

Schema Created by Portal

At the time of Oracle Portal installation, five new schemas are created; the default is *portal30*, which you can change to a more meaningful name at the time of installation. The schemas created are shown in Table 19-1.

Schema Name	Purpose
portal30	Account for Oracle Portal DBA; highest privileges
portal30_admin	Account for administration of Oracle Portal; no privileges for creating and managing schemas
portal30_public	Unauthenticated account for all end users
portal30_SSO	Login server application account
portal30_SSO_public	Non-authenticated sessions for login server application

TABLE 19-1. *Oracle Portal Schemas*

PL/SQL Gateway

The PL/SQL gateway provides support for building and deploying PL/SQL-based applications on the Internet. The PL/SQL stored procedures and packages can retrieve data from tables and generate HTTP responses containing data and code to display in a browser. The PL/SQL gateway is critical to any Oracle Portal implementation and is also part of the Oracle technology stack.

Oracle Mods

Oracle has enhanced several standard mods and provided more specific mods in addition to the Apache modes. Table 19-2 shows the mods with their purposes. Oracle mods extend the functionality of the language used for Internet-based development. For example, Mod PL/SQL has additional commands to generate and display dynamic HTML pages.

Integrating Oracle Portal in an Oracle Application Environment

Integrating Oracle Portal to an existing Oracle application environment is relatively simple. Make sure that you have a development, integration testing, and production environment and that your development process passes through the process of development, unit testing, and user acceptance testing before moving over to the production environment. Oracle Portal installs the five schemas and the PL/SQL toolkit in the Oracle8i server, and it installs specific components at the middle-layer tier. Make sure you choose an appropriate name for the Oracle portal schema, such as *papps*.

Mod Name	Purpose
mod_ssl	Standard HTTPS fully supported by Oracle; ensures secure listener connection with encryption mechanism.
mod_plsql	PL/SQL requests are routed to the 8i server to be serviced by PL/SQL programs; similar to the PL/SQL cartridge technology of earlier times.
mod_perl	Perl requests are forwarded to the Perl interpreter.
mod_jserv	Servlet requests are routed to Apache JServ servlet engines.

TABLE 19-2.   *Oracle Mods and Purposes*

Oracle Portal can be installed via two methods: automatic and manual. The manual method could be a preferred method for the purpose of integrating Oracle Portal with the Oracle Applications 11i environment. This method involves installing the following pieces:

■   PL/SQL Web toolkit

■   WebDB packages

NOTE
Listener need not be configured separately since it is already configured as part of the application setup.

Setup Issues and Workarounds

When using Oracle Portal on UNIX, even though you are installing Oracle Portal on the same ORACLE_HOME as the database server, make sure you correctly set up your tnsnames.ora for Oracle Portal. If you do not do this, Oracle Portal may fail with a "TNS could not resolve service name" error. If you encounter this error, check to make sure that the connect string, server name, and port ID in tnsnames.ora correspond to the DAD information in Oracle Portal, like so:

 `http://servername:port/admin_/gateway.htm`

You should then be able to connect to Oracle Portal.

Depending on your usage, the system administrator may have to size the portal30 tables—i.e., tables owned by the user portal30*. This is required because Oracle Portal stores information about the application in the database itself. You should check various extents on various objects, and resize the objects using the export-drop-import method if required. In this context, it will be advantageous to create a separate tablespace for Oracle Portal objects. You can also consider using locally managed tablespaces.

In addition, if a user is not able to connect to Oracle Portal to access the application, the application DBA could use the following checklist for troubleshooting:

1.   Check to determine whether the listener is up and running. If it is up, check to determine whether the listener logs are showing any specific errors. Start the listener using the **apachectl** start command.

2.   Try to access a static HTML page on the server to see whether it will be displayed. This will ensure that the listener is up and running.

3. Check to determine whether PL/SQL packages are installed correctly. You can also check for invalid objects by running a command like this in the respective portal* schema:

```
SELECT OBJECT_NAME, OBJECT_TYPE FROM USER_OBJECTS WHERE STATUS<>'VALID';
```

4. To determine whether Oracle Portal is installed properly, connect to SQL*Plus as portal30 and run the following code:

```
Set serveroutput on
Execute webdb.home;
Execute owa_util.showpage;
```

This should execute successfully and display the HTML tags.

5. Finally, check the connectivity of Oracle Portal from the database.

Restrictions

The following restrictions apply to Oracle Portal setup:

- Oracle application modules are developed in forms and reports. There is no clear migration path for moving Oracle Portal applications to a developer environment. This means that if you have certain customizations built into Oracle Portal and you would like to develop them further, your only choice is to rewrite the customization in forms and reports.

- Oracle Portal is suited for relatively simple customizations. Consider using Oracle development tools for customizations that involve more complex business logic and user interfaces.

Examples

This section attempts to present some examples for building applications to be used with the Oracle Application Suite. It also lists the implementation activities.

Example 1: Expense Reports for Oracle Web Employees

This example demonstrates a method of creating an expense analysis reporting system using Oracle Portal. Expense-related transactions and payment information from the AP (Accounts Payable) module will be used in this reporting system.

In this example, a menu screen is used to show the available reports. Upon choosing the expense analysis reporting, the user will be prompted with a dynamic list of all the expense types and their descriptions. This list is created using PL/SQL packages referring to specific application tables.

The user can click on a particular expense type and navigate further in the report to obtain more information. The next level reports the details of a particular expense report, employee information, and relevant amounts. At this level, the user can click on the expense report number to look at the entire expense report or employee name to see a list of all expense reports for that employee. Refer to Figure 19-2 to see the reports hierarchy.

Example 2: Forms and Self-Service Registration

This example describes a forms-based application that is used for setting up a self-service user registration application that could be included in any Oracle Web

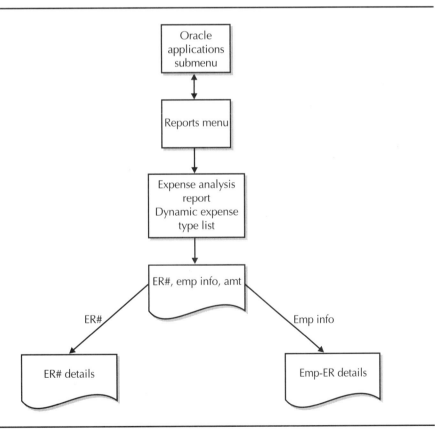

FIGURE 19-2. *The reports hierarchy*

application. Users can sign on to the application using a prescribed user name and password. First-time users need to register before they can sign on. To register, the user clicks on a Register Here icon. A form containing all the relevant information is then displayed. Information entered by the user is validated using PL/SQL packages with the application data. The system makes required entries to add the user to the application. In addition to saving setup time, this form can also help capture valid user information in the application.

Figure 19-3 shows the self-service user registration hierarchy using Oracle Portal.

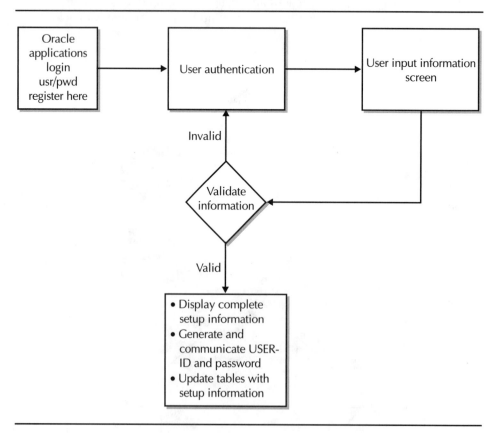

FIGURE 19-3. *Self-service user registration hierarchy using Oracle Portal*

Summary

This chapter provided some insight into Oracle Portal technology and how it can be used for implementing self-service customizations as also numerous enhancements in the area of the Oracle Application Suite. As you have seen, Oracle Portal is based on PL/SQL technology and provides an easy method for displaying content from the application to the Internet. Oracle Portal is available with Oracle9i; however, Oracle Portal is available as a component of Oracle9i Application Server.

Oracle Portal provides many features like multiple files upload, multilanguage support, export/import scripting, and search capabilities, which can also be leveraged when developing custom applications in 11i. Oracle Portal can be a good tool for developing add-on modules in the Oracle E-Business Suite in situations where there is a need to publish a number of critical details from different sources. Some of the examples where Oracle Portal solutions can be used could be implementing system performance charts, critical management reports, and so on.

Oracle Portal is secure and does not require skilled technical knowledge for implementation. In fact, if developed properly, functional representatives in charge of specific modules can maintain Oracle Portal enhancements. Note that it is critical to document these enhancement and customization efforts because such documentation will help you redeploy these enhancements after any major upgrade without surprising the users with unexpected changes. Refer to specific Oracle documentation for detailed information about implementation and usage of Oracle Portal.

CHAPTER 20

Oracle Financial Analyzer

- Introduction to Oracle Financial Analyzer
- Components of Oracle Financial Analyzer
- Installation and configuration of Oracle Financial Analyzer
- Implementation tips and recommendations

n this chapter, we will review an introduction to OFA and how it can be used with the Oracle application modules to enhance the user's ability to analyze and utilize the data more effectively. Oracle Financial Analyzer (OFA) is a tool provided by Oracle for forecasting and analyzing multidimensional data.

Oracle Financial Analyzer (OFA) is a very powerful tool for performing complex financial analysis, budgeting, and forecasting. Oracle easily links with Oracle General Ledger; its database engine is Oracle Express, which is an OLAP (online analytical processing) database engine. An OLAP database is different from a relational database process as it stores data in the form of cubes to facilitate advanced drilling and rotation. This feature allows an OLAP database like Oracle Express to quickly and easily process certain types of queries that will take much longer to develop and execute in the usual relational database server. OFA uses this power of Oracle Express to perform advanced analysis on Oracle General Ledger data.

Online analytical processing (OLAP) establishes the need for special technology to cater to day-to-day reporting and analysis requirements of a certain category of users. OLAP does not replace existing operational and database systems but complements them. Most often, by creating OLAP, the overall load on the operating system can be reduced by redirecting reporting and analysis users to point to the OLAP server.

The main target for OLAP applications are power users or users with knowledge of the application. OLAP applications do not target operational support users. Using an OLAP application, users can view a cross section of any multidimensional data. For example, in a retail industry, users can view data by product, store, and time and can perform various types of analysis of this data. In addition to this, OLAP applications provide the following functionality:

- Forecasting, statistical estimation, and extrapolation

- What-if analysis, slice-and-dice capability, and consolidations

- Moving averages and complex ratio calculations

- Standard deviation and statistical analysis of the data

Introduction to Oracle Financial Analyzer

The Oracle Financial Analyzer tool is useful for "what-if"-style analysis. OFA (not to be confused with Oracle Flexible Architecture) provides tools for planning, analyzing, and reporting corporate financial data. It uses the Express multidimensional server and lets you customize individual requirements of data for all levels of business users. It handles organizational consolidations across multiple hierarchies and automatically performs line-item and time aggregations.

OFA is a powerful software package used for centralized budgeting, forecasting, and analysis. OFA links seamlessly with the Oracle General Ledger and has as its database engine Oracle Express, the best OLAP engine on the market. OFA provides security for financial information stored in the database, is Web-capable, and contains expected OLAP functions such as drilling and rotating. OFA grants the user access to the Selector, a powerful and easy-to-use query tool. There are several benefits to implementing an OFA system and the Financials administrator needs to know about its abilities and configuration details.

OFA uses *dimensions* to provide the organization with financial data. A dimension contains a list of values that identify the elements of the dimension. Dimension values not only identify your data, but they provide an easy way to target the data you need for a particular purpose. For example, some of the common examples of dimensions are location, region, and time. Selecting different dimensions has no effect on the database. Also, every dimension has a certain value when the database is started. A financial data item can have up to 10 dimensions. Each dimension is stored as a separate object in an OFA database.

When you create a report, graph, or worksheet, you select the values to work with. Selecting dimension values has no permanent effect on your database. Every dimension has all its values available whenever you start up your database, and you can change the selection at any time as you work with OFA.

OFA has many benefits:

- Provides access to summary of multidimensional data for reporting and analysis

- Helps decision-makers solve their day-to-day problems by providing them with their day-to-day reporting needs

- Helps administrators and executives make strategic decisions

- Provides financial reporting, analysis, planning, and forecasting help

OFA supports write-back to the database. This is indeed an expectation from an application capable of doing budgeting, financial reporting, and forecasting. OFA contains a number of interface features that support things like asymmetric reports and the generation of new report line items and the models behind them, on the fly. OFA uses a distributed data model, which allows end users to work on a budget without affecting any other users and then update a shared database, making the results available to others.

Steps to Build OFA

Here are some of the broad steps to build a Financial Analyzer model from an existing GL (General Ledger) or operational model.

- Define structures using DBA Workstation.

- Define dimensions, hierarchies, and attributes.

- Define Financial Data items (Metrics or Measures).

- Load structures.

  - Enter values through the DBA Workstation.

  - Load from files using the Data Loader or Express Loader program.

- Create models.

- Solve the data.

  - Transform data along the hierarchies.

  - Solve the model.

- Distribute data and structures to users.

Components of Oracle Financial Analyzer

Before you can create a user of any type, you must first use Installer to install an environment for that user. This environment, called a *component*, contains shell databases and configuration files for that user. The task is to identify which component you want to install. The following components are available in OFA:

- Super Administrator

- Administrator

- Cluster

- Web

- Single Sign-On

Super Administrator Component

You must install a Super Administrator component before installing any other component type. After installing this component, all other users of this component will be created through the Super Administrator workstation using the Users option from the Manage menu. You can refer to the topic called "Creating Users" in the Financial Analyzer Help system for more information on this task.

Administrator Component

If you install an Administrator component, you must create the personal database for that component by creating an Administrator workstation using the Super Administrator workstation. You can refer to the topic called "Creating Users" in the Financial Analyzer Help system for more information on this task.

Cluster Component

If you have installed a Cluster component, you can install the Budget workstation personal databases for that component by creating Budget workstations in the Administrator of that component. You can refer to the topic called "Creating Users" in the Financial Analyzer Help system for more information on this task.

Web Component

You should install the Financial Analyzer Web component separately if you want to place the Web component on a different computer than the one that Express Server is running on.

Single Sign-On Component

You should install Single Sign-On only if you plan to use this functionality with Oracle Applications for Financial Analyzer Web users.

OFA Web Client vs. OFA Windows client

This section provides a comparison of features and functionality of the OFA Web client versus the OFA Windows client.

Web Client Unique Features

Let us first review the features and functionality specific to the Web Client.

- Reporting/Graphics
    - Drill across in reports
    - Drilling on nested edges

- No dimension nesting limits (three dimensions for down and across edges on the client)

- No edge values limit (5000 on client)

- Drilling in graphs

- Data values on graph

- Change view type without creating a new document

- Graph types such as

  - 3-D

  - Stacked line

  - Stacked line dual-Y axis

  - Stacked line

  - Stacked line dual-Y axis

  - Percentage line

  - Stacked area

  - Scatter dual-Y axis

- Selector

  - Sort by depth

- Data Entry Form (vs. Worksheet)

  - Multiple FDIs

  - Cell locking

  - Asymmetric edge

  - Combined input of text and numeric data

  - Controlled usage for end user—no selector, rotation, or calculation change

Windows Client Unique Features

Now let us review the features and functionality specific to the Windows client.

- File menu

  - Document management—creating, saving, renaming, and deleting documents

- Print capabilities
- Export to XLS format
- Export a custom selection of logical pages
- Selector
  - Create saved selections
  - Sort dimension values manually using drag and drop
  - Change combinations for asymmetric edges
- Worksheet (vs. Data Entry Form—End User functionality)
  - Ability to rotate and change selection
  - Grow and increase data options
  - Spread data options
  - Change calculations used in worksheet
- Edit menu
  - Inserting and deleting rows and columns
  - Edit dimension label descriptions in a document
- Format
  - Formatting options—Web supports only font and row/column width
  - Report calculations—Enter report calculations directly into a report
- Tools
  - Solve Definition function
  - Solve Group function
  - Copy Data function
- Maintain
  - Ability to define dimensions
  - Ability to define FDIs
  - Ability to add dimension values
  - Ability to create and edit models, hierarchies, and attributes

- Manage (Administration Functions)
  - Ability to distribute structure and data
  - User maintenance and reporting
  - Task Processor management
  - Write Access management

Installation and Configuration of OFA

Installation of OFA involves installing the proper server and client components that are needed, setting the directory and file structures, and also setting up Web clients so that users can access data using the Internet. Note that OFA can be installed as a single-user installation on shared installation on the PC. For details about installation of OFA, refer to *Oracle Financial Analyzer Installation and Upgrade Guide for Release 11i*, Part # A87523-01. In this section, we will present an overview of the installation and configuration procedures.

For minimum client hardware requirements, please refer to the *Oracle Financial Analyzer Release 11i Installation and Upgrade Guide*.

Minimum UNIX server requirements:

- Dual processors and 512MB of extended memory

- Minimum Windows NT server requirements: Pentium Pro dual processors and 128MB of extended memory

Installed Server Directories and Files

After the required components of OFA are installed, a default directory structure and set of files is set up for each component type. The following default directories are set up beneath the standard root directory for each component type:

- **CODE directory** Contains the code databases for the application.

- **SHARED directory** Contains the shared databases for the application and subdirectories that contain files for Financial Analyzer Web access.

- **TEMPORARY directory** The location for temporary files that are created by the system as it runs.

- **TASKFILE directory** The location for tasks that are created by users and processed by the system.

- **SHELLS directory**   Contains a set of EIF (Express Interface File) files used by the system to create personal databases for user workstations.

- **USERS directory**   For the Super Administrator installation, contains the Super Administrator personal database and a Task Processor personal database. (The Task Processor database is used only if the Task Processor is running in standalone mode.) This directory is created as a suggested location for personal databases.

Oracle Financial Analyzer Database Security

It is important for the Financials administrator to ensure that unknown users without proper access rights are not able to get into the environment. The OFA setup provides security levels that can be implemented to secure the environment.

Shared Database

Access to a Financial Analyzer shared database ofas.db is controlled through the PERMIT_READ and PERMIT_WRITE functions of the Express Server *PERMIT* command. To attach the shared database in read/write mode, the connection to Express Server must be made using an operating system user name that is associated with the Financial Analyzer Administrator workstation user for that shared database. Once attached in read/write mode, all the objects in the database are available to the user. When you attach the shared database read-only, the connection to Express Server must be made using an operating system user name associated with a valid Financial Analyzer user who is defined by the Administrator for that shared database. The user will be able to access only the dimensions, dimension values, financial data items, hierarchies, and attributes that have been distributed to that Financial Analyzer user connected with that operating system user name. If the operating system user name is associated with more than one Financial Analyzer user, the database objects available to the user will be those distributed to the first instance of that Financial Analyzer user in the list of users.

Workstation Personal Database

Access to a workstation's personal database is controlled by the operating system user name entered in the Connect to EXPRESS Session dialog box when starting Financial Analyzer. The operating system user name must be associated with a Financial Analyzer user. For detailed information about associating operating system user names with Financial Analyzer users, refer to the topic "Creating Users" in the Financial Analyzer Help system.

Configuring Financial Analyzer for Web Access

Follow these general steps to configure Financial Analyzer for Web access:

1. Ensure that you have installed all the necessary components that are required to run Financial Analyzer through the Web. These include:

   ■ Express Web Agent 6.3.3

   ■ Web listener software (Oracle's Application Server is recommended)

2. Enable Web Agent security in Oracle Express Instance Manager.

3. Modify the Web listener.

4. Provide the URL for the shared database to the users who need Web access to that database. By specifying this URL in their browsers, users will be able to see everything that the administrator has distributed to them.

Financial Analyzer Configuration Files

The Financial Analyzer configuration files control system communication in the following ways:

■ They control how workstations communicate with their associated shared and code databases.

■ They control how Administrator workstations communicate with super or subordinate administrators.

There are three types of configuration files in OFA:

■ System configuration file: ofasyscf.cfg

■ Code configuration file: ofacdcf.cfg

■ Personal configuration file: personal_database_name.cfg

System Configuration File

The system configuration file (ofasyscf.cfg) contains information that is used to populate the ofasyscf.db database at runtime. The file contains three sections, which specify the following information:

■ The location of the shared database associated with a workstation

■ The location of the superior super administrator's shared database

■ The location of the CODE, TEMPORARY, and TASKFILE directories

Code Configuration File

The code configuration file (ofacdcf.cfg) contains information about the location of the code databases and allows the declaration of a primary custom database. It also contains information that is used to populate the ofacdcf.db database at runtime.

Personal Configuration File

A personal configuration file (database_name.cfg) exists for each personal database in a Financial Analyzer system. It contains information about the location of the system configuration file that is used by that workstation. The personal configuration file for a Super Administrator workstation also specifies whether the Oracle General Ledger Integration Module is installed.

Implementation Tips and Recommendations

In this section we will discuss some tips, techniques, and recommendations that can help when working with the Oracle Financial Analyzer tool.

Creating External Users in OFA

To create external users in OFA follow these steps:

1. Review the Oracle Budgeting & Planning Reference Guide (Part # 82945-01) and see Chapter 3 for a discussion on Distributing Express Database Objects and Data.

2. Refer to the appropriate sections in the Oracle Financial Analyzer (OFA) User's Guide for information on creating external users and transferring structures and data.

3. Log into OFA as the Super DBA user by attaching the OFA super personal database (../super/super.db) using the same NT/UNIX server account that was used for the initial login to OFA after installation.

4. Select the Users option from the Manage menu to open the Maintain Users dialog box.

5. Add your NT/UNIX server account user name as a user for the Super DBA by performing the following steps.

6. With **Super DBA** in the User box in the Maintain Users dialog box, click Edit.

7. Enter the NT/UNIX server account Username in the top section of the Specify Usernames box and click Add. The Username just added should move to the bottom section of the box. Repeat the process to add any other NT/UNIX accounts to the list for the OFA Super DBA user or remove any unneeded ones that may appear in the list.

8. Click OK to exit the Edit User dialog. The Username(s) added should now show up in the User Information box for user type DBA. Repeat the preceding procedure to create other external users while in the Maintain User dialog.

9. Run the Task Processor when finished, or proceed directly to running the Task Processor and add external users later. To run the Task Processor, go to the Manage Menu --> Task Processor dialog. Upon completing creating users through OFA, be sure to distribute structures to all users and data to be shared.

Starting OFA Without the Front-End

Upon starting the Financial Analyzer Super Administrator workstation, several programs are executed that set up temporary value sets and variables in the OFA databases. For this reason, it is relatively difficult to script a routine that will attach the OFA databases and start executing queries against them. You need to be able to start OFA in the batch programs. You can start OFA in your batch program by simulating the startup of a OFA Super Administrator using the following commands:

```
dtb attach /<SuperDBAPath>/<SuperDBAName>.db rw
dtb attach /<ExpressDBPath>/xpdb.db ro last
call init.main('/<SuperDBAPath>/')
call da.set.lang('ENU')
call fms.startup
call dir.startup
where
SuperDBAPath is the path of your Super Administrator personal database,
SuperDBAName is the name of your Super Administrator personal database,
ExpressDBPath is the complete path of your Express Database
```

Now you are ready to run programs that will query against specific objects, just like using the OFA front-end.

Integrating General Ledger with Financial Analyzer

We will discuss a generic procedure for integrating General Ledger with Financial Analyzer. Some variations to this procedure could be necessary, depending on the version of Oracle Application or Oracle Financial Analyzer used.

1. Ensure that the versions of General Ledger and Oracle Financial Analyzer are certified. You can do this by reviewing the certification matrix that is available on the Metalink. This step is critical and will help get support from Oracle before going forward.

2. Refer to the document called *Oracle Financial Analyzer: Oracle General Ledger, Integrating Oracle Financial Analyzer with Oracle General Ledger, Release 11i*, Part # A86564-01. This manual has specific details on the following:

   ■ Defining metadata in General Ledger

   ■ Extracting Financials data from General Ledger

   ■ Loading Financials data into Financial Analyzer

   ■ Using the data in the Financial Analyzer

   ■ Writing Budget data back to General Ledger

NOTE
To integrate General Ledger and Financial Analyzer, the order in which they are installed does not matter.

Monitoring User Connections in OFA

The Financials administrator can use this section to monitor and control user access to OFA. Monitoring user connection is also required when the Financials administrator needs to apply a patch or perform an administration task on the OFA, which requires that all users are logged out of OFA. To monitor users in OFA, complete the following steps:

1. In the directory <ofa_server>/code, create a custom database called, for example, Log1.db.

2. In this database, create a program named **LC.STARTUP.PRG** (exactly this name). Include the following in this program:

```
DATABASE ATTACH '<ofa_server>/code/Log2.db' FIRST -
RW CALL P.User UPDATE DATABASE DETACH Log2.db
```

3. In the directory <ofa_server>/code, create a database called Log2.db.

4. Create a dimension entry (Type=TEXT, Width=variable) in the database Log2.db.

5. Create a program called P.User in the database Log2.db. Include the following code in P.User:

```
VARIABLE _host TEXT VARIABLE _user TEXT VARIABLE _date -
TEXT VARIABLE _tod TEXT DATEFORMAT = '<DD>/<MM>/<YYYY>'  -
_host = SYSINFO(HOSTNAME) _user = SYSINFO(USER) _date = TODAY -
_tod = TOD MAINTAIN Entry ADD -
JOINCHARS('Hostname:',_host,' Username:',_user,' Date:',_date,' Time:',_tod)
```

6. Modify the file ofacdcf.cfg in the directory <ofa_server>/code as follows:

```
[Primary Custom Database] OFALCNAME=Log1.db
```

7. If you specify the OFALCNAME database (custom OFA database, Log1.db in the above example) in the file ofacdcf.cfg, after each OFA workstation startup (including Web), this database is automatically attached and the program LC.STARTUP.PRG is automatically submitted. The program LC.STARTUP.PRG attaches the second database (Log2.db) in read-write mode (OFALCNAME database cannot be attached read-write) and submits the program P.User. The program P.User finds information about the new session (host name, user, date, time) and saves the information in the dimension Entry. By reviewing values in the dimension you can see how users connect.

Summary

OFA provides a mechanism for users to perform multidimensional analysis on Financials data available in Oracle General Ledger. OFA is useful to the end user because it helps them perform analysis, forecasting, and complex reports and what-if analyses. Oracle Financial Analyzer is also useful from the administrator's point of view, because by creating another multidimensional schema, the administrator is diverting a group of users away from the production database that is used for day-to-day operations. This leads to better management of available resources as well as improved performance of the operational database. In this chapter, we reviewed OFA and its components. We also touched on integrating Oracle Financial Analyzer with Oracle General Ledger.

Index

511

F

Fast REFRESH of a materialized view, 166–167
Fast Requests Manager, 145
FGAC (fine grained access control), 426–429, 440–449
    benefits of, 427–428, 440–441
    how it works, 446–449
    implementing, 428–429, 443–446
    overview of, 427
    terminology, 427, 441–442
    user layer, 442
File Character Set Conversion (adncnv) utility, 116–117
File system, 14–19
File system tasks (AD Administration), 106
Financial Analyzer. *See* OFA
Financials administrator
    characteristics of, 33
    vs. database administrator, 26
    finding success as, 34–35
    required skills of, 32
    responsibilities of, 25–31, 33, 366–370
    roles of, 23–26
    toolkit for, 365–391
    types of, 35–36
Fingerprint (message digest), 432
Firewalls, 421
FIRST_ROWS parameter (optimizer mode), 203
Fixed memory utilization, 352
Flint60 upgrade utility, 98–99
Fnd (foundation) directory, 16
FND_DUAL table, 139
FND_FUNCTION package, 424–426
FND_HISTOGRAM_COLS table, 209
FNDLIBR process, 138
FND_PRODUCT_INSTALLATIONS table, 209
FND_STATS package, 152–153, 203, 206–209, 241
Forms, using Oracle Portal for, 493–494
Forms client, 5–6
Forms 4.5 form, migrating to Forms 6i, 98–99
Forms server, 5–6, 47–49
Fragmentation, 154–157
Front office functions, 5
Full table scan, 205
Function, defined, 225
Functional environment, creating, 53–54

Function-based indexes, 161–162, 274–275, 477–478

G

Gather Schema Statistics Concurrent Program, 203, 206, 209
GATHER_ALL_COLUMN_STATS procedure, 207–208
GATHER_INDEX_STATS procedure, 207
GATHER_SCHEMA_STATS procedure, 207
GATHER_TABLE_STATS procedure, 207
General Ledger, integrating with OFA, 509
Global indexes, 454
Global prefixed index, 454
GLOBAL QUERY REWRITE privilege, 165
Global temporary table, explained, 477

H

Hardware components
    and Oracle 11i upgrade, 59
    stress testing, 354
    that may need backing up, 394
Hash clusters, 275
Hash partitioning, 452–453
Hash values, generating, 275
High-availability (application), 396–403
Hints, 202–203, 213, 305–306
Histograms, 205, 242, 280, 303–304
Historical processing information, 22
Hot data files, analyzing, 341–343
Hourly average instance efficiency, 338–341
Html directory, 17
HTML-based products, 6–7
HTTP home, 17
HTTP (Hypertext Transfer Protocol), 6
HTTP requests, 4
HTTP servers, 4, 6
Hybrid systems, tuning, 269–270

I

ICA (Internet Computing Architecture), 4–5
ICM (Internal Concurrent Manager), 134–135
IDBA (Internet Database Administrator), 244
IN operator, using in RBO, 300
Index categories, and standard extent size, 155
Index clusters, 275

T

INTERNATIONAL CONTACT INFORMATION

AUSTRALIA
McGraw-Hill Book Company Australia Pty. Ltd.
TEL +61-2-9417-9899
FAX +61-2-9417-5687
http://www.mcgraw-hill.com.au
books-it_sydney@mcgraw-hill.com

CANADA
McGraw-Hill Ryerson Ltd.
TEL +905-430-5000
FAX +905-430-5020
http://www.mcgrawhill.ca

**GREECE, MIDDLE EAST,
NORTHERN AFRICA**
McGraw-Hill Hellas
TEL +30-1-656-0990-3-4
FAX +30-1-654-5525

MEXICO (Also serving Latin America)
McGraw-Hill Interamericana Editores S.A. de C.V.
TEL +525-117-1583
FAX +525-117-1589
http://www.mcgraw-hill.com.mx
fernando_castellanos@mcgraw-hill.com

SINGAPORE (Serving Asia)
McGraw-Hill Book Company
TEL +65-863-1580
FAX +65-862-3354
http://www.mcgraw-hill.com.sg
mghasia@mcgraw-hill.com

SOUTH AFRICA
McGraw-Hill South Africa
TEL +27-11-622-7512
FAX +27-11-622-9045
robyn_swanepoel@mcgraw-hill.com

**UNITED KINGDOM & EUROPE
(Excluding Southern Europe)**
McGraw-Hill Education Europe
TEL +44-1-628-502500
FAX +44-1-628-770224
http://www.mcgraw-hill.co.uk
computing_neurope@mcgraw-hill.com

ALL OTHER INQUIRIES Contact:
Osborne/McGraw-Hill
TEL +1-510-549-6600
FAX +1-510-883-7600
http://www.osborne.com
omg_international@mcgraw-hill.com

**The Largest Single Community
of Oracle Applications Users
in the World**

- Collaborate with fellow members

- Obtain the latest product information

- Receive implementation and usage tips

- Learn about Oracle Services and Partners

http://appsnet.oracle.com

ORACLE

Knowledge is power. To which we say,

crank up the power.

Are you ready for a power surge?

Accelerate your career—become an **Oracle Certified Professional (OCP)**. With Oracle's cutting-edge *Instructor-Led Training*, *Technology-Based Training*, and this *guide*, you can prepare for certification faster than ever. Set your own trajectory by logging your personal training plan with us. Go to **http://education.oracle.com/tpb**, where we'll help you pick a training path, select your courses, and track your progress. We'll even send you an email when your courses are offered in your area. If you don't have access to the Web, call us at 1-800-441-3541 (Outside the U.S. call +1-310-335-2403).
Power learning has never been easier.

University

Get Your FREE Subscription to *Oracle Magazine*

Oracle Magazine is essential gear for today's information technology professionals. Stay informed and increase your productivity with every issue of *Oracle Magazine*. Inside each **FREE,** bimonthly issue you'll get:

- Up-to-date information on Oracle Database Server, Oracle Applications, Internet Computing, and tools
- Third-party news and announcements
- Technical articles on Oracle products and operating environments
- Development and administration tips
- Real-world customer stories

Three easy ways to subscribe:

1. Web   **Visit our Web site at www.oracle.com/oramag/. You'll find a subscription form there, plus much more!**

2. Fax   Complete the questionnaire on the back of this card and fax the questionnaire side only to **+1.847.647.9735.**

3. Mail   Complete the questionnaire on the back of this card and mail it to P.O. Box 1263, Skokie, IL 60076-8263.

If there are other Oracle users at your location who would like to receive their own subscription to *Oracle Magazine*, please photocopy this form and pass it along.

□ **YES! Please send me a FREE subscription to *Oracle Magazine*.**   □ **NO**

To receive a free bimonthly subscription to *Oracle Magazine*, you must fill out the entire card, sign it, and date it (incomplete cards cannot be processed or acknowledged). You can also fax your application to **+1.847.647.9735. Or subscribe at our Web site at www.oracle.com/oramag/**

| SIGNATURE (REQUIRED) | X | DATE | |

NAME	TITLE
COMPANY	TELEPHONE
ADDRESS	FAX NUMBER
CITY	STATE	POSTAL CODE/ZIP CODE
COUNTRY	E-MAIL ADDRESS

□ From time to time, Oracle Publishing allows our partners exclusive access to our e-mail addresses for special promotions and announcements. To be included in this program, please check this box.

You must answer all eight questions below.

1 What is the primary business activity of your firm at this location? *(check only one)*
- □ 03 Communications
- □ 04 Consulting, Training
- □ 06 Data Processing
- □ 07 Education
- □ 08 Engineering
- □ 09 Financial Services
- □ 10 Government—Federal, Local, State, Other
- □ 11 Government—Military
- □ 12 Health Care
- □ 13 Manufacturing—Aerospace, Defense
- □ 14 Manufacturing—Computer Hardware
- □ 15 Manufacturing—Noncomputer Products
- □ 17 Research & Development
- □ 19 Retailing, Wholesaling, Distribution
- □ 20 Software Development
- □ 21 Systems Integration, VAR, VAD, OEM
- □ 22 Transportation
- □ 23 Utilities (Electric, Gas, Sanitation)
- □ 98 Other Business and Services
  _____

2 Which of the following best describes your job function? *(check only one)*
CORPORATE MANAGEMENT/STAFF
- □ 01 Executive Management (President, Chair, CEO, CFO, Owner, Partner, Principal)
- □ 02 Finance/Administrative Management (VP/Director/ Manager/Controller, Purchasing, Administration)
- □ 03 Sales/Marketing Management (VP/Director/Manager)
- □ 04 Computer Systems/Operations Management (CIO/VP/Director/ Manager MIS, Operations)
IS/IT STAFF
- □ 07 Systems Development/ Programming Management
- □ 08 Systems Development/ Programming Staff
- □ 09 Consulting
- □ 10 DBA/Systems Administrator
- □ 11 Education/Training
- □ 14 Technical Support Director/ Manager
- □ 16 Other Technical Management/Staff
- □ 98 Other _____

3 What is your current primary operating platform? *(check all that apply)*
- □ 01 DEC UNIX
- □ 02 DEC VAX VMS
- □ 03 Java
- □ 04 HP UNIX
- □ 05 IBM AIX
- □ 06 IBM UNIX
- □ 07 Macintosh
- □ 09 MS-DOS
- □ 10 MVS
- □ 11 NetWare
- □ 12 Network Computing
- □ 13 OpenVMS
- □ 14 SCO UNIX
- □ 24 Sequent DYNIX/ptx
- □ 15 Sun Solaris/SunOS
- □ 16 SVR4
- □ 18 UnixWare
- □ 20 Windows
- □ 21 Windows NT
- □ 23 Other UNIX _____
- 99 □ **None of the above**

4 Do you evaluate, specify, recommend, or authorize the purchase of any of the following? *(check all that apply)*
- □ 01 Hardware
- □ 02 Software
- □ 03 Application Development Tools
- □ 04 Database Products
- □ 05 Internet or Intranet Products
- 99 □ **None of the above**

5 In your job, do you use or plan to purchase any of the following products or services? *(check all that apply)*
SOFTWARE
- □ 01 Business Graphics
- □ 02 CAD/CAE/CAM
- □ 03 CASE
- □ 05 Communications
- □ 06 Database Management
- □ 07 File Management
- □ 08 Finance
- □ 09 Java
- □ 10 Materials Resource Planning
- □ 11 Multimedia Authoring
- □ 12 Networking
- □ 13 Office Automation
- □ 14 Order Entry/Inventory Control
- □ 15 Programming
- □ 16 Project Management

- □ 17 Scientific and Engineering
- □ 18 Spreadsheets
- □ 19 Systems Management
- □ 20 Workflow
HARDWARE
- □ 21 Macintosh
- □ 22 Mainframe
- □ 23 Massively Parallel Processing
- □ 24 Minicomputer
- □ 25 PC
- □ 26 Network Computer
- □ 28 Symmetric Multiprocessing
- □ 29 Workstation
PERIPHERALS
- □ 30 Bridges/Routers/Hubs/Gateways
- □ 31 CD-ROM Drives
- □ 32 Disk Drives/Subsystems
- □ 33 Modems
- □ 34 Tape Drives/Subsystems
- □ 35 Video Boards/Multimedia
SERVICES
- □ 37 Consulting
- □ 38 Education/Training
- □ 39 Maintenance
- □ 40 Online Database Services
- □ 41 Support
- □ 36 Technology-Based Training
- □ 98 Other _____
- 99 □ **None of the above**

6 What Oracle products are in use at your site? *(check all that apply)*
SERVER/SOFTWARE
- □ 01 Oracle8
- □ 30 Oracle8*i*
- □ 31 Oracle8*i* Lite
- □ 02 Oracle7
- □ 03 Oracle Application Server
- □ 04 Oracle Data Mart Suites
- □ 05 Oracle Internet Commerce Server
- □ 32 Oracle *inter*Media
- □ 33 Oracle JServer
- □ 07 Oracle Lite
- □ 08 Oracle Payment Server
- □ 11 Oracle Video Server
TOOLS
- □ 13 Oracle Designer
- □ 14 Oracle Developer
- □ 54 Oracle Discoverer
- □ 53 Oracle Express
- □ 51 Oracle JDeveloper
- □ 52 Oracle Reports
- □ 50 Oracle WebDB
- □ 55 Oracle Workflow
ORACLE APPLICATIONS
- □ 17 Oracle Automotive

- □ 35 Oracle Business Intelligence System
- □ 19 Oracle Consumer Packaged Goods
- □ 39 Oracle E-Commerce
- □ 18 Oracle Energy
- □ 20 Oracle Financials
- □ 28 Oracle Front Office
- □ 21 Oracle Human Resources
- □ 37 Oracle Internet Procurement
- □ 22 Oracle Manufacturing
- □ 40 Oracle Process Manufacturing
- □ 23 Oracle Projects
- □ 34 Oracle Retail
- □ 29 Oracle Self-Service Web Applications
- □ 38 Oracle Strategic Enterprise Management
- □ 25 Oracle Supply Chain Management
- □ 36 Oracle Tutor
- □ 41 Oracle Travel Management
ORACLE SERVICES
- □ 61 Oracle Consulting
- □ 62 Oracle Education
- □ 60 Oracle Support
- □ 98 Other _____
- 99 □ **None of the above**

7 What other database products are in use at your site? *(check all that apply)*
- □ 01 Access
- □ 02 Baan
- □ 03 dbase
- □ 04 Gupta
- □ 05 IBM DB2
- □ 06 Informix
- □ 07 Ingres
- □ 08 Microsoft Access
- □ 09 Microsoft SQL Server
- □ 10 PeopleSoft
- □ 11 Progress
- □ 12 SAP
- □ 13 Sybase
- □ 14 VSAM
- □ 98 Other _____
- 99 □ **None of the above**

8 During the next 12 months, how much do you anticipate your organization will spend on computer hardware, software, peripherals, and services for your location? *(check only one)*
- □ 01 Less than $10,000
- □ 02 $10,000 to $49,999
- □ 03 $50,000 to $99,999
- □ 04 $100,000 to $499,999
- □ 05 $500,000 to $999,999
- □ 06 $1,000,000 and over

If there are other Oracle users at your location who would like to receive a free subscription to *Oracle Magazine*, please photocopy this form and pass it along, or contact Customer Service at **+1.847.647.9630**

Form 5

OPR